Conservative Islam

Conservative Islam

A Cultural Anthropology

Erich Kolig

LEXINGTON BOOKS
Lanham • Boulder • New York • Toronto • Plymouth, UK

Published by Lexington Books
A wholly owned subsidiary of The Rowman & Littlefield Publishing Group, Inc.
4501 Forbes Boulevard, Suite 200, Lanham, Maryland 20706
www.rowman.com

10 Thornbury Road, Plymouth PL6 7PP, United Kingdom

British Library Cataloguing in Publication Information Available

Library of Congress Cataloging-in-Publication Data

Kolig, Erich.
Conservative islam : a cultural anthropology / Erich Kolig.
p. cm.
Includes bibliographical references and index.
ISBN 978-0-7391-7424-1 (cloth : alk. paper) -- ISBN 978-0-7391-7425-8 (electronic)
1. Islamic fundamentalism. 2. Islam--Customs and practices. 3. Islam--Social aspects. I. Title.
BP166.14.F85K65 2012
306.6'97--dc23
2012001547

Printed in the United States of America

Contents

Acknowledgments

I am grateful to many Muslims and non-Muslims who in one way or another over many years have been helpful in shaping my views on Islam and have stimulated my interest in how people live guided by this fascinating religion. They brought to life the rather dry matter published in books, journals, newspapers, on the web, and in blog sites. But they are not responsible, of course, for my interpretations and for the views that inform my analysis and description. Any shortcomings and errors in this study cannot be blamed on them. There are too many people to name them all. In many cases I do not know their names, but their kindness or their views, sparking my interest, have remained in my memory. (Muslims would be less than human though—and my ability to remember would be rather deficient—if some of them would not have left rather negative impressions. But even being threatened with a knife in the holy city of Qom by a fanatic who did not want my infidel feet to touch sacred ground was instructive and valuable in a way.)

Through my research in Afghanistan and Indonesia and the travels in the traditional Islamic world (in Turkey, Iran, Pakistan, Kashmir/India, Malaysia, Morocco, Egypt, and the United Arab Emirates), I could become acquainted with the many faces of Islam. In Austria and New Zealand I received interesting insights into Muslims as a religious minority and how the diaspora in a Western secularized liberal democracy influences the lives of the devout. This has always been the angle of my interest in Islam: as an anthropologist, my approach focuses on the social aspect rather than the purely theological one.

I could repeat much of the litany of gratitude expressed in my previous book *New Zealand's Muslims and Multiculturalism* (Brill, 2010), but I will refrain from doing so. Instead I want to acknowledge a much wider circle of people. Conversations, seminars, lectures, and research projects of my colleagues, research assistants and associates, and graduate students at Otago University, in New Zealand, over many years have been invaluable in stimulating my interests and deepening my insights into Islam and Muslim cultures. From among them, I would like to thank Professor Rex Ahdar, professor of law, for focusing my interest on the sharia; Dr. Joko Susilo, for his ever cheerful guidance around the not-so-harmless cliffs of Indonesian radical Islam; Drs. Najib Lafraie and William Shepard, for helpful suggestions from their font of knowledge of Islam; and Professor Paul Trebilco of the theology department at Otago University, for providing me with some logistic support in his capacity as director of the Centre for Studies of Islam and Muslim Cultures. My (late) friend Dr. Assadullah Baha has taught me much about Afghanistan and pashtunwala. Abdullah Drury, a Muslim convert, has supplied me with information about Islam in New Zealand, my home for the last forty years. I also thank the Department of Cultural and Social Anthropology at Vienna University, my alma mater, which provided me with several appointments as Visiting Professor and thus allowed me to observe firsthand the growing Muslim diaspora in Europe and reactions to it. (My teaching duties were in the area of indigenous politics, theory of religion, and Australian Aboriginal studies, but unofficially I could engage in my "hobby" of "Muslim studies," observing multiculturalism and culture politics.) In this context I owe Professor Em. Karl Wernhart, as (former) Rector of Vienna University, a debt of gratitude.

My fieldwork in Afghanistan as a graduate student at Vienna University (my thanks go to the anthropology department at Kabul University) and later in Indonesia intermittently over the last fifteen years (my thanks to Universitas Kristen Satya Wacana and Badeni) were profoundly important to my professional interests. Perhaps somewhat unusual for Islamology, I am also drawing on my research experience among Australian Aborigines over a period of thirty years (a special thanks to Ron and Catherine Berndt who initially gave me the big chance) and experiences collected in several other places (in Melanesia, Polynesia, Europe, Asia, etc.). For these experiences, gathered over a period of forty years, I owe so much to hundreds of people. I cannot even begin to name them. I can only silently encompass them in my acknowledgements for the kindness they have shown me.

Last but not least, I thank my wife Nicole for her understanding and forbearance when I was preoccupied with this work.

***

I am not an Arabic speaker. For that reason and to avoid getting into an argument about the correct rendering of terms of that language,[1] unapologetically I place the emphasis on simplicity and ease. Arabic words are presented therefore in the simplest or most commonly employed English rendering, and without using the letters hamza and ayn, usually shown as upper case inverted commas. Thus it is simply Quran and not Qur'an; sharia and not shari'a, and so forth. However I will retain, for instance, Shi'i or Shi'a as this is in common use.

References to the Quran are made using the official Saudi version and translation *The Noble Qur'an*, produced in Madinah. Its English is not necessarily always the most elegant rendition, but it has the official stamp of approval of the authorities most closely associated with world Islam.

In most cases in which news items and current affairs have been referred to, I have not listed the media source where I obtained this information. Important news is reported world wide in many different languages and in various media (internet, newspaper, television, radio, etc.) and not always exactly at the same time and in identical detail. Such information is usually retrievable through Google or other search engines and can easily be checked this way. Similarly, I have been sparing with my references to the anthropological literature, confining myself only to the most outstanding literary contributions. Otherwise the footnotes would easily have swollen to double the volume.

NOTES

1. For a very recent and brief explication see William Shepard, *Introducing Islam*. London, New York: Routledge, 2009; p. xvi–xviii.

Introduction

Islam has become an object of fascination in the Western world, inspiring hundreds of new studies, books, and learned articles every year. This is the harvest of a continuous and tireless rethinking and reinterpreting of Islam from the point of view of Western scientific analysis trying to capture the essence of Islam. This religion and its manifold expressions have been in the limelight of academic and journalistic enterprise for years, but especially since the beginning of the twenty-first century. The reasons for this—above all the attack of 9/11 and the growing Muslim diaspora especially in Western Europe—are too well known to require belabouring. Leaving aside the prolific literature produced by Muslim theologians and jurist-scholars exploring "their" Islam and its intricacies, this religion is being theologically and analytically dissected, examined and probed, by scores of non-Muslims who have no interest in converting or confirming their personal faith. Very important in this enterprise is that many Muslim intellectuals are working now in the Western academic tradition in universities, research institutions and publishing houses.[1] If Edward Said's classical complaint[2] of the bias of Western Islamic studies ever had justification, the picture has been more than balanced now through the heavy involvement of Muslims.

The deeper reason for this heated intellectual production, above all, is because Islam sociopolitically is of immense relevance in the modern world and its various, and not always very pleasant, expressions are of enormous topicality. Many big ideological battles—from the most extreme "socialist" to the most fascist and also the most unfettered, rapacious capitalist ones—have been fought and then the combatants were consigned to the scrap heap of history. They were found to be cul de sacs, to bring no major improvement in the human condition, or were rejected for other reasons. Yet it seems humanity cannot steer itself into ideologically calmer waters and turn to

1

more pragmatic pursuits to ease and secure its existence on earth. As trans-continental, indeed global, problems loom affecting the physical well-being, even survival, of our species—or so it seems at least—radicalized Islam, the ugly proboscis in the face of this world religion, emerges as an unwelcome distraction.

Much attention is directed towards the current radical ideology Islam inspires and which seems to sprout militant and extremist action. What some claim to be a religion of peace is convulsed by ideological ructions of regressive conservatism, uncompromising rejection of the West and its modernity, political fanaticism, religious fascism, and bloodthirsty terrorism. Needless to say that in no small measure this has been responsible for the suspicion under which Muslims and Islam sui generis suffer in the West. Humankind always seems to have had a fascination with the bizarre, the cruel, and the bloody, and so unsurprisingly the violence Islam seems to be spawning provokes the study of these phenomena with an intensity ranging from clinical detachment to morbid fascination.

Undoubtedly, studies abound of Islam and Muslims in the modern world. The vast majority seems preoccupied with the political or ideological conflict discourses in which this religion and those who profess to it are embroiled. Probably among the most influential frames of reference is Samuel Huntington's, by now, famous (or infamous) ouevre *The Clash of Civilizations and the Remaking of World Order*.[3] Its significance as an intellectual milestone, both in a positive and negative sense, is too well known to make an explanation necessary here. For many it has become the baseline from which they view Islam as an antagonistic force hostile to the West. What is undoubtedly true even from a moderate viewpoint is that as both sides are being forced now into ever closer proximity through globalization, significant problems arise.

Extremism and violence aside, Islam is being studied, above all, in relation to world politics, globalization, distribution of global power, human rights, gender relations, resistance to secularization[4] and democratic governance. It has extensively been discussed for its mysterious ideational relationship with modernity and postmodernity and in relation to humanity's epistemological, social, and ethical progression in general. In a paradigmatic fashion these analytical concepts are treated heuristically as causative givens, as a kind of agens movens with the same degree of reality as the moon or the weather, but their effects on Islam remain enigmatic. Whether globalization with its cultural, epistemological, and ideological pressures has evoked Islamic fundamentalization and whether the radicalization of Islam is to be seen as a response to, or a consequence of, globalization are indeed interesting, even pressing questions.[5] Has the weakening of the Western hegemon[6] and the West's global decentering invited a strengthening of an oppositional Islamic identity; does fundamentalization represent a "cultural closure" against global homogenization;[7] and has postmodernity with its epistemological liberation brought about the reindigenization of knowledge? Does this encourage Islam, in an act of self-preservation, to stand up against the globalizing universalization through rationalism and secularization? Is it the last hurrah of religious conservatism against processual epistemology—the endless evolution of knowledge—that rejects final truths revealed by supernatural intervention? These are some of the fascinating questions to be asked. Few conclusive answers have been provided, in particular with regard to reasons for the violence that seems to sweep the Islamic world. The question what causes this extraordinary flowering of violence that seems to emanate from Islam has been framed in the way that it may be "a plea to reinstate the religious narrative in a world increasingly seen as secular, disenchanted, and lacking moral values."[8] Other answers blame the interventionism of the West, from twentieth-century colonialism to the most recent militaristic adventures, which causes anomie and provokes a counter-push by the less powerful who cannot resist on equal terms. Subterfuge and terrorism must be their answers. All these paradigms presuppose the existence of orderly and universal causal chains, which admit to objective assessment. And, of course, there is also an intricate web of contemporary contexts of a political, economic, and ideological kind that also exert their influence. A valid explanatory perspective must attempt to encompass much of that, even if this goes at the expense of methodological purity. And, of course, one has to bear in mind that in trying to grasp this complexity, inevitably ideological viewpoints, values, and aesthetics of the observer color and govern the perception and evaluation of the observed.

In this book I look for characteristics of today's Islam and the Muslim life world, to relate them where possible to what may be referred to as behavioral and epistemic universals, but also, equally importantly, to trace them to ancient cultural and social peculiarities and symbols extant at the time of Islam's emergence. Cultural phenomena have a communicative aspect, symbols carry a message, but exactly that semiotic function can lead to misunderstandings. The encrypted meaning may be enduring, but as it fades with the passage of time, lack of comprehension, derision, and rejection may result. Over time the reason for the emergence of ideas, and the symbolic values of thought and action, once self-evident and precious, may be lost and their original message misinterpreted. In a new context—such as that provided by globalization—they may come to seem out of place, adversarial, and hostile.

Popular (Western) perception sees Islamic culture as a cohesive, characteristic entity, or, more carelessly, as a grab-bag category into which everything to do with Islam can be put. In this regard, this perception meets with the Muslims' who also, glossing over differences, see themselves as a seamless and global class of people adhering to one particular faith across and beyond nationality, ethnicity, and race. Not many anthropological studies, however, elevate the global uniformity of Islam to prime importance.[9] Attempts are rare to analyze Islam simply as a specific "culture" with a specific set of symbols and shared meanings—a culture which unifies the Muslim umma, the community of believers, in a coherent worldwide "society" with specific features and characteristic interaction patterns, valid irrespective of national or ethnic boundaries. Even fewer studies do so with the tools of traditional anthropology, bestriding the path of how in the traditional discipline of anthropology a tribal society and a tribal culture would have been scrutinized, analyzed, and comprehended. Here I try to address this manko by unashamedly using a traditional anthropological, methodologically "conservative" angle. This harbors a danger. Taking recourse to a "traditional-type" anthropology and its methods provokes the hackneyed notion that an academic tool employed in the study of so-called "primitive" or "tribal" cultures and societies is being used. It needs to be pointed out, therefore, that if it ever was true that anthropology studied only "primitive" societies, it certainly is so no longer. And anyway, using a "traditional" anthropological approach is by no means meant to imply that Islam is a "tribal" religion and that its study would require methods and perspectives different from those applied to Western society and culture.

To subject all of Islam and its cultural patterns to a closer inspection, or to try to encompass all of Muslim society, would be too ambitious a project. Instead this study is confined to a selection of patterns and features; namely those considered by the contemporary West to be characteristic, remarkable, or controversial; and to symbols, which—at least to an outsider—appear to have iconic status or some elevated significance. (They may not necessarily be regarded the most important ones from a Muslim perspective.) Admittedly, here we run into the problem of stereotyping and essentializing. Trying to elicit the essential Islam or the typicality of Muslim society from among the many variants in which they appear is fraught with many pitfalls. Avoiding them is a daunting task. Naturally, given my self-imposed task, my focus is on "conservative" expressions of Islam, and not so much on the very extremes of radical modernism or militant regressivism.

Islam, of course, exists in several versions, from the radically modernist to the ultraconservative, "medievalist." By concentrating on patterns that appear to be characteristic for the conservative version of Islam, we may gain a better understanding of the matrix from which Islamic radicalism springs. For it is this version of Islam that provides the reservoir from which radical expressions by a small impulse of existential, intellectual, and political circumstances can emanate.

A BRIEF REFLECTION ON METHODS

Methodologically, I cannot claim to follow a purist legacy. In talking about characteristic patterns I owe some inspiration to Ruth Benedict's *Patterns of Culture* (1934). Especially when I am trying to link Islamic patterns to characteristically panhuman expressions and panhuman experiences, I am connecting with the German idealist tradition of anthropology manifested in Wilhelm Dilthey's and Hans-Georg Gadamer's work. There are also inspirations from Adolf Bastian's Elementargedanken, elementary ideas, and James Frazer's cross-cultural analytical method. In a broad sense, I am also drawing on Max Weber's methodology concerning social action by placing the accent on motivations that cohere to systems of meaning. In an ambivalent sense they are sociologically formed on the basis of independently emerging ideas and a process of selection by elective affinity, and guided by interests that are largely determined by material conditions. Weber's work stands out among the classical studies of Islam also in another respect. In the fragments of thought on the subject, Weber's respect for Islam is transparent. It does not fit Edward Said's views of the biased and Eurocentric Orientalist scholarship—as Said himself later seems to have admitted.[10]

Weber did not live long enough to complete his project of analyzing Islam in the same way as he did with other world religions. He left his thoughts on Islam in fragments that others were attempting to put together to form a picture of some coherence.[11] Even so, it is clear his mission in studying Islam was to show its relationship to his understanding of rationalism. The culture producing capacity of Islam generated characteristic shapes in politics, economics, and social conditions, which he could compare with the emergence of scientific rationality as a life condition through Protestant fundamentalism and pietism.

In this sense this book is a study of ideational conditions, rather than of institutions, social and political courses of interaction, and sociopolitical process. A perspective that draws on Islam's history of ideas and their formative influence on dogma, culture and society, however, if it is to explain today's situation, cannot ignore the present-day international context of economy, society, and politics. How do Islamic ideas, meanings, and values react to the world context today?[12] This de rigeur must be an important question begging to receive an answer.

UNDERSTANDING ISLAM'S MOTIVATIONS AND ORIGINS

In discussing the interrelationship between Islam and the modern world, the question is challenging: what are the formative issues of Islam at its inception; how are the original motivations expressed today; and what impact do they have on current conditions? What response do ideas and symbolic meanings, conceived and formulated centuries ago, elicit in the world today? Why do they sometimes seem to be ill-fitting in the modern world? This is not to forget that Max Weber warned that "a Geist is not confined to the religious formation that brings it into existence"[13] —in other words, Islam today is not reducible to the ideas that stood at its cradle. But exactly that difference is of interest here.

In selecting outstanding features of modern Islam for closer scrutiny and tracing their meaning back in history to their origins in social and intellectual circumstances in the seventh century, one must remain aware that this is a highly conjectural enterprise. This kind of analysis attributes importance to intentions and motives extant centuries ago and now subliminally manifest in cultural patterns. Much of the very beginnings of Islam, the Prophet's life, let alone his innermost thought, is shrouded in enigma. The first written source, conventionally accepted as the oldest biography of the Prophet Muhammad, *Sirat Rasul Allah* (Biography of the Messenger of God),[14] by Ibn Ishaq, is extremely controversial as to its veracity. Written about one hundred years after the Muhammad's death by an author who did not know the Prophet, this work relied entirely on oral traditions. There was no proper historiography in the modern sense and the transmission was not in the form of a coherent narrative. Information was handed on in truncated and fragmented form as far as it seemed relevant at the time.[15] What is even more problematic is that Ishaq's biography exists only insofar as it seems to have been copied, more or less faithfully to the original, by a later author, Ibn Hisham.[16] Some modern authors researching the topic have cast aside conventional understanding of the origins of Islam and the Muslim Arabic sources on which it is based and have rewritten early Islamic history profoundly.[17] However, this challenge to received knowledge is not universally accepted as valid. By and large it seems the scholarly community remains divided.

Taking the more conventional route here nevertheless is still like walking on thin ice, being acutely aware of the possibility of misinterpretations. Original intentions and motivations, standing at the cradle of Islam, are at best frozen in semiotic cryptograms. The Prophet's personal ideas and motives, intriguingly, entice guesswork, debate, argument, and even controversy but engender no certainties. Some scholars sympathetic to Islam but slightly critical of the form it has assumed since its inception, ascribe humanist intentions to the Prophet. His purpose was honorable and kind, they argue, but his ideas and social rules were later hijacked and corrupted by prejudiced or less well-meaning Muslim leaders. Owing to their influence, Islam partially reverted to pre-Islamic patterns of misogyny, brutality, and inegalitarianism. Especially caliph Umar, allegedly an arrogant and violent man, as well as an Arab arch-conservative, comes in for heavy criticism. This strand of thinking is particularly noticeable in Fatima Mernissi's ouevre, but is not confined only to it. However, the hard facts are that little can be said with absolute certainty as the Prophet left no personal record[18]—unless one commits the ultimate sacrilege by suggesting that the Quran contains the Prophet's own musings rather than divine inspiration. The question of whether Muhammad was instrument or author creates a dilemma, which the believer may prefer to avoid altogether.

Sunna (tradition) and ahadith (the records attributed to the Prophet) can supply only very limited enlightenment regarding the innermost goings-on of the Prophet's biographical life story, the sira. Even the most detailed and careful tafsir and asbab an-nusul (licit exegesis and considerations of historical circumstances of origin) cannot provide certainty. The ahadith are a chronically uncertain source in illuminating the foundation spirit of Islam. The record of traditions, customs of the early Muslim community and sayings of the Prophet, from the point of view of strict historiography, are unable to produce an unimpeachable, immaculately truthful picture. Not even ahadith labeled sahih (true), and possessing the endorsement of the highest accredited authority, Sahih Bukhari, escape completely the shadows of skepticism.[19] Sigmund Freud drew our attention to the failings of memory, to its unintended selective working and the distorting effects this has, not to mention the all-too-human failings of deliberately falsifying recollections and adding inventions made for reasons ranging from the opportunistic to the malicious. Hard-core historical analysts may even entertain the possibility that misunderstandings and small changes over time may have crept into the revelations themselves.[20] (For Muslims, it pays to entertain such doubts in secret—either for fear or courtesy.)

Hermeneutic approaches seeking to contextualize elements of the sacred scriptures also are fraught with difficulties, though of a different kind. They run the risk to be seen to go beyond the legitimate asbab an-nusul and to adversely affect theological substance. The result is that explanatory assertions seeking to illuminate motivations at the cradle of Islam cannot go beyond a broad generalization as to how and why comparable patterns do emerge in humanity at large or at best may be derived from a broadly based understanding of Middle Eastern culture. In other words, some understanding of Islamic foundational motivations may legitimately be inferred from the general epistemes of the region at the time and of the milieu in which the formulation of the doctrinal basis occurred. In some instances it is useful to compare Islamic cultural patterns with patterns of other cultures, and in considering their universality derive some understanding in this way. Then, contextualizing them in the modern world, one can better grasp why and how a sura, a tradition, a behavior pattern has become influential, and is shaping attitudes, values, and features of social intercourse in modern Muslim society; and also why it should be ill-fitting in the context of modernity.

One of the "hottest potatoes" in Islam is the exact status of the Quran. The historian Simon Schama,[21] known for his eclectic choice of words, described it as having "a lyrical softness combined with a fierce sword-sharpened intemperance." There is an "utter certainty about the Quran" that he finds disturbing. But divine revelations, one may object, are always exuding certainty and an uncompromisingness of the "take it or leave it at your peril" kind. A Muslim friend enthused about its poetic quality expressed in perfect Arabic, in addition, of course, to its absolute unshakable veracity: formal perfection meeting absolute truth. This contrasts somewhat with another interpretation that attributes linguistically a Syro-Aramaic origin to the Quran and locates the beginnings of Arabic language literacy about two hundred years later.[22] According to this interpretation, the original Quran contains terms and concepts alien to classical Arabic. There are obviously quite different ways in which people are impressed by it and understand it. Another view I have heard is that as a text, taken by itself, it is extremely boring, not least by the endless repetition of pious formulae. A Muslim scholar of some renown once told me that only a relatively small percentage of the text has any specific and meaningful information, such as regulative instructions. He put a precise percentage on it and suggested the rest, consisting of poetry, pious phrases, and redundancy, could be safely discarded. Not surprisingly, he thought that even the useful portions have to be reinterpreted to make them relevant to the modern world.

Leaving totally aside non-Islamic views that the Quran is a psychological phenomenon, that it is a collection of human inspirational endeavor, of illusions, if not hallucinations, and contains a plethora of ancient superstitions common at that time in this region, there are several more respectful interpretations. It is not my purpose here to enter into a theological debate. The question whether the Quran is preexisting—and thus an attribute of God—or a creation is of immense importance to Muslims. Mutazilah tradition, for instance, emphasizing the Oneness and indivisibility of God, the tawhid, argues that giving the divine word timelessness means exalting it to the same level as God himself, while the Hanbali school defends exactly this position.[23] Related questions are the following: is it a text in human language phrased for human, and therefore limited, understanding—which would give it a hint of imperfection; is it a flexible polyphone discourse addressing different people, at different times and in different situations? Such questions are not given any space here. These are important questions for the believer, but are outside our purview. Some of these views earn the distinction of being derided as heretical. For instance, the Islamic scholar and erstwhile Al Azhar scholar Nasr Hamid Abu Zayd (1943–2010),[24] was declared an apostate and had to flee into exile in Europe because of his hermeneutic interpretation of the Quran. His is a fate not unusual among bold Islamic thinkers. Secularized, ex-Christian West has to come to the rescue to allow a more wide-ranging fertile debate internal to Islam. But instead of earning praise for granting asylum to Islamic "free-thinkers," its facilitation is, unsurprisingly, often seen by Muslims as a Western ploy to undermine and weaken Islam.

On a somewhat less explosive level is the debate about the status of sharia, the rules and laws for proper, divinely prescribed human conduct. Fiqh, the systematised sharia, clearly is a human product, reflecting human understanding. But is any understanding of the sharia automatically a human understanding, even as some articles are spelt out relatively clearly in the Quran, which of course is supposed to be God's word verbatim? [25]

The present work pointedly abstains from engaging in this debate. It is not for anthropology to get into a theological dispute and into what essentially is a matter of religious belief. An argument about the nature of the divine, the supernatural, and revelation is beyond the purpose here.

A CHILIASTIC DREAM

What can be said, in a much broader sense, refers to what I see as Islam's cryptic sociological message—possibly one of several imputable ones. In a sweeping way one can almost sense that the original intention of Islam lay in creating the ideal society by perfecting human conduct. In this respect, by propagating the social medium designed by higher intervention for humans to achieve perfection, its intent as well as its design plan is utopian or, to pay homage to its religious nature, millenarian (or chiliastic). No motto can express this better than "kuntum khaira ummatin," "You are the best community" (Quran 3/110). It is not too farfetched to assume that it was not only meant as complimentary in a spiritual sense, referring to a perfection of faith and a select group of people holding it in trust, but literally addressing people living in a perfect society. In order to achieve that blessed condition laws and regulations had to be put in place to transform human asocial, selfish, immoral nature into divinely inspired and guided sociability, to hone social impulses and direct behavior into ethically effective channels. Equally important was to overturn entrenched undesirable social patterns, or at least give them a new meaning expressive of disapproval. The Prophet's inclination towards social regulation, was later carried on in spirit and letter by a succession of caliphs, legal scholars and so-called law schools, refining and honing his legacy in recognition of the founder's original intention. This intent is clearly discernible in the emergence of the complex Islamic doctrine and in the intricacies of the hierocratic sharia. Most religions have a more or less strong socio-regulative aspect—that is, before the onset of secularization—but few go to the extreme as Islam does in its attempt to create the God-society on earth.

There is also another piece of evidence attesting to the Prophet's personal disposition towards juridical and socio-regulative authority underpinned and mandated by a higher legitimacy. The Dustur al Madina, the Madina Charter is an early piece of Islamic legislation authored by Muhammad.[26] It is a kind of constitution for the town of Yathrib before it became known as Madina (which simply means city). The city contained eight tribes of "pagans," Muslims, Christians, and Jews. Designed by Muhammad, the charter intended to regulate the social interrelationship within the religiously pluralist local community and place it on a legal footing under his leadership. Putting the accent somewhat differently: it meant to place the relationship of his small Muslim community on a firm basis with the local polity. Madina's original citizenry was not only of different faiths (polytheists, Muslims, and other pre-Islamic monotheists) and therefore followed diverse forms of worship, but also adhered to somewhat different laws and customs. While Muslims lived under the rule of the incipient Islamic law, this document literally laid down the law with regard to pluralistic conditions. With some hyperbole it could be called an ancient multiculturalist charter. It shows clearly the Prophet's serious intent to remove pluralist conditions and multi-religious social intercourse from chance, randomness, whimsicality, and chaos, and thus lessen the likelihood of destructive conflict arising.

Islam pressed eschatology into service to justify the ideal society, as envisaged by Muhammad, and to elevate it from among the pluralist conditions of the time to unique, singular importance. It did not seek, however, to repress other ways of ordering society —this is made clear in the Quran verse (2/256) where it says there is no compulsion in religion—and in this sense Islam, at least in the way it emerged, evinced a spirit of tolerance. This was not always obvious in its history, but initially at least, and to some extent later on, Islam was content with regulating the relationship between Muslims and other-religionists (most conspicuously with the dhimma system and the Ottoman Empire's millet system), but in some cases eschewed forcible conversion or extending the sharia in its entirety to (recognized) religious minorities.[27]

Ethics were devised in a down-to-earth spirit and rules extended over time to regulate every kind of behavior. The ultimate aim was to harness it for the benefit of the perfect society, a society in which its functions and individual conduct were streamlined "to please God," but cryptically meant to create the perfectly functioning human conviviality on earth. Enhancing cohesion, internal solidarity, and harmonious coexistence through strict regulation became important guiding principles. Vague moral imperatives were not enough—they had to be underpinned by precise rules of interaction. Underlying the vision of this chiliastic utopia is a theory of how society works and a theory of human nature. Both are important to make the vision work. In constructing and attempting to implement a theory of the perfect society and placing it into a transcendent framework, Islam can be compared with grandiose schemes the social sciences produced. Marxism comes to mind—despite the glaring differences between materialism and the spirituality of theology of any kind—in which a theory of society is piggybacking on the Hegelian "phenomenology of spirit" for transcendental underpinnings. And in Marxism, as in Islam, the notion of societal functioning is drawing on an implied theory of human nature. There is also a hint of Emile Durkheim's organismic conception of society and the importance he attributed to religion as a vital precondition for society's (of the premodern kind) smooth functioning. The Marxist scheme also shares with Islam a preoccupation with the purifying social process that enables the emergence of the ideal human being when it is embedded in an ideal social aggregate. They share the view that perfection—a God-pleasing existence, or in a secular sense the fulfillment of human potential—lies in being part of an ideal form of collectivity.

In Islam, social interaction is constrained to follow the ethical rules and laws laid down by a supernatural agent and thus are beyond questioning and doubt. Countless prophet's and charismatics over time have attempted this extraordinary feat of establishing a perfect conviviality of like-minded individuals, or on a grander scale have attempted to mold civil society, or a whole nation, to their vision by appeal to a higher authority.[28] In trying to lead the way to a promised, divinely ordained existence, most have failed utterly, enjoying no or only short-lived success, or being derided as crackpots and criminals. Over the centuries, hundreds of charlatans and false prophets have made claims of this nature. Only very few stick out for having made a lasting impression. Among those, even fewer can boast as spectacular a success as the Prophet Muhammad. His was a remarkable triumph in convincingly presenting what "Essential Man" could be if cleansed of moral imperfections, bad behavior and ignorance. His plan was that given time and the encouragement through Islamic law it will happen; as human beings, unless diverted by evil influence, have a natural, innate propensity to recognise and accept the supreme authority of God.[29]

The Prophet Muhammad represents a fascinating example of the social workings of charisma. The concept relies on Max Weber's definition of charisma[30]—meaning gift of grace or in a secular sense, a special ultimately undefinable quality. It is

> a certain quality of an individual personality by virtue of which he is set apart
> from ordinary men and treated as endowed with supernatural, superhuman, or
> at least specifically exceptional powers or qualities. These are . . . not access-
> ible to the ordinary person, but regarded as of divine origin or as exemplary.
> And on the basis of them the individual concerned is treated as a leader.

The range of responses to the attribution of charisma is huge. Once charisma
is attributed, the madman's ravings may become epiphanies; personal whim-
sies become eternal, divinely inspired exemplifications; murderous esca-
pades may become apocalyptic necessities—any foolish strategy a building
block to install the divinely willed communality. Of course not all utopians
are charismatics in the true sense. In the Age of Reason such society-building
plans have to be phrased differently to satisfy intellectual requirements. The
elevation of reason to intellectual and social importance has brought about a
profound distrust in epistemological methods which draw on altered states of
consciousness from glossolalia to hallucinatory visions, from trance to sei-
zure, while in premodern society and many tribal societies such extraordinary mental conditions were attributed with higher wisdom and greater truth
than empirical knowledge. Especially secularization has introduced skepticism towards an overly religious type of leadership that claims revelatory
experience and prophetic vision.[31] Hitler, Stalin, and Mao Zedong had to
draw on different paradigms and avoid the supernatural mandate (although
Hitler alluded to the course of destiny). And so did the luddites, Adam Smith,
and Buckminster Fuller. His "communes of networked, non-hierarchical,
self-organising individuals held in equilibrium by the self-correcting influence of feedback loops [paraphrased]" also holds up a vision of the perfect
society but on "rational," scientifically sounding grounds. Any such "vision"
to have traction in the modern globalized world and to be more than a blip in
history requires adjustment to dominant epistemes, rationalism, global value
systems, ethics, and science-infused worldviews. It even has to carefully
avoid giving the impression that it has charismatic origins. Artificial and
ephemeral as such epistemological hegemony may be, even the most conservative Islamic vision will eventually have to bow to it—unless of course
those who see signs that the Enlightenment Age is coming to an end are
correct. If indeed there is such a phenomenon of a post-rational and postmodern flowering of religion, charisma—in the religious meaning of the word
and not simply referring to attributes of a prestigious, flamboyant person—
may well come into fashion again.

From an anthropological point of view, charisma is not written on a
person's forehead—even though devotees having been converted to the
cause may see a certain aura surrounding such a person. Charisma, being
invisible, is therefore not easily acquired. As a quality which sets certain
persons apart through an act of faith and trust, it must be earned somehow:

this may be through the gift of revelation, credible prophesy, through miraculous, seemingly superhuman deeds, through exemplary, inspiring, and successful leadership, and the like. Especially performing miraculous deeds of either curative or magical magnificence is a sure path towards gaining credibility. Muhammad fits this profile of a charismatic career as the tradition recounts several miraculous deeds of healing and procuring water.[32] It is not difficult to understand that mysteriously producing rain or providing water for drinking or for ritual ablution in an arid environment is of special significance. The attribution of deeds like these must be an important signal of outstanding personal qualities. By general agreement Muhammad is credited with two major miracles, which overshadow all others: the biggest being the conveyance of the Quran, receiving the word of God and bringing it to humankind; and the smaller of the two being his journey to the heavens. By disregarding the minor miracles and emphasizing the relative absence of spectacular miracles of healing or other impressive demonstrations of superhuman magical potency, which for instance are woven into the Christian tradition, some scholars and Muslims feel encouraged to regard Islam as a "rational" religion.[33]

Charismatics usually do not emerge in a social vacuum.[34] Usually there are social, or sociopolitical circumstances—crisis conditions, cataclysmic change, and the like—which produce a need, not necessarily consciously perceived, for radical and bold leadership to take society into a new, more promising or redemptive direction. It may produce rebellious social activism, even militaristic features, or alternatively escapism to the point of mass suicide. The emergence of a charismatic may also be facilitated by a preexisting cultural tradition congenial to the belief in special capabilities of outstanding individuals. As Reza Aslan[35] argues, at Muhammad's time there were many prophets who were claiming a mandate from God, gathering adherents, and declaring sanctuary cities obeying divine laws. Apparently, Arab culture at the time provided a rich matrix from which personal charisma could arise. There were traditional roles of kahins as poets, seers, moral philosophers, announcers of salvation, and social commentators. In the ecstatic tradition the kahins revealed divine will in various forms. Muhammad combined all of these functions in his person, absorbing and incorporating these role models in his function as Rasul Allah, "the Messenger of God." In fact, one might observe that the function of prophecy, social critique, and leadership by supernatural, charismatic means, is deeply rooted in the Middle Eastern culture and thus characterizes also the Judeo-Christian heritage of historical times. The prophetic figures of Abraham and Moses, John the Baptist and Ezekiel, and many others[36] belonged to Jewish and Christian monotheism but no doubt contributed to Muhammad's career their shining example. The Prophet also made use of the, for this region, typical techniques of inviting divine inspiration through seclusion, fasting, and thirsting—in other words subjecting himself to physical and sensory deprivation to invoke communication with supernatural powers such as angels, the devil, and God. Here is an important connection with the shamanistic syndrome. Producing altered states of consciousness through these techniques is part of the equipment of universal shamanism, which is used for the purpose of receiving higher wisdom.[37] It surely is one of those human epistemological universals to assume that through nonempirical means even greater, more profound and meaningful insights might be gleaned. The vision quest of shamans, search for personal totems that guide a person's life, dream and trance experiences are thought to produce an intuitive form of knowledge that is both individualistic and superior to empirical-observational forms. Shamanism usually augments its techniques with the use of psychedelic or intoxicating substances, which the Prophet seems to have shunned. Muhammad's journey to heaven also conforms with another standard feature of shamanism: the vision journey in which the shaman by traveling spiritually to a distant destination receives deeper insights.[38] Traveling to the abode of the spirits is often combined with suffering, but the gain in valuable information (about practical issues like the future, healing, hunting predictions, or issues relating to the meaning of human existence, etc.) makes it worthwhile. On the whole, however, Islamic nonmystical mainstream eschews the ecstatic conditions of classical shamanism, both as a way of life or as an avenue to higher knowledge.[39]

On this rich background of charismatic phenomena being available in the cultural repertoire at his time, Muhammad could draw on impressive precedent in claiming an exalted position. Certain times of social upheaval and cataclysmic change provoke the emergence of such persons who feel qualified, and are acknowledged as such, to show the way to a better existence.[40] Just as Christ was believed to have an answer to Roman colonialism through a message of salvation and was building on Jewish messianic beliefs and charismatic traditions, Arab society seems to have offered the necessary preconditions through upheavals of tribal warfare and religious tensions.

Aslan also emphasizes that Arab society, contemporary with the Prophet, was replete with adherents to monotheistic and henotheistic religions. There were Jews and Christians, Hanifists, and Zoroastrians, in addition to Sabians,[41] Mandaeans, and polytheists, some of whom worshipped a supreme deity above others.[42] Thus Islam's conversion struggle was only to some extent aimed at suppressing polytheism, as there seems to have been a wider range of monotheistic and pseudo-monotheistic religions at least as influential as polytheism. Though monotheistic rivals in one respect, in another they were useful to emergent Islam. A theological path in fact appears to have been cleared by them for the embracement of Muhammad's strictly monotheistic message.

Be that as it may, the Prophet was successful above all others. His charismatic persona was modeled on a rich tradition of similar and related roles. However, sociologically, he is outstanding in one respect. Except for a few in the Judeo-Christian millenarian tradition, virtually all other erstwhile charismatics have disappeared, often nameless and without leaving identifiable cultural traces. (This goes especially for the Third World untouched by anthropological recording.) As Christians do, Muslim believers take the power and endurance of their charismatic founder's message as proof of the truly divine nature and veracity of the revelation. From the Muslim devotee's standpoint, other charismatics, being false, have been consigned to the scrap heap of history, or in a few cases are believed to truly have had charisma, the gift of grace, but are only of lesser eschatological importance as earlier harbingers and heralds of the "final seal ."[43]

NOTES

1. Just to name a very few: the works of Tariq Ramadan, Bassam Tibi, Sami Zubaida, Tariq Modood, Amina Wadud, Fatimah Mernissi, Mohammed Arkoun, and Abdullahi an–Naim fall into this category. Many of these intellectuals, in one form or another, pursue an "apologist" agenda by explaining the difference between what they see as the "real" Islam, peaceful and adaptable, and its modern objectionable, fanatical, and radical expressions.

2. Edward Said, *Orientalism*. Numerous editions.

3. New York: Simon and Schuster, 1996.

4. See Ernest Gellner's, *Postmodernism, Reason and Religion* (London, New York: Routledge, 1992), which gives a succinct summary of the major ideological streams of modern times.

5. See Olivier Roy, *Globalized Islam: The Search for a New Ummah*. New York: Columbia University Press, 2004.

6. Jonathan Friedman, *Cultural Identity and Global Process*. London: Sage, 1994.

7. Simon Harrison, "Cultural Boundaries." *Anthropology Today* 15/5 (1999): 10–13.

8. Madawi Al-Rasheed and Morat Shterin, Introduction. In *Dying for Faith: Religiously Motivated Violence in the Contemporary World*, M. Al-Rasheed and M. Shterin (eds.). London, New York: Tauris, 2009; pp. xvii–xviii.

9. In fact, some specifically reject this approach. See, e.g., A.H. El-Zein, "Beyond Ideology and Theology: the Search for the Anthropology of Islam." *Annual Review of Anthropology* 6 (1977): 227–254.

10. Ernest Wolf-Gazo. "Weber and Islam." *ISIM Newsletter* 16 (Autumn 2005):43–45.

11. Brian Turner, *Weber and Islam*. London, Boston: Routledge, 1974.

12. See, for instance, Reinhard Schulze, *A Modern History of the Islamic World*. London: Tauris, 2000.

13. *Sociology of Religion*. Boston: Beacon, 1996; p.151.

14. Ibn Ishaq (c. 704–768). His work is also know as Al Sirah Nabawiyah (The Prophet's Life). Translated by Alfred Guillaume, *The Life of Muhammad*. Karachi: Oxford University Press, 1955.

15. As Patricia Crone notes in *Slaves on Horses: The Evolution of the Islamic Polity*. Cambridge: Cambridge University Press, 1980.

16. Died 833 AD. It also contains 600 hadiths of questionable isnad (chain of transmission). This may say something about the reliability of the work.

17. See, e.g., Patricia Crone and Michael Cook, *Hagarism: The Making of the Islamic World*. New York, Cambridge: Cambridge University Press, 1977.

18. Interestingly, few charismatic figures wrote their personal memoirs, revealing the motivations and innermost thoughts that inspired their teaching.

19. See, for instance, Alfred Guillaume, *The Traditions of Islam*. Beirut: Khayats, 1966; p. 9–36. Fatema Mernissi, *Der Politische Harem*. Freiburg: Herder, 1992.

20. The so-called Satanic Verses, deleted later from the official version of the Quran, give an indication of the meandering path of revelation.

21. Lecture held at the Hay Festival on June 6, 2011, as reported in the press and online.

22. Christoph Luxenburg, Die syro-aramäische Lesart des Koran—ein Beitrag zur Entschlüsselung der Koransprache. S.l.: Verlag Hans Schiler, 2004. (Translated as "The Syro-Aramaic Reading of the Koran: A Contribution to the Decoding of the Language of the Qur'an," 2007.)

23. See, eg., Anna Gade, *The Qur'an: An Introduction*. Oxford: Oneworld, 2010; p.164.

24. In his quest towards a humanistic hermeneutics of the Quran interpreting it as an utterance of its time to be understood in historical and cultural context, he came in grave conflict with more conservative theological views.

25. Tariq Ramadan (*Islam, the West and the Challenge of Modernity*. Leicester: Islamic Foundation, 2001; p. 47) sees sharia as *derived* from Quran and Sunna. Abdullahi An-Naim (*Islam and the Secular State: Negotiating the Future of Shari'a*. Cambridge MA: Harvard University Press, 2008; p. viii) goes further in regarding it as human interpretation in the context of the time, and, therefore, amenable to change.

26. It exists only in the form of a reconstruction through Ibn Hisham"s work (833).

27. Jews and Christians, though as monotheists not forced to convert, were evicted from the Islamic heartland and had to move to the periphery in the decades following the Prophet"s death. In many cases territorial conquest meant more or less forcible conversion.

28. There is a huge body of literature on charismatic leadership. This phenomenon is not confined to the Western and Islamic world or European and Middle Eastern culture (where it spans the medieval Christian era to modern times; see Norman Cohn, *The Pursuit of the Millennium*. 1st ed. London: Secker, 1957) but can be found in abundance in Third World societies, from colonial times to the present (e.g., Peter Worsley, *The Trumpet Shall Sound*. 1st ed. London: MacGibbon, 1957; Bryan Wilson, *Magic and the Millennium*. London: Heinemann, 1973; Kenelm Burridge, New Heaven New Earth. Oxford: Blackwell, 1971). Some such millenarian movements assumed explicitly religious guises while others pursued a secular, political thrust.

29. The concept of fitrah, referring in the narrow sense to divine creation, is widened to encompass the innate pure nature of humans and their ability to recognise the workings of God.

30. Max Weber, *The Theory of Social and Economic Organization*. New York: Glencoe, Oxford University Press, 1947; p. 358.

31. This is not to say that it does not exist any more. Small groups are still attracted to the most bizarre and implausible forms of charismatic leadership involving UFO beliefs, incredible apocalyptic and redemptive expectations, and blind obedience to the prophetic leader. See the enormous literature on NRMs (New Religious Movements).

32. This, however, is not universally acknowledged by Muslims.

33. Other reasons are, of course, the absence of ingredients of magical transformation such as the sacraments and the relative lack of iconic symbolism in worship except for the qibla (kiblat in Malay language) and the sacred book of the Quran, items endowed with numinous power and requiring special ritual attention. Folk Islam, though, contains much magical thinking and many magical practices, as well as a belief in the miraculous deeds of saints.

34. Weber (in his *Sociology of Religion*) distinguished several forms (or ideal types) of charismatic leadership. I am referring here to the religio–politically active form.

35. *No God but God: The Origins, Evolution and Future of Islam*. New York: Random, 2006; p. 42, 110.

36. Christianity recognizes sixty major prophets who are mentioned in the Bible.

37. See chapter 3.

38. This shamanistic motive recurs in the trope of the witch's travel—in stories often undertaken on a broomstick—to a secret place to meet with demons and the devil. (See, e.g., Hans Peter Duerr, *Dreamtime: Concerning the Boundary between Wilderness and Civilization*. New York: Blackwell, 1985).

39. Sufism is the major exception in that it uses trance conditions for dhikr (remembrance of God) to communicate with God. The practitioner believes himself in the presence of God. The ritualized dhikr ceremony of the Mevlevi Whirling Dervishes is well known.

40. Western colonialism has produced preconditions of this kind and there is a rich body of literature on this topic. Within Islam Mahdism provides a good example.

41. Sabians are mentioned together with Jews and Christians (Quran 2/62, 5/69, 22/17) as acceptable monotheists.

42. Henotheism is the worship of a pantheon of divinities among whom one is exalted and revered as the supreme deity. Such High God beliefs were predominant among sedentary Arabs at that time, according to Aslan, *No God but God*, p. 8.

43. See Quran 33/40. However, Shi'ism with its messianic emphasis on imamism has produced the belief in post-Prophet charismatic figures who rival the Prophet Muhammad in importance. Together with the veneration of Imam Ali and Hussein the eschatological expectation of a millennial end-time and salvation through a messianic figure has produced variations ranging from, Alawism, the Druze belief system, Ahmadiyah, to Bahai'i, which are only some prominent examples. In Sunnism a belief in the coming of the Mahdi can also spontaneously arise.

Chapter One

Unity in Plurality

ONE GOD, ONE CULTURE, ONE SOCIETY

The umma—or more correctly: umma-al-munimin (community of believers)—the globally spanning "fellowship" of believing Muslims, for the purposes of this study, is treated as possessing one culture, sponsored by a particular religious dogma, and living in a social context that exhibits some characteristic shapes.[1] The embracement of the fundamental religious doctrines of Islam, despite many regional and sectarian differences and internal variation, gives Muslims collectively a certain distinctiveness of an international kind. Islam has a tendency to put a strong and characteristic impress on otherwise quite diverse local or regional cultures. Its culture-formative ability is Arab in provenance and draws much on Arabic culture, mentality and the Arabic language as a sacred medium of communication. The sacred texts at the heart of this religion and a belief in a particular divine revelation inspire and even dictate certain distinctive epistemes, unconscious or barely conscious epistemic configurations of apprehending the world and human existence. These causally relate to the religiously required, observable behavior, to symbolic formations and characteristic social and cultural patterns. Despite ethnic, national and regional variations and peculiarities, in conjunction they produce a sociocultural "habitus" that is unmistakably Islamic. The attendant sociocultural reproduction seems to have a particularly strong self-replicating impulse that permits only limited deviation from the foundational, religiously prescribed precedent. This persistence produces the image of constancy that supports the notion that secularization has had ostensibly less effect on Islam and the Islamic world than in the Christianity-derived West.[2]

While the West must define itself by two counteractive phenomena—Christianity and its rejection through secularization—no comparable paradox has so strongly enriched the Islamic past.

Ernest Gellner's[3] audacious enterprise to "explain" Muslim society in one keen sweep of bold generalizations has failed—if we are to believe Sami Zubaida's insightful critique.[4] Gellner's essentialization is to be rejected, he argues. Too many and too important exceptions have been glossed over. The Ottoman Empire, for example, does not fit in many ways into the Islamic frame. Ibn Khaldun's cyclical model of sedentary people and nomadic tribes alternating in dominance is too flawed to make it useful as an explanatory tool. And too simplistic is the division between purist high Islam and syncretistic folk Islam. Islamic and Muslim reality does not comply with Gellner's characterizations. One cannot help but respect the erudition of Zubaida's argument, and yet this will not stop the search for adequate comprehension of what are the defining characteristics of the so-called Islamic world. It cannot all be illusion, or simply geography. Even when avoiding gross generalizations—whether they be of the Gellnerian or Huntingtonian kind—there are undoubtedly communalities to be recognised and acknowledged, though they be of a more cryptic, amorphous, and less concretely expressed kind. They may be found in ideal types of a very subtle kind, arising from underlying shared epistemes that are vitally inspired by Islam. Rather than plain correspondences and distinct likenesses, one should expect less clear evidence. The result, more likely, is "family resemblances" in the Wittgensteinian sense and transformations on features of a common thematic origin, rather than eye-catching strong similarities. Indonesian Muslims are embedded in a social and cultural context obviously very different from say Gulf Arab Muslims or Bosniaks—yet in a global perspective, they do exhibit resemblances they do not share with Papuans.[5]

Max Weber treated the world religions as cultural phenomena—distinct cultural entities that had emerged under certain historical conditions and had developed characteristic shapes in the contemporary world. As he seems to have intended to argue, Islam was driven by a kind of rationality at its inception. As a method of thinking about the world and as an ontological tool a belief system contains an element of cognitive and social inertia that compels it towards resistance to change. But the world does not stand still. As Karl Popper has shown in its broadest sense, cognition as a method ensures fluidity and change thus is inherently inimical to the long-term retention of customs, dogmatic beliefs, traditions, and entrenched socializing habits. While religious doctrine, well adjusted to the intellectual and social conditions it may once have been, remains static, other forms of knowledge move on, opening up gaps of incongruities and lack of relevance. This contradiction between cognitive method and product crystallized over time in this way can be noticed clearly in Islam and its culture formation, where original rationality had turned into fixed patterns that do not fit smoothly into a modern, globalized world governed by hegemony of a different kind.

One of the Islamic world's characteristics is that when compared with the West, religious considerations play a relatively greater role. This not only hints at the stronger social relevance of Islam than Christianity has, it has led to speculations about the reasons for the lesser impact secularization has had in the Islamic world. It has also encouraged some scholars to posit a quasi universal evolutionary scheme in which the West being more secularized is more advanced and the Islamic world is lagging behind. Zubaida[6] excuses religious zealotry of Islam (death fatwas, book burnings, sectarian warfare, etc.) by pointing to the West's history which exhibits the same features and turns out to be not so distant in the past. This is exactly what Muslims resent and reject: placing them into a timeframe in which they scrabble behind the West and are expected that they have yet to pass through exactly the same sociocultural phases. I agree—there is no proof for this assumption. The real question is why has the West dismantled the preeminence of religious thinking and elevated anthropocentricity, hedonism and socio-political pragmatism to primacy? Why is individualism cherished and the bondage of communitarianism and groupism despised? Why is material gain valued more highly than spiritual perfection? The West-internal ideological dominance of materialism, creature comfort, this-worldliness, and God-doubting empiricism has risen to become the global hegemon (increasingly embracing a host of client cultures), thus accentuating the alterity status of the religion-infused Islamic world. Even when the Western example is ostensibly being followed as in the current so-called "democratization movement" (or "Arab Spring") sweeping the Arab world, the religious component is still noticeable. Mass demonstrations of thousands of Syrians demanding freedom usually follow Friday's salat-al-jummah as people stream from the mosques after prayer, ready to protest. Individual actions of a militaristic kind by Lybian fighters were punctuated with shouts of Allahu akbar. Thus firing a rocket or cannon into the far distance, its success in striking the enemy decisively is delivered into the hands of God. Observe the pictures of devout "rebels" prostrating themselves in long rows and facing the sacred qibla, the direction towards Macca, next to tanks and machine guns mounted on pickup trucks. In some respects, and by looking at some images, the Lybian "freedom fighters" seem little different from the Taleban.

Leaving aside Sufi mysticism, Islam has a transcendental framework, but puts a heavy emphasis on esoteric traditions, which in their reference are this-worldly in that their theological contents manifest themselves in everyday practices and responsibilities. Islam's ontological emphasis produces a condition in which orthopraxis shares importance with orthodoxy. While Christianity morphed into an amorphous, yet defining dedication to love, charity, and compassion as the highest principles of man's God-pleasing existence, in Islam the highest devotion means obeying specific divinely commanded rules laid down in minute detail. Man is created to worship God through their social conduct—not just by prayer. Society is religious belief made manifest by the lawful interaction of the believers. Suzanne Haneef[7] expresses this in the following words:

> Islam is not a mere belief-system, an ideology or a religion in the usual sense in which these words are understood. Rather it is a total way of life, a complete system governing all aspects "of a man's existence, both individual and collective . . . "

It is exactly this condition that distinguishes Islam from, especially, Protestant Christianity and leads to certain difficulties in a multiculturalist situation in Western society. Sebastian Poulter[8] couched it in the these words referring to the Muslim minority in the UK: "[I]t is inevitable . . . that [Muslims living in the UK] will have to accept that in England Islam can only be followed as a religious faith and not pursued as an all-embracing way of life." Islam has to recast itself as one religion among others in a secular space. In other words, it must change and it must follow at least one aspect of secularization: in some parts of doctrine it has to retreat into the private sphere;[9] and other parts of the doctrine, those that intersect too strongly with the public sphere, will have to be abandoned altogether. Not surprisingly, as this demand cuts into the very essence of Islam, it poses some considerable problems for devout Muslims—and for the encapsulating majority society as well. Ultimately, the problems do not just play out within a multicultural state in which Muslims form a religious minority, but also in a multicultural globalized world. (As will be argued later, on an international plane the official politics of Muslim majority countries usually are of the realpolitical kind, but whenever the grassroot level or popular groundswell is involved, the ensuing dynamics assume a more distinct Islamic flavor.)

Adjustment and change are demands in the modern world that are not easily met by Muslim society—less so than in the West—for one particular reason. The thoroughness of the Prophet, his companions, and the madhahib (schools of Islamic interpretation and law) has left to modern devout Muslims little room to maneuver by way of cautious qiyas (inference) and ijtihad (interpretation). There are few unoccupied scenes, which they can fill with the images of their own creativity. The tyranny of exegesis in the religious and cultural sphere has stifled to a large extent creative modernizing impulses. These shackles can only be effectively removed now at the risk of becoming a nominal or laissez-faire Muslim or being branded a heretic, or worse, an apostate. A culture is a ground of continuous contestation, but

Islam contains doctrinal mechanisms that resist innovation and change to a greater extent than the normal conservative persistence and unchanging replication that lies in the nature of a dogmatic system.

Implicit in Islam, as it was conceived, is the attempt to create a synthesis of Abrahamic individualism with Asiatic collectivism, in which religion arises not solely from an individual, creaturely dependence on the goodwill of a single divinity, and from the relationship of an individual with a divine entity, but from the collective conduct and the cumulative human experience. Individual devotion can only work if it is shared, and responded to, by others, like-minded in pursuit of the same goal. The interdependence of community members determines the quality of religious life. Blessing arises from the quality of collective living and the sum total of individuals' conduct. Exoteric practices of roles, duties, rituals, ethics, and customs, all of which ultimately are instrumental in achieving social integration, are enriched with esoteric meaning. In the Islamic synthesis, the theistic assumptions are heavily weighted with a particular social ideal to achieve a transcendental purpose. Social living is tantamount to worship.

What may be called "the mainstream" of Islam is only minimally mystically inclined,[10] almost "positivist" in pronouncing that the nature of God is beyond human knowing. As "his" exaltedness exceeds human comprehension, speculation in this direction is considered pointless. Instead the important aspect in a Muslim's life is to be closely guided by the ethical and social rules God demands. Following the difficult maze such rules entail for human existence has its rewards. Closely observing them is not just an abstract ethical imperative but will be tangibly rewarded in the afterlife with (what seem to be) earthly delights and privileges that are highly desirable from a very human point of view. That is to say, the rewards are conceptualized in terms of a human value system. Whether this system of rewards is to be understood in its literal sense, or only metaphorically so, is open to debate.

The close social instrumentalization of dogma has distinct effects. Especially in mainstream Sunnism, theology is almost tantamount to jurisprudence and as a rule book to lawful social conduct and interaction should, ideally, be closely wedded to politics. In particular Islamism has adopted the mantra of din wa daulah (belief and state) expressing the fundamental doctrine that the two entities be coterminous and coextensive; in fact demanding the close wedding of religion and politics to the point of becoming one. Even in a less radical hymn book, the ideal and essential message of mainstream Islam is of the complementarity of belief and lawful social conduct. Of course this is not totally shared by all Muslims. Some theological spin-offs, like the mysticism of Sufism and the rationality of Mutazilah, place slightly different accents. Shi'ism also offers a slight peculiarity insofar as it incorporates a charismatic aspect, which provides for some whimsical, non-scriptural phenomena in politics. However, in another respect, Khomeini's radical theology, despite its creativity, is leading back to a close union between belief and political action in encouraging a greater involvement of the ulama (clerics) in political leadership.

Islam can be taken as a Durkheimian example of a religion performing a profound and explicit socializing function in accordance with a grand, masterly blueprint of the ideal society. It is designed to produce an orderly, ethical, and lawfully regulated society with a high degree of predictability in social conduct and internal cohesion. While "custom" is usually loosely defined and allows for a wide range of social action, the probability of how specific patterns of interaction internally operate under given circumstances is much higher through this religious intervention. It provides a strict social reglement more wedded to social conduct than engaging in philosophical speculations about the transcendental meaning of human existence, which would hand to believers a greater degree of optionality regarding social action. In Islam, eschatology is subordinated to the demands of the perfect society. This religion is ontology, more than metaphysical speculation, with the clear aim—one might even say preoccupation—to provide a smoothly functioning society by supplying it with a thoroughly comprehensive code of conduct. Every aspect of social interaction and personal conduct is fixated law-like or potentially amenable to be so regarded and treated. Through certain interpretive techniques (of qiyas and ijtihad) some doctrinal reassurance can also be gained with regard to modern circumstances and sociocultural patterns, which are not specifically included in, or foretold, or foreseen in the scriptures. These also have to be subjected to principles and guidelines laid down, be it implicitly only, centuries ago.

As I have said before, theology, in having this ontological thrust, is largely identical with jurisprudence, much more so than a far-flung web of cosmically applicable ethics. I think this allows the generalized conclusion about the inherent intent: that it was designed for the purpose of creating the perfect society—and not primarily as a universal ethical system—no matter whether one believes that this happened through divine revelation or through the ingenuity and inspiration of a charismatic, brilliant human leader and a few of his almost equally gifted successors. The course of history is strewn with millenarian prophets who tried to create the perfect human society—but few succeeded in having a lasting effect; most disappeared, becoming the subject of historical and anthropological curiosity. Islam—like the other world religions—by its lasting success sticks out among myriads of zany beliefs and superannuated doctrines that have fallen victim to humanity's insouciance.

How effective Islam is in its socializing function is a matter of debate, but it can hardly be disputed that it tends to generate universal patterns of conduct and attitudes among its adherents. Put in other words: Islam tends to produce characteristic sociocultural patterns which, though expressed in different degrees of intensity and apparency, tend to be present in all regional Muslim societies and cultural variants.

It may well be that this is more true nowadays than was the case for centuries previously. The reason is the broad re-Islamization trend and the phenomenon of fundamentalization, which tend to accentuate communalities in the world umma (the global community of believers) more sharply now; communalities that reach back to the early (foundational) scriptures rather than relying on later accumulated traditions. The mobilization of the sharia and what may be considered basic principles of Islam have gained traction across the traditional Islamic world and partially also, through migration, in the West. A kind of remoralization according to Islamic doctrinal principles, the reinvigorated use of the sharia to regulate human interaction contributes to commonalities becoming more prominent in Muslims' social and cultural milieus, and producing—and reinforcing—characteristic patterns.

Treating "Islam" as a coherent "culture" and as informing a particular, characteristic "society of Muslims" cannot rely on a purist approach. In the age of globalization that seems now even more justified than before. This society is not territorially definable, it is not co-local or co-residential, and only in a loose arc is vaguely geographically contiguous reaching from Morocco in the West to the southern Philippines in the East. Accentuating its deterritorialized condition, especially in recent years, it has spread beyond its traditional "territory" of the Middle East, northern Africa, South and central Asia, and the Balkans in Europe. In a diasporic sweep, Muslims have moved to many other parts of the world (not to forget the emergence of black Islam in America) where they form easily distinguishable communities. In some countries, where they had not been previously, they represent now significant minorities, whose presence begins to influence the cultural composition in the respective host countries. In particular, considerable numbers of Muslims have settled in Western Europe, North America, and Australia; and to a smaller extent as part of the legacy of European colonialism in South Africa, New Zealand, the Pacific, and many other places. But on account of a common religion and its culture-producing properties, these many diverse local communities form a meta-society, which is what the umma, the community of true believers, really is.

Today's reality makes it clear that Muslim society de facto is neither a homomorphic nor a monolithic entity. Its many manifestations can be very different. There is no inner coherence in the same sense as a "conventional" society possesses. The global Muslim society can best be seen as approximating an "imagined community" in Benedict Anderson's[11] sense. By referring to a "Muslim society" one simply relates it to two things: the existence of a common identity and the commonalities in some basic life patterns that all Muslim majority societies and Muslim communities share. The reason for this is grounded in the fact that they are subject to the strong culture-formative influence of Islamic dogma.

The needed essentialization that treats Islam as culture-producing and regards Muslims as members of a single meta-society, I believe, is well justified as an heuristic anthropological construct. Although essentialization is much opposed now within anthropology for the danger that it alienates description and analysis from reality, it is still useful in the attempt to gain a wide-angle perspective on the many diverse forms of human existence in a globalized world. It also has the advantage of approximating an "emic" category as Muslims themselves tend to have a perception of themselves as essentially linked through salient features of faith and doctrinally enforced, or strongly encouraged, behavior forms. The de-territorialized Islamic world, in other words, in a self-reflection possesses features of both "culture" and "society." As cultural and social reproduction is strongly guided by religiously derived epistemes, it tends to produce similarities of an "organic," not accidentally convergent, kind.

MUSLIM IDENTITY

About a fifth of the world population (between 1.2 and 1.6 billion people) identify as Muslims with greater or lesser conviction. Islam quite clearly is identity-defining: being "Muslim" not uncommonly overrules national, ethnic, and other personal identities. Depending on circumstances of course, from the many identities available to every person, [12] Muslims will frequently select the religious identity over others. In the identity pastiche every person draws on, giving preference to a particular option in a certain situation is significant. Muslims will in many circumstances give preference to their religious identity where "Christians" for instance will not. The strong religious orientation in identity formation and self-identification is rare among "Christians." [13] The vast majority of Westerners will not reach for a religious identification to define themselves, unless specifically required or encouraged in narrow, purpose-specific areas of social discourse. Declaring oneself "Christian" is usually done when this identity is counter-juxtaposed to "Muslim," a situation that is more often provoked by Muslims than by Christians. With people, who among Muslims would be labeled Christian or Western, the preferred self-identification is more in terms of nationality, or—depending on circumstances—ethnicity, or location of residence, or belonging to a profession.

The labels Muslim and Christian have really become categorizations of very different gravity. While the former is still very relevant, the latter has strongly declined in importance as a result of secularization. The identity of being Muslim has not undergone such a process of decline, at least not to the same extent; it is used more widely and frequently and, in fact, in very recent years has received a strong ideological boost by regulating people's lives more emphatically and consciously. Identification in terms of nationality (largely introduced in the Muslim world in the twentieth century through Western influence), traditional ethnic identifications (such as Arab, Kurd, etc.), and sectarian differences (as Sunni, Shi'a, Sufi, Ismaeli, etc.) do, of course, impact heavily on Muslim identity. However, Islam's dialogue with globalization has provided an incentive for emphasizing the ancient concept of umma. This is to say, Islamic universalism is not only ideologically still very vibrant, globalization and the cultural melting pot it augurs have presumably contributed to the revitalization of the "pan-Muslim" identity.

The unity of Islam is ubiquitous in the scriptures, but especially so in Quran 23/52: "And lo, this religion is one religion." It emphasises the indivisibility of Islam whose monolithic nature is further emphatically underpinned by the concept of umma, the community of believers. Its oneness, with strong connotation of cohesiveness, is further underlined by a strict delineation against nonbelievers, whose emphatic otherness is used to enhance and throw into sharp relief the in-group identity. Shutting non-believers out so decisively by saying, for example, that friends should not be made among Jews and Christians (Quran 5/51)[14] is more than just a strategic device to prevent infiltration and avoid harboring the enemy within, but insinuates a pan-Muslim identity that must not be compromised by obscuring the boundaries. Its potential effect of creating in-group solidarity may be less tangible in actual life, although one may sense that this was the original intention.

A Muslim identity today is still capable of glossing over language differences, ethnicity, and political boundaries, even at times over sectarian differences. In today's world, despite globalization, respect, solidarity, and empathy still do not easily osmose through language and national borders. Yet in Islam the acceptance of the centrality of one divine revelation and one sacred language, allowing the common appreciation of the revered texts, are congenial to the maintenance of a meta-identity that is largely missing among the "Christian world" or among other major religions.[15] By recognizing the valorization of a Muslim identity, which in some situations tends to hold primacy over other identity choices, I do not mean to express agreement with Huntington's thesis[16] of the existence of an "Islamic civilization," which is one among several monolithic, coherent, and to a large extent, religiously defined cultural blocs. This very coarse-grained reading of world cultures, religions, and identities allows him rather crudely to prophesy major political difficulties ahead engulfing whole "civilizations," but none more severely than between the West and the Islamic civilization. [17] My largely heuristic essentialization of "Muslimness" is not intended to support this thesis by hypothesizing a political coherence of the Islamic world, as will be discussed later.

Huntington's thesis superficially though conforms with the classical Islamic world view of a dichotomous global situation separating Dar-al-Islam, the realm of Islam, from Dar-al-Harb, the belligerent world of the infidels. (Although this conception is a ninth-century addition, it is firmly part of today's Islamism and even Salafism, even when it ideologically rejects Islamic thought and tradition younger than the times of the Prophet.) [18] This classical Islamic perception pared down to its essential function can be seen in the same terms of the confrontation of "Western civilization" with the Islamic one. It implies Manichaean proportions of good and evil locked in an eternal mutual antagonism that resonates with Huntington's thesis. The world of Islam, inhabited by the umma, is conceived in terms of a cohesive civilization founded on shared principles and doctrines—all of which are good since divinely inspired and commanded, and stand in stark contrast to the dubious and evil ways of the non-Islamic world. Region-specific cultural features in the Islamic world that are not shared, from an Islamic point of view, are not considered indicative of a profound bifurcation, but are non-essential, negligible, or aberrant. They do not go to the essence of Islam or to what it means to be Muslim. (Sectarian differences though cannot so easily be glossed over and are readily subsumed under "heresy.")

The reality, however, is that the appeal to common Muslimhood has consistently failed to succeed in uniting Muslims in practical action. Scriptural and doctrinal exhortations for absolute solidarity are rarely translated into actual life. Despite much admonishment in the Sunna for Muslims to practice unity among themselves—a hadith says for instance, "it is sinful for Muslims to insult each other and unbelief to fight each other"—political reality looks quite different. In the face of ethnic, sectarian, economic, and national interests, the common religious identity usually is set aside. On the whole, as Halliday [19] claims, international relations cannot be adequately explained solely by cultural and ideational approaches that allot primacy to ideas, perceptions and cultures. A good example is the deep division between the Sunni Arab and the Shi'a Iranian worlds that was again laid bare by the WikiLeaks revelations in 2010 and 2011. [20] The friction between Saddam Hussein's Iraq and Iran and more latterly between Saudi Arabia and Iran (as well as internally in Bahrain) were constant reminders. The cleavage between the Shi'a spirit of social revolution and the Sunni monarchic traditionalism is just too great, seeing sectarian difference reinforced by incompatibility of political systems. Iraq's and Syria's internal strife emanates from the same sectarian divisions. Another example is al-Qaeda. It is appealing to

Muslim identity, proclaims a jihad as a religious fardh (duty) incumbent on all Muslims so as to reclaim former Islamic pride, regain preeminence of Islam in the world, purify the Islamic world, and recapture Muslims lands. Yet by appealing to pan-Muslim solidarity, it has little success in galvanising the masses and creating a popular movement, although it does attract a steady stream of individuals from various nationalities and ethnicities who are prepared to fight for the cause. On the other hand, it is true to say that a common identity as Muslims can at times create unlikely bedfellows united in brief alliances. Mutual dislike between al-Qaeda and the Baathist regime of Saddam Hussein, for example, was at least temporarily suspended at first in the Gulf War of 1990 and then again in resisting the invasion and subsequent occupation of Iraq by coalition forces. While the U.S. administration's claim of a link between the Baathist regime and al-Qaeda—and the presumption that they jointly were hedging terrorist plans—which served as one of the rationales for the war, was patently wrong; it later briefly turned out to be true when both sides realized they fought a common enemy and joined forces. But this coalition of the desperate did not last long, bringing home the fragility of the Muslim identity.

ISLAM'S DIALOGUE WITH GLOBALIZATION

In many respects the so-called Islamic world, by containing the starkest contradictions and incongruities often visibly side by side, does not make it easy to perceive unity. While some parts of the Islamic world palpably reject globalization, others manage to selectively assimilate some of its aspects to spectacular proportions. Dubai in the United Arab Emirates, containing in many respects a very conservative Muslim society, is a good example. It has chosen to copy Western economics and to imitate classical capitalism, setting aside Islamic economic, trade, and banking principles, and effectively casting off the conservative sharia shackles. Dubai's economy treats the imported work force—mostly fellow Muslims—as an expendable commodity so that in terms of labor relations it can be compared, if not with a classical slave economy, then certainly with the rapacious, exploitative capitalist system Europe practiced in the nineteenth century and which spurred Karl Marx to write his communist manifesto. In financial terms, it seems to be a shining poster example for the boom-and-bust mentality of the more recent Western brand.[21] Islamic fiscal prudency and caution, which at least in spirit condemns usury and gambling as immoral and against God's law, seems to have taken a backseat.

In January 2010, the Burj Khalifa was officially opened; a proud symbol of financial daring and cutting-edge construction technology, standing there like a huge needle in the brown-gray heat haze, head and shoulder above Dubai's skyline, in which tall buildings seem to jostle for a place in the abundant sunshine. During planning and construction it had been named Burj Dubai (Dubai tower), but then was renamed after the ruler of neighboring Abu Dhabi, Sheikh Khalifa bin Zayed al-Nahyan, who came to Dubai's financial rescue. The tower's construction costs no doubt having contributed to Dubai's financial woes, the project was apparently close to collapse—sharing metaphorically the fate with its predecessor, the ambitious Biblical architectural marvel of the Tower of Babel. Indeed, not even three months after (near-) completion, it was closed down (though as it turned out to be only temporary), among rumors of technical faults and financial difficulties. At least for the time being, the skyscraper of 828 meters remains the world's tallest building and shows some interesting novel features. Mohammad al-Qubaisi, Dubai's top Muslim cleric, was reported in July 2011 to have decreed that the people living above the 80th floor have to wait two additional minutes to break the Ramadan fast, while those above the 150th floor must wait three extra minutes because they will see the sun longer than those lower down. This extravagant monument to modern architecture and financial might—as much as a sign of the vainglorious alliance of capitalism and nepotism—is effectively juxtaposed with the Spartan life in Bedouin camps only a few kilometers away, where people follow life patterns fundamentally not much different from centuries ago. Apart from its record-breaking features (in terms of office space, the number of apartments, length of elevators, etc.), the Burj Khalifa is said to contain the world's most elevated mosque. Ironically, on the opposite coastline of the United Arab Emirates, only a few kilometers from Dubai city as the crow flies, is one of the oldest mosques in the world, Al Bidyah Mosque in Fujairah, dating back to the fifteenth century. It is a small modest adobe structure devoid of minarets and other ostentatious artistic or architectural features that would single it out from other mud huts.

In terms of socioeconomics, surely the Islamic world contains some of the most stunning and polarized features in the world. If anything, globalization has accentuated these internal differences. Compare the stunningly hypermodern patterns of central Dubai, its futuristic monorail (under contraction), the wheeling and dealing in air-conditioned glass and concrete palaces, the opulent life style of rich Arabs to the life style, social patterns, and the level of everyday technology in remote valleys of the Hindukush, or in the central Asian steppes, or in African villages. Compare the commodious palaces of Arab princes with the squalor of shantytowns anywhere in the Middle East and Bangladesh. Nowhere is this antinomious difference more obvious than, again, in Dubai where the upper classes of Arabs are practically next-door to the ramshackle accommodation of foreign workers, many of whom are also Muslims. Dubai is a perfect welfare state—any social worker's dream, but only so for its citizens, the indigenous Arabs. They are about 10 percent of the population, while imported laborers and expatriate experts enjoy no social security whatsoever. There are none of the family reunification programs, medical care, low-rent housing, prospect of naturalization, financial support, and advisory services Muslims enjoy as migrants, refugees or guest workers in most Western countries. Globalization obviously can be playing out quite differently.

Globalization in the optimistic perspective of recent times seemed to promise a homogenized world culture, economic prosperity for all, individual and collective interconnectedness, and weakened nation-states in favor of strengthened panhuman administration and internationalized human rights legislation, eventual emergence of an identity as citizen of the world, and legal and ethical rules that give peace and security to humankind. Although one might say this vision is not an unattainable utopia, at the present time, it does seem to be lodged somewhere in the distant future beckoning like a shimmering, insubstantial mirage. Multiple new fissures have opened up, counter-globalization movements and forces that are trying to resist what no longer seems so inevitable.

Pessimistic views argue that globalization provides the means of spreading capitalism in the form of neoliberalism across the globe, and thus extending and entrenching exploitation and marginalization of large sections of humanity even further. This perspective means ceding the moral highground to globalization-resistance movements, whatever their methods may be, such as those of radical Islam. Some scholars have identified a trend by which the center of globalization is shifting from the West "eastward"; at least in an economic sense decentering the West and handing the momentum to East and South Asia.[22] At the same time the resistance towards globalization seems to grow. It strives to shift the world's accent away from materialism, from chasing after the vague notion of "progress," to other concerns such as culture, religion, and identity. Yet, relentlessly grinding on, globalization makes it difficult for nations and ethnicities to retain substantive distinctiveness and to maintain credible myths of national or ethnic specificity, if not superiority. Processes, which are hard to stop, cause national cultures to become more similar through overt or clandestine infiltration of specific culture elements. This may lead to identity crises and the perceived need to develop new strategies for generating time-appropriate images of self-worth in this global arena. Even anthropology in reflecting and analyzing these global changes falls in line with these developments:

> If the late 1950s and 1960s were characterised by the development of a domi-
> nant cultural materialism [and the development of anthropological paradigms
> to reflect this] . . . today's emergent themes [reflecting "progress" resistance]
> are culture as text, culture and identity, ideologies, culture and history etc., all
> pervaded by a relativist or even primitivist standpoint.[23]

Professional interests and sympathies have clearly shifted in line with the shifting sands of hegemonic ideologies.

A major source of resistance to globalization has been identified as emanating from Islam. (This much at least seems to be a vague consensus among experts, although about the reasons there is much less unanimity.) However, speaking of an Islamic resistance to globalization and its homogenizing effect is itself homogenizing, Pasha[24] argues. There is no single form of resistance, as its many forms spring from the enormous diversity in the present-day Islamic world. One must also bear in mind that resistance does not necessarily mean rejecting all features of globalization. With reference to Muslim politics, Habib[25] distinguishes several forms of resistance with partly overlapping and partly divergent goals. The political left concentrates on refusing the importation of the economic neoliberalist features of which it fears it will lead to further exploitation and economic domination by the capitalist West. While the West undergoes the third industrial revolution harnessing vastly improved means of telecommunication and information to its advantage, the rest of the world will slide into ever greater poverty and powerlessness. On the other hand such aspects as rationalism, secularism and technical modernization are welcomed. The nationalist and fundamentalist rejection of globalization is based on other considerations. Fearing loss of cultural substance and a historical grudge (concerning the troublesome relationship between Occident and Orient going back in time as far as the crusades) combine to a basic mistrust of innovations that seem to emanate from the West. Such entrenched patterns as patriarchal and feudal structures as much as illiteracy resent enlightenment improvements and prevent any respect for human rights or democracy, let alone the wish to adopt these Western features.

Let us explore for a moment this dimension: the—partly heuristically and partly realistically—constructed Muslim identity being linked in a peculiar way with the process of globalization. It becomes quickly apparent that the relationship between globalization and Islam (or rather Muslimness, i.e., being a devout Muslim in abstracto) is extremely multifaceted, in some respects contradictory, and in effect surprisingly amorphous. It is immediately clear that Muslimness is simultaneously rejecting globalization and itself is potentially globalizing.

Islam could be completing its globalizing mission in tomorrow's world—if humankind can be persuaded to unite under the banner of Islam or at least would acquiesce in humankind's division into believers and infidels. Islam had been set on this course in the past. Today, as Islam is being drawn into this globalizing vortex from which it cannot entirely stay aloof, it becomes a truly global doxa. Muslims dwell now in all corners of the globe thus physically transporting Islam beyond its traditional boundaries. Since its inception, Islam contains a globalizing impulse, which it has demonstrated for several centuries in the past. Reaching beyond its cultural origin on the Arabian peninsula, it has not only spread to what historically became known as the Islamic world, but has poured beyond it in the attempt of creating an even larger religiously coherent realm. Only by dint of applying concerted military means in the West—through the reconquista in Spain, the Norman intervention in Sicily, by stopping the Ottoman army's advance through the Balkans, and through Tsarist Russia's conquest in the Caucasus—was it possible to dam in the vigorous expansion. In Asia, the Turkic Khazars and Mongol expansion provided a counter-push and at first contained Islam's expansionism. South Asia's Hinduism also proved to be a stumbling block. It is clear that Islam's energy was only dammed in by the rather patchy European resistance in the West, by the Mongol counterattack in the East, by uncongenial circumstances in Africa and a somewhat passive resistance to conversion in India from where Islam's fingers were already eagerly grasping at the Southeast Asian archipelago.

In Southeast Asia, though, and along the Silk Road into China, Islam was successfully spread more by peaceful proselytization. Succeeding in stamping its creed on many diverse regional cultures, Islam has managed to create a cultural, though not a political, empire. Geographically at least, it is now again expanding, deep into the midst of the Occident (to the chagrin of many non-Muslim Westerners). On an ideological level, the dream of a world caliphate is kept alive today by some extremist groups, though it is only loosely connected with the real world. To what extent Islam will succeed in guiding globalization to its advantage remains to be seen.

At the same time, Islam emits now, culturally and ideologically, one of the strongest anti-globalization impulses.[26] This has obvious reasons that derive from hegemonic implications of the globalization process. Neither in theory nor in practice does globalization rely on a process of a harmonious growing-together, a gradual fusion of equal cultural constituents to form a synthesis to which all will have contributed in equal measure. From a non-Western perspective, globalization is usually perceived as a form of Westernization, an instrument to impose Western cultural domination and to lead to a future world that is essentially "Western." Some openly hostile arguments even present globalization as a reincarnation of European colonialism.[27] In the Islamic rhetoric of rejection, globalization is labeled Westoxification, or

Westoxication, and subsumed under the rubric of evil influences bringing with it all the amoral, antireligious impulses of Western civilization. A coterie of evils accompany it: consumerism, materialism, egotism, rapacious capitalism, decadent aesthetic regimes, the deluded selfishness of anthropocentrism, and the like. Leaving aside more obvious signs of Western hegemony (in financial, economic, and military matters), in a cultural sense it cannot be denied that globalization hides a plethora of Western influences and openly or subliminally suggests to other cultures the adoption of Western patterns of social interaction, juridical principles, and the like. As many of today's international processes and features are largely determined by Western ways, values, and cognition, globalization insinuates, stamps, and perhaps even crudely enforces Western cultural features on the rest of the world. An example is the Human Rights agenda. The abstract concept of this legal corpus (attributing the possession of inalienable rights to individual human beings and the rights of emphatic individualism) as well as the juridical flavor of it (of which it is often claimed that it arises from Christianity's ethics and the Western tradition of jurisprudence, which is rooted in this religion), as well as the history that gave rise to it (the history of genocide in Europe during the era of World War II), are undeniably of Western provenance. From an Islamic point of view, globalization is loaded with a moral and historical baggage that is both alien to the Islamic world and difficult—and undesirable—to assimilate. Not surprisingly, the Islamic world has been slow and cautious in signing up to various international agreements, compacts, and conventions, which represent and elaborate on human rights. Even when it obviously attempts to imitate global human rights, the Islamic world comes up with quite different legal perspectives to which a distinct Islamic aroma adheres. The Cairo Declaration of Human Rights in Islam of 1990 makes that quite plain. This is so despite Riffat Hassan's claim that the Islamic human rights declaration contains many, if not most, of the legal principles addressed in the international human rights proclamation: such as right to life, to respect, justice, freedom, privacy, knowledge, sustenance, work, protection from slander, defamation and ridicule.[28] However, despite similarities with the UN charter, the flavor of sharia is unmistakably present in the Cairo Declaration.

Globalization is inextricably connected with blunt issues of domination. In this sense, the success of European colonialism in subduing much of the rest of the world was clearly the pathfinder of the contemporary processes of globalization. (To speak of success in this context is a highly subjective notion referring to a political process that has left a morally dubious and highly ambiguous legacy as well as implanting a sense of resentment in much of the world that can still be felt today.) Islam in its history had displayed similar impulses, only that in a contest of strength with the West, its ambitions were forestalled from reaching the same global proportions as Western colonialism. Islam, too, was once a colonizing force with superiorist attitudes, a sense of pursuing a civilizing mission, and claims to moral and spiritual dominance. Considering itself the harbinger of a superior civilization, its colonizing impact on vast areas in Asia and Africa impressed an indelible cultural stamp on them. For a while Arabization and Islamization, propelled by an aggressive dynamic, were spreading with breathtaking speed out of the Arabian peninsula, later to be carried on by the Ottoman empire. In a move that seemed unstoppable, Islam rapidly metamorphosed from a desperate struggle, at the Prophet's time, to defend a small community of religious outcasts into a world-conquering juggernaut. The whole of the Middle East, Egypt, and North Africa fell to Islam within a few years. Only the inaccessible areas of the Hindukush resisted well into the nineteenth century allowing the first European observers to assemble a written record of the colorful culture and religion of Kafiristan—today's province of Nuristan, "the land of light." In the Maghreb, only Berbers in the inaccessible mountain areas have retained their language and traces of their pre-Islamic culture, while in other respects they have wholly embraced Islam. Southeast Asia, too, has resisted to some extent becoming Arabicized despite being Islamized to a large extent. Without Islam's push in the seventh and eighth century, Egypt would even be prouder of its ancient, pre-Islamic culture, relating its national identity entirely to the distant times of pyramids and pharaohs instead of uneasily juxtaposing that with its Muslimness. One can have similar expectations for the Eastern Mediterranean Levant and Western Turkey, if the Byzantian empire had not fallen to the Islamic onslaught. Indigenous pre-Islamic culture and language—and religious remnants—survived only in small enclaves here and there. Though not Arabicized to the same intense extent, amazingly large parts of Asia and Africa, and a corner of Europe, have been brought under the Islamic umbrella. Seen in this way, what may be called Islam's religious colonization in effect differs little from Europe's colonialism. The economic circumstances may differ somewhat, but in terms of cultural expansion through raw political power, there are unmistakable parallels both with European colonialism and modern-day globalization.

The rivalry between the contenders for globalization, the West and the Islamic world, has been settled—at least for the moment. The momentum belongs to the West (if we ignore the signs of its growing eccentricity and economic power slipping from its grasp). Occidentalism now believes it has the panacea for the world and feels justified in insinuating or forcing, as the case may be, its patterns on the rest of the world. Such is the depth of the missionary zeal that this effort often assumes the complexion of evolutionary inevitability. However, from a purely sociological viewpoint, this seems much less clear. At the very least, current global dynamics do not show clearly that the cultural future will be of a Western type. Above all, in the medium term, it must be realized that the Islamic world is not bound sooner or later to follow the same developmental path as the West. Islam may well prescribe a different road. It is tempting to rate the sociocultural differences between the West and the Islamic world as an evolutionary lag on the latter's part and to expect that global homogenization will mean that Islamic patterns will pull in line with modern Western ones—and perhaps even entertain the hope that this will produce a spiritual, ethical, and legal concordance that will eliminate serious global conflict. Islamic self-understanding is far from having adjusted to Western teleological assumptions. The notion of a universal sociocultural evolution that leads humanity along one preordained linear path is lacking. Francis Fukuyama's *End of History*[29] —though much less all-comprehensive than Marx's development theory or Durkheim's—was one of the more recent attempts, modernizing social teleology, to grasp political and ideological processes in terms of a universal development. But the hope it propagated for the emergence of a democratic world polity has yet to be realized. Globalization, although undoubtedly advancing Western patterns in the world, is not a guarantee for sociocultural synchronization, let alone uniformity, at least not in that part of the future that is foreseeable by a stretch of the imagination. Although, for instance, there is a tendency towards more secularization, more freedoms and enhancement of individual and collective liberties, more political actions based on law and legality rather than on whimsicality, what exactly these dynamics in detail may bring remains highly and dramatically uncertain. Islam certainly prescribes different ideals and priorities. The move towards universal acknowledgement of human rights does tend to have a unifying tendency, but there also are other ideological forces, which exert a different pull, as mentioned before. Western society, for example, propelled by a momentum of individual freedoms in the area of thought, belief, and values, experiences a deepening social paradox. Mounting intellectual freedoms and freedom of physical movement and expression, because of the desire for collective security encounters, increased state surveillance, and an erosion of privacy by the use of ever more sophisticated devices, to the extent that it begins to resemble thought control. Again, Islam channels this momentum into different pathways. Later on, we will touch on this issue in the context of prohibitions on female veiling. Modern communication technology allows masses of people to rally, which facilitates the dynamics of the so-called Arab Spring. However, it also facilitated the English riots in August 2011. The drive to engage with global networks and ideas comes with disadvantages, not the least of it is the increasing impossibility to absent oneself from them. It raises questions whether overall there is an enhancement of personal freedom or loss of it.

Muslim conservatives in pointing out that there are no grounds on which Western claims of legal and ethical superiority of the globalizing patterns can be justified, find an unlikely ally in some of Western social philosophy. Max Horkheimer,[30] a leading exponent of the Frankfurt sociological school, looking at the ruins of postwar Europe, very pointedly said, "The assertion that justice and liberty as such are better than injustice and oppression is scientif-ically not verifiable and worthless. As such it sounds as senseless as the statement that red would be more beautiful than blue or an egg would be better than milk." As social science leaves us in the lurch, aim and direction of sensibly improving the human condition can still be derived from the endeavour to implement the "ethically necessary" as Horkheimer suggests. This is based on convention, vague as it may be, and often shifting. At the present time, the convention is contained in the process of globalization and its ethical hegemony. To its credit, much of its momentum is not the result of blunt coercion, militarily or economically. Rather than being enforced by subduing the unwilling, compliance with the processes of globalization is brought about by their persuasiveness and desirable example, by the promise of enfranchisement and respect, affluence and power flowing from consent—just as Antonio Gramsci had argued about hegemony, how it is brought about and maintained. To paraphrase a current—and in the Islamic world some-what malodorous—slogan: it is a coalition of the willing. But should those who are not willing be allowed the freedom to stay apart? Or to phrase it even more bluntly: should conservative Islam be accorded the freedom to stone adulterers, execute apostates, amputate hands, and force women to cover their faces?

SITUATING ISLAM IN THE WORLD TODAY

Islam is far from being contained by globalization just as much as it was not contained by Western colonialism. It is spreading—not only in the Third World, but most importantly in the West, mainly through migration and to a lesser degree by proselytization. In January 2010 the New Zealand press[31] announced that Invercargill, the country's (and almost the whole world's) southernmost city, will shortly have the southern-most mosque in the world to service one of Muslimhood's smallest local communities, a mere fifty. A few months later, in November of that year, the northern-most mosque (the Midnight Sun Masjid) was inaugurated at Inuvik in arctic Canada, a town of some four thousand inhabitants and eighty Muslims.[32] This surely speaks to the rapid expansion of the Islamic faith to the far corners of the world. It speaks also to the tolerance of Western societies and the strength of legisla-tion securing cultural and religious freedom. Somewhat incongruously, roughly at the same time Switzerland in a not-so-well-attended national refe-rendum—a hallmark political institution of Swiss democracy—overwhelm-ingly resolved to prohibit the further erection of minarets on mosques to mitigate the architectural impact of Islam on the cityscape and to preserve its Middle European appearance. Grotesquely, traditional bastions of reason, freedom and democracy seem to rush to dam in what is seen as the tidal wave of Islam's advance and to start a cultural reconquista. The national identity appears to be at stake, demanding that the thrusting, phallic towers of Islam be curtailed to stop them from growing into the Swiss sky. France, no less a pillar of democratic freedom and freedom of expression and religion, after having banned the partial veil in the public education system, is giving in to widespread opprobrium and enacts a general prohibition on wearing the full face-veil, the burqa, and niqab, in public, thus adding to its previously enacted hijab interdiction in the public education system. Masquerading as liberation for women and as a protection of the country's official laïcité, such laws, easily recognizable as Islamophobic as they are, sit rather poorly in a juridical landscape that pretends to glory in personal liberties, unparalleled in the world. However, these moves are not without initiatives to the contrary. Recognizing that Muslims form a sizable religious minority, especially in Western Europe, some public figures have advocated various ways of better enfranchising the Muslim minority. Especially bold was the suggestion by the Archbishop of Canterbury, Dr. Rowan Williams, to give the sharia official status as an optional, alternative justice system in the United Kingdom. To some extent, the sharia is already alive there; as equipped with very limited jurisdiction, some sharia tribunals apparently are already operating in a few cities. Dispensing Islamic justice of a minor gravity, they enjoy official recognition as long as their verdicts do not contradict human rights and domestic laws and can be appealed in English courts. Other European countries defer to Islamic laws in matters concerning Private Law or have other mechanisms by which multiculturalist provisions are satisfied. However, so far Dr. Williams' advocacy going against growing public sentiments has met with concerted rejection.[33] After all sharia, female sartorial code, and minarets are characteristic features of Islamic culture, their presence clearly signaling the advance of Islam and, as some fear, the concomitant, proportional loss of national identity. This may not be everybody's view, but enough experience a sense of threat to allow parties and movements located at the extreme right of the political spectrum to advance Islamoskeptic, if not Islamophobic ideas and anti-immigration programs. With some hyperbole it may be said, the West begins to feel under threat and starts to react as Islam reaches ever more deeply into its domain. Prominent scholars such as Francis Fukuyama and Bernard Lewis[34] have warned of the advance of Islam and the loss of Europe's cultural identity due to its lethargy in protecting itself. Others[35] base their Islamophobic litany on security fears about the supposedly aggressive and treacherous nature of Islam.

Regardless of the fact that Islam, having spilt hugely beyond its traditional borders, is now a religion of the West, the largest minority religion in Europe (behind Christianity), and represents a sizable minority religion in North America, Australia, and New Zealand, it is not regarded part of the

West. Still considered as cultural Other, it remains subject to xeno-suspicion, more so than Judaism. (After having had a home in Western society for about two millennia, Judaism finally appears that it is becoming an integral part of the narrative of the West.) Muslims tend to accept the classification as "Others" assigned to them by the dominant Western discourse because it resonates with their predominant self-identification. Their self-imposed strong delineation towards non-Muslims is expressed forcefully in the classical dichotomy between believers and kafirun (infidels). Being a member of the umma rivals in importance to being English, or Dutch, or French. The dimension of religious belonging at best admits to a hyphenated identity such as French-Muslim or Muslim-German.

Contemporary Islam ideologically and in the way it reacts to globalization is, of course, a multifaceted and multidimensional affair that does not easily submit to a succinct characterization. One characteristic feature of Islam in the globalizing world is its fundamentalization by accentuating traditional doctrinal aspects and elevating them to conspicuous significance. Taking the sum total of learned arguments, it is totally unclear whether Islamic fundamentalization is a sign of protest against globalization because it is happening on Western terms, or whether it is an inevitable consequence of it (i.e., marks the consequent de-territorialization of Islam),[36] or whether it is a form of indigenization consequent on postmodernity and its search for spiritual certainty. To many Muslims, globalization is not only an intrusion of a foreign culture and its dictates, norms, and values, it has the religious flavor of an attack on Islam; for them, Islam is tantamount to a particular culture and a particular form of society, both of which are changing under the West's onslaught. Both are governed by doctrinal imperatives derived from Islam and which now are being undermined and threatened by this intrusion. Thus Western impositions are like an enforced conversion, a pressure to accept infidel terms. The present world order seems to contradict claims of Islam's superiority.[37] Resistance to globalization is whipped up by an elite that is not necessarily paramount in theological terms, but is adroit in combining religious doctrine, appropriately interpreted, with political ambitions and elevating this explosive mix to the normative Islamic viewpoint. Violence becomes a designated theologically sanctioned part of the strategy. Rejecting what is seen as oppression and protecting Islam and Muslims against the corrosive infidel influences, aggressive tactics are not only allowed but seem called for. The doctrinal notions of jihad (holy war) and taqiya (covert action through dissimulation) provide a useful ethical rationale.

Like a religious surfer, Islam is also riding the wave of globalization utilizing it to its own advantage. Islam is not just a passive recipient, or a victim, of the effects of globalization; there is also a dynamic aspect to the relationship between Islam and the present-day non-Islamic world. From the beginning, Islam had an expansionary energy, which was greatly aided by the assimilatory capacity of this religion. Early Islam was prepared to incorporate people of different culture and leave much of their customs intact as long as doctrinal essentials of Islam were preserved. Islam has a potential to absorb foreign cultures into a religious template that allows for considerable cultural hybridity. As said before, globalization is implicit in Islam's proselytizing ambition, and historically it has given an impressive demonstration of its potential. From the seventh to the seventeenth century it showed an aggressive dynamic to spread well beyond the region of its origin, the Arab peninsula, advancing into and throughout the Middle East and Northern Africa. It smashed the Persian empire, mortally wounded Byzantium, and wrested Asia minor from its grasp. It reached deep into central Asia and India, advancing into South East Asia and into the Philippines. On its Western flank on at least two occasions, it thrust into Europe and politically retained a religious foothold in the Balkans for centuries to the present day. The recent massive migration of Muslims into the Western world, though motivated by economic and political concerns, may have similar effects. Muslims for the most part do not migrate for religious reasons. Search for better economic opportunity for themselves or their children, flight from political upheaval and war are the major reasons. Yet by sheer force of numbers, they manage to give Islam a noticeable presence in the Western world, which may be mistaken for a continuation of the historical expansionism of Islam.

Growing numbers of non-Muslims in Western Europe begin to perceive the massive immigration of Muslims as a surreptitious attempt to complete the conquest of Europe at which earlier Islam has failed to succeed. This view, strongly informed by Islamophobia, paradoxically is supported by Tariq Ramadan's lesson to regard the Western diaspora as a religious opportunity. His missionary exhortation may be seen as a call to active proselytization to convert Europe to Islam. It fits into the conservative Christian perceptions that a morally enfeebled Europe, hollowed out by agnosticism and atheism, is fast becoming a religious vacuum—a vacuum that could be filled by Islam without offering much resistance. Ramadan's remarks may have been intended to be much less calculatingly strategic, perhaps meant to remind Muslims only that they are not living a life in Dar-al-Harb, a hostile environment ultimately requiring of the devout to become muhajirun (seeking emigration to a Muslim country); and that instead they should think of the West as Dar-al-Dawa, the realm of proselytizing opportunity.[38] If Islam has similar worries of being weakened by secularization, it does not show it. Muslims come well armed spiritually with their religion, which simultaneously is their culture and a guarantor of internal solidarity. Minarets penetrate the sky, hijabs appear in the streets, hundreds of Muslims stream towards a mosque for Friday midday prayers, the all important salat al jumma, backroom sharia courts begin to operate, religiously inspired domestic violence is rumored to be rife. For some non-Muslims these are warning signs of a cultural invasion: a significant cultural Other swamping a traditional European identity. North America with proportionally fewer Muslims does not exhibit the same fear. Its apprehension about culture loss is focused on the Latin-American immigration[39] and as far as Muslims are concerned, almost exclusively on the security risk posed by a small extremist minority.

Part of the reason why some non-Muslim Westerners fear that Muslim immigration is not just adding another religion to an existing pastiche—socially unimportant though expressive of religious and personal freedoms—is because it is believed a cultural invasion is taking place. As mentioned before, Poulter[40] speaks for many when he said that Muslims in the West can practice Islam only in the same terms as other religions. In other words they cannot transpose Islam as a characteristic culture and society from their homelands, but have to fit it in the rather more narrow confines of the Western conception of a religion, that is to say, a system of metaphysics and transcendental assumptions which find only limited application in daily life. A centuries-old process of secularization having whittled away at Christianity means now that the contemporary Western concept of religion refers to a belief system whose ethical commands and metaphysical speculations have only a strongly reduced weight in social life and do not exert a noticeable influence on politics. In other words, the normative dominance of religion has been reduced to the point of having almost vanished. The religion's erstwhile controlling influence on all public matters of society and nation has become relegated to backroom lobbying, media discussions, and the political action of influential personages who privately happen to be believers but publicly would lose kudos were they to openly ground their views in religious dogma.

The United States though has taken a course slightly different from the rest of the Western world insofar as the religious influence on politics is more overt and public and is also noticeably more vigorous. In my experience this has encouraged some radical Muslims to perceive America's propensity to intercede in Muslim affairs as a continuing Christian crusade. From another angle, American politics may be seen as slightly quixotic in view of the first amendment that is meant to provide a firewall between religion and politics and in its intent seems glaringly antinomious to radical Islam's motto of din wa daulah, belief and state being coterminous. It says something about the convoluted, yet sophisticated, nature of radical Muslims' thought processes that they are fully cognizant of Western politics, constitutional circumstances, and historical facts, and are able to combine all that in a paradox that makes sense to them.

Bassam Tibi's vision of a Euro-Islam emerging—an Islam conforming with the Western concept of religion—is based on the prerequisite that Islam shed its sociocultural all-comprehensiveness, abrogate any political ambitions, abandon its intolerant superiority complex, and provide only a backdrop of benign—as some would say, emasculated—ethical recommendations. Western Muslims, he argues, have the chance to effect a profound reform of Islam and to bring it into the twenty-first century. Freedom of speech and freedom from religious persecution create opportunities for Muslim intellectuals in the West to create a new Islam. Yet, as Tibi pessimistically remarked in an interview (in early 2011), the few reformers are missing out against the Islamists.

As Samuel Huntington[41] has perceptively remarked, "People came to America to become Americans. But Turks are not coming now to Germany to become Germans." As anti-immigrationists insist with a sweeping generalization, invitations to participate actively in democracy remain stubbornly unanswered, and offering the benefits of a humanist, people-centred sociability elicits no grateful response in the majority of Muslims. Thus the voices proclaiming the end of multiculturalism are growing louder, spreading beyond the far right of the political spectrum. Politicians and social scientists alike, picking over the detritus of failed policies, have pronounced multiculturalism a failure. It has allegedly produced parallel societies living side by side in a nation, harboring mutual hostilities against others not sharing a particular religious, cultural, or ethnic identity, encapsulating themselves within their self-imposed segregation, retreating into their own residential ghettos and deepening their isolation through their exclusivist education. This has created fears that society's internal cohesion is being dangerously eroded. While America has retained much of its traditional melting-pot ideology, Europe takes its human rights obligations of granting cultural freedom more seriously. The age-old maxim "when in Rome do as the Romans do" legally does not hold true any more. Even the conferment of citizenship does not come with a legal obligation to assume the culture of the country and embrace its core values.[42] Assimilation is not legally enforceable, making it easy for immigrants to retain their cultural Otherness and to insist on the recognition of a special status. In other words, Muslims make use of the freedom to reject the host societies' identity and culture. Thus from a position of strength Muslims exert influence—beyond their actual numbers as a minority, some claim—on the host society and its culture.

Right-wing, anti-immigration voices in Europe claim Muslims do not assimilate; they do not even wish to integrate—even when offered the possibility through a host of incentives and cultural compromises. Offers of cultural accommodation on the basis of tolerant public policies do not seem to work. It seems to support such alarmist sentiments when Tariq Ramadan rejects the offer of tolerance. Judging it an unequal relationship, offered by the more powerful as a charity to the weaker, he demands greater recognition.[43] The relationship should be based on a sense of equality and the recognition of the religious rights of Muslims as citizens and residents. Nothing less than complete acceptance of Otherness will suffice—thus, in fact, transforming Otherness into We-ness. Given this attitude, it sounds somewhat implausible then that the majority of Muslims would be content with the (reversed) status of dhimmi (tolerated religious minority), as some have argued. An apparent acceptance of dhimmitude as religiously and culturally tolerated, but politically disempowered (as dhimmis were in the classical Islamic civilizations), is occasionally reported.[44] One must assume that a dhimma system would look like the Austro-Hungarian solution before the end of World War II. It offered to the Muslim Bosniaks of Bosnia-Herzegovina a limited internal legal autonomy while externally making them subject to normal state law.[45] Needless to say, that even if this would be acceptable to a majority of Muslims—which seems doubtful—it would be inadmissible by any standard of human rights application.

These, in a rough sketch, are the sociopolitical forces, ideologies, and problems Muslims face in the modern world. Globalization may provoke rejection, but also the clever use of opportunities; it may confer important stimuli and activate collective historical memories of past vigor and glory that may be replicated in tomorrow's world. Most or all of these issues adhere to Muslimness, form part of a Muslim identity, or are somehow connected with it, either from a Muslim perspective itself or imposed by expectation and image non-Muslims have of Muslims. Through common self-identification and the ascribed one which stereotypes them, all Muslims are confronted in one form or another by these ideological forces and issues sketched above. Some of them belong into the identity's historical dimension (being centuries old), others are newly acquired and now add an odious reputation to Muslimness. Somehow Muslims have to face their demons. Being Muslim also defines stereotypical expectations how Islam constrains them to deal with issues of globalization. Whichever way Muslims respond, both they and the West have become intensively and irrevocably aware of their mutual interdependence in a globalized world and of the very need to understand each other.

NOTES

1. This goes vastly beyond the observance of the five pillars of Islam. See Andrew Rippin, *Muslims: Their Religious Beliefs and Practices*. London: Routledge, 1990–1993; pp. 127–141. Frederick Mathewson Denny, *An Introduction to Islam*. New York: Macmillan, 1985; pp. 105–129.

2. See Ernest Gellner, *Postmodernism, Reason and Religion*. London, New York: Routledge, 1992.

3. Gellner, *Muslim Society*. Cambridge: Cambridge University Press, 1983.

4. Sami Zubaida, *Beyond Islam: A New Understanding of the Middle East*. London, New York: Tauris, 2011; pp. 31–76.

5. Clifford Geertz's classical work *Islam Observed: Religious Development in Morocco and Indonesia* (New Haven: Yale University Press, 1968) demonstrates the point of unity in diversity.

6. Sami Zubaida, *Beyond Islam*; p. 11.

7. From her book *What Everybody Should Know about Islam and Muslims*. Quoted in John Wolffe, "Fragmented Universalism: Islam and Muslims." In *The Growth of Religious Diversity: Britain from 1945*, vol.1, Gerald Parsons (ed.). London, New York: Routledge, 1993–1994; p. 156.

8. Sebastian Poulter, *Ethnicity, Law and Human Rights: The English Experience*. Oxford: Oxford University Press, 1998; p. 236.

9. Olivier Roy (*Secularism Confronts Islam*. New York: Columbia University, 2007, 1st French ed. 2005) sees this already happening in France.

10. By excluding mysticism from "mainstream," I do not mean to imply a value judgment or to apply theological censorship.

11. Benedict Anderson, *Imagined Communities: Reflections on the Origins and Spread of Nationalism*. London, New York: Verso, 1983.

12. See Amartya Sen, *Identity and Violence: The Illusion of Destiny*. New York, London: W.W. Norton, 2006.

13. The religious declaration (as Catholic, Protestant, etc.) that had still been demanded in official discourses (forms, applications, etc.) up until the 1970s in European countries, has by now almost totally disappeared. Religious affiliation, so far as it is still relevant, has become a private affair.

14. The prohibition on fraternization with non-Muslims seems to belong to a later phase in the development of Islam under the Prophet's leadership, reflecting a rising hostility towards outsiders.

15. Judaism appears to have a potency similar to Islam's. A victim mentality adds to it.

16. Samuel Huntington, *The Clash of Civilizations and the Remaking of World Order*. New York: Simon and Schuster, 1996.

17. See Erich Kolig, Sam Wong, and Vivienne SM. Angeles, "Introduction: Crossroad Civilizations and Bricolage Identities." In *Identity in Crossroad Civilizations: Ethnicity, Nationalism and Globalism in Asia*, E. Kolig, V. Angeles, and S. Wong (eds.). Amsterdam: Amsterdam University Press, 2009.

18. It is not part of Quran or Sunna. Asma Afsaruddin, "Demarcating Fault-lines within Islam." In *Shari'a as Discourse*, J. Nielsen and L. Christoffersen (eds.). Farnham: Ashgate, 2010; p. 34.

19. Fred Halliday, "The Politics of the Umma: States and Community in Islamic Movements." In *Shaping the Current Islamic Reformation*, B.A. Roberson (ed.). London, Portland, OR: Frank Cass, 2003; pp. 35–37, 39.

20. I am referring here specifically to the revelation that the Saudi monarchy urged the United States to attack Iran in order to thwart that country's nuclear ambitions–as revealed by WikiLeaks in 2010.

21. Timur Kuran, *The Long Diversion: How Islamic Law Held Back the Middle East*. Princeton: Princeton University Press, 2010.

22. Jonathan Friedman, *Cultural Identity and Global Process*. London: Sage, 1994.

23. Jonathan Friedman, *Cultural Identity* p.79. See also Ralph Grillo, "Cultural Essentialism and Cultural Anxiety." *Anthropological Theory* 3/2 (2003):157–173.

24. Mustapha Kamal Pasha, "Globalization, Islam and Resistance." In *Globalization and the Politics of Resistance*, B. K. Gills (ed.). Basingstoke Hampshire, New York: Palgrave, 2000.

25. Kadhim Habib, "Globalization and the Fears of the Arabic and Islamic World." www.qantara.de; accessed February 2004.

26. The remainder of the Communist World (the countries that have changed their ideological-economic colors, and even those that nominally remain Communist), has for the most part given up its resistance.

27. This is not to deny that even within the so-called West there are distinct anti-globalization phenomena of cultural conservatism, separatist ideologies, and the like.

28. Riffat Hassan, "Rights of Women Within Islamic Communities." In *Religious Human Rights in Global Perspective*, J. Witte and J. van der Wyver (eds.). The Hague: Nijhoff, 1996. See also J. Witte and J. van der Wyver, Introduction. In the same volume.

29. Francis Fukuyama, *The End of History and the Last Man*. New York: Free Press, 1992.

30. *Zur Kritik der instrumentellen Vernunft*, (ed. by A. Schmidt). Franfurt a.M.: Suhrkamp, 1967; p. 33.

31. See, for example, *Otago Daily Times* January 12, 2010; p. 8.

32. *New Zealand Dawa eNewsletter*, December 1, 2010. Other websites give slightly different numbers.

33. See Rex Ahdar and Nicholas Aroney (eds.), *Shari'a in the West*. Oxford: Oxford University Press, 2010.

34. Francis Fukuyama, "A Year of Living Dangerously," *The Wall Street Journal*, November 2, 2005; p. 5. And "Identity, Immigration, and Liberal Democracy," *Journal of Democracy* 17/2 (2006): 5–20. His argument addresses the concerns that massive Muslim immigration in the West brings about a shift in cultural identity. Bernard Lewis has expressed similar fears with regard to Europe. (In the Jerusalem Post, November 2, 2009, www.jpost.com.) Earlier on, he had already predicted that "by century's end Europe would be Islamic" (www.weeklystandard.com , accessed October 2004).

35. E.g., Melanie Phillips, *Londonistan: How Britain Is Creating a Terror State Within*. London: Gibson Square Books, 2006.

36. See Olivier Roy, *Globalized Islam: The Search for a New Ummah*. New York: Columbia University Press, 2004.

37. Bassam Tibi, *Political Islam, World Politics and Europe*. London: Routledge, 2008; pp. 37–38.

38. Tariq Ramadan, *Western Muslims and the Future of Islam*. New York: Oxford University Press, 2004.

39. See Samuel Huntington, *Who Are We?* New York: Simon & Schuster, 2004.

40. Sebastian Poulter, *Ethnicity, Law and Human Rights;* p. 236.

41. Samuel Huntington, *Who Are We?;* p. 191.

42. Some European countries do, however, now demand from immigrants a larger demonstration of commitment to the host nation in terms of cultural acceptance.

43. Tariq Ramadan *The Quest for Meaning: Developing a Philosophy of Pluralism*. London: Allen Lane, 2010.

44. For example, Jørgen Nielsen, "The Question of Euro-Islam: Restriction or Opportunity." In *Islam in Europe: Diversity, Identity and Influence*, A. Al-Azmeh and E. Fokasi (eds.). Cambridge: Cambridge University Press, 2007; p. 36.

45. This was anchored in the Islamgesetz of July 1912, which officially recognized Islam (of the Hanafi school). This in principle was already done in 1874 when the Ottoman empire ceded the province to the Austrian monarchy. The juridico-political situation then was akin to the millet system of the Ottoman empire, giving a degree of self-governance and limited autonomous legislation to various ethnic and religious communities.

Chapter Two

Islamic Law

STRENGTH AND FLAW OF THE SHARIA

It is impossible to consider Islam and not delve deeply into Islamic law, the sharia. Most of what constitutes the perceived unity of Islam and Muslims hinges on the shared acceptance of sharia—although one has to add immediately that the shared ingredient may be no more than a vague similarity of practice and customs and a whiff of scriptural doctrine. The sharia exists in so many different versions that some scholars refuse to acknowledge its communality in more than just the name. The communality lies more in a diffusely underlying episteme of justice and ethics, of evaluating in a particular way social conduct as to its appropriateness, in setting accents in what is considered correct behavior and how incorrect behavior is to be punished, rather than rendering concrete rules and fixed laws, which would exactly be the same everywhere in the Islamic world. For instance, rating apostasy as a heinous act and considering blasphemy a severe crime, in gravity equal or even surpassing murder, is such a communality, which distinguishes the sharia from other judicial systems. However, these "crimes" are not punished with exactly equal measure everywhere where Islamic justice is being practiced. The sharia simply, and more diffusely, delivers the distinct and particular aroma of human sociality and social order that pervades the so-called Islamic world.

In actual empirical reality, the exposition of sharia ranges from the strict, "medievalist" version the Taleban instituted to a very liberal, relaxed interpretation proposed by some leading reformers (especially the neo-modernist school in Indonesia[1] and some Muslim scholars living in the West), from the conservative sternness of the official Saudi law to the hybridity practiced by "acculturated," diasporic Muslims in the West, and from the conservative tenacity of ancient village custom to modern state law barely infused with the flavor of Islamic ideas. In its purely doctrinal, abstracted form, sharia is one of the main defining aspects of this religion, in dogmatic importance second only to the concept of tawhid, the oneness and indivisibility of God. The significance of this concept gives Christianity in the eyes of Islam a suspect tinge of not really being monotheistic and surrenders to (some) Muslims the justification to look down on Christians as mushrikun, polytheists. For the concept of the holy trinity, which is considered shirk, unlawful association of the oneness of God with other entities, comes dangerously close to the worship of three divine entities.[2]

In its ideal form sharia, closely regulating the believers' conduct, is the code to guide the faithful on the "straight path to the well"—a very apt metaphor for a desert culture to describe a resolutely "correct" approach to a God-pleasing existence. Sharia is the orthopractic face of the religion, of equal importance to orthodoxy. Close adherence to it is the guarantee of salvation for the believing Muslim, its existence the proof of God's love of humanity, and its uncompromising sternness the appropriate penalty for straying from the way. The "straight path" paraphrases the social, juridical and ceremonial reglement believed to have been revealed by God and exemplified by the Prophet in his words and his life. It is the sum total of commandments, laws, ordinances, rules, and recommendations overtly or cryptically laid down originally in the Quran, exemplified and elaborated on by the Prophet in his personal hagiography, and laid down for all eternity in the Sunna (the traditions and the Prophet's commentary, the ahadith). The Prophet's whole life and conduct is an epiphany of law-giving importance, to be revered and emulated to the smallest detail—as especially the Salafis try to do. The Quran[3] contains several references specifically to this effect, commanding the believer to obey the Prophet and follow his example. This original body of revealed information has been further refined through the intellectual efforts and "deductive reasoning" of the madhahib (so-called law schools) in the subsequent centuries and preserved in the fiqh, the codified law system. Some extreme Salafists though dispute the validity of the latter source and endeavour to find back to the purity of the Prophet's revelations and his exemplary life, and that of the al-salaf al-salih, the pious forefathers and compatriots of Muhammad, who serve as paradigmatic role models.

Islamic law as we know it today was profoundly shaped by the labors of the so-called law schools (madhahib), aggregates of eminent scholastic minds systematizing scriptural hints into comprehensive law codices (fiqh). In the centuries following the Prophet's life, they were instrumental in codifying and, through exegesis, elaborating the revealed rules, often to the outsider's eyes no more than vague hints, into systematic form thus transforming divine commandment into formal law.[4]

Apart from many cul-de-sacs, there are four major Sunni schools: Maliki, Shafi'i, Hanafi, and Hanbali; and three major Shi'a schools: Jafari, Zaidi, Ismaili,[5] which created the bodies of legal scholarship that are still recognized today. Although sharia in its classical shape is being emulated relatively faithfully only in Saudi-Arabia, to some extent in Sudan, and Yemen, and (with a large dose of Khomeinism) in Iran, it does inspire to varying degree the legal systems of most Muslim-majority countries. In less conspicuous ways, the sharia still determines life in large parts of West Africa, central Asia, and southern Russian areas.[6] It also underlies, of course, more or less faithfully, the customary life at every level of Muslim society except its most secularized or westernized sections.

As a body of knowledge, the sharia is indispensable to living a God-fearing existence. Through divine revelation and the Prophet's divinely guided and inspirational life, more or less clear guidelines are supposed to have been given as to how to lead a God-pleasing life. Straddling and obscuring the dividing lines between orthopraxis and orthodoxy, between strict law and recommendation, between canonical legality and ethical ideal, sharia in its functionality spans the regulative ontological aspects of human existence in its entirety. Islamic doctrine goes vastly beyond mere ceremonial rules of worship and articles of faith. Like all religions, Islam delivers a sense of the meaning of human existence, but it goes further by giving a strict and very detailed blueprint for how to conduct oneself in order to fulfil this role. The requirement to closely espouse the rules of sharia applies to individual lives as much as in a structural sense to the society of believers (the umma) as a whole. For the collectivity, too, in its communal functions, should be guided and organized by doctrine and divine principles, thus molding theology, divine law, and politics into one. Moral theology virtually becomes the law as well as the foundation of political action. By and large, being human finds fulfilment in the duty to please God and achieving this by following closely the divinely devized rules of social conduct and being mindful of God's designs for man. At the end of a life of obedience, at divine pleasure, lies the prospect of heavenly reward in a paradise, which for the benefit of the less sophisticated is conceived in fairly earthly-minded terms. Alternatively, ignoring and violating these rules beckons with assurance of eternal damnation—and, of course, also with prospects of harsh punishment in this world as prescribed by divine decree and administered by worldly authorities.

Few if any other religions pay such enormous attention to correct conduct to the smallest detail.[7] This gives a ceremonial, sanctifying gloss to actions of social intercourse, which in other religions would remain entirely mundane and untouched by the religious brush. Especially the five daily prayers (salat) structure that punctuates the everyday life of the devout and remind them in short intervals of their duty to God—or in an abstract sense, of the transcendent quality of their existence. The relevance of this interconnected-

ness is that in the modern world it gives society—as well as the culture that
provides the motivations for social conduct—a greater degree of viscous
inertia than society would have otherwise. In other words, it increases the
resistance to social change when through its societal and cultural ramifications this change tends to touch on the very essence of religion.

The shariatic rules that ideally regulate a devotee's life have an ontological span from the very private to the very public; they implicitly or overtly
prescribe everything from conducting personal hygiene and sexual activity,
to risking one's life in God's service. Laws of proper diet and inheritance,
punishing a thief, conducting business and dealing with an enemy, giving
witness in a court of law, divorce, political leadership, polygyny and gender
relationships—every conceivable aspect of human life is at least potentially
if not succinctly and clearly contained in the fiqh, the systematic collection of
shariatic rules. Supported by exegetical interpretations of qiyas and ijtihad, or
by wide consensus, ijma, rules can be extended to conditions and matters that
clearly did not exist at the time of the Prophet nor in the centuries after him
when the original revelations were codified by the law schools. Thus for the
strict believer even the ringtone of one's cellphone, the brand of toothpaste to
be used, or whether it is permissible to breathe in vaginal fumes,[8] requires a
legal-theological decision by experts. Many eminent scholars and theologians maintain websites or blogs to answer such enquiries by the devout.
How a Muslim should respond to friendly wishes for a merry Christmas or
what a Muslim astronaut orbiting earth should do with the required five
prayers at specific times when every ninety minutes the sun comes up, become serious issues for experts to contemplate.

Some aspects of the sharia are spelled out in relative clarity, while others—despite the collective efforts of brilliant jurist-scholars in classical
times—are obscure or vague and are open to a wide range of possible interpretations. (There are also significant differences in the legal interpretations
of the various madhahib.) Hand amputation for theft, for instance, is unambiguously commanded in the Quran, which being God's word "verbatim" all
Muslims accept as the most authoritative source of legal wisdom. Yet, juridical and aesthetic globalization often intervenes and in less hard-line state law
systems this draconian punishment is not applied. Other rules, if not formalized in current law, emerge only after lengthy and laborious interpretation,
requiring consultation with the experts in individual cases to achieve clarity.
Agreement among experts though is rarely achieved. In virtually any matter
expert views on shariatic application diverge widely, often in personal affairs
giving a choice which view or fatwa (ruling, opinion) to adopt. In the absence of a hierarchy of authority among those who by general consensus are
regarded as legitimate sources of legal wisdom, a range of other criteria come
into play as to which opinion should be followed. And adding to the complexity surrounding the issuing of legal opinion, expert assessments can be

treated as recommendations or as strict commands or, if not backed up by temporal power, can be ignored entirely depending on the inclination and receptivity of those affected.

Another complicating yet defining feature of the sharia is the multitude of regional variations. Differently expressed, there is a considerable breadth of variation in scriptural normative Islam and customary sharia. Islam spreading over a vast geographic expanse in its history has incorporated regional customs and pre-Islamic belief elements as part of the sharia. This has engendered quite different notions of authenticity and the proper normative function of Islam. Such differences in perceptions of what constitutes authentic sharia, what is correct orthodoxy of scriptural Islam and what is the required orthopraxis can be area- or ethnicity-specific or relate to sectarian divisions. For example, it is fair to say that the vast majority of Muslims have little appetite for the Talebanic version of sharia and consider it an anachronistic misinterpretation, a regression into barbarity, or worse, a perversion. This extremely draconian version of sharia is apparently still practiced in isolated areas and in some village communities in defiance of state law, but is rejected even by the most conservative official law. This often brings the customary sharia practiced in the social intercourse of some local communities in direct conflict with the official jurisprudence, although both sides claim to be espousing shariatic principles. Such a clash was glaringly exemplified for the whole world to see in a case in Pakistan a few years ago, when a young woman, Mukhtar Mai, was gang raped by four men by order of the village council. This was done to punish some transgression by her brother— the young man apparently had an ill-conceived dalliance with a higher-class girl. (The news reports unfortunately were not specific enough.) In a Western sense of justice this would hardly be considered a punishable transgression at all, and even if it were the case, his sister would not be considered the appropriate recipient of the punishment. After the event, rather than submitting and living quietly the life of shame she had been sentenced to for no fault of her own, the woman bravely sought redress through Pakistan's official law which, although also based on shariatic principles, condemns the act of "judicial" rape—and provides for capital punishment of any rape. Shortly afterwards, in July and August 2002, pictures of the perpetrators (those having committed the rape and those having ordered it) being shepherded into the courtroom in chains went around the world, publicized through the electronic and print media. In August of the same year, a court sentenced six men, responsible for ordering and carrying out the rape, to the death penalty. On appeal, in 2005, this verdict was overturned. Not long afterwards, through the intervention of yet another juridical angle, all the culprits, except one, were quietly released. (The fate of this man remains uncertain.) This event shows that the normative function of Islam and its judicial arm can vary to some considerable extent according to context, area, community, and country and not least which particular version of sharia is brought to bear.

However, the question arises, what then justifies considering the sharia as one of the most important unifying factors for Islam and Muslims? The reason is, that despite great variability in detail, in its fundamental epistemic form the concept of sharia does produce a degree of (for the most part subliminal) uniformity revealing itself, though reluctantly, in fundamental features of jurisprudence, ethics, and social conduct, and their patterning, be it at the village level or the official, state level.[9]

Rudolph Peters[10] distinguishes four types in the relationship between sharia and modern state law in the Islamic world. One in which the sharia has been totally eliminated from state law: as in Turkey (but in rural areas and in family law matters shariatic views still prevail). Second, as in Saudi Arabia and Yemen where the sharia is the law of the land and official jurisprudence is exercized on this basis. Third, countries in which Western law prevails with some exceptions (in family law, waqf) and the sharia supplies principles on which state law is based. And the fourth type exists in countries in which criminal law has been re-Islamized (such as Iran, Sudan, Libya, northern Nigeria, and Pakistan). If we leave aside the juristic detail, the fact remains that in one form or another the dominant ethical viewpoints and common social practice are still derived from or influenced by the sharia, though in varying degree of intensity. Although the sharia is re-codified by the state and the state determines what sharia norms are—and not the uluma (clerics)—the influence of the sharia as a body of ethics and normative regulator has been retained in jurisprudence and even more strongly in the daily social discourse. Thus there is a degree of secularization to be noticed, but it is by far not as intensive as in the West.

An important factor of globalization is the impact of Western juridical dominance and of Western aesthetic regimes on the practice of sharia. In some cases, this has pushed Islamic law into comprehensive modifications and adaptations. More than the rather diffuse Western aesthetic dominance in the world, it is the existence of human rights provisions supported by the United Nations that has had a major impact on the Islamic world. Even Saudi Arabia, despite espousing very conservative shariatic principles, does not stand totally aloof in its official legal practices. Often it is the intervention by the royal house that seeks mitigation in cases of capital crimes. Saudi interpretation of hakimiya, governance, by statute allows the king to vary the implementation of sharia in actual cases. Whether the reason, when he does so, is the concern for international opprobrium or a humanist streak of the royal house is debatable. Iran, on the other hand, which also bases its jurisprudence strongly on the sharia, delights in its independence and does not allow the West to take credit for exercising any influence. Capital punishments (for homosexuality, marital infidelity, blasphemy, or prostitution, for instance), retributive qisas forms of mutilation, and harsh imprisonment for what is regarded as female insubordination are carried out despite Western protests. In several Muslim countries significant disharmonies between Western-influenced and perhaps even partly secularized state law, and customary law as practiced by rural or remote communities or less Westernized social classes, have come into the spotlight (for instance, in so-called honour killings). In some cases this has opened up sizable rifts between official jurisprudence and communally applied rules of conduct and punishment, especially those practiced by Salafist sections of society who in various way are trying to recreate what they regard as the shariatic purity of early Islam. On the whole, however, and despite various differences, and despite many concessions the Islamic world has made to globalization, it can be said that the sharia—especially its penal aspects, responses to offenses against divinity and sacred personages, gender-related aspects, and grotesquely also its dietary rules—still expresses the major difference between the Islamic world and the non-Islamic world more than anything else. Every feature that seems to define Islam's authenticity or to characterize Muslim society can be traced back to the sharia. This warrants a closer look at the nature of this legal body in relation to human universals and to enquire into the effects of juridical globalization. Although all of humanity seems to share innately a concept of justice, it differs strongly in content and meaning. As is abundantly clear, the shariatic sense of justice, adl (or adil), is noticeably different from the Western one.

TRIBAL LAW, MODERN LAW, AND GLOBALIZATION

At the time Islamic law (or less forcefully expressed, rules of social conduct) was initially formulated through revelation and exemplification, it had been surpassed in sophistication by far by Roman law which had been devized already centuries before and survived the demise of the Roman and Byzantine empires. Yet, historically, there is great value in the sharia. Islamic law in its original formulation in Quran and Sunna takes a decisive step away from relatively "informal," customary or tribal law and moves towards a more formalized and systematized law.[11] Some scholars refuse to recognize sharia as codified law in reference to its flexibility and the role ijma (consensus), ray (personal opinion), ijtihad (interpretation), and qiyas (analogy) play in giving Islamic law much fluidity.[12] Ultimately, it is a matter of interpretation what may be considered as codified, in the sense of systematized. Certainly, Muslims believe sharia to be so. From an anthropological angle considering the vast variety of legal systems throughout human cultures—and especially by comparison with tribal or customary practice of law—sharia in the form of fiqh seems highly systematized. A certain whimsicality of definition in scholarly understandings of the sharia is also reflected in the fact that Snouk Hurgronje[13] considered it to be revelation and thus in his mind does not qualify terminologically for the same status as Western law. Max Weber[14] also had difficulties in according it equal status with Western law, because to him it was of lesser rationality. And Joseph Schacht[15] saw it more as ethics than law.

Customary, and newly invented, rules of behavior and forms of collective retribution for their violation were cast by sharia in more explicit form than is normally the case in "tribal" societies. Early Islamic law, by superseding Arab tribal law, placed social intercourse on a more predictable basis than earlier, more informal law systems might have provided. The subsequent step towards complete systematization was taken then by the madhahib, the various law schools, by amplifying and codifying the beginnings made by the Prophet and his successors, the Rashidun caliphs. This groundbreaking work retained its direct validity until the present day and in doing so overtakes Roman law in longevity. It also surpasses Christian (Catholic) canonical law in the sense that sharia has retained a greater degree of social relevance by withstanding the forces of secularization more successfully. At the same time it remained more static, unchanging. Essentially, conservative jurisprudence, notions of appropriate conduct, and ethics remained at the stage they were centuries ago, in their principles unchanged until the present time, through the doctrine of juridical immutability. As divinely revealed law it is only subject to exegesis, but not revision. It is certainly true to say that Islamic law (to the extent that it is till practiced today) has not undergone a rapid and profound evolution of juridical principles relating to justice and propriety to the same degree as Western justice systems.

Leaving this very modern difficulty aside, the Middle East in general and Islam in particular can be celebrated for having forged a tight union between religious belief, generalized moral principles, and codified law. This effort not only removed the definition of lawfulness from the vagaries of customary practice and from the tyrannical whimsicality of despots, but also achieved a fundamental measure of equality before the law regardless of social status or tribal affiliation. Another merit of the emerging Islamic law was that, although a profound distinction between believer and infidel was made, the latter were not people outside the law who could be treated at will. This is an important difference to tribal law, which normally does not extend to outsiders. Customary rules and tribal "civility" thus do not apply to them.

The first attempts at codification of law are ancient in the Middle East, reaching back to Hammurabi[16] and the Mesopotamian civilization. The Old Testament is part of, and heir to, that stern regional legislative tradition, but while urbanization facilitated a clearer codification, the nomadism, and in some periods downright peripatetic existence, of the original monotheistic Hebrews seems to have prevented that.[17]

Although still couched in terms of divinely received rules, thus giving it an axiomatic gloss, law being articulated in some detail made it accessible and subject to closer scrutiny. This opened the gates to informed legal argument and enhanced transparency as to the consequences of social, or asocial, conduct. Importantly, it also removed law to some extent from the grasp of capricious power and tyrannical rule. Insistence on the possession of precise rights and duties—as different from being dependent on the whim of despotic social agents or on diffuse tribal tradition, which is amenable to being interpreted and bent in accordance with sociopolitical interests—can rightly be considered a very progressive step for the time. It enhances predictability and thus security of existence; especially when the laws' universal nature—which includes at least theoretically the rulers—is spelled out. (Practically, of course, the ruling elite were still often beyond the reach of the common law and its enforcement, and were practically subject only to "divine" intervention.) Not surprisingly, Britain still considers the Magna Carter as a milestone in the development of British law without which society's enjoyment of impartial legalities would not exist in their present form. Codified regulative functions to which all members of society are subject are one of the building blocks of a "civilized" society. At least in principle this distinguishes such a law system from tribal or customary law, which is exercized from unformulated traditions whose definition, application and enforcement lay in the hands of elites who often had the kind of unquestioned authority that enabled them to use "customs" to their advantage.

Recognizing this should not mislead one into the assumption that there ever were "lawless" societies that is to say, groups of people of some coherence who were devoid of any rules of interaction. Even so-called outcasts of society, pirates, groups of escaped slaves, and the like, devized, usually unwritten, rules of conduct and interaction and punished transgressions within the group. Human sociability is not thinkable without laws, however formal or informal they may be. A condition of "lawlessness," the total absence of rules of conduct, as it allegedly has been observed in some societies in historical times, more often than not is the result of displacement and social uprootedness; in other words the observed chaotic forms of social interaction are symptoms of acute anomie. (Quite possibly, the lack of finely honed analytical powers of the observer, failing to see some order behind the apparent chaos, may also be to blame.) This seeming condition of lawlessness in historical times, occasionally described in the ethnographic literature, was often the result of herding tribal populations into reservations with confined spaces and severe limitations on traditional activities.[18]

Often the exercise of violence makes it appear that no laws apply. However, the existence of cyclical vengeance and recurring blood feuds, for instance, does not indicate a state of lawlessness and may occur in accordance with relatively strict customary "laws."[19] Pre-Islamic Arab society, like neighboring societies, seems to have had similar social mechanisms of regulated revenge-induced violence—which only from an outsider's point of view would have appeared "lawless." On this point there is a logical contradiction in sharia law. Revenge violence certainly seems to sit well in an "eye-for-an-eye" justice philosophy that underlies the sharia. The provision of the concept of "blood money" (diyah) to settle a homicidal culpability—and obviate the need for execution or a chain of vendetta-like killings—does not. It was probably already a pre-Islamic legal mechanism to stop chains of violence extending over generations. This provision has existed in other pre-modern societies also and probably for the same reason, namely, to put a stop to the socially very disruptive, internal bloodletting.

The lex talionis aspect of appropriate retribution to punish a crime, is an important element of sharia and warrants a closer look. Most conspicuous for Western sensibilities is the juridical principle of qisas based on the notion of measured equality between crime and punishment. As the Quran (16/126) phrases it, "If you punish . . . then punish with the like of that with which you were afflicted." For the time, it probably seemed a sound juridical basis regulating punishment and removing the undesirable and socially disruptive consequences of violent crime by a simple and relatively uncomplicated mode of retribution. Qisas, the principle of "eye for an eye" is fairly concisely stipulated as well as more obliquely referred to in several Quranic verses[20] indicating the importance attributed to it. Verse 5/45 spells out the principle very precisely:

> Life for life, eye for eye, nose for nose, ear for ear, tooth for tooth and wounds equal for equal. But if anyone remits the retaliation by way of charity, it shall be for him an expiation. And whosoever does not judge by that which Allah has revealed, such are the zalimun (wrong-doers . . .).

And in equal detail, Verse 2/178:

> Al-Qisas . . . is prescribed for you in case of murder: the free for the free, the slave for the slave, and the female for the female. But if the killer is forgiven by the brother . . . of the killed against blood-money, then adhering to it with fairness and payment of the blood-money to the heir should be made in fairness.

Importantly, there is reference to the payment of blood money, diyah,[21] to discharge homicidal culpability. It seems almost a recommendation, if not an entreaty, to accept such a settlement. And not least there is also a suggestion of the possibility of penance and forgiveness.[22] It is clear, as Donner[23] suggests, that the vengeance system was too deeply entrenched in Arab society for the Prophet to suppress totally. But he placed restrictions on it: that only the killer be killed,[24] and thus ending the crime by appropriate punishment, instead of setting in motion a chain vendetta by killing arbitrarily a kinsman of the killer, which would then require an appropriate reprisal. Although the idea of collective guilt and shared identity among social units, which would favor this kind of unfocused retribution, is not alien to Islam; the sharia obviously seeks to dam in the eruption of further violence which could rupture the social fabric of the umma.

It is doubtful there ever was a human society that did not have conventions on correct modes of interaction. The narrative of a lawless original social existence belongs to the realm of scientific mythology. The brutish condition of "a war of all against all" (as proposed by Thomas Hobbes' *bellum omnium contra omnes*), the proverbial "law of the jungle,"[25] and of the sex-driven "Primal Horde" (a la Sigmund Freud) in which patriarchy was libidinally defined, does not even apply totally to animal primates. But by taking "lawful" interaction out of the reach of brachial force and customary convention based on habituation, and placing it in the supervisory hands of supernatural forces guarding the sanctity of rules, an important step is taken. Attributing the origins of rules of proper behavior to supernatural forces, "legality" became tantamount to moral theology. Making human interaction and its patterns lawful or unlawful, as the case may be, under the rubric of proper morality and obedience to divine will is one of the greatest civilizing gifts a divinity could bestow on humanity. Thus forging law, belief, and morality tightly into one became a defining factor of human society until very recently when through the influence of secularization not only the supernatural ingredient of legislation is diminished, but the concept of legality or lawfulness, as defined and exercized by the modern state, is taking increasingly little recourse to religious viewpoints. Religion relying on traditional doctrinal interpretations has an increasingly tenuous hold on current ethical and moral standards applied by state law, as in fact the state is redefining the concept and content of morality. In this sense sharia's original merit has become an encumbrance: its divine origin resisting its adaptation to globalizing aesthetic and legal sensitivities that have been subjected to intense secularization.

Having said this and elevated the codification of law to special importance, it seems necessary to put the Middle Eastern specificity into a pan-human perspective that avoids premature valuation. Drawing an even deeper division between societies with law that is codified and those without, some scholars refuse to call tribal law "law" in the contemporary legal sense and prefer to refer to it as "custom." In their view, law proper is social control exercized through the systematic application of the force of politically organized society and through law-enforcing institutions. So-called "custom" or customary law, in this view, is in principle different from real law, not because of its lack of codification, but because of a deficiency in social institution.[26] Put differently, a social norm is legal if its neglect or infraction is regularly met, in threat or in fact, by application of physical force by an individual or group possessing the socially recognized right (duty and privilege) of so acting.[27] In the absence of such an instituted role (of judge and police), behavior is subject only to custom or convention and not to law. (It avoids the question how to classify the belief that breaches of customs may be punished by supernatural intervention.) This leads to the conundrum that customs clearly have different degrees of gravity. Violating the homicidal taboo on a clan member is different from not washing one's hands after going to the toilet. Both may be covered by the sharia, but in the first case there is a reaction by the judicial system and in the latter the reaction is disgust and contempt. It is interesting that Islamic doctrine in itself does not recognize a law-enforcing profession—although traditionally there is a judiciary (kadis) and modern fundamentalist states even have a religious police—yet it has a tendency to regard even seemingly minor customs as subject to enforceable laws. The agencies of justice, however, may be quite different ones.

In this definition some societies—and classical Muslim society among them—then do not have law as they lack judiciary and police, which enforce the rules, although they may have definitive rules of interaction. This introduces an unjustifiably deep delineation separating societies with law from "lawless" ones. Against this view Leopold Pospisil[28] argued that all societies have "law" by dint of four major attributes: social rules have authority and gravity, they have generalized applicability, there is an understanding of right and obligation between members of a society, and breaches of rules entail sanctions.

Leaving aside the law's regulative functions relating to proper, lawful, and acceptable behavior, defining it and identifying breaches, there is also the punitive aspect. Failing to meet the obligation of acting in accordance with the customary regulative laws attracts punishment: quantifying it, controlling its execution, and making its extent predictable is another important function of a proper law code. A characteristic that distinguishes tribal or customary law from codified law is that tribal law usually is not precise about punishment. Even if there is a fairly clear sense of what constitutes crime, the precise quantification of punishment may be absent. Much depends on circumstances, the persistence and effort necessary in pursuing a miscreant, the intensity of sentiments of revenge, the social position of the offender, and the like. A refugee from justice may also enlist the help of kinsmen (for protection or advocacy) and thus escape from justice—and that in itself may be considered lawful. The old adage "blood is thicker than water" extends to the obligation of affording physical protection and support to kin in a time of need. This "law" may cut across other conventions about lawful conduct. Which is given priority in a given situation remains in the discretion of the affected parties. Alfred R. Radcliffe-Brown,[29] an early anthropologist, reported from the Andaman Islands that local conventional law had no agreed mechanisms of punishment. Retribution for malfeasance and crime depended entirely on the injured party taking action or on an aggrieved person seeking retribution. In pursuing a case a person could enlist support from third parties as much as the miscreant may have protection and support from others. There was no socially unanimous, coordinated, orchestrated, and generally agreed on reaction to a misdeed, although it seems that there was at least a vague conventional sense of right and wrong and of what constitutes justice. Although all else being equal there may have been consensus in condemnation of a deed, other mechanisms (of loyalty, kinship, etc.) seem to have outweighed impartial legal action and pursuance of abstract "justice."

When considered in this light, the advance sharia introduced can be appreciated. However, it is not necessarily justified, though tempting, to attach an evolutionary scheme to such conditions and thus distinguish more ancient, primitive forms (of spontaneous and arbitrary retributive, vengeful reaction to perceived injustice, which some scholars may not even consider to be "law" in the proper sense of the word) and more progressive forms of an orderly judicial process. For instance, Australian Aborigines, though possessing no codified jurisprudential system had clear notions of what constitutes crime and conventional responsive mechanisms prevailed. Although their society is often—and wrongly—taken as a paragon of primitiveness, it had relatively concise concepts of "crime" and appropriate punishment. But legal viewpoints as to the severity and appropriateness of punishment could be individually bent (for sentimental or nepotistic purposes or for convenience's sake), although only to a limited extent. Verdicts were communally sought and pronounced, authority and responsibility to execute punishment could be delegated (almost like appointing deputy sheriffs to hunt down a criminal). Execution then could be carried out in a kurdaitja raid, by a posse of deputies waylaying the culprit in a surprise attack, or could be done through a stealth magical act. In rudimentary form particular kin groups of the accused could represent the defense, both physically and verbally. Of course, individuals may also have, in a manner of speaking, "taken the law into their own hands," but pursuing "justice" without approval of the council of elders lay a person open to collective retribution. (There were exceptions where a person might have to take immediate action to punish a wrongdoer or spontaneously come to the defense of a wronged person, compelled to do so by kinship rules.) However, by and large, the judicial system allowed for considerable flexibility, which did not make it entirely predictable.

There is another strong point in favor of the sharia as initially formulated. Historical features indicate the absence of commonly binding laws across Arab society in pre-Islamic times. This society seems to have been rent by many and deep divisions. Tribalism was an important dividing factor, further splitting society into clans, lineages, families, and "houses." The chronic tensions between urban or village dwellers and Bedouins makes it doubtful that there was an agreed-upon code of laws shared between the two sides, even though the sedentary and the nomadic groups in a conveniently vague sense were part of one society—and sometimes even may have shared a tribal identity—and were culturally akin. (In fact the two sides were not as diametrically opposed as is often suggested. They represent only the opposite ends of a wider spectrum where the majority were engaged in both settled farming and pastoralism with features of semi-nomadic herding. Goat and sheep herding was somewhat less extensive than camel herding, but both could be combined with varying degrees of settled agriculture. A tribe could contain both agriculturalists and nomads.)[30] Even during the widely respected time of the pre-Islamic pilgrimage to Macca, when hostilities should have ceased, Bedouin raids on pilgrim caravans seem to have been the order of the day. Religious diversity, through the differences in legal customs, was probably also a major factor of interaction, as Jews, Christians, other monotheists and polytheists were living side by side. Adding to the complexity, regional and local polities presumably observed their own legal conventions. Kinship rules also seem to have shared co-importance with communally observed laws. Islam changed all that and boldly cut across this bewildering and often conflicting maze of "legal pluralism." Sharia abolished this multitude and clearly intended from the beginning to universalize its juridical code. This has encouraged some modern scholars to see in Islam, at least by its potential, a globalizing force.[31] This is true, but with the huge proviso that globalization on Islamic terms also draws a definite and unbridgeable line between believers and infidels across the world. An embracement as equals of non-Muslims, the kafirun, being unthinkable, Islamic globalization would also universalize a fundamental division of humanity with potentially important legal ramifications. Globalization would occur at the cost of barring non-Muslims from full legal enfranchisement. Not surprisingly, the Islam-inspired human rights agenda (e.g., the Cairo Declaration)[32] contains some fundamental differences to that sponsored by the United Nations. One difference, which makes it unsuitable as a globalized code, is that the Cairo Declaration addresses only Muslims.

Another factor that limits the appeal of Islamic law as a globalizing force is the historical precedent of the legal status granted to non-Muslims under Muslim rule and governance. Where Islam permitted the continuation of other laws and legal conventions (of the dhimmi, recognized religious minorities), it severely reduced their status against Islamic law. (There is a faint similarity with tribal law in the sense that people outside in the in-group remain peripheral to the aegis of the law and only are legally enfranchized, or not, at the discretion of the dominant group.) Legal pluralism came at a severe cost to permitted minorities (the ahl al kitab, people of the book),[33] whose judicial autonomy in any case of conflict with matters Islamic was rendered inert and, in fact, relegated to irrelevance.[34] However, this issue is capable of revealing the ambiguous nature of a paradox par excellence. Viewed differently, the concept of dhimmitude can also be regarded as a major achievement of tolerance, a concession unparalleled at the time in Christian Europe. By a stretch of the imagination, it can be seen as an early version of multiculturalism. Even in modern times supposedly tolerant Western society has not embraced the idea of legal pluralism for the sake of culturally enfranchising minorities.[35] The use of sharia aspects in law and under the umbrella of Western jurisprudence does exist in a few countries of the West. However, it is very limited in application: usually only in matters of Private Law or within family affairs and as long as it does not contradict dominant law and constitution.[36] Some Western countries have totally and emphatically rejected the idea of even the slightest concession to sharia law.

CANONICAL LAW AND MODERN TIMES

In terms of a rough taxonomy (with or without evolutionary undertones), one can distinguish canonical law and secular law in reference to the extent the legal system is believed to be of divine instigation or is under divine oversight. Canonical law, by referring to its divine origin, draws on transcendent ethical principles inaccessible to empirical reasoning. The Quran often includes the phrase "for this is better for humanity," but fails to explain why. There is no need: it is decreed by God and therefore beyond human understanding and volition. Moral philosophy and ethical principles are axiomatic and beyond human reason to comprehend, amend, or change them. (My imputing society-building motivations and socialization functions to Islamic doctrine and sharia rules, as I have set out earlier, is based on analogical, anthropological reasoning and is not explicitly suggested by Islam itself.) The more prominent the religious rationale and the stronger the religious ingredient in law is, the less amenable to fundamental, non-exegetical change it will be. As the religious aspect of law retreats the more fluid it becomes in line with social, cognitive, and ideological changes. This may open up a gap between canonical regulations and the moral principles they are intended to uphold, and changing sensitivities and preoccupations in the wider, progressively secularizing society. Social conventions tend to be more open to changes over time than doctrinal principles, which may erupt in bitter dis-

putes about ethical principles. Recalcitrant fissures in the notion of religiously dictated ethical propriety, appropriate justice in social life, and actual
practice are the consequence. The scientific advance of capabilities also
tends to increase the gap. Especially in the medical field this becomes glaringly obvious nowadays. Sexuality, family planning, and surgical and genetic interventions are areas where this has become particularly apparent in
recent years. Cutting-edge family planning strategies are subject to much
acrimonious debate. Crude state-run eugenics have been resoundingly rejected, but individual freedom of choice together with scientific advances has
opened up a new front. Techniques of gene manipulation, in utero sex determination, pregnancy termination because of impending birth and genetic
defects or simply for reasons of limiting family sizes, "designer babies,"
cloning, sex change, and so on, create an ever widening gap between scientific capability, legal acceptability, and religious conservatism.

The notion of crime is no longer chiefly linked with violation of divine
ethics, but has become a problem of asociality, or antisociality, a violation of
social order and convention, a breach of social contract and anathema to
social cohesion. Crime bears less of a stigma of immorality in the transcendent sense, but is simply a breach of socially agreed-on norms. Concomitantly, ethics, so far as they are expressed in law, have become more closely
aligned with social pragmatics and changing aesthetic regimes.

In the West, conventional ethics as espoused by state law, more implicitly
than explicitly encoded there, have separated from religion and undergone
their own separate development. Guardianship of social ethics consequently
has passed into the hands of secular agencies and institutions, which sometimes now feel called upon to exert strongly supervisory functions over religious institutions. The formulation of ethics binding for society as a whole has
been transferred from divine revelation to social discourse. The highest
church authorities, previously considered the guardians of public morality,
have hesitatingly adjusted to that and reluctantly submitted to secular agencies of justice. In very recent years, the numerous cases of child abuse committed by ecclesiastical functionaries and brought before secular courts have
made that glaringly obvious. A novel conflict situation has emerged in which
the Catholic church, traditionally the most powerful ethical influence in the
Western legal and political processes, has to defend itself vis-à-vis the moral
authority of secular law and popular opinion. As Catholic priesthood and
celibacy come under close scrutiny, the church is feebly attempting to retain
moral control within its own ranks and avoid submitting to secular authority.
However, secular law now clearly manages to overrule canonical rule. This
clearly is a social novelty. Similar charges for immorality have been made
against Christian churches in previous years, accusing them of inertia in
preventing or speaking out forcefully against the Holocaust. Some detractors
even went as far as accusing churches of complicity, in which political and

racist-based prejudices met with the age-old religious bias against Jews as the Jesus-killers. Yet, the institutional framework remained relatively unaffected and strong and human rights legislation could not successfully be employed to challenge the moral authority of church authorities.

These most recent events clearly demonstrate that in the Western world secularization has wrested moral authority—and the explication of ethics—from the Christian churches and handed it to secular jurisprudential institutions. It is now a combination of the various democratic parliamentarian functions, responding usually to a majority among the plethora of ethical viewpoints in society, as well as professional judicial and expert forums, which are charged with the responsibility of collective ethical oversight. Scientific advances also tend to create their own ethical systems, which, albeit with some lag, move along with innovations. In very recent years, especially the revision of medical ethics has been lodged in academic university circles as a separate discipline or as adjuncts to (secularist) philosophy and medicine, with advisory functions and appendices to lawmaking political processes. The hierocratic aspects of legal mechanisms and the ethical principles they defended, employed in the oversight of intellectual activity in Western society, have all but disappeared. Without having to reach back to the beginnings of the sciences and the fates of Galileo Galilei and Giordano Bruno, in past decades the careers of academics could suffer if their intellectual products met with church disapproval. (Sigmund Freud, and in anthropology, William Robertson Smith, are probably among the best known, but by far not the only examples.) Dangers to academic careers and to the promulgation of new knowledge, posed through control mechanisms, are completely differently situated now.

This is, of course, not to deny the Christian origins of modern Western ethics and the laws they have spawned—or to deny that through that descent Christian ethics are now of globalized importance and infused in the wider human rights discourse. But the once clear derivation becomes more and more obscured. Church doctrine and traditional religious viewpoints may still be infused in the secular ethical discourse, but rarely openly so on an institutional level. In previous centuries churches had set standards in ethics, not only by defining them, but partly even by supplying the functions and rationale of enforcing them in society. Until more recent times, conventions still allowed for a greater role of religion in the juristic discourse by consulting with church authorities who were in a position to influence the law more openly and decisively. This is no longer the case in secularized Western democracies, as theocratic features have declined drastically, the prerogatives of state churches have dwindled, and compacts between churches and states have been dissolved. (The obvious exception is the Vatican state.)

This problem is relevant to Islam because transcendental ethics and (secular) laws based on changing social conventions have not separated to the same extent as they did in Western society. Islam has not undergone similar developments in which religious ethics are becoming emasculated. As a sweeping generalization it can be said that ethical influence has been retained to a much greater extent than in the West by Islamic spiritual authority and the shariatic sense of justice. This is clearly expressed in the fact that scientific advances and their acceptability come under the legitimate scrutiny of theological authorities who may try to reconcile them with scriptures[37] or, as in most cases, reject them as un-Islamic. Although state law in Muslim majority countries, being influenced by Western juridical notions, not unusually deviates strongly from the classical shape of sharia, traditional religious jurist-scholars have managed to retain some influence on the collective Muslim consciousness to a much greater and socially more decisive degree than is the case with churches in the West. Leaving aside the formalities of the legal systems in Muslim majority countries, which may be heavily influenced by Western secular law, the social discourse—at grass-root level—is still strongly infused with ethical viewpoints derived from the sharia. Where the division most clearly shows nowadays is in the treatment of Islamic extremism. In some traditional and popular Islamic conceptions of justice it appears to be at least faintly justified by taking recourse to religious doctrine, while in state law—as much as in Western law—such action and the ideology inspiring it are simply and unceremoniously placed in the rubric of crime.

The concept of sharia, defined more narrowly as formal Islamic canonical law, has retained several characteristics shed in Western culture. Above all, law being a divine creation is sacrosanct; it eludes human tampering through the lawmaking capacity of experts and elected representatives. Law-giving sovereignty rests in God and not with human agencies whether elected or unelected. The perception that divine law by definition is fundamentally eternal and unchanging poses another considerable difficulty when it goes beyond some vague moral principles and enters into legal detail. To the extent that sharia is at all capable of adaptability, the traditional concepts of darura (necessity) and maslaha (common good) will be strained to the limit so as to generate the needed flexibility, sanctioned by Islamic authorities, to allow some rapprochement between conservative Islamic justice and globalized, West-dominated juridical provisions.

It follows that from an Islamic viewpoint if state law deviates from the letter of sharia, it should at least be grounded in sharia and reflect its spirit; which is to say, it should implicitly contain the ethical principles that are enunciated in the sharia. (For instance, if homosexuality and apostasy are not punished by death, they should at least be punished severely.) The interpretation of law properly belongs in the hands of religious experts, rather than secular legal agents; jurists should possess and carry out a religious mandate rather than just possessing a diploma from a secular law school. Social ethics applicable in daily life should be grounded in divine imperatives rather than human-made social conventions that are subject to the changing vicissitudes of ephemeral social aesthetics and fickle politically driven notions of right and wrong. On this basis it seems a fallacy to argue, as some scholars have done, that an Islamic democracy in the true sense of the concept is possible.[38] If a polity is meant to be Islamic—regardless of this being so with or without the wishes of voters—the ultimate supervisory function in state business, jurisdiction, and social interaction has to remain in the hands of the clerics and theology experts. Thus such a political system would at least have the flavor of theocracy.[39] It could be truly democratic only if by general consensus the clerical elite is democratically recognized and specifically authorized to perform a political and juridical supervisory function. This would have to be freely acknowledged by subjecting religious authority also to electoral processes. Needless to say that this seems hardly possible, as the separation of church and state, dividing spiritual and political functions, is one of the preconditions of a functioning modern democracy. Existing examples of Islamic republics do not provide convincing evidence that this is possible. Even if one discards formal electoral processes as a precondition for a functioning democratic system, the Islamic concepts of ijma (consensus) and shura (consultative council) are too nebulous, lacking in precise democratic mechanisms, and are still too dependent on elite leadership to satisfy the aspirations of a polity as diverse, disharmonious, and not infrequently contrary as modern day populations are. General homogeneity of aspirations and ungrudging malleability of the masses through persuasion of an elite are things of the past. Islamic criticism of democratic principles as "the terror of 50 plus one percent" refers to the principle that a majority overrules the minority simply through its numbers, and the dominant viewpoint does not emerge and prevail through reasoned argument. At least superficially this point resembles the political concept of the "terror of the majority," that is the dubious yet legitimate domination of majority society over minority aspirations even in the best democratic system. (The topic of governance, leadership, and democratic system will again be briefly discussed later.)

Globalization in juridical matters facing Islam in today's world is based more on Western patterns in which the original religious (Christian) viewpoints and principles have been sidelined in favor of secularized legal viewpoints and their implied ethics, and pragmatic, world-immanent functions. In international juridical discourses the internationalizaton of (non-religious) ethics becomes apparent. The human rights charter, having been inspired by the horrors and genocide of the era of World War II, makes no reference to divine law or ethical commands apart from a nebulous backdrop of the right to life and justice, which may vaguely have Christian roots. In contrast, the Islamic human rights have the stamp of Islamic theology all over it.[40] Many

Western state constitutions do still make reference to God, but more as a formula-like bow to tradition, and less emphatic than those of Muslim-majority countries.

In the relentless globalization process, since it is mostly Western controlled and, therefore, acts as vehicle of secularising initiatives, juridical and religious viewpoints tend to become separated. Harsh views on blasphemy, apostasy, homosexuality, and adultery, which in an Islamic gradation of severity sit right at the top as capital injuries to ethical standards, fit uneasily in a world of increasing personal liberties of choice and expression, flexibility in ideological allegiance, equality, and growing, legally enforceable tolerance. Prevailing aesthetic regimes of globalization also shudder at some methods of meting out justice in accordance with conservative Islamic jurisprudence. The moral sense of outrage at certain types of behavior enshrined in the concepts of abomination, blasphemy, and offenses against divinity can have only an increasingly precarious hold on today's secularising world. Notions of criminality in these regards are losing validity as religious rationales for social behavior decline in significance. The same goes for notions of what constitutes appropriate forms of punishment. Many forms of penalty under the aegis of an "eye for an eye," prescribed by the principle of qisas—a concept that suffers profound universal rejection because it lacks the moral distinction between crime and punishment—fall now under the rubric of torture.

From July to August 2011 a case of qisas was widely reported in the world media. A young Iranian woman had been completely blinded and severely disfigured through an acid attack by a jilted admirer. A court sentenced the attacker to have the sight of one eye destroyed through a medical intervention in which a surgeon would administer some corrosive acid to the eye. In terms of strict equality of repayment for the injury the culprit had inflicted, the verdict seems even relatively mild. Literally, then, in the last minute, the woman in whose hands it lay to forgive and spare the man the ordeal, pardoned the offender, settling instead for a fine. Compared with the loss she had suffered, the sum (roughly USD 200,000) seemed paltry. Pre-attack pictures of her shown on television portrayed a young woman who by most accounts and across cultures would be considered good-looking. Newspaper reports described her as a university student with a bright future prospect. Through the attack she was condemned to a loss on both counts and quite possibly to an existence of emotional loneliness and physical dependency. As this case demonstrates, a perfect balance of crime and punishment through qisas is difficult, if not impossible, to achieve. It is not even likely to satisfy a sense of natural justice, even though it may purport to do so.

This provides an impressive example of the particular sense of justice of "Biblical" proportions couched in the legal principle of qisas. It is closely related to the Old Testament notion of adequate retribution, but time has eroded the attendant notion of penal justice and inherent ethics. The "an eye for an eye" slogan has totally disappeared from Western law, where restorative principles and resocializing functions are considered preferable to simple retributive punishment and its function of deterrence. (It is debatable whether this has a Christian root in compassion and forgiveness or hinges on rational sociological insights into cost-effect relations of conventional forms of punishment such as imprisonment.) Such considerations are absent from conservative interpretations of sharia.[41]

The sharia's ethical principles, expressive laws, and forms of implementation all contribute to bringing it in conflict with Western, globalized and hegemonic views of ethical priorities, proper justice, and its enforcement. The definition of significant crime demanding of the severest punishment, has also changed so that conservative sharia deviates much from the humane trajectory legal globalization appears to be taking.

For one, the conservative Islamic sense of justice (adalah, adil) disagrees in important aspects with the globally dominant juridical discourse. Legal and philosophical sensitivities have changed, so that in human rights, great value is placed on the preservation of individual life and the integrity of personhood. (The Quran 5/32 superficially agrees by declaring "if anyone killed a person not in retaliation of murder or to spread mischief in the land— it would be as if he killed all mankind.") In the West, as a consequence juridically sanctioned punishment by death has become rare and has a connotation of being rather exceptional. Execution by public spectacle—a form of gruesome entertainment in European medieval society—has been abolished in the West centuries ago; execution, when and where it is still practiced by the state today, has become a semi-secretive affair, uneasily combining officialness and privacy. Only conservative Islam resorts to the ancient recipe of using public execution as a deterrent, didactic experience, and entertainment in tri-symbiotic conjunction. Other countries, which practice executions for capital crimes do so in seclusion. If the sanctity of human life is breached by official law and the state, it is to be done hidden away from the public discourse as if to uphold the myth about the sanctity of human life.

The forms in which Islamic punishment is carried out (beheading, stoning, hanging, execution by shooting, amputation) involves aspects of public spectacle for its exemplary value. This aspect, and with it its presumed didactic value, have also disappeared from Western justice. Aesthetics and the sense of justice, appropriate punishment, and standards of legality have vitally shifted over a period of centuries. This is particularly noticeable in regard of the Old Testament, which is of much greater antiquity than the revelation of the Quran but bears resemblance in many judicial respects to sharia. The insistence on "Biblical" forms of punishment has virtually disappeared from Christianity. Not so in Islam. Instruments of justice called for in conservative perspectives of sharia, such as stoning, hand amputation, harsh treatment of marriage infidelity and homosexuality, toleration of female circumcision, owning slaves (despite the scriptural demand of humane treatment), and the like, do not sit well in today's world and in globally dominant, elite driven discourses on justice and propriety. This suggests that the reintroduction (or retention, as the case may be) of such instruments of justice and moral aesthetics are bound to come up against strong global opposition and do certainly run counter to human rights provisions. The Quran admonishes against female infanticide,[42] but does not specifically forbid it. It is quiet on female circumcision. Objecting to it is left to a hadith, which only cautions "do not cut severely." Shariatic law does not condemn these customs in such strong terms as are used in relation to, for instance, alcohol and pork consumption,[43] adultery, prostitution, or theft.[44] This certainly is a strong indicator of the difference in a sense of justice, propriety, and proportional punishment opening up a gap between conservative Islamic views and globally dominant juridical regimes.

Islamic law, true to its charismatic inspirational source, places its emphasis on fardh, duty, the obligation to fulfil obligations posited by the divine source of laws. Obeying these laws "to the letter," as it were, is tantamount to meeting one's duty. Modern Western law places the accent on rights of enjoyment (the "pursuit of happiness" and individual fulfilment) and balances that with obligations vis-à-vis the collectivity. The essence of this constellation is summed up in Immanuel Kant's concept of "asocial sociability." It means, phrased very simply, man seeks society but does so for selfish reasons; society then is entitled to curtail some personal liberties for the common good, which in turn is ultimately in the interest of the individual. This view also harks back to notions of a "social contract." The contractarian philosophies of Thomas Hobbes, John Locke, and Jean-Jacques Rousseau differed as to the extent individuals have to surrender sovereignty so as to have ordered society through proper governance, but their principle idea is the same. Sociability has to be observed, not because it has been commanded by a divine agent, but for the sake of a cohesive social entity, which in turn is to the benefit of everybody. The resulting contract is between "men" (I am purposely replicating here the seemingly sexist language used in the philosophical language of the day), and not between God and men. Individualistic and opportunistic impulses innate in human beings have to be overcome—on rational grounds—to create a functioning social aggregate that allows humans to exist, to survive, and to "enjoy." Human rights reflect this on an international level: guaranteeing individual rights and thus enabling a global community to exist. Islamic human rights are different in placing emphasis on collective identity (of the umma) arising out of the individual's observation of duties towards God. Only obedience to divine law, its god-fearing nature, ensures a functioning, cohesive sociability. Thus Islam also emphasises the need for a cohesive community of humans, but the reason for this demand—implicitly given—is because of a transcendentally orientated obligation and not because this serves the practical interests of men. Divine rules create a regulated hence cohesive society, not primarily because this is good for humans, but because it pleases God. (It is my sociological interpretation, which causes me to presume an underlying, cryptic practical purpose of theology.) The outcome is superficially similar to the Western contractarianism in that it recognizes the need for ordered society. The difference lies in that in one case the contract has to be unquestioningly obeyed, in the other it has to be reasoned; the former demands obedience, the latter intelligence.

This underlying philosophical difference reflects the basic world view of the secularized West, the pragmatic anthropocentrism that inspires it, and Islam's theocentrism. In the Western anthropocentric perspective observation of ethics is meant to serve the interests of the individual through constraining society to adhere to some rules some of which are supported by shared ethics and some are not. The common good's raison d'etre is to maximizes the chances of happiness and freedom for the individual. Although sacrifices have to be made, ultimately it is done for selfish reasons. What serves society is good only insofar as it enables the individual to pursue its interest. This reflects the idea that the measure of all things is the singular human being: it has an interest in maintaining control over life and limb, in possessing reasonable personal security, it is entitled to the legitimate pursuit of happiness and well-being, and to possessing a guaranteed supply of food so as to satisfy all creature comforts without duty of gratitude to a greater power being required. Islamic theocentrism does not recognize human entitlement nor does it ask whether the individual's interests are served by the adherence to legality. God, for whatever reasons, wants a functioning, cohesive society in which everybody obeys the rules regardless of whether their sense and meaning is understood. It is also beside the point whether individual expectations of personal well-being are met; a good life is a grace granted out of God's beneficence and can be withdrawn or withheld for reasons unknown to man. Human existence as a whole is by the grace of God for which man has a duty, a fardh, of gratitude, which is to be shown by adhering to the divine reglement.

By placing the emphasis on duty—duty to God being tantamount to a duty to adhere to divine rule, duty to obedience, recognizing an obligation to meet God's standards—the dimension of rights and entitlements is severely diminished. Under the aegis of human rights, what may be considered enjoyment as of a right, in the Islamic perspective at best is considered a privilege, a rare blessing, an added bonus, a special gesture of divine favor never to be taken for granted. It is no coincidence that universal human rights, inspired by Western views and decisively shaped by secularization, attribute to humans inalienable rights, anchored in the human condition, and autonomous of divine dispensation. In line with the overwhelming hedonism of modernity, even the enhanced spirituality of postmodernity does not demand sacrifice, nor duty, in acknowledging superior powers; nor does it demand the denial of individual rights to happiness for the sake of the obedience to a divinity or the self-denying uncomfortableness for attaining eventual bliss. A characteristic ascetic strain is still present in Islam while it has been wiped from the remains of practiced Christianity and even more from the secularized Weltanschauung that has conquered, or at least is about to conquer, the world. Having said this, one has to admit that on the level of actual reality, millions of Muslims live successful and fulfilled lives, well-adjusted to modernity and obviously able to build a syncretistic form of existence based on a hybrid form of Islam. Even fundamentalization, in many cases, generates a personal kind of piety and morality—not militancy—that in actual practice works well in a globalized world. It can even be at the beginning of a process of privatization of Islam, indicating its retreat from the public into the private sphere as a person's personal choice.[45]

It would be unrealistic if all of Muslimhood would be assessed through the prism of the abstract reflections on sharia. It is a general feature of humankind—perhaps a species-typical feature—to show a resilience in the face of cognitive and social disharmony, to live with the ideational hurdles it creates and to meld it with the demands of real life in a real world. For some Muslims the hadith that religion is not meant to impose hardship on believers is an important, ubiquitous guiding thought in working out personal compromises without having to make the painful decision of deliberately setting their religious convictions aside in the interest of pragmatics. There are other parts of the ahadith, which in a roundabout manner hint at this strand of pragmatism. For instance it says if one sees injustice one should take action; but also that if doing so would put one's life in peril one should keep one's own counsel. Real life does demand at times a deviation from "the straight path." From a realist's point of view, it speaks for Islam that it has even developed doctrinal points that express this very dogma of pragmatism that springs from a realistic appraisal of human existential vicissitudes. Islamic jurisprudence has developed several mechanisms and concepts that facilitate compromise, such as duress (ikrah), necessity (darura), and public welfare (maslaha). For diasporic Muslims, for instance, the political concepts of Dar-al-ahd (country of treaty or covenant), Dar-al-amn (country of security), Dar-al-sulh (country of truce), and Dar-al-darura (country of necessity) have been advocated to recognize situations of practical necessity and adaptation—areas in which Muslims are doctrinally allowed to set aside the requirement of living only under Muslim governance.[46]

It is above all the concepts of darura (existential necessity) and maslaha (common good or best interest) which give Muslims, if they so wish, the free space of individual discretion to make decisions that are not strictly in accord with the sharia or the religiously prescribed ethics. Even though it is debatable what degree of priority or significance in the hierarchy of Islamic ideas necessary adjustments and concessions enjoy, or to what extent they can ease a painful conscience, they are part of the doctrinal repertory and can be elevated to importance in people's individual lives. They are being used in an opportunistic sense to sanction compromises and give religious meaning to individualistic, existentially prudent decisions. While ideally, in individual cases, the opinion of experts should be sought to reconcile deviation from doctrinal norms and grant dispensations, if necessary; this is not always the case. Especially if a quick decision is required, the devout will see a salat-al-haja (a prayer out of need) as sufficient to give moral strength to the perceived deviation from the "straight path."

NOTES

1. Nurcholish Madjid, Harun Nasution, Abdurrahman Wahid, Djohan Effendi, Taufik Abdullah, Ahmad Wahib, and others.

2. The Catholic veneration of Mary, the "Mother of God," the Madonna cult as some call it, adds to the gravity of shirk. Especially Wahhabism is relentless in its condemnation of it as idolatry. To avoid shirk and bida (incorrect belief), Wahhabism also rejects the veneration of Islamic saints, even the celebration of the Prophet's birthday, eid-al-nabi, which to Wahhabis (and others) means elevating a person to a status rivaling God's. The division between those who celebrate the birthday (the Miladis) and those who do not, creates another, informal split in Muslimhood.

3. Quran 3/32, 4/80, 33/21, and 36, 48/10.

4. In actual fact, the "formal" nature can range from the recommendation of convention to strictly formulated law (as in penal law, family law, civil law, etc.).

5. Only the most important ones are mentioned. There are so many subdivisions based on small doctrinal differences as to make it impossible here to enumerate them all.

6. I am ignoring here regionally applicable and acknowledged sharia laws, for instance, in the northern parts of Nigeria, the province of Aceh in Indonesia, the Taleban-controlled areas of Afghanistan and Pakistan, in parts of Somalia, and so on.

7. From my personal experience, traditional Australian Aboriginal religion shows similarities insofar as many traditional activities have a narrative precedent in the sacred mythology and contain an aspect of divine creation. But this belief system lacks the strict juridical dimension that makes following precedent the law, as is the case in Islam.

8. In case the reader should wonder, I have found this question posed on the blog site of a famous jurist-scholar giving advice and fatawa (rulings) on all kinds of existential problems.

9. For the variability of sharia see, for instance, Erich Kolig, "To Shariaticize or Not to Shariaticize." In *Shari'a in the West*, R. Ahdar and N. Aroney (eds.). Oxford: Oxford University Press, 2010. Abbas Amanat and Frank Giffel (eds.), *Islamic Law in Contemporary Context: Shari'a*. Stanford: Stanford University Press, 2007. *Shari'a as Discourse*, J. Nielsen and L. Christoffersen (eds.). Farnham: Ashgate, 2010.

10. Rudolph Peters, "From Jurists' Law to Statute Law or What Happens When the Shari'a is Codified." In *Shaping the Current Islamic Reformation*, B. A. Roberson (ed.). London, Portland OR.: Frank Cass, 2003; p.91.

11. Ann Elizabeth Mayer "Islamic Law as a Cure for Political Law." In *Shaping the Current Islamic Reformation*, B. A. Roberson (ed.). London, Portland, OR: Frank Cass, 2003), following the Italian law scholar Ugo Mattei, distinguishes traditional law systems, political law, and professional law. In this taxonomy the sharia has not reached stage three on its evolutionary course. In another taxonomy sharia is "common law," not "codified law."

12. See, e.g., Jørgen Nielsen, "Shari'a between Renewal and Tradition." In *Shari'a as Discourse*, J. Nielsen and L. Christofferson (eds.). Farnham: Ashgate, 2010; p. 3, where he calls it "common law" in reference to Lawrence Rosen. Also, Dorthe Bramsen, "Divine Law and Human Understanding—the Idea of Shari'a in Saudi Arabia," in the same volume; p. 157. Only siyasa shariya, the authority of the governing body to supplement the sharia, she argues, is at least partly codified. This reflects a special definition of what codification means.

13. Snouk Hurgronje, *Mohammedanism*. New York, London: Putnam & Sons, 1916.

14. Max Weber, *Wirtschaft and Gesellschaft*. Tübingen: Mohr, 1972.

15. Joseph Schacht, *Introduction to Islamic Law*. Oxford: Clarendon, 1964.

16. Babylon's king Hammurabi (1792 BC – 1750) "published" a code of law by inscribing 282 laws on a publicly displayed stone stele. Most were of the lex talionis (law of retaliation) kind and based on the philosophy of "an eye for an eye." Other city states (Ur, Eshnunna, Lipit-Ishtar, and Hittite cities) too had apparently law codices of a similar kind.

17. Another complex codified law system in written form was, however, devized and implemented by nomads, namely the Mongols under Gengis Khan and his successors. This was the Yassa (or Yasya) law underpinning the Pax Mongolica of the thirteenth and fourteenth century. Significantly, and characteristically for nomadic herders, it treated livestock rustling as a capital crime.

18. See e.g., Colin Turnbull, *The Mountain People*. New York: Simon & Schuster, 1972. Jules Henry, *Jungle People*. New York: Vintage Books, 1964.

19. Vendettas and similar "chain crimes" do not occur randomly but follow conventional patterns.

20. Al-qisas, the law of equality in punishment; Quran 2/178,179, 194, 5/45, 16/126, 17/33, 22/60, 42/40.

21. Quran 17/33.

22. Quran 42/40.

23. Fred McGraw Donner, *The Early Islamic Conquests*. Princeton: Princeton University Press, 1981; p. 58–59.

24. Quran 17/33.

25. Not in Rudyard Kiplings' sense of anthropomorphizing animals by ascribing a law code to jungle dwelling creatures in his *The Jungle Book*.

26. It needs to be said that in practice settler states, like Australia (in its Native Title legislation), do in certain issues (like property law) recognize customary or tribal law of the indigenous people. This, however, does not amount to full legal pluralism. Tribal penal law is usually not recognized.

27. See E. Adamson Hoebel, *The Law of Primitive Man*. Harvard MA: Atheneum, 1954.

28. Leopold Pospisil, *The Kapauku Papuans and Their Law*. New Haven: Yale University Press, 1958.

29. *The Andaman Islanders*. Cambridge: Cambridge University Press, 1922.

30. Fred Donner, *The Early Islamic Conquests*; p. 16.

31. For instance, Jocelyne Cesari, "Islam in the West: Modernity and Globalization Revisited." In *Globalization and the Muslim World*, B. Schaebler and L. Stenberg (eds.). New York: Syracuse University Press, 2004.

32. *The Cairo Declaration on Human Rights in Islam*. Adopted at nineteenth Islamic Conference of Foreign Ministers in Cairo August 5, 1990.

33. Initially, it seems only Jews, Christians and Sabians qualified as "people of the book." Later, however, Zoroastrians and others were included, even Buddhists and Hindus at least nominally fell under "tolerated religions."

34. See Donna Arzt, "The Treatment of Religious Dissidents under Classical and Contemporary Islamic Law." In *Religious Human Rights in Global Perspective*, J. Witte and J. van der Wijver (eds.). The Hague: Nijhoff, 1996. And several books by Bat Ye'or, esp. *The Dhimmi*. Rutherford NJ: Farleigh Dickinson, 1985. The dhimma system in the Ottoman Empire was somewhat modified to the millet system.

35. Some tentative steps have been taken by some settler states (like Canada, Australia and New Zealand) towards giving a very limited juridical autonomy to their indigenous minorities. The UK has tentatively allowed Islamic tribunals to operate in a narrow range of jurisdiction. In matters of Private Law several Western judicial systems also make concessions and defer to Islamic viewpoints.

36. See Erich Kolig, "To Shariatizise" p. 271. A request for recognition of limited sharia jurisdiction in early 2011 by the Australian Islamic umbrella organization to the Australian government was curtly dismissed by the Federal Attorney General.

37. For examples relating to Indonesian Neo-Modernist interpretations see Taufik Abdullah and Sharon Siddique (eds.), *Islam and Society in Southeast Asia*. Singapore: Institute of Southeast Asian Studies, 1986. Family planning and restricting family sizes through birth control, for instance, is justified with the hadith: a strong Muslim is better and more loved by God than a weak Muslim (p. 150).

38. See Mostapha Benhenda, "Liberal democracy and political Islam: The Search for Common Ground." *Politics Philosophy & Economics* 10/1 (2011): 88–115. Vali Nasr, "The Rise of Muslim Democracy." *Journal of Democracy* 16/2 (2005): 13–27.

39. Whether the moderate Islamist parties emerging from the Arab Spring will be able to plot a course that aligns them more with democracy rather than theocracy, remains to be seen at the time of writing. Some have already declared that their function will be based on the sharia.

40. An interesting example is Riffat Hassan's "Rights of Women Within Islamic Communities." In *Religious Human Rights in Global Perspectives*, J. Witte and J. van der Vyver (eds.). The Hague: Nijhoff, 1996).

41. A few Quranic verses do relate to forgiveness and repentance followed by waiving punishment. Verse 42/40, e.g., relates to forgiveness instead of qisas retribution.

42. Quran 16/58-59, 81/8–9.

43. Quran 5/3.

44. Quran 5/38.

45. As mentioned before, Olivier Roy (*Secularism Confronts Islam*. New York: Columbia University, 2007, 1st French ed. 2005) sees this already happening in France.

46. See Bernard Lewis, "Legal and Historical Reflections on the Position of Muslim Populations under non-Muslim Rule." In *Muslims in Europe*, B. Lewis and D. Schnapper (eds.). London, New York: Pinter, 1994.

Chapter Three

Islamic Commensality

SACRED, GLORIOUS FOOD, AND ITS OPPOSITE

Meeting physical needs is undoubtedly one of the universal givens of human existence, and yet there is no easy one-to-one relationship between potential resources and hunger and thirst. Rarely is there a social approach to food and drink that is entirely governed by practical considerations. In other words, pragmatism does not appear to rule supreme in satisfying hunger and slating thirst—except of course in situations of extreme crisis.[1] Karl Marx elevated meeting bodily needs to a prime social agens movens in his materialist scheme, which recognizes that like all resources, food and drink are amenable to social controls and manipulation. The joy of the primary, innate tastes of sweetness, saltiness, or spiciness is not unusually a luxury that is easily won. However, I am not referring here to the intervention of social power and egotistical or sectional interests in controlling the production, distribution, and availability of food—hanging the food basket high, as Marx called it, which undoubtedly plays an enormous role and makes it a fascinating topic in sociological studies. Of interest in this context is the fact that dietary considerations unusually are not connected and intertwined with religious beliefs. I am referring to the sacralization and symbolic value of food and drink, to the ritualization of food production and consumption, to the mysterious tabooization of edible resources, and to enigmatic religious rules and interdictions hedging in what on first sight looks like the simple satisfaction of bodily requirements. Mundane though as it may appear on first glance—sustenance to stoke the furnace of the body—food is amenable to attracting epiphany and becoming the object of hierophany. Ingesting sustenance turns out to be vastly beyond the simple maintenance of physical existence by any means, and may assume the trappings of a prayer or may require negotiating a maze of religious rules.

Nutritional considerations and availability of consumable resources (their rarity or difficulty of production or procurement) undoubtedly have some considerable influence on the social and economic value attributed to edible and potable resources in a society. However, not entirely so. It is not unusual that these considerations are overruled or considerably bent in favor of criteria that are entirely cultural, not to say whimsical. Selective and quite arbitrary tastes and fickle fashion trends, status considerations, highly artificial and impractical culinary traditions, the search for the rare, even if it is tasteless and of low nutritional value, and not least, religious doctrines all influence the human approach to food and drink. Hierarchies of the status of certain foods and drinks may be totally divorced from their nutritional or health value or the reliability of their supply. Caviar, old whisky, and select champagnes and wines are prestige foods and drinks today in Western society. In the Elizabethan era it was ambergris sausages. Ambergris, being a kind of whale's vomit, still has curiosity value because of its rarity, but would hardly be considered a delicacy today. Bird nest soup is both rare and expensive, though being basically the spittle of a species of swallows. Good Muslims have to shun many of the luxuries rich Asians and Westerners can enjoy. Indonesian coffee beans that have gone through the digestive tract of marsupial civet cats and are gathered from their dung are transformed into a highly prized luxury. This kind of luxurious, very expensive coffee is now also allowed to Muslims for whom it had been forbidden previously. Indonesian Islamic authorities have recently certified the brew made from these beans as no longer "haram," forbidden, as long as they are washed thoroughly. Clearly, food and drink, as status symbol, can be totally divorced from nutrition or from a notion of what is appetizing. Food aesthetics and preferences are highly whimsical, turning sometimes what ordinarily is attractive and what is revolting on its head. There seem to be no limits to the whimsicality with which food is being treated and how aesthetics and esteem intertwine with it. In all matters of food and drink religious belief also may heavily intervene, adding approval or disapproval, and surrounding them with symbolic meaning.

While elevating some foods to a higher plane of culinary delight, others of equal or even better nutritional value are treated with disdain and revulsion. Western culture despises locusts, grubs, crickets, termites, and ants despite their ready and plentiful availability and their high nutritional value. The UN Food and Agriculture Organization is beginning to look seriously into this natural abundance, one of whose advantage is its low carbon emission. Their plentiful existence will make it increasingly attractive as a food source in so-called developing nations in which starvation is a "normal" problem. The West may have to learn to consider this food source with less haughty condescension—and may be able to do so unencumbered by religious sentiments. Culinary conservatism may put up some resistance, but Christian traditions will hardly be the major stumbling block. Islam—as much as other religions with dogmatic views on food—will most probably resist the widening of the resource base because of its strict and doctrinally prescribed dietary rules. (Despite the fact that locusts are considered edible by some Muslims, other insects are forbidden.) What is considered fit for human consumption is not based on natural criteria. Where the quality of edibility in effect is dictated by revelation and long-standing religiously sanctioned tradition, flexibility according to need and practical reason is not easily achieved.

Some hunter-gatherer societies in the recent past—before Western civilization and technology profoundly, and on a global scale, changed traditional lives and with it the use of foods as well as tastes—came close to making use of all resources nature is offering effectively and without impractical limitations. The attempt to sustain themselves and achieve a degree of resource security in a sparse and harsh environment (as especially in the arid center of the Australian continent or the Kalahari desert in southern Africa) imposed a certain "rationality" on them, which would have been absent in situations of greater choice and abundance. Yet, even in these socioeconomic systems in "normal" times (i.e., when unusual weather, climatic, or environmentally catastrophic events did not impinge on the normal availability of resources in the requisite area) the maxim "beggars can't be choosers" did not entirely reign supreme. Symbolic systems, religious beliefs, and values kicked in and caused procurement and consumption of food to depart significantly from the rational and pragmatic behavior one might expect. In other words, hunter-gatherers too—as ethnographies recorded in historical times show—observed special rules in the selection of food and drink: some foods are tabooed, or tabooed at certain times or under certain circumstances, water may be sacred and approached only in certain ritualistic ways no matter how great one's thirst, some foods and delicacies may be reserved for certain sections of society. The beneficiaries of a rare edible commodity (in a Western perspective) may not be the most deserving or the most vulnerable groups, for example, pregnant women, the very young, the elderly, and the sick. Modern Western ethics of food consumption do not apply. Religious and ritual experts, shamans and powerful leaders, may enjoy privileges others do not have, contrary to Marx's notion of the original "primitive" communist society sharing everything equally. Religious experts had to be humored with choice food to use their—one is tempted to say imaginary—powers to secure good fortune for the group. Animal fat, a highly prized nutritional luxury among the Aranda of Central Australia, was reserved for the socially and ritually important "old men" (i.e., men of mature age who were ritual leaders); it was forbidden for women of whom it was said that eating it would give them beards. (Had he known it, Karl Marx might have pounced on this ethnographic information as a good example how the grossest superstition cleverly built into the ideological superstructure may be used to create social privilege.) Vice versa, special experts, constrained by religious rules, may be bound to observe even more food restrictions than others or may have to do so at certain times. For instance, in some traditional societies shamans may avoid "hot" foods because they are believed to destroy their spiritual powers; or they may have had to practice selective abstinence or fasting before a vision quest or a curative ceremony. In some tribal societies a person may not have been allowed to eat their personal totem, even if it was the most delectable food. Perhaps best known is that the highest castes in Hinduism abstain from the consumption of meaty foods to maintain ritual purity. Other Hindus confine themselves to a taboo on beef.

Harvesting of food species in hunter-gatherer societies was also not necessarily a straight-forward "rational" predatory or acquisitive matter. In some societies hunters may have had to undergo ritual cleansing, and after a successful kill the prey had to be appeased and thanked for its sacrifice. In some societies the successful hunter may not partake of the meat and other restrictive customs may have to be observed. Among Australian Aborigines, for instance, certain (terminological) kin groups were entitled to receive specific parts of the prey. After sharing the kill, as prescribed by unwritten rules, the hunter may have ended up with some morsels that were not necessarily the choice parts. Seemingly pointless and impractical rules relating to the harvesting of edible resources abound in virtually all societies. In agricultural societies traditionally there are pre- and after-harvest rituals to observe, fertility and rain magic and the like.[2] Even European peasant culture, until recent decades, practiced many ritual and sacrificial customs relating to the fertility of the fields and domesticated animals. The hunt—at least that of a highly traditionalist, stilted type—is often still surrounded with much decorum and ritualized custom, which from a rational point of view serves no purpose other than gladdening the heart of the inveterate traditionalist and snob. In pre-modern times, the poacher in Europe was not just a common thief, but somewhat of a violator of ritual protocol and often punished more harshly than a common petty criminal.

Seemingly ordinary food may be subject to many religiously prescribed arbitrary rules and doctrines, which, though pointless from a practical point of view, have to be strictly obeyed. Judaic dietary rules and restrictions (kashrut) are especially stringent and complex. To satisfy the religiously prescribed concept of kosher, for instance, animals destined for human consumption have to be slaughtered in a particular manner. Nowadays this Jewish slaughter method, shechita, in which the animal has to be alive and fully conscious when its carotid arteries (and, in fact, the whole throat) are cut, has become controversial. It is heavily criticized by animal welfare groups in the West, but generally the practice continues protected by mantras of religious freedom. Hinduism's and Jainism's vegetarian preference and absolute prohibition on beef are well known—a taboo difficult to fathom from a practical point of view given the great need for nutritious food in a burgeoning population.[3] Buddhism frowns on the harvesting of animal protein and leaves it to a special, disrespected class of butchers to do so.

Islam is not only no exception to this universal picture, but is exemplary in the complexity and stringency of its dietary rules. Its distinct approach to potential food sources is already laid down in the Quran. Some of sura 5 is devoted to food and eating and so are other ayas interspersed in the text (especially 2/173, 5/3, 16/115). The Quran's interdiction on pork consumption and pork products is particularly prominent and generally well known (Quran 2/173, 5/3, 6/145, 16/115).[4] Also forbidden is blood, carrion (maitah), animals not slaughtered in the prescribed way, and meat (al-ansab) hallowed for others than Allah (i.e., sacrificial meat for divinities other than God). An exception is made in cases of starvation (16/115). Good food (attayibat) is mentioned in 5/4 as milk, fats, vegetables, and fruit. Food other monotheists (Jews and Christians) consume is allowed in principle, while meat slaughtered in a sacrificial manner at pagan an-nusub (stone altars) is strictly forbidden (5/90). The kill trained animals like hounds and birds of prey bring in may be consumed after consecrating it in the name of Allah (Quran 5/4).

The flesh of animal species and even some other foods, traditionally known in the Middle East, are ordered by Islam in certain rubrics according to their religiously prescribed use value. Meat of "allowed" animals has to be harvested in a special, ritually prescribed manner to make it halal, "allowed," "lawful," or "pure" (Quran 23/51).[5] Failing that, it may not be consumed by the believer, unless in a situation of utter starvation. Some potential foods, labeled makruh, are permitted, but not recommended to be consumed; others are totally forbidden, haram, unless their use is absolutely essential for physical survival. The Quran and further generally accepted elaborations are very explicit and uncompromising. Only when consuming haram (forbidden) substances or drinking blood is the sole means of escaping death, does the Quran make concessions (16/115). The guiding maxims in such cases are that there should be no hardship in religion (Quran 22/78) and that the preservation of human life is a high priority.

THE PORK PUZZLE

Among the strictly forbidden foods pork sticks out. The whole pork avoidance syndrome is remarkable, insofar as in many societies pig rearing and eating is not only allowed and pork is highly appreciated as food, but forms a ceremonial, ritual, and sacralized cluster of great cultural importance in resource management.[6] This is the case above all in the Pacific region; especially in some Melanesian societies where pork is not only highly prized, but pigs are the avenue to social power and prestige. Eating pork is surrounded with much decorum and has supernatural implications. Leading personalities, the so-called Big Men, acquire and maintain their status by giving lavish pork-feasting parties in which the size of the supply of pigs determines the sponsor's social standing. Slaughter and consumption of the pork are highly ritualized affairs. Also in other respects are pigs lifted out from among the animal kingdom and other food sources. Papuan women suckling piglets is not unusual and point to a culturally high appreciation of the pig. In terms of the human world population, pork eaters outnumber pork avoiders (for doctrinal reasons) who seem to be concentrated in the Middle East, throughout Muslim and Muslim-majority regions into Hindu India, and into non-Muslim Africa. In central and Southeast Asia, pork-eaters and pork-avoiders meet face to face.[7] In Indonesia, where pre-Islamic Hinduism and tribalism have survived the wave of Islamization (in a more concerted manner from about the thirteenth century) in enclaves (for instance, on the island of Bali), pig eating has ceremonial significance.

The meaning of the pork taboo has abundantly been speculated about and produced a host of explanations ranging from the purely symbolic to rational-medical ones centered on perceptions of hygiene and the fear of parasites. The very devout Muslims are content to know that God has forbidden it in his wisdom, regardless of any reason humans may contrive. Nowadays, rationalist explanations are popular among educated Muslims because they justify on a scientific basis why pork is forbidden in Islam. Such explanations refer to the flesh of swine containing parasites, a high concentration of uric acid, and other things detrimental to human health.[8] Whether this information was imparted by God or derives from ancient human wisdom is open to debate. Other explanations of the porcine taboo relate to the dirty habits of the animal, which creates disgust and may explain why its flesh is avoided—ingestion being the ultimate contagion. The animal's filthy attributes may easily translate into a symbolic blemish in signaling an abstract quality of uncleanliness that needs to be avoided. Disgust with porcine filth may be further heightened to become a fear of spiritual impurity and sublimated as the horror of ritual pollution some people feel. While this sounds plausible enough, explanatory extravagance has taken the matter further. Among anthropological hypotheses, the argument that pigs are in direct food competition with humans has also been advanced, and that this would be the reason for the disappearance of pig rearing in the Middle East.[9] Another theory, of a symbolist-intellectualist bent, refers to the swine's taxonomic anomaly in being a cloven hoofed nonruminant, thus sharing some physical characteristics with sheep and goats, but not their digestive anatomy and ruminant habits.[10] Whether taxonomic discomfort is enough to reject a vital food source is wide open for debate.

In Islam swine is considered "unclean," in the ritual sense even more than simply referring to hygiene, and consequently pork is closely associated with ideas of ritual pollution. Both Judaism and Islam in sharing this idea have doctrinally strictly tabooed not only pork consumption, but also any contact with this "unclean" animal and its products. The tactless joke about Jewish and Muslim soccer football players trying to avoid coming in contact with the ball made from pigskin is close to reality. It is a good example of how in cultural conceptions a substance's spiritual quality—in this case that of uncleanliness and its capacity to pollute—can be transferred by physical contact. Magical practices (so-called contact magic) make use of this belief in many different forms and so do beliefs that touching or rubbing over a spiritually powerful object can transfer this power or its forceful spiritual essence. Icons and sacred stones are treated in this way in many cultures. Kissing sacred objects, such as crosses or the Blarney Stone, is more than a mere gesture of deep reverence; it also contains an ingredient of the belief that the power, special quality, or blessing somehow contained in an object can be transferred to the devotee by physical contact. In a negative sense, the transferability of pollution makes the contact with swine and pork unwelcome.

Early Christianity, due to its Middle Eastern roots, was also inclined towards porcine disdain. However, despite deriding the swine, once Christianity had emancipated from Judaism it was not forbidding pork as a food source. Later, the Middle Eastern roots of pig prohibition had sufficiently weakened when Christianity spread throughout Europe.[11] It may be surmised this facilitated the spread of the new religion. For central and northern Europeans in pre-Christian times held pork in the highest esteem; it was much more highly prized than beef, poultry, or the flesh of sheep and goats. (Given this culinary predilection perhaps an ecclesiastical ban would have been too difficult to enforce and may have reduced the acceptability of the new faith.) Slaughtering a pig, in the peasant culture of medieval times up to the modern era, heralded a festive occasion and usually was celebrated with feasting and merriment. (A pig's carcass was rather economic as virtually all parts—blood, lard, organs, intestines, trotters, skin, and so on—were eaten, bristles were used, guts served as sausage skins, etc.) Nordic and Celtic mythology (like Hindu and ancient Egyptian mythology) did not stigmatize pigs and

folklore similarly was not prejudiced against things porcine. Roman civilization and its latinized outliers were also not adverse to the consumption of
pork. Beyond a taste for pork, wild boar was a symbol of strength and
courage and could be found on standards of Roman legions.

In wide parts of European folklore, the pig was elevated above the pre-
conception of representing swinish, unclean, and repulsive behavior to become a symbol of good fortune. In this capacity the animal is often associated with good wishes exchanged at the time of New Year's eve. In idiomatic
expressions, too, the pig enjoys rather positive connotations, at least as much
as negative ones. Gluttony and greed as well as dirtiness—these attributes are
referred to when calling someone a "pig" in a rather unflattering sense,
because of their unclean habits or foul morals—may be associated with it,
but not exclusively so. While to be called a swine, and the epithet "pigs" for
the police, surely are not compliments, to call someone a "lucky pig" is
rather a term of endearment or perhaps sincere envy. In the German idiomatic use "schwein haben" (in literal translation: "to have pig") means to have
good luck or to have a lucky break. Despite sharing with Muslims a recognition of the unclean, and in some respects unsavory, habits of pigs prevailing
attitudes hint at least obliquely at a deep appreciation for this animal and its
culinary status.

It is intriguing to speculate why the porcine syndrome has suffered this
religious degradation in the Middle East. While pig rearing seems to have
originated in this region about 13 millennia BC, it later disappeared entirely
from there. Reasons for the specific pig symbolism and its strong prohibition
must be searched for in an historical context that goes beyond the emergence
of Islamic doctrine. Its roots seem to reach back into the prehistoric past of
that region. Most likely, the symbolic transition from pig appreciation to the
tabooization of pork and avoidance of porcine husbandry arose in the course
of profound social transformations in which loosely connected autonomous
local peasant communities developed into city states. In other words, culinary traditions developed and changed in tandem with social and economic
conditions, and were heavily influenced by them. The status of pigs may
originally have been high as vital food source, and serving also as symbolic
pillar of autonomy and self-sufficiency of local peasant communities. But
then for larger social units to take hold the pig's status may have had to be
undermined for the sake of entrenching new sociopolitical conditions. The
formation of city-based states with a centralized administration, James Frazer[12] argued, was that vital social innovation. I am not certain whether Frazer
had this in mind, but by extending his argument one could understand that
the imposition of centralized authority—involving land registration, some
form of recording property title for land-based taxation purposes, and so as to
enforce other forms of social control (levying labor and military services)—

is much easier in a peasant economy based on the husbandry of ruminants. They need relatively larger tracts of land as pasture, which makes it easier to control people's property and livelihood.

The economic benefit of pigs was not amenable to centralization of authority to the same extent as that of ruminants and grazing animals. So as to achieve a fundamental sociopolitical transformation from small communities to a state society under central leadership, the swine's symbolic status had to be lowered from a desirable commodity to one of polluting and undesirable nuisance. This can only be a matter of conjecture, as much as the question whether emergent ideas about contact magic or homeopathic effects (according to Frazer)[13] also played a role in attributing to the unclean habits of pigs an undesirable magical efficacy on the human consumers.

An additional straightforward explanation may be that the increasing urbanization and density of human cohabitation, as it happened six or seven millennia ago in the Middle East, made pig husbandry undesirable, and it eventually had to be abandoned because of the pig's unsanitary habits. Especially in a domestic style in which the stables and the people's living quarters were in close proximity—virtually sharing living space one on top of the other[14]—keeping pigs may have posed a serious olfactory nuisance and created health problems. Compounding the situation, the relatively dense clustering of houses in the emergent city would have intensified the pigs "nuisance value."[15] The mounting urbanization would have exacerbated the olfactory offensiveness of pig keeping by comparison with ruminants. Also the difficulty in containing pigs outdoors because of their burrowing habits all may have militated against porcine husbandry. In a society in which laws and rules in order to be effective had to have divine or supernatural sanction, there was good reason to discourage pig husbandry by giving it the connotation of spiritual uncleanness and pollution and underscore it with divine command. Perhaps, in addition, one should not underestimate the level of knowledge such societies may have had about parasitology (especially trichnosis) and the transmission of diseases through lack of cleanliness.[16]

For herders and nomadic animal pastoralists living in arid and semiarid environments, such as Bedouins, the reason for pig avoidance is self-evident. Pigs are unsuited to long-distance herding and overall are a drag on economic patterns of transhumance in an environment of scarce vegetation.

These explanations, superficially plausible as they seem, are based on the empirically unverifiable assumption that some form of social rationality guides the process of cultural formation. Inventing porcine husbandry seems easy to understand on this basis. The Neolithic "revolution" and its agricultural innovations are perfectly comprehensible as feats of human practical rationality, which we can rationally comprehend and empathize with. But the pig's disappearance and pork prohibition is much less clearly accessible by way of some kind of rationally based reasoning. Some arguments may appear to possess plausibility; however, there is a large ingredient of uncertainty in explanations of how symbolic systems come into existence. Causation in the emergence of culture may be far from and beyond what is recognizable to human understanding as rational. Although culture, and especially symbolism, are human products, oddly we are on terra infirma when it comes to explaining them. The believer is in an incomparably more comfortable position.

THE MEANING OF HALAL

Halal basically means permitted or pure, as opposed to haram, forbidden. There is another major category, makruh, discouraged as distasteful but not strictly forbidden (such as crocodile, carrion-eating birds, etc.). It is generally well known that Islam observes a requirement to sanctify food and make it spiritually ready for human consumption. Some foods are naturally halal, such as sea food (finfish, crustaceans, shellfish), being pure and clean by its nature due to the pure environment from which it comes. (Environmental pollution and degradation was obviously no problem at the Prophet's time.) Other foods have to be transformed through special ritual techniques. Potentially consumable meats (excluding above all pork, dog, and blood products) have to be processed in a special way, imparting a blessing on them to make them ready for ordinary, everyday consumption (not in a crisis situation when survival is at stake). In rendering meat halal, three basic requirements have to be observed. When slaughtering the animal, its value as a gift from God has to be acknowledged by orientating the act of killing towards Macca and accompanying it with the ritual bismillah formula that honors God; the blood has to drain from the carcass as completely as possible so as to avoid consuming it with the meat; and the slaughterer has to be ritually pure and a Muslim.

The first requirement imitates the prayer situation and sanctifies the act by which a living animal is transformed into food. While this step is purely symbolic, the next is of practical significance though also performed in order to meet a symbolic requirement. Emptying the carcass of blood avoids a possible violation of the strict prohibition on its consumption. (Nowadays, "rationalist" Muslims like to explain this prohibition as divine foresight in preventing the transmission of diseases carried in the blood.) So as to bleed the animal as completely as possible it must be alive and its organs still working. Above all, the heart must be still beating when the animal's carotid arteries are being cut. "Humane" slaughter methods prescribe nowadays that stunning should precede bleeding and actual slaughter. In principle Islam is not as adamantly against pre-slaughter stunning as orthodox Judaism is.[17] In modern slaughterhouses various methods of pre-slaughter stunning are allowed to achieve a halal result, in contrast to Jewish shechita prescriptions, which insist that an animal be alive and fully conscious at the moment of slaughter. However, even with Islamic slaughter methods much argument may arise as to what degree of stunning, to invoke unconsciousness and make the animal insensitive to pain, can be administered to make the method still capable of delivering a fully halal product. The scriptures are not oblivious to the humaneness of the slaughter: they prescribe that a very sharp knife be used to minimize the suffering of the animal. However, the suffering of animals may in reality not always be eliminated when, for instance, inexperienced lay people perform the ritual slaughter for the eid-al-adha (commemorating Abraham's sacrifice). In respect of humaneness, the highly trained Jewish shochet, who is supposed to cut the animal's throat in one swift stroke, has the advantage.[18]

The third requirement, the purity of the slaughterer, means that in modern meat works, which produce a commercial halal product, slaughterers should be employed who can boast an impeccable Muslim lifestyle. In the West this disqualifies men who have succumbed to the allure of alcohol and in a wider sense have followed the path of secularization in the form of adopting un-Islamic morals, abstain from prayer, and have acquired un-Islamic eating habits. It also means that women may not be employed in this role as they are at times ritually impure.

Each of the three requirements is of equal importance. When Western abattoirs are expected to deliver an impeccably halal meat product for export to Muslim countries, any of these steps can give rise to serious problems. When accusations are raised that the process is not followed correctly it can have a dire economic impact. Problems can arise from various issues. The slaughterers may be laissez-faire Muslims and, therefore, through their conduct impart their personal lack of purity on the meat, or they may be found to be negligent in offering the correct prayers at the correct, prescribed time. The management may be reluctant to stop the slaughter chain to allow the slaughterers enough time to pray at the prescribed times, as the whole production process is impeded by such interruptions and entails economic losses. Equally unacceptable may be the work habit by which only one of the slaughterers prays as a substitute for the whole gang. The method of stunning may come under close scrutiny when it is criticized for making the animal too comatose to bleed out properly. Some time ago, a problem arose in New Zealand with a slaughter chain that processed chickens the halal way. Fully automated, the prayers were delivered by an audiotape while the chickens were transported along on a chain inexorably moving to their demise by an automatically activated blade. On inspection of the plant by Islamic authorities, it was found that the actual and highly mechanized slaughter was happening too fast for the tape to keep up with the speed with which the chickens were dispatched. The full ritual formula was completed only after every six chickens had passed, so that each killing missed out on being impeccably blessed.

The term "halal" has changed considerably from its classical meaning to become all-encompassing. It refers now to all sharia-compliant products. It is no longer confined to meat and meat products. Over the last few decades, halal products have evolved from meaty things to product ingredients, to pharmaceuticals and cosmetics, to service industries such as Islamic finance, logistics, and retailing, to healthcare and tourism. The requirements of the modern Muslim consumer for products and services that serve to enhance their total Islamic lifestyle is estimated at USD 2.1 trillion. No wonder the concept of halal, its production processes and methods, and its products and services have suddenly captured the attention of leading global industries.

Considering food and its sacral aspect in a global context, it can be said that concepts of purity, ideas of purifying or blessing food to make it ready for human consumption, and elements of sacralizing food are widespread if not universal. The sacralization of food and its production, relevant ritual techniques and ceremonial procedures can be detected in many and various cultural features and in many permutations on the basic themes involved. It is probably no exaggeration to maintain that with some interpretative imagination, an element of symbolization and ritualization of food, its production and its consumption can be found in most, if not all, past and present cultures. Sacralizing food may be connected with magical expectations that through ritualized manipulations its nutritional value and wholesomeness may be enhanced and that it energizes the consumer through its spiritual dimension. In any case food goes vastly beyond the act of simple ingestion of substances for life sustaining purposes. The indiscriminate gobbling down of nourishment may possibly have occurred in the prehominid phase of evolution, but ever since has been confined more or less to crisis situations when starving individuals were reduced to utter pragmatism.

In the West, although it is performed increasingly rarely owing to secularization, praying over food or blessing it is a familiar traditionalist Christian part of dining culture. The table prayer of the devout, offering it over the food to be consumed, is a remnant of the traditional practices of conjoining sacredness and the divine with food and drink, their production and consumption. The sacralization of food on the table valorizes the act of eating to a communion with the divine. This is particularly prominent in food and drink that is doctrinally elevated to the status of sacrament. Even the act of eating itself may be subject to divine rule and fall under divine auspices. The Sunna, for instance, has something specific to say about the proper, God-pleasing way of eating: one should avoid filling oneself to bursting; "a few morsels are enough to sustain the eater's spine" the scriptures proclaim; and "Let a third be for food, a third for drink and a third for breathing."[19]

Some monasteries, since medieval times up to the present day, produce certain kinds of food and drink, which not only have a reputation for healthy wholesomeness, but are considered blessed and of particular spiritual quality. In pre-secularization times in Europe, the blessing of food production, and of the means of production (implements, fields), was important in peasant cultures. Blessings and prayers were offered to fruit trees, domesticated animals, grape vines, and fields of grain; the hunt as a means of procuring meat was blessed; and so was wine, beer, and bread in various ceremonies. In Catholic rural custom, practiced in some regions up until recent times, sacred icons were carried in solemn procession through the fields. Libations and food offerings were not uncommonly made to the supernatural forces responsible for fertility and harvest. Most of these ritual customs were lost in the process of secularization and commercialization. (Partly also Protestantism, which had a more "rational" approach to such worldly matters, initiated this decline in the ritualization of food production.) Thanksgiving celebrations are left nowadays as a reminder of erstwhile pious attitudes to food production.

On the topic of the procurement and production of food under a sacred aegis, let me briefly refer to other cultural ways of dealing with food resources, giving them special symbolic meaning, and paying ritual attention to how they may be won. Drawing on my own research over many years among Australian Aborigines I can find many fine examples. One might expect that these Australian hunter-gatherers, as they once were, in their everyday traditional existence, were forced by their environment and their level of technology to adopt a very pragmatic stance. Yet, traditionally—that is, before Western colonization changed their lives irreversibly—they did not have a completely utilitarian approach to natural food resources. Beyond a clear "rational," empirically based understanding of nature and its workings—and using this vast store of knowledge to wisely work with nature's grain rather than against it—there were elaborate symbolic means of dealing with an altogether not very benign environment and the foods it may yield. Special rituals (so-called fertility or maintenance rituals), thought to enhance nature's fertility, were considered vitally important as virtual guarantors of human survival; for they were believed to have the effect of replenishing useful resources—each ritual for a particular species or phenomenon. They had to be performed regularly for animal and plants species, for rain, and even human fertility, as it was believed that without them a species or natural phenomenon could not thrive and, in fact, would not survive in the long run. These rituals constituted a form of blessing of natural resources—a kind of Thanksgiving in advance, and a variation on the theme of sacralizing food production.[20]

In traditional Maori society and several other Pacific societies the sacralization of food and its procurement had an inverted effect. Establishing, by ritual means, a conjunction between sacredness, tapu, and food made it nonconsumable, forbidden. In New Zealand's traditional Maori culture there is an antinomious relationship between tapu and ngoa, sacredness and non-sacredness (or mundaneness). Food being ngoa, mundane or of an everyday quality, makes it consumable. But when it is transposed into sacredness it becomes too powerful (mana) to be treated as an ordinary commodity. For example, a person being in a (temporary) condition of tapu touching food, through contact charged it with so much power as to become inedible. A tapu placed on an area (declaring a rahui) made its resources practically inaccessible: they became sacred and therefore inedible and untouchable. Fish or shellfish could not be harvested on a coastal area over which a rahui had been declared, fruit may not be taken from such a tree, vegetable resources may not be gathered, and the like.[21] In this way, "blessing" of food had the inverse effect to enhancing its beneficence.

The sacralization of food and its consumption does not only result in ceremonialization of resource management and symbolic elevation of foodstuffs, or the tabooization of potential nutritional substances. The action of partaking in food can be sanctified to such exalted proportions that the act of eating is believed to be a communion with the supernatural. Lifting nourishment and its act out of the ordinary is spectacularly expressed in ritual cannibalism, but also in the eucharist and the consumption of holy foods in other religions. (Beliefs in holy water, which has special curative, salvific, and other mysterious powers, falls into the same category.) This special quality is also implicit in the idea of the "last supper" or the "last meal" of the condemned—a custom that goes back in Europe to before Christianity as the stomach contents of (ritually disposed) corpses found in bogs testify.[22] All of this is evidence that the act of eating is lifted out of the ordinary and is more than the simple meeting of bodily needs. Secularized Western culture has shed much of this deep-rooted panhuman attitude, leaving only the whimsicality of valuing some foods and disdaining others and a special etiquette of eating at special ceremonial occasions. Islam has preserved to a much greater extent these panhuman ideas around the sacredness of food and its ingestion.

In Islam the ceremonialization of the act of eating is reinforced by the prescription that only the right hand may be used. In greeting the right hand touches the heart (or rather the left side of the chest) in (almost) universal language signifying sincerity and affection.[23] The left hand is considered the "toilet hand," used for impure purposes. Thus the left hand should not be used for important purposes like touching another person or one's head, handling the Quran, not even waving at an esteemed person. The left is used for monetary matters and other "unclean" or dubious activities. This is not simply done for reasons of hygiene that relate to the specific customary toilet habits of the Middle East, but has also symbolic significance of a kind that is widespread in humankind. In several cultures the right hand is considered "the good hand," associated with positive attributes, while the left is loaded with negative connotations. Even in Western culture, supposedly liberated by the Enlightenment and boldly freeing itself from blind superstitions, until recently the education system saw a need to recondition left-handers. Naturally left-handed children were reeducated to use their right hand and sometimes were even punished for lapsing back into old habits. The very terms left and right—in some languages—are connoting negative and positive attributes respectively. Seen against this cultural background, the tabooization of the left hand in Islam for the important task of ingesting nourishment can be assumed that it is not solely done for the sake of reserving one hand for dirty, unhygienic activities (such as cleaning oneself after defecation) and the other for clean ones, but that it has its origin in the widespread, almost universal symbolic dichotomy associated with right and left.[24]

By mentioning the ethnographic example of traditional Maori culture and its notion of tapu, I have touched on the feature of ritualization and sacralization leading to food avoidance. This is the reverse side of sacralizing food and symbolizing the act of eating in order to improve their quality and beneficial effect. Related to this cultural syndrome is the temporary ceremonial abstention from food. Ritual abstention from food may serve the same purpose of establishing a synergy between divine purpose and human existence; connecting life-sustaining activity with the ultimate causality of human existence. Fasting may be done for purposes of personal or collective purification, to stimulate reflection and intuition, perhaps to the point of inciting deprivational delusions believed to be supernatural revelations. In Islam observing sawm (fasting) in the month of Ramadan, the ninth of the lunar calendar,[25] is considered one of the five pillars, a sacred duty to be performed by every Muslim. Several ayas (2/183–187) refer to the holy month of Ramadan and the required behavior underlining its significance. The rules and laws surrounding the observation of fasting (sawm or siyam) are complex. Some of the rules have obvious "rational" grounds. Most interpretations of the Ramadan rules grant exemptions to the sick, the elderly, the frail, the insane, women who are pregnant, nursing, or menstruating, to travelers or those feeding thirty people or more. The daily fast lasts from sunrise to sundown, or as it specifies in the Quran (2/187), from the time a black and a white thread can be distinguished to the time in the evening when this is no longer possible. Nowadays, tables with exact times are issued by the Islamic authorities in every Muslim country (and countries where there are sizable Muslim minorities) so as to coordinate the observance of fasting and fixate the end of this period. These instructions remove the guesswork in observing light conditions, the sun or the moon, and also unambiguously regulates the prayer times from fajr (morning prayer), before which the sahur meal is to be consumed, to maghrib (evening prayer) after which the iftar is taken, which breaks the fast for the night. The very devout even interrupt their brief sleep period with additional prayers around midnight (tarawih) and make an effort to read the Quran even more assiduously than normally. (When in subantarctic conditions—where Muslims now also live—Ramadan falls into the brief summer months, the time of darkness is much reduced and it needs a kindly interpretation to make this bearable for the believers.)

Nowadays, in a slightly more secularized and urban environment, these rules may have become more relaxed and obedience to rules assumed less stringency. I remember Cairo during Ramadan when in the evening restaurants were full with people sitting with filled plates in front of them, anxiously eyeing the sun as it disappeared under the horizon. The religious duty being reduced to the minimal requirement, no prayers were offered before greedily breaking the fast.

Ramadan celebrates the time when the first verses of the Quran were revealed to the Prophet. The abstention from food is a symbolic sacrifice, reminding people of the duty they have to God, but also to impress social virtues such as patience, humility, modesty, gratitude, peacefulness (despite the fact that the important battle of Badr was fought in that month), pure thoughts, and remembering the poor and starving. An empty stomach, so to speak, concentrates the mind on spiritual matters. Nowadays, fasting is sometimes styled as a health issue, a religious habit, wisely dictated by Islam, because it is beneficial to personal physical well-being. In a world in which the so-called developed part is increasingly suffering the scourge of obesity, with all the attendant health problems, and where chronic overconsumption and seemingly boundless food indulgence are being more and more clearly recognized as a health risk, occasional fasting makes good rational sense. (What is disputed, however, is the length of the fasting period. It has also been pointed out that while fasting people are in a weakened condition, which makes them incapable of performing to normal standards. Especially physically demanding performance may be suffering and some Muslim countries make appropriate concessions. In the Western diaspora Muslims are, however, at a disadvantage.)

As Ramadan is a period of purification, not only food and drink is forbidden to be consumed during daylight hours. Tobacco smoking falls under the same rule as well as sexual activity and music and dance. Harsh and injurious words, quarrels, and asocial acts are to be avoided, at least during fasting hours. It is considered bad taste to engage in wars and hostilities during Ramadan. In some excessively devout interpretations even taking of medicines is not allowed. Eye drops, for instance, in this view are nourishing a body part and therefore should be avoided. The fasting period ends on the first day of the following month, the Shawwal, with a big festivity, the eid-al-fitr, with feasting and gift giving.

Ramadan is a highly ceremonial period, enriched as it is with more than five prayer times, the taking of food in a very structured manner and saturated with sacred meaning. The provision of common ceremonial activity engaged in by everybody with few exceptions and designed to instill and reinforce socially valuable values certainly acts in a manner that enhances intra-Muslim solidarity and reinforces social cohesion. The spiritualization of a relatively long period of the year intensifies the lesson of bonding and enculturation, made even more effective by renewing it every year. Today, keeping the fast is considered a cultural marker of Muslimness, an overt statement of a person's faith, and an important symbol of commitment to Islam. Although statistics are not available on this issue, the overriding impression is that even in the diaspora modern and Westernized Muslims take pride in adhering to this religious custom in fulfillment of one of the five pillars of Islam. The Beur culture of some French Muslims, though, has made some adaptive concessions to the national French ethos, by shortening the fasting period to three days and also taking the alcohol prohibition more lightly, but this is certainly a minority phenomenon.[26] On the whole, it can be said that keeping the fasting restriction is becoming a signal marker of global Muslimhood.

HEDONISM AND TEMPTATIONS OF INTOXICATION

Among the striking dietary rules in Islam, some of the strongest regulations, heightened to strict prohibition, refer to intoxicating drinks and stimulants; or to phrase it in modern jargon, psychoactive substances that alter the chemical milieu of the brain. As this prohibition is both characteristic for Islam and highly unusual in the context of general human behavior, it warrants a closer look. (The alcohol prohibition, in some sense, constitutes an exact opposite to the previous consideration of the universalist character of sacralizing food and drink. Alcohol is demonized in Islam and in respect of the uncompromising rejection of its much sought-after effect doctrine and Muslim custom show a singularity unmatched by the rest of humanity.) Abstinence of this kind is an identity marker of modern Islam, but is not as strong a feature of historical Muslim society as is usually believed.[27] Its increased emphasis today seems more a return to the puritanical spirit of the original Islam. It is reasonable to see a connection with tendencies toward fundamentalization and its search for Islamic authenticity. The spread of Wahhabism with its ascetic features and strong rejection of earthly hedonism also helps to lift the prohibition to focal prominence.

Few societies traditionally do not produce, through fermentation or distillation, intoxicating drinks (such as wine, beer, or liquor). As far as can be ascertained, humanity seems to have done so for millennia. Wine making is supposed to have been invented in Asia possibly as long as eight thousand years ago and there is no reason to believe that some form of beer brewing is much younger as both processes involve knowledge of methods of controlled fermentation. Oldest methods may have been to induce fermentation and to free narcotic chemicals through chewing—as has still been done in historical time with kava[28] —until the beneficial effects of sugars and yeast were discovered.[29] In addition there is a whole range of other drinks and substances with special effects on human metabolism, performance, mood, and mental conditions. Many of them are naturally occurring in plants and are available without requiring longwinded processing techniques. Universally seen, narcotics and pharmaceutical stimulants are treasured in most societies. Appreciated for their mind-altering, euphoric, or relaxing effect, the relevant substances inducing such mental and physical responses usually enjoy a certain, elevated social status. Not unusually, such substances are not indiscriminately accessible, are considered a luxury, and may come under very special rules. In some societies their consumption is restricted to religious experts or shamans in their capacity as healers and communicators with the divine or spirit world; in others it is reserved for privileged groups. Australian Aborigines in precolonial times treasured so-called "native tobacco," a green leafy weed that released its special properties when chewed. It grows in shady places and before the introduction of other stimulants and intoxicants such as chewing tobacco, "smokes," alcohol, petrol-sniffing, and street drugs, it was considered a special treat. Especially in the arid interior of the continent, Aborigines traditionally made use of almost every conceivable nutrient including grubs, ants, lizards, snakes, and the like; but "native tobacco," pitchuri,[30] was elevated from among natural resources and especially prized as a luxury for its mildly narcotic properties. But only the gerontocratic elite, the older men, being the religious experts and considered ritually important, "officially" had access to this stimulant. Younger men and women usually had no right to consume it and had legitimate access only when they received it as a special gratuity from an older male.

Transcending pure hedonistic and practical reasons, more often than not religious and spiritual aspects adhered to such substances, the plants from which they are won and their consumption. Both raw material and the act of using it could be endowed with awe and reverence. In the Pacific region, the production and consumption of kava (piper methysticum) are traditionally hedged in with ritual decorum and even nowadays, when it is consumed more widely and in a more secular social context, it has still retained some of the spiritual mystique. In other parts of the Pacific region it is betel, a nut fortified with lime, that enjoys much popularity as a mild stimulant. Ritual smoking of the peace pipe in the American Plains Indian culture has romantically been popularized through movies and adventure novels. Many more examples could be cited. Coca in South America seems to have been socially more widely accessible and whole prehistoric Andean empires seem to have been fueled by it. It was known and used for its effect of giving physical endurance beyond normal human capacity. Consumption of the peyote cactus extract has become the central symbolic act around which a religious belief system has been devised. Rastafarians consider cannabis as the "holy weed" and smoking it has ritual significance. These are just some prominent examples. South American shamans smoked rolled-up tobacco plants. Yage, an extract from a South American jungle vine, traditionally is the drug of choice for shamans to enter a hallucinogenic condition to heal and prognosticate the future. Yopo, the hallucinogenic drug of the Yanomamo is won also from a jungle vine mixed with some herbs. The powder blown through a long pipe into a man's nasal cavity by another man causes nausea and blinding headaches, but puts the recipient into a trancelike altered state of consciousness in which he is capable of communicating with the spirit world. In Mexico and Siberia, mushrooms served a similar purpose, and possibly still do. The list could be extended considerably even without going into the present-day situation where dozens of different street drugs are on offer, legally and illegally. A wide range of synthetic drugs—scientifically produced—are commercially available purely for the euphoric effect they induce. It almost seems that they have become part of today's youth culture. (As critical voices complain, without these legal and illegal drugs young people seem unable "to have a good time.") An equal if not greater scourge is excessive consumption of alcohol in the form of "binge drinking" (episodic overindulgence) leading to serious health problems, asocial behavior and criminality. Islamic culture (which is not quite the same as actual practice), however, cannot be found on a register of cultures using intoxicating, hallucinogenic or even stimulating substances to such an exorbitant extent. While alcohol abuse has become a serious problem in Western society and many Third World countries have adopted a Western lifestyle including the prolific use of alcohol, Muslim majority societies by and large remain untouched by the social and health problems that afflict the West as a consequence.

From among world cultures Islam sticks out by its reputation of enforcing absolute sobriety and being doctrinally and implacably opposed to intoxication of any kind.[31] So-called altered states of mind brought about through the use of mood and mind altering substances of any kind are strictly forbidden. Straddling the line between its dietary restrictions and behavior rules particularly, the consumption of alcohol is strictly labeled haram (forbidden). In a sense this is ironic as etymologically the word alcohol is said to derive from the Arabic al-kuhl, which relates to the semantics of essence and its derivates.

Although it is not as expressly forbidden as eating pork or consuming blood—which are the object of a special and emphatically explicit aya (2/173) in the Quran, imbibing alcohol is considered sinful and therefore prohibited. This prohibition enjoys profound, if not total, respect in today's Muslimhood.[32] Indeed it is customary in Muslim-majority countries to not only frown on the consumption of alcohol but to punish it, in some countries severely. Under the Saudi Arabian legal system, which generally is considered to come closest to the ideal type of Islamic law, sharia, wine drinking is punished with between forty and eighty lashes.[33]

In July 2009, the world media reported that the Malaysian sharia high court sentenced a beauty queen and part-time model Kartika Sari Dewi Shukarno, a Muslima, to a substantial fine and six lashes with the rotan (rattan) whip for drinking beer at a night club. Her case made headlines in the West, even though it is by far not a singular or isolated incident. It is not implausible that the Islamic world network was not unhappy in broadly publicizing the sentence to demonstrate the complete impartiality of a sharia-type justice system. Not even beautiful women are exempt from punishment and, in fact, are likely to be made an example of for the sake of publicity. (However, in January 2010 media reported that the woman has been given a reprieve.) Even in diasporic conditions, Muslim communities may try to enforce the alcohol prohibition. The media reported in July 2011 that in Sydney, Australia, a recent convert who had lapsed back into what seems to have been a pre-conversion "weakness," was punished with forty lashes with an electric cable. A posse of Muslims broke into his house and meted out this punishment, which prompted the police commissioner to reiterate that sharia law would not be tolerated in Australia. Only a few weeks earlier (in May 2011) the Australian media reported just such a proposal by the Australian Federation of Islamic Councils to the Federal Government's enquiry into multiculturalism. The suggestion was to acknowledge the right of Islamic tribunals—more in the sense of arbitration councils—to pronounce in family matters (i.e., divorce, inheritance), business disputes, and neighborhood conflicts and for sharia to coexist with Australian law. In fact it was said that such tribunals were already operating (unofficially) in certain mosques in Sydney. (Perhaps punishing the alcoholic recidivist may have been a verdict imposed by an unofficial sharia court.) The media also reported that any further discussion was immediately quashed by the Federal Attorney-General, reiterating what several politicians before him had already emphatically declared: there was no place for sharia in Australian society, and if people wished to live under sharia law they better not come to Australia in the first place.

The courtly culture of the classical caliphs may not always have set a good example for the Islamic world. It did not strictly observe the alcohol prohibition and arrogated some privileges and exemptions to itself. Guillaume[34] refers to the Umayyad and Abbasid caliphs' lifestyle as "Wein, Weib und Gesang (wine, woman and song—an aphorism for debauchery and a decadent, overly hedonistic lifestyle) practiced in their palaces. Umayyad caliphs not only indulged themselves, but even tolerated wine booths in mosques. Medieval Muslim poets and writers praised wine in exalted tones and even questioned the religious doctrine of abstinence. There was also considerable and relatively open wine consumption in the urban Arab middle classes—even the ulama and qadis—similar to the habits of the rising bourgeoisie in Turkey.[35] These times of the elite flaunting Islamic prescriptions are past. The Muslim elite and even members of the general public may still indulge their taste for alcohol, but it has to be done more or less secretly.

Bosnian and Albanian Muslims, and more generally Muslim minorities in the Balkans, probably influenced by the drinking culture of all other ethnic groups in the region, seem to have a somewhat more relaxed attitude. Autochthonous Islam, the Bektashi version of the Bosniaks above all, has assimilated local non-Islamic drinking customs (involving strong liquor) and in general do not practice the same degree of puritanical strictness as other, recent immigrant Muslims, now living among them, do.[36] There are deep roots of alcohol consumption in the Balkans, going back to the times of the Ottoman empire. Bektashi Turks were known as drinkers and in more recent times incline towards Kemalism, the Turkish version of secularism, which has abandoned the religious alcohol prohibition. In the times of the classical Ottoman Empire taverns were heavily frequented by the soldiery, especially the janissaries (of whom many though were Christians). Not only wine but also arak or raki, a strong liquor, was very popular, even outside Turkey proper. Banquets of Sultans offered champagne, as consuming alcohol became a sign of being "civilized," modern and desirably Westernised in the nineteenth century. In more recent times a public (male) drinking culture developed in the Turkish urban centers, until it was curbed again later in the twentieth century by the rise of Islamic nationalism and the growing influence of Islamic political parties.[37]

French Beur Muslims of North African descent, finding themselves under ideological pressure from France's eminent cultural icon of wine consumption, also do not appear to observe the alcohol prohibition as religiously as other devout Muslims. However, these are exceptions produced by a situation of diasporic minorities under cultural pressure from engulfing populations with different culinary and taste traditions and different value preferences. Some Muslim-majority countries, like Morocco, Turkey, and Indonesia, produce alcoholic beverages (such as full-strength beer and wine), but usually only so-called nominal Muslims (in Indonesia jokingly called Muslim statistik) or "secularized" ones do consume it. Officially, however, consumption is restricted to resident non-Muslim minorities (and non-Muslim tourists), while Muslims are expected to abstain from it totally. This is not always strictly the case—despite the trend of fundamentalization. Statistically alcohol consumption has gone up significantly in recent years in more liberal Muslim countries such as Morocco, which cannot be explained through the presence of an expatriate Western community or tourism. Even in religiously stricter Muslim countries, unofficially alcohol consumption has increased, though officially, of course, these countries are "dry." Thus alcohol may be taken to symbolise both advancing globalization and resistance to it at the same time.

Theoretically at least, not only consumption of alcohol is prohibited in Islam, but also trading with it and even carrying it for someone else as though its impurity would rub off on anyone coming into contact with it. Even purchasing stocks to do with the production or distribution of alcoholic beverages is forbidden. Of course daily life is riddled with exceptions to the doctrinal rule as some "good" Muslims flaunt it and surreptitiously do drink, trade, or otherwise come in contact with the forbidden drink. Places frequented by tourists and Westerners (such as resort hotels, bars, and restaurants) often make an exception and custom-free shops at airports and elsewhere are well stocked with liquor even in the Islamic world. Even in Saudi Arabia alcohol is tolerated when Westerners consume it privately (i.e., in nonpublic situations and "exclusion zones" such as private clubs), although officially it is not legalized. Well-to-do Muslims visiting the West are said to be enjoying the odd alcoholic drink seduced by the" forbidden fruit." As rumor has it rich Muslim visitors on mercantile or political business in the West favor a good shot of expensive whisky as a mark of daring adventurism. But such indulgence has to be done anonymously or secretly.

The interdiction on alcohol is usually understood to extend beyond ordinary intoxicants to all mind- and mood-altering drugs, narcotics, and hallucinogenics. Mild narcotics such as coffee, tea, and tobacco are not included, although the earlier excessively purist version of Wahhabism tried to suppress coffee drinking and smoking, but without lasting success. Tobacco was unknown at the Prophet's time and, therefore, is not mentioned in the fundamental sacred scriptures and in the exegeses of the law schools. When it became available, tobacco was not judged to be intoxicating or hallucinogenic, or to be an addictive drug. The notion that its consumptions would pose a health risk is relatively recent and though known has not penetrated deeply into the non-Western psyche. Regarding smoking as a "filthy habit" is a very fashionable Western perception that has no currency outside the West.

Modern Muslim purists will abstain from cigarette smoking, but not simply for health reasons. Their main motif is based on a religious interpretation. Sometimes the two aspects are practically conflated in the sense that it is considered God-pleasing to maintain a pure and healthy body by abstaining from "polluting," "toxic or "impure" substances. Imbibing or coming into close contact with haram substances has a spiritually polluting effect the devout is keen to avoid. Not only psychopharmaca are likely to be rejected by the devout; extremely strict Muslims will even abstain from painkillers and sedatives that are opiate based or codein derived. The position of performance-enhancing drugs such as smart drugs and steroids is ambiguous and open to interpretation whether they are included in the ban on intoxicants or not. The devout interpretation would be to abstain: what God has given (i.e., the physical and mental abilities) should not be altered. Another important criterion in separating allowed substances from those banned, is their addictive quality (which will be referred to below).

It is on religious grounds, that in the Muslim world drug addiction is even more despised than in the more liberal West, where addicts are often treated as victims and in need of help. Muslim addicts are deemed to commit a religious crime; and if an addict's asocial lifestyle makes them an outcast, they can count on little support or compassion. Again to cite the example of Saudi Arabia, drug use as a first offense is treated as "wine drinking" and like all consumption of alcoholic beverages is punished with lashings; recidivism is punished with death—as only death is considered that it can stop addiction. [38]

On the other hand, a series of stimulants, mild intoxicants, and narcotics may occupy an ambiguous position persisting in a grey area where their consumption is considered traditional and customary, incurring no stigma, despite the fact that in principle it is violating Islamic doctrines. If we leave aside tea, coffee, and tobacco as mild stimulants, which do not fall under the Islamic interdiction, there are other drugs traditionally consumed in the Muslim world. The best known is qat (quat, khat) used predominately in Yemen [39] and the horn of Africa. A green leafy plant, when chewed it acts as a stimulant, but its effects are not considered intoxicating. In 2010, a local Somali community in the New Zealand city of Hamilton came under suspicion of secretly importing khat (or chat), which is officially considered a class C drug, prohibited under New Zealand law. [40] One can have some sympathy for the fact that for Somali refugees this is part of their lifestyle and in a diasporic situation is a luxury of some nostalgic value. Their desire can be compared with Westerners living in a "dry" country being tempted to smuggle in whisky or beer. However, under present conditions there is little chance that the use of khat where it is forbidden may fall under the aegis of tacit cultural tolerance, let alone under legal provisions of cultural freedom. For the Muslims involved in khat smuggling, it must seem absurd that their activity is illegal when the whole country is "high" on legal alcohol consumption.

In Morocco connoisseurs of mint tea like to add a little absinth herb for its mildly narcotic effect. Another drug widely used in the Middle East is cannabis, commonly known as hashish; from which the word "assassin" is said to derive. hashish is believed to have been used by the medieval Islamic sect of Hashshashin (or hashishin, Hashasheen) whose name is derived from hashshash, a hashish user. The Nizari branch of Ismaili Shi'a, which became known by this name, had gained a reputation of carrying out religiously motivated assassinations during the Middle Ages. It is believed that its assassins were sent on their missions while under the influence of this drug. The effect was meant to make them bold for their daring attacks, which usually were suicide missions. However, more recently, expert opinion tends to with-draw from this view that the sect used psychoactives to induce the ecstasy necessary for equipping its emissaries for their deadly missions.

Among Muslim countries Afghanistan is considered to have the highest proportion of drug addicts and an especially high addiction rate to opium. It is ironic that this staunchly Islamic country is the world's most prolific poppy grower and opium producer.[41] Of about 30 million, a staggering 1.5 million are considered addicts.

Opium traditionally is less widely used in the rest of the Islamic world, although poppy cultivation is a traditional agricultural activity not only in Afghanistan. It was even tolerated by the Taleban as a revenue-generating crop, after an initial period of trying to suppress its cultivation had failed. After coming to power the Taleban government at first had applied harsh methods of prohibition, but by and large these proved unsuccessful. When financial strains began to bite into the regime's coffers and no kudos for the prohibition was to be earned with Western powers, the Taleban relented. Taxing poppy production allegedly became an important source of revenue for them in the later years of the regime—and allegedly even today. Today, in the regions of Afghanistan still under Taleban control peasants engage in significant poppy cultivation.

Addiction to hashish is often politely overlooked. As I could observe, hashish was widely used in Afghanistan in the twentieth century although a mild social stigma was attached to overindulgence. On the whole it was tolerated just as in a Western rural context people might more or less condes-cendingly or derisively smile about a village drunkard so long as his—the gender specificity is deliberate as women usually enjoy less tolerance—intoxicated behavior is still considered socially tolerable by being nonaggres-sive and relatively good-humored. Once a person begins to routinely over-step that mark of inebriation, there is little compassion for them. In the 1960s and 1970s the notorious Hippie hashish trail extended from Europe to Af-ghanistan and Pakistan where large numbers of Western youths traveled in search of the cheap, high-quality cannabis more or less openly available in that region. As I could observe on numerous occasions, the police did not interfere.

HISTORY AND DOCTRINE

Let us return to the less harmful drug—although this may be disputed—of alcohol. Archaeological evidence suggests that wine production through fer-mentation of grapes may go back eight millennia in China and may be of similar ancientness in Persia and the Middle and Near East. From there it seems to have later spread into the Mediterranean region—from where, mainly through the good offices of the Romans, it was transported into central Europe and Britain. More recently viticulture seems to conquer the more moderate climate zones of the world. For several countries wine has become a major export article and revenue earner, and viticulture has become a part of the repertory of a modern, civilized, and high-class lifestyle.

If one looks at Arab culture of the seventh century it is fair to assume that the consumption of wine was relatively widespread, in fact, may have been a salient element of Arab culture. (It is reasonable to assume that sedentary populations had grape wine, while nomadic people of the desert relied more on date wine.)[42] Communal meals and banquet feasting with liberal wine consumption seems to have been a routine event in some pre-Islamic cultures such as the Nabataeans'. Petra and Palmyra society was well known for lavish banquets in honor of the gods. Pre-Christian authors, such as Herodotus, refer to the cult of Dionysus in the Middle East. This is the Greek transliteration of the veneration of a divinity with Dionysian features in which wine consumption played a ritual role. Such information clearly hints at the existence of religious beliefs that supported liberal wine drinking.[43] References to the lifestyle of the times in which wine seems to have been fashionable can be found in other sources too. The hedonistic cultural features of high-class society seem to have raised the ire of Spartan Israelite prophets. "Lying on ivory beds and sprawling on their divans, they dine on lambs from the flock and stall-fattened veal. They bawl to the sound of the lyre . . . they drink wine by the bowlful and lard themselves with the finest oils" says a Ugarit text of the thirteenth century BC.[44] However, the picture is not unambiguous. Classical authors also distinguish gods, such as the god Theandrites, who do not drink wine, and are opposed to Dionysius. There seems to have been a dichotomy between wine drinkers, venerating specific wine-loving gods, and "teetotalars" who did not participate in orgiastic rites, nor seemingly indulged a liking for alcohol.[45] The hedonistic, epicurean streak in Middle Eastern culture disappeared with the spread of Islam, although in some noble households, even caliphate palaces, such patterns seem to have persisted into medieval times.

One might say, wine—made from grapes or dates—at the Prophet's time was the cardinal drug of choice, although heavy intoxication appears to have not been appreciated socially. A certain stigma or at least humiliating social derision was probably attached to heavy intoxication and the eccentric behavior incited by it. One of the oldest records of wine consumption and viticulture is the Old Testament. The Biblical incident of Noah (Nuuh in the Quran) being naked in a state of intoxication provides a clear testament to that (1 Mose 6,7,8,9). After the great flood, as the Old Testament relates, he planted vineyards and at one stage obviously enjoyed the fruit of his labors to excess. He sheds his clothes forcing his embarrassed sons to cover his nakedness with averted eyes so as to preserve their father's dignity. Similarly the character of Lot deals with this intoxicant less than wisely. With the divine destruction of Sodom and Gommorrha almost all its inhabitants perish. Only Lot and his two daughters survive in the end, which under the incest rules of the time would have meant the end of his tribe. The two women cunningly hatch a plan to ply him with wine so that being drunk and senseless he does not notice that they have coitus with him (1 Mose 19/32–38). As planned, they become impregnated by the patriarch, and by turning incest into a survival mode enable their tribe to survive. The Bible abounds with references to wine and does so mostly in a positive sense. It is obvious that Middle Eastern culture for a very long time had a central and fond place for viticulture and the enjoyment of grape wine. The traditional eucharist with wine (which in some churches in more recent times has been replaced with water or fruit juice) is a faint Christian afterglow of the ritualist esteem wine enjoyed in Middle Eastern culture. Islam changed that profoundly by overturning what seems to have been a deeply entrenched and cherished custom at the Prophet's time.

Grapes—as well as other fruit—seem to have been fermented and made into wine and other alcoholic drink apparently throughout the Middle East and adjoining areas. In the Hindukush mountains of Afghanistan I remember frequently coming across "vats," rectangular depressions carefully cut into grown rock (often with a drainage hole and channel into a lower-lying chamber, presumably so arranged to clarify the fermenting grape juices.) Local people were aware of their original purpose but steadfastly denied that they themselves or their forebears had ever used them. Instead they attributed wine making to people of another ethnicity, an earlier population of kafirun (infidels) not related to the present people who were all "good Muslims" and therefore "religiously" abstained from such devilish drink. This clearly was a denial of their own history, determined by a strong religious creed that easily overrode reasonable empirical evidence. The Islamization of large parts of the Hindukush had happened only towards the end of the nineteenth century when so-called Kafiristan (the land of infidels) transmuted into Nuristan (the land of light or enlightenment), but hedonistic paganism had profoundly and in very short time turned into a history-denying Islamic conservatism. The Afghan example may be taken as a microcosm of the history of Islam as a whole: it too destroyed, as Patricia Crone[46] suggests, its early history as well as the pre-Islamic past, rewriting and creating new relevances and new meanings. By this process not only was the past cast aside on the scrap heap of history—condemned as jahiliyah, barbarity, and ignorance—but it was totally denied as the matrix from which the new faith sprang. Islam, after it had consolidated its hold, became the new dawn for humanity, emphatically rejecting its own roots.

Despite the strict rejection of alcohol by Islamic doctrine today, the scriptures are ambiguous about it. Only by attaching a diachronic dimension to the revelation does a clearer picture emerge. From this one may surmise that the Prophet originally felt to be called upon to condemn intoxication, but not necessarily the modest consumption of wine as such. One could speculate that he saw the immodest consumption as too closely related with the orgiastic veneration of some gods of polytheism. It is commonly assumed that only later revealed verses of the Quran call wine drinking a sin (ithm) and alcohol a tool of the devil, thus more indirectly than directly advocating its prohibition.[47] Alcohol is not the object of explicit prohibition to the extent that pork is. Yet, in a generic sense all intoxicants are now believed to have been strictly forbidden through several separate Quranic verses. They seem to have been revealed at different times over a period of years and show a gradually changing, and hardening, attitude towards alcohol.

At first, it was forbidden for Muslims to attend to prayers while in an intoxicated condition. Sura an-Nisah (4/43) says, "Approach not the prayer as-salat when you are in a drunken state." This verse raises no in-principle objection against the consumption of intoxicating drink. Only the combination of intoxication with worship is discouraged—perhaps to distinguish Islamic worship from the pagan one or perhaps in response to actual scandalizing events in the Muslim community. Then later apparently a verse was revealed which said that alcohol contains some good and some evil, but the evil is greater than the good (al-Baqarah 2/219): "They ask you O Muhammad concerning alcoholic drink and gambling. Say: in them is great sin and some benefit for men, but the sin of them is greater than their benefit." This was the next step in turning people away from wine consumption. Finally, in al-Maidah (5/90-91) "intoxicants and games of chance" are called sins (ithm) and "abominations of Shaitan's handiwork." Just as gambling, alcohol was seen as part of a Satanic plot intended to turn people away from God and forget about prayer, an important religious duty demanded to be carried out at least five times every day. As this obligation is jeopardized through intoxication, Muslims were ordered to be totally abstinent. Quite reasonably it can be surmised by this progression that at first the Prophet did not feel emboldened enough to forbid the consumption of wine completely as it was deeply entrenched in Arab society. Perhaps beyond its purely hedonistic function, it also had religious significance as a medium of communion with divinity and in a quite generalized sense applied to all forms whether polytheistic, henotheistic, or monotheistic. Only later, when the new doctrines were more firmly entrenched and the Muslim community was consolidated enough was it possible to insist on the total ban on alcohol. A process of gradual and increasing doctrinaire strictness is observable also with regard to other revelations (for instance, in the hardening of the rejectionist attitude towards Judaism and Christianity). Above all, alcohol prohibition can be seen to be in line with the major thrust of Islam of encouraging useful socialization. In order to create a strong and cohesive community, disturbing and disruptive social features would have to be suppressed. The socially negative effects of alcohol leading to quarrel and violence may have been seen in an exaggerated light and seen to outweigh the beneficial, bond-strengthening effects of drinking commensality, thus labeling intoxication a sin and an instrument of Satan bent on destroying the Muslim community through internal quarrels. Yet, infractions still did not invoke a particular form of punishment (unlike theft, for instance). According to the Sunna, this was added later, under the rule of the Rashidun, the rightly guided caliphs.

The Quranic gradualism in reaching a firm doctrinal conclusion about alcohol and its shifting focus can also be observed in other ways. In the first verse cited above, the word for "intoxicated" is sukara, which is derived from the word "sugar" and means drunk or intoxicated. That verse does not refer to the drink—wine or anything else—that causes intoxication. In the next verses cited, the word, which is often translated as "wine" is al-khamr, which is related to the verb "to ferment." Although this word strictly refers to grape-wine, it was extended to other intoxicants such as beer or liquor.[48] Already at the prophet's time the term seems to have been extended indiscriminately to all forms of intoxicants whether made from grapes, dates, wheat, raisins, or honey, such as bita and nabidh (fermented honey drinks).[49] Even though grape wine is the most literal meaning of the word, through qiyas khamr in fact is today extended generically to all alcoholic drinks. Today, most Muslims understand the intent of these relevant verses to forbid any beverage and substance with intoxicating effects, not just wine. The result is the same sinfulness for all of these, as the Qur'an insists that it is the intoxication that makes one forgetful of God and prayer. In recent years, the list of intoxicating substances has come to include modern street drugs and other mind- and mood-altering substances available throughout the world.[50]

As described above, there is fairly clear evidence that in Middle Eastern society at the Prophet's time alcohol consumption was not an unusual social activity, nor was it stigmatized. In fact it may have enjoyed an elevated social position. This can be gleaned from some verses, which, in contrast to the eventual prohibition, are referring to the desirable qualities of alcohol. For instance, the aya (An-Nahl 16/67) refers to "strong drink" derived from grapes and date palms as a "good provision" and obliquely connects its use to a sign of wisdom. In the light of the prevailing strong prohibition, it must strike one as unusual that the Quran contains several verses in which among the delights offered by paradise, there is mention of wine. One promises that there will be not only rivers of pure water, honey, and milk, but also of wine (47/15). There is also mention of pure (unadulterated?) wine being available (83/25); of white wine (37/45,46), and of ginger-spiced wine (76/17). Presumably the devout are promised that they will be able to partake of these delights to their hearts' content.[51] Whether or not at the Prophet's time this was taken in its literal sense as a desirable and integral part of the redemption doctrine must be open to debate. [52]

One New Zealand imam whom I asked to interpret this apparent logical contradiction between the profound prohibition and this "promising" vision of the afterlife had no difficulty in reconciling it. To him it seemed quite obvious that in paradise bodily functions and desires are suspended, hence there are no intoxicating effects and no desire or need to drink in the first place. Instead of mundane extrusions of excrement and urine that inevitably follow digestive processes, the devout will exude an aroma of sweet-smelling musk. In sublimating this image further it might be said that the graphic description of sensory delights is to be understood only as a symbolic function in which culinary items are used as metaphors for a delightful form of existence. Without such metaphoric crutches presumably it would be impossible for the human mind to grasp this vision in its divine magnitude and refinement. But even in this sublimated sense, this notion is evidence of the high value ancient Arab society must have placed on wine and its consumption to make them serve as a metaphor for a delightful existence and spiritual wellness. It may not be too far-fetched to see this as an ascetic characteristic in Islam. Doctrinally denying oneself an obvious delight, clearly recognized as such in Arab culture at the Prophet's time, underlines the puritanical thrust of belief in the interest, as I would argue, of enhancing sociality.

As mentioned before, making the sin of alcohol consumption a punishable crime appears to have been added later to Islamic doctrine. The punishment traditionally inflicted on alcohol imbibing Muslims—usually lashing—relates to an incident described in the Sunnah. Under the caliphate of Umar ibn-al Khattab a notorious, drunken troublemaker among the Muslims was made an example of. (Apparently up to that time the consumption of wine although declared a sin had not been punished.) When intoxicated he would curse at and slander others, thus notoriously stirring up trouble in the Muslim community. The social disruption his behavior caused could no longer be tolerated. At the caliphs order he was beaten with hands and twisted cloth—presumably as punishment as much as a "cure." The Quran itself, however, does not prescribe a punishment for intoxication or consumption of alcohol beyond labeling it a sin. Today's caning or whipping is a modern adaptation of the historic precedent. Although based on the textual precedence of the Sunna, a closer reading would suggest an important in-principle distinction between alcohol consumption and undesirable social consequences. The first is a sin and entails a stigma but attracts no specific punishment; it is only when excessive consumption brings out antisocial behavior that a punishment is warranted. However, in the application of sharia justice today, commonly the two positions are merged, while it could be argued that as long as asocial behavior can be avoided, alcohol consumption itself when done in moderation does not warrant punishment.

The sharia interpretation subtly shifts moral reprehension (vis-à-vis the sinful consumption of alcohol) to being a punishable crime (insulting speech and bad behavior). Sin and antisocial behavior are treated identically. Moral culpability is amplified into social crime. (In the case of alcohol, of course, the Prophet's original revelation had to be extended by his successors, perhaps with the intention to clarify and eliminate ambiguities.) Many doctrinal rules are amenable to the interpretation that they are designed not only to condemn sin but in a practical sense to suppress all kinds of behavior that causes social tensions. The purpose, whether intended or accidental, is to prevent behavior that may lead to rifts and a breakdown of cohesion among the believers.

To fortify the prohibition against the smallest temptation current interpretations include even the most modest quantity of alcoholic drink. It is made an inviolable principle. According to a hadith, the Prophet Muhammad had instructed his followers to avoid any intoxicating substances even in the smallest amount: "if it intoxicates in a large amount, it is forbidden even in a small amount." Thus even moderate drinking, even tasting and sampling out of curiosity, or using small amounts in cooking or eating anything that has come in contact with alcohol is out of the question for devout Muslims—even when there is no danger of alcohol-fueled socially disruptive behavior to occur.

THE WIDER PICTURE OF PROHIBITION

Statistics are not available for the Arabic region at the Prophet's time, making the degree of alcohol consumption a matter of speculation. Whether Arab drinking culture encouraged excess, tolerated, or frowned on inebriation can only be guessed at. What evidence there is points to wine drinking and viticulture being important ingredients of the culture in the Middle East. Despite some pockets of nondrinkers such as some Bedouin tribes,[53] among sedentary populations wine consumption was probably part of secular and daily social discourse and very likely also had ritual and religious overtones in at least some regional cults. It is possible that the Prophet was concerned with the abuse, which would indicate that intoxication was a social problem; alternatively his concern may have been with wine being part of pagan rituals and by arguing against inebriation he intended to damage the religious rationale behind it. More unambiguously the prohibition refers to abuses he seems to have observed in his community of believers leading him to tighten controls at first within a religious context to be followed later (under his successors) by a total ban. As the revelations gradually turned from recommendation to mild proscription and on to a strict and absolute prohibition, alcohol consumption graduated from a faux pas in ritual protocol to a misdemeanour that may be tolerated at times to a major sin and lastly to an unpardonable crime. Imposing a blanket ban has had a major effect on Islam and abstinence constitutes today one of its major doctrinal characteristics. Here I would like to look at the issue of intoxicants in global terms of human culture as well as tentatively weighing the social effects of alcohol consumption. Looking at humankind as a whole, Islam's doctrinal abstemiousness in matters of narcotics and pharmaceutical stimulants must be seen as unusual and indicative of an ascetic streak unparalleled in most other human societies.

In very conservative interpretations of the Islamic prohibition even synthetic drugs with psychosomatic functions are viewed with skepticism. While anaesthesia for surgical purposes is certainly permitted, it is more doubtful whether the use of sedatives for persons sentenced to death by stoning or other forms of capital punishment is permitted; and whether the use of anaesthetics in hand amputation can be seen as related to this issue is open to debate. There are indications that in some jurisdictions women due to be stoned have been sedated, but the Taleban seem to have executed people without this small mercy. Faintly related to the issue of intoxication—but without the substance abuse—is the use, in a ritual context, of rhythmic drumming, motion, or the endless repetition of words, which can also produce a trancelike condition of changed brain activity superficially resembling intoxication. Well known is the turning motion of Turkey's Whirling Dervishes, whose ritual displays have now become a tourist attraction. In some African Sufi forms drumming is used for the same purpose. The mesmerizing purpose in these cases is clearly not for the sake of personal hedonism, although participants may derive a sense of gratification. Conservative Islam frowns on such techniques exactly for the reason of their similarity with states of intoxication. Such borderline cases are interesting but cannot be considered here.

It is no exaggeration to recognize Muslims as the only "society" today that totally and doctrinally rejects the use of any stronger form of intoxicant and pharmacological stimulant (excluding, as said before, tobacco, tea, and coffee). In terms of humankind's general behavior patterns, this must be considered unusual as it runs counter to the strong hedonistic predisposition that seems innate in humanity. No matter whether one accepts the Freudian concept of Lustgewinn (pleasure principle) as a potent factor of the human psyche, or in more general terms sees the human species as pleasure seeking by nature, the gratification that comes through chemically induced euphoria has been a powerful motivator for thousands of years.

The consumption of beer, wine, liquor, mead, or other fermented alcoholic substances is so widespread throughout humanity (both currently and historically; and, of course, prehistorically as far as one can surmise) that it defies a succinct enumeration. Beyond the usual alcoholic beverages, most societies as far as is known also used, or currently use, other narcotics, pharmacological psychoagents, hallucinogens, and stimulants. Some societies previously had only limited or no access to fermented intoxicating substances for environmental and climatic reasons. In arctic conditions fermentation is not easily possible, but concoctions of herbs and mushrooms still have been used to produce trancelike psychedelic states as part of shamanistic practices. The Maori and Moriori, who through their Polynesian extraction probably would originally have been familiar with tropical plant stimulants such as kava, when they migrated to the cooler climate of New Zealand and the Chatham Islands, they seem to have lost that knowledge (because the relevant plants did not grow there) and at the time of European contact were another stimulant-free society. [54]

The use of alcoholic drink has exponentially and dangerously increased in recent times, especially among populations that traditionally had no experience with the very effective intoxicants and substances available now. Western society is no exception having to cope now with an avalanche of health problems, inflated rates of drink and drug related criminality, and deaths. (It seems unbelievable when I read that in Russia eight people die every hour from alcohol misuse.)

The purpose of using mind- and mood-altering drugs (including alcohol) can be divided into two categories in terms of ideal types (in Max Weber's sense). Some drugs with special mood-altering properties are either purely used for hedonistic purposes, as a luxury simply for extravagant enjoyment savoring the drug's euphoric effect, or, closely related to that function, to engage in escapism from the drudgery, hardship, or monotony of daily life. The current binge-drinking behavior among Western youth—more prevalent in some Western countries than in others—may have to do with relative material affluence, but principally probably serves as an avenue to escape boredom and material saturation. In a more practical sense psychosomatically effective drugs may be used to stimulate endurance in work, bravery, and even bravado in battle. The drug-induced battle rush of the Germanic berserkers is one example; the use of Coca in South America spurring people to extraordinary efforts and facilitating feats hardly achievable under normal circumstances, is another. Modern Western society has developed this hedonistic category of drug use to extraordinary proportions, not only pushing the boundaries of legality and health, but also touching on issues of ethics. The spectrum reaches from excessive alcohol consumption to chemically performance-enhancing drugs in sports (so-called steroids) and even "smart drugs" (or cognitive-enhancement drugs). Huge societal energies and resources are invested in this area—both in researching and producing the drugs, and policing, containing, and combating them—while largely neglecting the other function much esteemed by many traditional societies.

In many societies the mind-altering properties of drugs were believed to open the way into another reality of a higher order. The psychedelic form of mental existence for the so-called counter culture (in the Western world of the 1970s) praised by hippie gurus imitated this traditional belief though mixing it with modern hedonistic motivations. "Blowing the mind" was recommended by philosophizing drug prophets like Timothy Leary and Jack Kerouac. In traditional societies drugs provided the entrance to the world of spirits and gods, gave access to the plane of a higher reality, and conveyed superior wisdom. Shamans and priests were meant to bestride this drug-induced path in search of the truth, existential and practical answers to be learned from spiritual beings. The shamanic flight to the spirit world was the geographical projection of this imaginary visit to the transcendental. The shamanistic experience was echoed by the witches' ride to the devil's meeting place in European medieval folklore (libeled as devil worship by the Christian church to discredit what was seen as a dangerous heresy). These are all expressions of, and variations on, this ancient trope. The shaman's enterprise, their vision quest, often involving pain and symbolic death is the counterpoint to the euphoria experienced by pleasure seekers who use drugs for hedonistic purposes. Some religions even used narcotics in religious worship and credited its effects with divine or spiritually blissful effects (e.g., the Bacchus and peyote cults). Shamans used it for healing purposes, to learn of essential causalities and to glean insights into the future. In these cases it was the narcotics' assumed truth-finding properties or their superior epistemological effects, not their hedonistic function, that was highly prized and sought after. Often the kind of usage in a truth-finding spiritual quest is based on hallucinogens, which effect trance or even induce epileptic, paroxysmal conditions. These often are not pleasurable, but are endured by the practitioner for the sake of a higher purpose. Through long and frequent use, there may also be an addictive result involved just as with hedonistic drugs.[55]

Some drugs straddle the line. For instance kava in the South Pacific is associated with ancestor worship. It is consumed both for its pleasure effect and for inducing a state of mind congenial to communing with one's ancestors. Even nowadays as the ritualistic-spiritual aspects of kava consumption are often downplayed in favor of the relaxed enjoyment aspect (especially in urban situations), a residue of traditional spiritual beliefs remains.

Humanity has searched after pharmaceutical ways to enhance its innate register of emotion and epistemological capability: in other words, to widen its experience, to extend its spiritual, physical, and cognitive existence, to extend its transcendental and metaphysical awareness, to lessen existential pain and deepen its emotional scale so as to derive delirious pleasures. (The discussion of chemical causes and effects pharmacological stimulation has on the brain and the body chemistry in general goes beyond the purpose of the book and shall not be entered into here.) Islam, or at least its conservative version, is anathema to this panhuman inclination by aesthetically and legally demanding sobriety and condemns any mind- and mood-altering consumption. Through its near-absolute and doctrinaire drug prohibition, it displays an ascetic streak that is almost unknown in human history. Forgoing drug-taking's euphoric as well as spiritual and religiously relevant effects, it is content with the very mild stimulants offered by coffee, tea, and tobacco, cherishing instead a sobriety that is supposed to lead to the divine.

Ignoring special forms of Sufi mysticism, godliness, proximity to God, is sought in a "sober" perusal of God's will as revealed in the sacred texts, and to be guided by it. Nearness to God is achieved by conscientiously adhering to the revealed truth, which is God's own word; it is to be rationally grasped with a clear mind, by careful study of exegetical texts and by following the lived example of the Prophet and his companions. The "straight path" as outlined in the Quran and elaborated on in the Sunna has no place for chemically induced intuition, no mind-altered communion with the divine sphere to penetrate God's inscrutability. Given the general human proclivities, it does not surprise that, partially at least, Sufi mysticism has broken ranks seeking transcendence in altered states of consciousness.

It begs the question not only why Islam for the sake of complete abstinence forgoes both of the basic functions, so much sought after by humankind in general, but also what broad social effect this may have. Insisting on complete sobriety and clearness of mind the sharia must have a specific social effect. Clearly, alcohol and other drugs, aside of their euphoric effect, have a series of negative effects, both in the area of health and social issues. Their main negative effect lies in producing aggressive, addictive, debilitating, and asocial behavior. Bringing out verbal or physical aggressiveness, withdrawal from society, and disinterest in ordinary social intercourse are perhaps the most destructive effects on a societal level. In the most acute form such socially disintegrative effects are now experienced by some societies that have profoundly been upset by colonization (Australian Aborigines, Inuit, First Nation People, etc.) and now are producing stereotypical images of social anomie. However, such problems are by no means confined to Forth World societies. Drug and alcohol related problems have become chronically acute in Western society, where they seem rampant regardless of economic conditions. Well-to-do sections as much as underprivileged sections of society are equally affected. Disruptive forms of behavior in the social discourse resulting from excessive alcohol consumption and drug use are clearly avoided through Islamic piety. Even as the rules of avoidance are broken by a minority of Muslims (despite the harsh punishment that beckons), by confining breaches, when they occur, to the private sphere Muslim society succeeds in preventing the alcohol and drug related social ills rampant and publicly noticeable in other societies. At the cost of personal liberty and freedom of choice, sharia's strict effectiveness succeeds in keeping at bay a social problem that besets modern societies on a global scale.

This is well known and we need not dwell on it. There is, however, also a reverse side to alcohol consumption: its beneficial effect as an aid to conviviality and as a ritual agent to seal social bonds. It is often claimed that in a culture of moderate and pseudo-ritualized drinking, alcohol may serve as a social lubricant, a medium to smooth social intercourse, and marking occasions with friendly mutuality. It may be seen as a "chemical release valve" useful by lessening personal tension in dispersing social tension. Especially when imbibed in a controlled and ceremonial context, alcohol can have a socializing effect in defusing conflict. Through its mood-altering properties alcohol—as much as it has destructive potential—is capable of enhancing social rapport and softening antagonism. When consumed in a ceremonialized manner, it can channel emotions in pathways that aid social bonding and engender the formation of solidarity among participants. Traditional student associations, sporting clubs, and other organizations use "liquid commensality" to create cohesion—an esprit de corps—among its membership by utilizing socially positive emotions generated by alcohol and its structured consumption. Related to this kind of regulated drinking is the ceremonial toast. Ceremonial occasions from weddings to state banquets use the toast with an alcoholic beverage as a declaration to seal a common bond. The symbolic meaning of official toasting with an alcoholic beverage is meant to foster diplomatic or economic bonds, reaffirm and strengthen the ties agreed upon, or simply underline the acknowledgment of friendship. The celebratory aspect of this symbolic act in part harks back to the spiritual, religiously motivated function of intoxicants as a communion with supernatural powers. An implied invocation of such powers, be it as witnesses or guarantors, may be highly symbolic and not meant to be effective in the literal sense (in the sense a religious ritual is meant to perform), yet in the background is the motive to strengthen and cement the bindingness of the social contract that has been entered into, by calling on a transcendent force. Thus, the ceremonialization of drinking, other than its emotionally hedonistic surface meaning, has the subliminally intended effect of actualizing the binding nature of a social arrangement by bringing in a supernatural agency. (In some societies, traditionally, the consummation of a sexual act may serve this purpose, a ritualized meal, drinking kava, or smoking the pipe. The globally hegemonic discourse has rejected these cultural options.)

Demonstrative of this function alcohol is able to perform is the traditional symbolism of the Eucharist; in particular the (Catholic) version which uses wine and is considered a sacrament that—after ritual transubstantiation—faithfully represents the sacred substance and is not just a proxy. Although often simply practiced as a ritualized tradition, it implicitly draws on the effectiveness of communal drinking as well as quite obviously invoking the divine presence. The holy communion is capable of strengthening bonds among the congregants, creating mutual goodwill (even though it may be ephemeral and needs to be renewed frequently); and it also performs the traditional function in connecting the drinker with the divine. (The difference to earlier Bacchanalia forms is that wine so consumed establishes the connection on a purely symbolic, less dramatic level, and does not have the depth of delirious emotiveness that arises from the mood-affecting, mentally debilitating effect of ancient ritual.) The sacrament's social importance is recognized in many Western countries by allowing—officially under the aegis of religious freedom—wine into prisons for this purpose.[56]

What appear to be sociological truisms about deep seated social effects of ceremonialized alcohol consumption emerge in exaggerated form as hedonist myths about the socializing, bonding effects of communal drinking. There are no hard-and-fast data that would support the contention that through (non-ceremonialized or pseudo-ceremonialized) alcohol consumption social cohesion and conviviality is measurably improved. Yet, just such themes playing on images of alcohol-fueled conviviality have emerged. Perhaps they are partly sponsored by the alcohol producing industry, but they are more than an advertisement for good wine and old whisky. It represents an important theme in an overarching narrative on the beneficial effects of moderate alcohol consumption and belongs in the same rubric as the stories that link moderate yet persistent alcohol consumption with longevity.

The measured consumption of alcohol for ceremonial occasions has become an integral part of globalized culture. Expensive alcoholic beverages have assumed the signal relevance as ceremonial seals affirming political and commercial deals. In the "cultivated" private sphere, alcohol is an international signifier of good taste, refined living, and sophisticated worldliness. The hip flask as a fashionable accessory, once part of the outfit of a rough journeyman rather than a lady of good breeding, can be found also in the handbag of a woman of power (such as allegedly Baroness Margaret Thatcher when she was prime minister). Oenophiliac tastes have become a mark of refined living and "class." The requisite knowledge in this field has become part of elite culture and a sign of good breeding. On the level of the international elite, alcohol use has become a ceremonial status signal, while for the broad masses it is affordable euphoria and bottled escape.

Alcohol consumption in Western society, regardless of whether it is to excess or not, or whether it has an iconic status in a regional or national culture or is just a means of blowing one's mind, is considered a basic right. For better or for worse, it forms an integral part of Western culture. For diasporic Muslims this creates a barrier. Muslims experience many difficulties in integrating, in gaining acceptance, and in forming emotional attachment to the encapsulating majority society. Not sharing in "liquid commensality" is one of the reasons—though trivial as it may seem—for Muslims to preserve a strongly separatist identity and for the Western host society to take this as a sign of rejection.[57] Drinking alcohol is among the bonding activities, which, though they seem informal, act as rites of inclusion in the social discourse. The inability of Muslims to participate heightens their sense of alienation, underlines their inability to even approximate majority society's identity and emphasizes the cultural distance between non-Muslims and them. Relevant observations have been made in several countries or subnational groupings in which alcohol consumption, whether this is conscious or not, constitutes part of identity, whether alcohol is consumed formally or informally. Muslims feel excluded,[58] and non-Muslims snubbed.

Even on a global level, alcohol serves as an important cultural barrier. Abstaining from alcohol in a world of "drinkers" requires some considerable cultural fortitude and individual discipline that reveals the ascetic streak of Islam. It stands in stark contrast to the spread of the Western drinking culture, which in its worst manifestation may be seen as the epitome of unprincipled immediate self-gratification and spiritual decay. Conservative Islam adds this judgment to the armory of moral condemnation of the West and at the same time as a device to underline its own superiority. Sympathetic voices agree: the doctrinal asceticism of Islam should serve as an antidote to the amorality of the present-day West that is poised to poison the rest of the world through the process of globalization; it can provide the moral discipline required to rescue the world from jahiliya, chaos, and immorality.

NOTES

1. Controversial cases have cropped up sporadically of survivors of plane crashes and castaways having resorted to cannibalism.

2. A classical study of this kind is Bronislaw Malinowski's *Coral Gardens and Their Magic*. London: Allen & Unwin, 1966 (1st ed. 1935).

3. Marvin Harris'explanation (*Cows, Pigs, Wars and Witches: The Riddles of Culture*. New York: Random, 1974), for various reasons, does not sound convincing. Effective milk production and dung use as fuel does not logically lead to sacralization of cattle and could easily be combined with meat eating as is the case in other peasant cultures. The superimposition of pseudo-rational motives on religious customs rarely sounds plausible from an instrumental rational point of view.

4. Pork prohibition is also contained in the Old Testament: e.g., Leviticus 11/7–8, Deuteronomy 14/8. Islam seems to have accepted its strict pig taboo from Judaism.

5. The Quran contains many references to halal (lawful, allowed, pure) and haram (polluted, forbidden) foods (2/168,172, 173; 5/1, 3–5, 88; 6/118,119,121,145,146; 16/114–118; 23/51).

6. See, e.g., Roy Rappaport, *Pigs for the Ancestors*. New Haven: Yale University Press, 1968.

7. In arctic areas and the Americas the pig was traditionally absent. However, in South America pig-like creatures such as the (rodent) peccary, guinea pig, and capybara, and also tapirs, were appreciated as food. In Indonesia, in areas where Hinduism survived the later introduction of Islam (mainly in Bali), pig eating is a ceremonialized and esteemed occasion.

8. Pigs are parasite carriers of trichinosis, brucellosis, and so on, and can transmit diseases to humans.

9. Marvin Harris (*Cows, Pigs, Wars and Witches . . .*) argues that humans and swine were food competitors and climatic and ecological circumstances in the Middle East militated against porcine husbandry. One might hold against that that feral pigs flourish in Australia and domestic ones in equatorial Pacific under similarly hot—and in Australia's case—semiarid conditions.

10. Mary Douglas, *Purity and Danger*. London/New York: Routledge/Praeger, 1966. And *Natural Symbols*. New York: Vintage and Harmondsworth: Penguin 1973 (1st ed.1970); p. 60–63. She traces pig prohibition to classificatory issues (cloven-footed non-ruminants did not fit the taxonomic scheme) and also holds that refusal to eat pork was a mark of distinction for Jews thus setting themselves apart from others. If pork prohibition is meant as a symbolic separation then it does not apply to Islam. The Prophet, in his later career, wanted to distance his teaching from Judaism, yet seems to have accepted the Jewish strict prohibition on pork. See also Paul Diener and Eugene Robkin, "Ecology, Evolution, and the Search for Cultural Origins: The Question of Islamic Pig Prohibition." *Current Anthropology* 19/3 (1978):493–540. This article provides a critique of the ecological approach.

11. Christianity also did not follow the Jewish custom of ritual male circumcision, while Islam adopted it. This is another important example of the selective approach of Islam towards pre-Islamic cultural traditions.

12. Sourced from Paul Diener and Eugene Robkin, "Ecology, Evolution, and the Search for Cultural Origins . . ." ; p. 501.

13. James Frazer, *The Golden Bough*. London, Toronto: Macmillan, 1967 (1st ed.1922); p. 649.

14. The living quarters usually seem to have been a level above the stables, both being under the same roof. This was at least the type of housing common in places like Bethlehem in Christ's time, which explains the Biblical theme of Jesus being born in a manger. Overcrowding may have forced his parents to share overnight quarters with domestic animals on the lower level.

15. The beginnings of urbanization may go back a considerable time. The remains of an eleven thousand year old tower unearthed at Jericho may give an indication of the social start of clustering people together in larger, permanent settlements.

16. However, a strong counter-argument refers to China, where similar sociopolitical developments did not lead to a pig taboo.

17. A ruling by Al-Azhar scholars permits electric stunning.

18. Traditional abattoirs in the Islamic world also usually use this method in the absence of electric stunning equipment. From the ordinary Western viewpoint concerned for animal welfare, this method seems cruel. In June 2011 publicity about this method in Indonesian abattoirs led to a temporary stop of live cattle exports imposed by Australian authorities.

19. Ibn Hanbal, Musnad IV, 132.

20. These rituals were also meant in a more general sense to maintain the world and its natural order. Not just resources of a utilitarian kind (such as edible and potable resources) were maintained by these rituals, but also nonuseful things. All things were considered an integral part of the world order. Their disappearance was feared that it would upset this order catastrophically and generally lead to human demise.

21. Some social scientists believe this was an early expression of the idea of nature conservation, a way to preserve valuable resources and protect them from overharvesting.

22. I am referring here to the preserved bodies of people who seem to have been executed in a ritual manner (either as sacrificial victims or criminals) and not victims of accidents or violent crime.

23. The heart in many cultures is associated with positive, socially valued emotions. However, in some cultures other organs (for instance, the liver) are considered the primary seat of emotions.

24. On the topic of the symbolism relating to right and left hand see Robert Hertz (transl. by Rodney Needham), *Death and the Right Hand*. Glencoe: Free Press, 1960; and Rodney Needham (ed.), *Right and Left: Essays in Dual Symbolic Classification*. London: Routledge, 1973.

25. The Islamic calendar is based on the moon cycles and is thus fifteen days shorter than the Gregorian.

26. Olivier Roy, "Islam in France: Religion, Ethnic Community or Social Ghetto." In *Muslims in Europe*, B. Lewis and D. Schnapper (eds.). New York: Pinter, 1994.

27. Sami Zubaida, *Beyond Islam: A New Understanding of the Middle East*. London. New York: Tauris, 2011; p. 205 fn 55.

28. Older ethnographic sources about the Pacific speak of the village virgins being delegated to this task of mastication through which enzymes in the saliva make the desired chemicals more freely available. The process caused some revulsion among European visitors.

29. I will not distinguish here between various processes such as brewing, vinting, steeping, distilling, and so on. Doing so would be superfluous to my purpose.

30. Also termed pituri, Duboisia Hopwoodii, a tobacco plant.

31. Only in the sense that rhythmic drumming or whirling motion and other techniques may induce ecstatic and trancelike conditions—as used in forms of Sufism (the Whirling Dervishes of the Mevlevi order), the breathless rapid recitation of the Quran in the Quadiri order, the ecstatic self-mutilation of the Rifa'i order—does one have to qualify this statement. "Motion intoxication" and other forms of trance inducement are, of course, in principle different from chemically based forms.

32. Wine making continues to be practiced among Christian groups (Assyrian Christians) in the Middle East (Turkey, Iraq, Syria) following time-honored methods and using ancient stone vats. Recently, tourism has discovered its interest in this survival.

33. Frank Vogel, *Islamic Law and Legal System: Studies of Saudi Arabia*. Leiden, Boston, Köln: Brill, 2000; pp. 242, 245. However, Vogel also writes (pp. xiv-xv): "Saudi Arabia no doubt does not perfectly apply Islamic law, and indeed according to the view of some . . . does not apply true Islamic law at all."

34. Alfred Guillaume, *The Traditions of Islam: An Introduction to the Study of the Hadith Literature*. Beirut: Khayats, 1966; p. 56.

35. Zubaida, *Beyond Islam*, pp. 57–60.

36. In the Austro-Hungarian Empire Bosniak troops (from Bosnia-Herzegovina), most of whom would have been Hanafi Muslims, were known to consume alcohol.

37. Zubaida, *Beyond Islam*; p. 144.

38. Vogel, *Islamic Law*, p. 257. He notes that the king in the 1990s was keen to introduce a drug rehabilitation programme to make the application of the death penalty superfluous.

39. According to unspecified news sources Yemenis, spends USD 7 billion a year on qat.

40. Internationally khat (or qat) has an ambiguous position: it is legal in the UK and banned in the United States, New Zealand, and Australia.

41. Only a fraction of opium is refined into heroin in the country.

42. Robert Hoyland, *Arabia and the Arabs: From the Bronze Age to the Coming of Islam*. London, New York: Routledge, 2001; p. 244.

43. However, this is a matter of interpretation. Jan Retsö (*The Arabs in Antiquity: Their History from the Assyrians to the Umayyads*. London, New York: Routledge Curzon, 2003; p.606) prefers a different interpretation that relates to the mysterious birth of the god.

44. Robert Hoyland, *Arabia and the Arabs*; pp. 134–135.

45. Jan Retsö, *The Arabs . . .* ; p., 604, 613.

46. Patricia Crone, *Slaves on Horses: The Evolution of the Islamic Polity*. Cambridge: Cambridge University Press, 1980. She argues that Islam was fluid especially in the initial oral phase until the Abbasid period when there was greater historiographical rigor.

47. Islamic tafsir and asbab an-nusul (history of origins) of the scriptures distinguishes nasikh (later, repealing verses) and mansukh (earlier, invalidated ones, superseded by nasikh).

48. See, eg., Anna Gade, *The Qur'an: An Introduction*. Oxford: Oneworld, 2010; p. 126.

49. Mona Siddiqui, "Clarity or Confusion – Classical Fiqh and the Issue of Logic." In *Sharia as Discourse*, J. Nielsen and L. Christoffersen (eds.). Farnham: Ashgate, 2010); pp. 23–25.

50. According to Mona Siddiqui ("Clarity . . ." ; p. 25), fiqh is more concerned with the definition of intoxicant than with moral defect, punishment, and social effect.

51. Cups "of wine" being served by servants (Quran 52/23; "wine" added to the verse in the official Saudi version).

52. I am drawing here on the officially approved English translation of the Quran issued in Saudi Arabia. Some translations avoid the term wine.

53. For obvious ecological reasons, Bedouins would have had little possibility of viticulture.

54. Maori used fermentation to alter the chemical composition of foodstuffs (kanga kopiro) but apparently not to produce intoxicants. Inuit traditionally seem to be in a similar position.

55. There is a voluminous literature on the subject of shamanism. See, e.g., Erika Bourguignon (ed.), *Religion, Altered States of Conscousness and Social Change*. Columbia: Ohio State University Press, 1973. Mircea Eliade, *Shamanism: Ancient Techniques of Ecstasy*. London: Routledge, 1964. Felicitas Goodman, *Ecstasy, Ritual and Alternate Reality*. Bloomington: Indiana University Press, 1988. Michael Taussig, *Shamanism, Colonialism, and the Wild Man*. Chicago: Chicago University Press, 1986. Ian M. Lewis, *Ecstatic Religion*. Harmondsworth: Penguin, 1971.

56. The Catholic church's success in having the alcohol ban partially lifted in prisons hints at a bigger issue: the criminalization of the use of intoxicants or psychotropic drugs for religious or cultural purposes may in some cases clash with religious freedom and human rights. This concerns above all the use of peyote in the Native American religion, cannabis for Rastafarians, and various other drugs for adepts of shamanism. In these cases the provision of religious freedom usually does not seem to be brought to bear.

57. As I could observe through my research among Austrian high school students. Erich Kolig, "Freedom, Identity Construction and Cultural Closure." In *Public Policy and Ethnicity*, E. Rata and R. Openshaw (eds.). Basingstoke: Palgrave 2006.

58. New Zealand's dominant culture has been defined to be resting heavily on "beer, rugby and racing" and this having a significant repulsive effect on immigrant Muslims. See Erich Kolig, *New Zealand's Muslims and Multiculturalism;* p. 27. William Shepard, "New Zealand's Muslims and Their Organizations." *New Zealand Journal of Asian Studies* 8/2 (2006): 8–44; p. 14. Apart from beer, betting at the races is forbidden in Islam, and rugby is not a sport Muslim immigrants are traditionally familiar with.

Chapter Four

Vexing Questions about Gender Relations and Women

ISLAM AND WOMEN

Strong emotions and images are invoked when Islam is brought into conjunction with women and gender relations. Islam is well known as a religion that has a decisive bearing on basic regulative functions relating to women's role and status in society. The position of women in Islam is a highly contentious issue, especially in terms of the question whether Islam is misogynistic and discriminatory vis-à-vis women in the practices it prescribes, or whether it is grossly misunderstood when approaching it with a modern Western perspective. In particular on this issue there is the danger that strong culture-specific biases on one side may meet equally strong and entrenched ones on the other side making it difficult to assume a sensitive, fair, and objective stance. To achieve a truly supra-cultural, "scientific" view and overcome the emotionality of this issue is well nigh impossible. In assessing and evaluating the relevant issues an a priori cognitive and ethical instrumentary deeply rooted in the analyzt's cultural background is all but indispensable as well as turning out to be unsurmountable. In addition, there is an acuteness and rawness to this issue which tends to create sharp partisanships unable to compromise or admit that opposing viewpoints may at least in part have some validity. Much of the acrimoniousness of debate thus generated arises out of the fact that women in Western society have, historically seen, only recently achieved nominal and legal equality, and according to cutting-edge advocates of gender equality, it is still a mission as yet not completely accomplished. As some see it, Western women are still far from having totally overcome gender prejudices and inequalities in letter of the law, let alone in social practice.

115

Especially when equipped with a gynocentric worldview, many bastions of male power and privilege remain yet to be vanquished. Laws need to be tightened to eliminate the last loopholes for men to withhold equal rights from women, and stronger gender affirmative initiatives have yet to be devised to clear out the last enclaves of stubborn male conservatism. The golden pot of true gender egalitarianism at the end of the social rainbow has yet to be found. One of the most recalcitrant preserves of male dominance is conservative religiosity and here in particular the cleric of almost all religions, including Christianity. While Protestant clericalism has softened considerably its male exclusiveness, Roman Catholicism sticks out for having made virtually no concessions. In fact in some countries it—and often other Christian churches as well—is exempted by law from the requirement of gender equality.

Some current Islamic gender practices and attitudes, and some features of the treatment of women, correspond with those valid in Western culture until about a hundred years ago, giving the whole issue a semblance of an evolutionary process in which Islam lags behind. In fact it creates the impression as though Islam deliberately drags its feet. This gives detractors of Islam the ammunition to argue that Islam, unwilling to go with the flow of social evolution, has to be dragged forcibly into the twenty-first century. However, there is no empirical ground on which a social evolutionary scale could be built convincingly, and humankind, when looked at from a purely cultural viewpoint, may just have two equally valid solutions to the gender situation. On the other hand, leaving cultural relativity aside, certain trends in the universalization of aesthetic and legal regimes strongly disadvantage the Islamic side in corroborating the view that Islamic gender relations are unsynchronized with the times. In other words, globalization—guided as it is by predominantly Western values and views—produces an increasingly influential internationalized discourse on gender rights, equality, personal freedoms and related issues. This process draws negative attention to conditions obtaining in the so-called Islamic world and puts considerable pressure on its gender situation to change.

Islamic "misogyny," alleged or true, is a difficult theme. Thus understandably, in a situation where a combination of missionary zeal and a goodly dose of frustration is arraigned against immovable religious conviction, there is hardly any middle ground. Usually in Western society the topic conjures up images of female bodies covered by the shapeless jilbab, women swaddled in tent-like coverings, the burqa, leaving only a slit for the eyes— brutally enforced in Afghanistan under the Taleban regime—the inhibiting and uncomfortable face veiling with the niqab, the ungainly abaya and the equally unflattering chador. At the very least there is the unmistakable religious gender-distinct hijab, covering a woman's hair and often much of the face too—and even when fashionably flimsy still remains as a stigma of female subservience. Male dominance and androcracy are blamed for forcing such sartorial traditions on women who otherwise would not acquiesce to such a barbaric and demeaning dress sense. Superficial information most non-Muslim Westerners have may also bring to mind the harsh practice of stoning of female prostitutes and female adulterers (based on Quran 24/2) in some Islamic justice systems;[1] and of honor killings and domestic violence that chronically go unpunished. Also, the rule of polygamy, enshrined in the Quran (4/3) and which allows men to marry up to four women, is seen as an insult to women and an expression of male power over women.

There is, of course, a vast variety of legal applications and customary social practices throughout the so-called Islamic world, but negative stereo-typing attributes all that and especially the worst features to Islam itself. Leaving aside urban "Westernized" conditions in modern Muslim society, which espouse as much practical gender equality as Western society, the conservative Islamic gender situation is difficult to essentialize. Profound differences have to be acknowledged between scriptural, normative Islam and customary practices, which also can vary widely from region to region. Although the practitioners of such customs may well believe they are in accord with scriptural Islam or its intent, they may not be (according to the interpretation of other Muslims). While in Saudi Arabia women are barred from driving cars (not even with tinted windows),[2] the sight of a heavily veiled woman riding a moped is not too unusual in Indonesia, the most populous Muslim country (of around 220 million Muslims in a total popula-tion of well over 240 million). Many forms of customary treatment of wom-en, especially the most notorious ones, are regionally confined and far from being shared by all Muslims. It is some particular customary forms of gender relations and treatment of women which are not demanded in this harsh clarity by Islamic law but create the impression of a strikingly inegalitarian and discriminatory approach to gender and may stand out as highly exploita-tive of women—in fact, may be regarded as criminal in the West. For in-stance, the Pakistan-Afghan border area (the reservoir from which the Tale-ban movement draws much of its strength) is notoriously known for custo-mary practices which in effect—in an unflattering reading—treat women as tradable chattel; where rape as reprisal for perceived wrongs is practiced; betrothing women, some of them children, is customary to settle feuds, to pay debts, and expunge other obligations. This is practiced under the guise of "tribal law" of which the people concerned believe that it is faithful to scrip-tural sharia. However, scriptural felicity does not support such practices and makes them lawful only by a severe stretch of the imagination. Yet, even by recognizing this cleavage between scriptural tenet and practical application, it is indisputably true that scriptural Islam is not gender-egalitarian or gen-der-indifferent in the rules it prescribes. The principle of Islamic law spec-ifies some legal responses and requisites to gender issues that clearly give women a different social and legal status from men. As the eminent British law expert Sebastian Poulter[3] expressed it, "sharia accords women not equality with men, but equivalent rights."

Thus several specific Islamic rules are in breach of human rights conventions; especially article 2 of the Human Rights Charter regarding the absolute, in-principle social and legal equality of the genders. And this violation of principle is quite apart from the fact that some of these gender prescriptions by most standards would have to be regarded as socially disadvantageous for women and unfairly empowering men. Blatantly giving men socially the upper hand sits poorly with dominant ethical tropes and themes of justice in Western society. Leaving aside the violation of abstract standards of gender relations in terms of absolute equality in all things, it is particular, notorious expressions of Islamic gender rules that fuel the claims that Islam is oppressive to women, that it hands absolute control of female sexuality and reproductive capacity to men, and that it inflicts an inordinate degree of cruelty, both physical and spiritual, on women.

Not surprisingly Islamic apologists take quite a different view on the matter. Apart from conservative-minded Muslim jurist-scholars and intellectuals to whom critical scrutiny of Islamic doctrine is an abomination, there are many Muslim women who fiercely defend Islam. The defense can be made on various grounds, from the ultraorthodox view that God's command has to be obeyed unquestioningly to modern rationalist arguments praising the advantages Muslim women enjoy over their Western counterparts. For instance, swaddled in fabric women remove themselves from lustful male inspection and from being degraded as sex objects. The gender division, giving privacy and refuge to women, is perhaps the most commonly cited advantage Muslim women are supposed to have over their "liberated" female counterparts in the West. According to this view, what may appear to be discriminatory rules do, in fact, mean making life easier for women. Burdening men with responsibilities (of a ritual, social, as well as economic kind) means taking this burden off women's shoulders, and the like. None of these arguments are totally absurd and just demonstrate that a different episteme—a deeply lodged different way of apprehending the world—is at work.

Riffat Hassan[4] admits that Human Rights are an internationally enforceable legality, but claims that they have only the flimsiest of actual reality and no bearing on real human lives. Human rights are a subject of political and popular discourse but make little difference to the lives of real women in a real world. In any case these rights have applicability only in a secular context, she claims, but have no validity within a framework of religion. In fact they are antithetical to a religious view and resist being combined. However, after having questioned the universality of these laws, she then, somewhat surprisingly, goes on to list Islamic prescriptions which resemble various clauses in the human rights declaration. And not only that, they seem to show a humanist concern.

Superficially seen, Hassan[5] is plausible when she points out—as have done many others before and after her—that the Quran shows good intentions towards women. Women were given rights and recognition as persons where they had none of that before. If they are deficient in rights now, she argues, it is because Muslim societies have perverted the scriptural intentions. Plausible as this may sound, this argument suffers from a serious weakness. A religion, even if codified in great detail, is always open to diverse interpretation. It is also ethically multifaceted. Christianity performed many good deeds while at the same time inflicting much cruelty—a judgment that has validity today. An argument about a religion's intent—benevolent or not—is hardly on terra firma. A limited measure of objectivity on the basis of empirical evidence is achievable through study of the scriptural evidence, but of equal importance is the observation of the religion's application in real life (i.e., its actions at a certain time and in specific situations and when seen and judged from a particular perspective). Indeed, a religion predominantly gets judged—appreciated or disapproved of—by the actual life patterns it inspires. A religion is perceived mainly through the lives and deeds of its adherents and exponents, while its implicit intent, supposedly standing at the cradle of the belief system, not least through the complexity and often contradictory nature of the foundational scriptures, is removed from unambiguous empirical verification and is subject to constant speculation, shifting interpretations, changing value judgments, ethics, and aesthetic regimes. On such grounds any certainty about a belief system's original intent can only be of a highly speculative nature, its assessment validity easily disputed and overturned.

The argument by Muslim apologists that early Islam, and especially the Prophet, was of beneficent intent vis-à-vis the social position of women, giving rights to them where they had none before, is well known. There is some considerable evidence of the original humanitarian attitude of the Prophet and his personal life, as preserved in the Sunna, bears testimony to that. A kindly man, rather than a tyrant, in family matters Muhammad's historical persona fits the image of a benevolent traditional father figure, kind and firm; but equally that of the Biblical prophet who loves and cherishes his wife and children, is kindly disposed towards his people, yet can make cruel decisions when asked by God to do so. The Prophet's first wife, Kadidja, seems to have been the dominant part in the marriage. A wealthy and influential widow, she employed him and most probably proposed marriage to him to seal a satisfactory work relationship. The trust between them appears to have been so deep that she often comforted him almost in a motherly fashion when he was distraught by his supernatural experiences and eventually, in a show of connubial loyalty, became one of the first converts to his divine inspiration and a staunch supporter. His later wives, within the context of the time, seem to have been well treated; Aisha especially enjoyed his deep respect. In the usual perception the sira and some features of the sharia, which grant women some rights, attest to some kindly intentions of the original Islamic revelation—which later, after the Prophet's death, may have been perverted, as some would argue. However, other interpretations are possible. Societal conditions in the Middle East, before and during the Prophet's time, offer some considerable complexity, which is not in every respect consonant with the usual perception that women were without rights, heavily disadvantaged and oppressed in social discourse, and desperately in need of liberation. In some Middle Eastern societies at various times there have apparently been features of matrilineality. In fact Kadidja's social persona as conveyed by the Sunna seems to attest to this. She was a woman of independence and considerable means over which, although they were inherited from her previous husband, she appears to have had total control. Also customs of uxorilocality existed (together with virilocality), customs whereby a husband married into the wife's clan or local group—thus strengthening the wife's social position. Other features that do not hint at total powerlessness of women were, for instance, that in childless marriages women could "advertise" for lovers to enable them to bear offspring (through a relationship to be consummated in a "one night stand"). Also other features seem to have existed which speak to a greater social freedom women enjoyed in some ancient Middle Eastern societies than is normally assumed. That women were able to inherit wealth, office, and leadership roles from their deceased husbands does not seem to have been unusual, at least among the social elite. The prophet's personal life story attests to these possibilities. Kadidja seems to represent the persona of a liberated woman. Some of the Prophet's other wives, especially Aisha and his daughter Fatima, exemplified the "liberated" life of women of consequence, a pattern which may have predated the emergence of Islam rather than reflecting the privileged position of the Prophet's women or being the result of the social innovations introduced by him. What appears at first sight to be the Prophet's personal kindness and deeply felt humanitarianism may, in fact, have been established social patterns in some Arab groups.[6] And what seems to be the original sharia's, relatively speaking, progressive gender rules (such as giving women the right to inheritance, to be recognized as a juridical persona, etc.) may in fact be more misogynistic than apologists would make us believe when compared with some gender-egalitarian social patterns that seem to have existed at that time. The existence of monogamous and polyandric patterns, women exercising rights of divorce and inheritance, matrilineality in which descent was counted in the female line, women as sponsors of ritual banquets (with wine consumption), and the like, paint a picture different from the usual one of an excessively misogynist, androcratic Arab society contemporary with the Prophet, which he supposedly substantially improved through his teaching. The reality may have been one of quite diverse societal conditions and groups with different social norms coexisting or possibly of a social stratification with a relatively high degree of diversification.

Hassan[7] is on firmer ground when she claims that the West's concern for the subservient position of women in the Islamic world does not reflect a genuine compassion for Muslim women, but is just another arrow in the amor of criticism towards Islam and Muslims. It fits into the prejudiced picture of Muslims being bad and Islam evil. How can that be?—Hassan wonders. After all the victims for whom there arguably is compassion are also Muslims and statistically form 50 percent of Muslimhood. It is a logical contradiction to presume they can be bad as Muslims and innocent victims at the same time.

Lila Abu-Lughod puts forward an apologist argument[8] that extols the virtues of cultural relativism and of withholding judgment on other cultures. She places her argument within the context of political rhetoric in the United States. The then first lady, Laura Bush, in a radio interview seemed to advocate the fantasy notion that American troops are fighting in Afghanistan to liberate women from the oppression by the Taleban.[9] Abu-Lughod hyperbolizes what probably was no more than an offhand remark meant for the consumption of American housewives, and builds on it her argument in defense of Islam. In Western prejudicial views of female oppression, it is symbolized by the requirement, strictly enforced by the Taleban, of wearing an all-covering burqa, a female garment that is usually derided in the West as a jail, a coffin, or a body bag for women. But surely the West's misinterpretation of Islam's sartorial code was not the true reason for America to enter into a war. Abu-Lughod attempts to demolish Western prejudice against Islam but bases it on the wrong assumption that any American first lady comes even close to articulating official United States foreign policy and its reasons or expressing the president's views. Setting up a strawman, as she does, then to be knocked over all too conveniently, does this kind of argument no service. Although the burqa does have a negatively "iconic" position in Western awareness and often does serve as a poster image of female oppression by Islam, it is not the only signal indicator of gender inequality, and not even the strongest.

To be fair, demonizing the Taleban and using this regime to condemn Islam per se sometimes is indeed based on the sensationalized and exaggerated exposé of harsh treatment of women. In this manner it may at times indeed be used as a pretext to justify the Afghan war and the West's involvement in it. Let me recall one particular event that showed this constellation quite clearly: where the horrific mistreatment of a woman was connected with the assertion that the West's fight is a moral duty to improve the lot of women under the Taleban. The front cover of *Time* magazine in August 2010 showed the horribly mutilated face of a young Afghan woman, Aisha. This image was widely bandied about in cyberspace for weeks afterwards. Her nose and ears had been cut off by her husband—years before the media grabbed hold of this image, it would seem—as punishment for insubordination. The case was presented as evidence of the Taleban's repulsive sense of justice. According to the media reports, she had tried to run away from her abusive husband and in-laws and had the misfortune of being caught inflagrante. Her brother-in-law had held her down while her husband exacted "justice" with a sharp knife. She had been left for dead but obviously had survived the ordeal. While some condemned the photo as an unfortunate example of sensationalized news reporting, others used it to press home the viciousness and moral depravity of the Taleban, thus emphasizing the need to fight the good fight, intended to liberate Afghan women from abuse. Unusually cruel, Aisha's case is not entirely inconsistent with the archaic sense of justice in the backblocks of this part of the world. However, nowhere in scriptural Islam does it prescribe this punishment for marital infidelity or a wife's "insubordination."

Aisha's mutilated face invites, to reflect on the propagandist value of impressive imagery. In particular photographic pictures of pretty young women in distressing situations can achieve considerable effects, particularly in the West. In this genre of a woman's portrait having a stunning impact was the haunting look of the green-eyed Pashtun girl Sharbat Gula. Her portrait stared from the cover of the *National Geographic Magazine* in June 1985. She was twelve years old at the time (when the picture was taken in 1984) and as a refugee in Pakistan she—and not least her luminous eyes of mesmerizing effect—became the poster image of the misery of Afghan refugees fleeing from the Soviet occupation. Termed the Afghan Mona Lisa, few photographs have had this degree of universal appeal and have ascended to such iconic value as this. It would go too far to ascribe to such images archetypal powers as the compelling reaction to this image is perhaps confined to Western aesthetic culture and only shared moderately in a universal sense. But it may be justified to speak of a Mona Lisa quality of such images, reminiscent of the enormous aesthetic effect and iconic prestige Leonardo da Vinci's portrait enjoys.[10] It is not so much the beauty of the face that attracts and fascinates, but a combination of pleasant features with the enigmatic facial expression and attributes that hint obliquely at an underlying intriguing condition, a puzzle, or in Aisha's case a tragedy. In a semiotic respect the mysterious attraction of such images can be used for the conveyance of quite diverse messages. The impact of Aisha's visage, though heavily damaged, still leaves the potential of beauty recognizable enough, to serve the same function. In a species-typical sense the human face, its shape and expression, is loaded with information that goes far beyond personal identity and individual recognition value. It offers itself quite obviously as a medium of enormous semiotic capacity.

Let us return to Abu-Lughod's paper on the misuses of Muslim gender relations for propaganda purposes. Her defense of women's position in Islam requiring no liberation negates the host of female Muslim authors and activists who deal highly critically with Islamic gender issues and demand drastic improvements. Abu-Lughod's desperate disputation reminds one of the anthropological insight gained in tribal societies whose discriminatory social systems are sometimes fiercely justified and defended by those discriminated against. A beacon in this respect is Maurice Godelier's[11] analyzis of New Guinea Baruya society. Extending the Marxist concept of class struggle[12] to gender relations, he analyzes a New Guinea tribal society. Using Marxist analytical tools to reveal how dominance and hegemony is achieved, Godelier uncovers the machinery of male domination and the ideological justification of the existing social order in which social power is highly inequitably distributed. On analyzis it turns out that some women take an active part in helping to uphold the myth of male superiority. Older women, especially, support misogynous gender inequality and contrive with men the continuing subservience of all women. They participate in the ritual deceptions concocted by the socially privileged older men to subdue younger men and women. Yet, their conspiratorial participation does not appear to be rewarded with better treatment, while boys and younger men have the consolation that one day they will be the beneficiaries of the ruse. Antonio Gramsci already theorized about such social constellations in which brute force and coercion between socioeconomic classes is replaced by persuasion to achieve hegemony. It seems to violate common sense and rationality when a client subsociety succumbs to hegemony, accepting the class-based ideology of the dominant group as its own. Its gullibility is apparently aroused by the lie that it is being enfranchised, or will shortly be, or, even more futuristically, that its rewards are awaiting an unspecified future time. This allows the subaltern group to live in hope and makes acceptable the ideology that actually justifies the iniquitous conditions.[13] This relates to a concept Max Weber developed and termed "hierocratic coercion": blessing is dispensed only on condition of obedience to the dominant ideology. Tribal societies lend themselves to such analysis relatively easily and, in fact, also more complex, post-industrial ones can render similar insights.[14] The ruse that lies in the promise of eventual rewards for acquiescence, can also easily be seen—by using the Marxist lenses—in revelatory religions and their doctrines of a posthumous better life for true believers. However, this approach, with its distinct Marxist tinge, although it yields interesting insights and much food for thought, will not be deployed here.

What seems to really justify being critical of Islam, is the fact that powerful criticism of Muslim society—if not Islam itself—also issues from Muslim women themselves. The chorus of female Muslims demanding changes in Muslim society—the more radical ones clamouring for a revision of Islamic tenet—can hardly be overlooked. Many are vociferously outspoken about the injustices they claim to suffer under existing gender relations and Islamic laws. Taking such a stance in the traditional Islamic world—though not for Muslim women living in the West—comes with great risks. Those who are not careful enough in couching their critique in moderate and circumspect language run the risk of becoming targets for religious zealots. Some suffer the fate of having a fatwa issued against them, some have to flee into exile or are imprisoned, and occasionally some are paying the ultimate price with their lives; for criticism of traditional gender patterns is considered blasphemy, a crime worthy of the death penalty. Even when blame is clearly laid at Muslim practice and not at scriptural Islam, the female critics may risk life and limb. Fanatics make little distinction between scriptural tenet and social practice, as they are firmly of the belief that their practice is the correct one and is totally supported by the scriptures. Most often, the (putative) normative function of textual Islam is uncritically merged with normative custom and tradition.

Some female detractors of Muslim practice and Islamic tenet have become well known in the West: the Dutch-Somali politician Ayaan Hirsi Ali, the Canadian feminist Irshad Manji, the American academic Amina Wadud, the Bangladeshi writer Taslima Nasreen, to name only a few from among the hundreds of authors, activists, journalists, and bloggers.[15] A more comprehensive list would be far too long. Among the more cautious detractors, only moderately representing a critical, feminist viewpoint, is the Moroccan author and sociologist Fatima Mernissi.[16] Here is a sample of her writing:[17]

> One of the distinctive characteristics of Muslim sexuality is its territoriality, which reflects a specific division of labor and a specific conception of society and of power. The territoriality of Muslim sexuality sets ranks, tasks and authority patterns. Spatially confined the woman was taken care of materially by the man who possessed her, in return for her total obedience and her sexual and reproductive services, The whole system was organized so that the Muslim "ummah" was actually a society of male citizens who possessed among other things the female half of the population . . . Muslim men have always had more rights and privileges than Muslim women, including even the right to kill their women. . . . The man imposed on the woman an artificially narrow existence, both physically and spiritually.

The thrust of Mernissi's argument[18] is aimed at pointing out a crucial difference between the Prophet's humanist intentions and the formation of Islamic tradition. Unfortunately for such arguments, not even the sira, the Prophet's biography, is unambiguous about gender issues—and much else for that matter. The Prophet, for instance, is said to have been torn between forbidding violence towards women and allowing it to placate the more conservative minded in his community.[19] Even the Quran vacillates on such issues as the Prophet received revelations relating to the pressing issues of the day, thus over many years adding in volume and in contradictions to the total body of revelation. As the wide diversity of expert views clearly demonstrates, not even a close and sympathetic reading of the Quran and the Sunna, as one must assume is done by Muslim sages, can give clear, unwavering, and precise answers to questions about the true intent of Islamic doctrine.

Among the women's issues that caught global attention and mightily stirred up questions about the treatment of women in Islam was the case of the Nigerian woman Amina Lawal who was sentenced to death by stoning in 2002 for adultery and for having a child out of wedlock. It rallied Muslim and non-Muslim women from all over the world to her defense. Islam does not look kindly on adultery; it is regarded as one of a few capital crimes that require the mandatory death penalty.[20] Pregnancy provides, of course, incontrovertible proof of guilt as far as an (unmarried) woman is concerned. Lawal's death sentence was to be carried out, according to Islamic law, but was postponed until after she had given birth and, in accordance with most sharia interpretations, after the baby had been weaned. However, the pronouncement of the death sentence led to a massive outpouring of universal protest and sparked off a campaign that united Muslim women's groups from around the world despite their many differences. They were united not only to protest this case but to use it as a platform for a concerted advocacy of women's rights. Eventually Lawal was set free by a presidential pardon, but through the mobilization on her behalf, a new meta-network of women's organizations had emerged that includes the Women's Human Rights group Baobab (Nigeria), Sisters in Islam (Malaysia), Shirkat Gah (Pakistan), Sisterhood is Global Institute/Jordanian Office, Women Living Under Muslim Laws Network, the Muslim Women's Research and Action Forum (Sri Lanka), the Muslim Women's League (America), and the Canadian Council of Muslim Women. Such a transnational coalition of Muslim women's groups and organizations was unprecedented and, given the ideological and cultural diversity of its constituent entities, is remarkable.[21]

IS ISLAM MISOGYNOUS OR HOMOSOCIAL?

Globally, the dominant discourse, ideologically, juridically, and politically, is on issues of equality, rights, gender, freedom, and the like. This discourse, though being essentially elitist and ideologically confined even in the West to a social minority who make themselves the torchbearers of dogmatic gender equality, does determine some of the official agenda of states and international relationships. And even though this may be more theoretical than practically serious—and is not pursued to the last consequence—it does set an important agenda and a mood that is all-pervading on the level of international politics. Although human rights laws were borne from the racially, ethnically, and religiously motivated atrocities of the World War II era, gender equality has become a significant ingredient in them. On the other hand, the New Age ideology and fashionable cultural tolerance encourage a cultural relativism, at the level of the social elite, which seeks to enfranchise and accept alien sociocultural systems regardless of their gender relations. And yet, despite the official world's earnest wish to sincerely embrace cultural Otherness, Islam finds it difficult to shed the stigma of being intolerably oppressive to women. It can hardly be denied that Islamic doctrine in some details violates domestic Western and international human rights that have great currency in Western nations and which insist on absolute equality of the genders, the right of personal choice in many matters, and the preservation of individual human dignity. Even in a fair-minded assessment infused by cultural relativism Islam comes under suspicion: being female is hedged in by a greater number of striking social rules (such as obedience, modesty, self-effacement, duties to husband, relinquishing control over her physiology, distance to the sacred sphere, etc.) than specific maleness. Women seem to be subjected to more restrictions on their freedom than men, and in various ways the sacred texts assign to them roles which appear inferior and more humble when measured against male privilege and outgoing assertiveness. Some doctrinal prescriptions clearly assign a subservient position to women vis-à-vis men and foist tasks on them that entail a lower social status. Others infringe on individual rights of choice and freedom when compared with male liberties, and in this way underline gender inequality. All this is apart from the fact that there are quite specific textual passages in the sacred scriptures that refer to the superiority of maleness and inferiority of femaleness—often almost next to an insistence that men and women are created as equals (for instance Quran 4/124, 33/35, 3/195; so equal that, as the hadith says, "none have rights over the other as they are as equal as the teeth on a comb") and are all the same before God.

Not surprisingly, the Islamic human rights agenda[22] is different in spirit and letter—which it owes to the sharia and only in a much smaller measure to Western humanist notions—from the human rights charter sponsored by the UN. Although it owes its existence to the example of the UN charter, which it aims to rival, in its contents it is clearly more inspired by the sharia and in its spirit in effect is distinct from Western secular humanism. Glaringly obvious is this through the rejection of the human rights' canon of the complete equality of all of humanity without exception. Neither gender nor race nor religion must be ground for discrimination. As Benson and Stangroom[23] point out, the Cairo Declaration right from the beginning in article 1 makes its bias clear: it refers to the superiority of Islam and sheds all pretense of universal human equality in that it divides humanity into Muslims and non-Muslims. Thus Islamic gender relations, whatever they may be, are shielded against critique arising from the universal human rights agenda.

If one applies a slightly different angle, perhaps unsurprisingly, a somewhat different approach to gender relations emerges. The dominant Western view on women in Islam is inspired by feminism and guided by the egalitarian discourse that registers and measures the smallest deviation in the balance of gendered power. For most non-Muslims, therefore, the issue whether Islam is misogynist or not is an open and shut book. Objectively, there is of course no absolutist benchmark to determine what exactly is discrimination and disadvantage, what constitutes a signifier of unilateral subservience, or indicates beyond doubt the one-sided exercise of power, and therefore should be condemned; and what is simply special gender-based treatment issuing from the recognition of the natural condition in which men and women are different. Proceeding from the premise of such a natural innate and unbridgeable difference it is logical that different social roles, rights, and duties must follow. For most Muslims there can be no doubt: men and women are naturally different anatomically, physiologically, and psychologically—even science admits that—;[24] so what could be more natural than assigning different roles to them, different duties and responsibilities suited to their innate abilities, and consequently to give them differential rights in society?[25] This does not sit well with dominant Western perceptions, though some of them may be hypocritical in accusing Muslims of a "flaw" Western society has not completely eliminated in its own ranks. Clearly, social gender difference lends itself to be interpreted in quite different ways. Under a modern Western prism, gender patterns prescribed by Islam appear discriminatory and inegalitarian, but with a panhuman, somewhat less critical perspective, this assumes the normalcy of a majority situation. Most human societies have instituted gender differences firmly in their social discourse and underpin it with ideological rationales of some sort. In most societies men and women carry out different, but complementary social roles from which usually different status, rights, and duties derive. Attempting to evaluate these differences in terms of supremacy or inferiority, unilateral exercise of power, notions of excellence and gradations of significance, reveals quite contrasting opinions. The women involved in the customary social patterns may hold quite different views from their men folk regarding their respective importance, freedom and status, their empowerment, and both men's and women's views may differ again from the considered findings of an outside observer.

In the social sciences the rise of feminism has focused attention on male-female interaction, a perspective much ignored previously when sociocultural homogeneity was taken for granted on the basis of the tacit assumption that gender specificity was irrelevant. Feminism also introduced a new sensitivity vis-à-vis a female point of view in the respective society, recognizing the fact that the two may be quite different. This has produced a demand for new paradigms to understand the social interaction of the genders and how gender specificities contribute to the defining shapes of a socioculture.

Academic anthropology, at home within the walls of university campuses and lecture halls in which an intellectual climate supportive of the rise of gynocentrism flourishes, has reacted in quite diverse ways to what may be a moral conundrum. How can respect for cultural Otherness be combined with a fashionable feminist viewpoint that fiercely rejects male domination? Most tribal societies—and not only they—by modern Western standards appear to be fortresses of male domination defying gynocentric demands. For many years I have been familiar with this conundrum through my studies of Australian Aboriginal society. Traditionally, women in this society perform the "pedestrian" jobs of child bearing and rearing, provision of the bulk of food through their gathering activity, but seem to earn little thanks in terms of social esteem; while men are proud to perform the "really important," "aristocratic" tasks of hunting and looking after religion through ritual and the cultivation of myth, which is supposedly necessary "to make the world go round." They are rewarded with higher status for their trouble, or so it seems when one asks the men. Women, as it turns out, see it differently but do not openly challenge the male point of view. Which side is right and represents the correct view? Which is the official version? Two schools of thought developed in anthropology: one subscribing to the autonomy model and the other to the oppression model.[26] The latter accepts the male domination paradigm, while the former offers a model of a more complicated interrelationship. It is not my purpose here to describe their thinking in great detail, but their analytical (and partly also ideologically driven) opposition can be seen to extend throughout the anthropological analyzis of most societies.[27]

The gender complementarity of social roles, the frequent absence of social competitiveness and the attendant notions of social significance (in which the genders often differ profoundly) suggest a model of homosociality underlying gender issues. The genders are meant to inhabit different, mutually autonomous social spheres (with their own separate value systems) and mix only in well-defined, circumscribed periods, situations, and spaces. (Sometimes additional constraints are imposed by kinship.) Both gender spheres have their own evaluative schema with which they regard their interactive relationship. (Recognizing this means accepting a much more complex picture of "culture," which lacks the homomorph and monolithic nature of traditional conceptions.) It seems to me this is a social ideal underlying

Islam. However, in the areas where the two sides do meet gender interaction patterns obtain—and attract much attention—which seem to favor the male side.

Professional ethics dictate avoidance of gross moral judgments (especially when they would seriously damage the reputation of a society), but intellectual integrity may exert a pull in the opposite direction. Observational honesty, subjective as it may be, may be suggestive of a situation of exploitation and oppression of one gender by the other. Mindful of this dilemma, by and large, academic Islamic studies have shunned describing with critical clarity what appear to be the official and undisguised androcentric, patriarchal features of contemporary conservative Islam, in actual life as well as in doctrinal exegetical provisions. Even those kindly disposed towards feminist-inspired academic discourses have skirted the issue and seem to have preferred to assuage the rivaling discourses that emphasize the equality of all cultures and bow to culture relativity. Shunning open critique has left some awkwardness. Describing gender relations in some detail requires an evaluative standpoint; it is impossible to maintain strict descriptive neutrality. Even the blandest description, through the choice of words, introduces at least a hint of bias. Yet anthropology's prevalent discourse has performed a delicate choreography so as not to break any ideological raw eggs. Pro-Islam scholars by and large, avoid the topic of gender relations and its hypersensitive points. Undisguised critique has been largely left to Muslim feminists operating on the fringes of the discipline and to non-Muslim populist writers. Not even the trope of Islamic masculinity, colorful as it may be, has been a popular object of study. Ingrained cultural relativism and political correctness have proved an effective barrier to analytical openness and imposed a harsh self-censorship.[28]

Before rushing to condemn what appears to be gender-biased Islamic orthodoxy, let us take a somewhat wider view. Islam is unambiguously strong in implying a distinct human nature to which social rules are attuned. The innate, divinely designed nature—which separates genders and in some respects divides them into a fundamental, unbridgeable male-female distinction—forms the basis of human existence and worship through social conduct. Such characteristic and integral elements of divinely consigned, unalterable nature relate to sexuality and genderedness, as well as the natural inclination of humans (fitrah) to recognize and acknowledge God and to be Muslim (i.e., to submit to the will of God). (It is only through life circumstances that people get diverted away from Islam. Thus not being Muslim is almost a perversion of nature.) Equally the capacity for sexuality is God-given and no reason to be ashamed or to renounce it. (Hence Islam does not support celibacy, nor does it have monks and nuns.) But being very powerful it requires hedging in as it can be potentially destructive. (Interestingly, this coincides with contemporary scientific theories of libido and totemism and will be discussed below.) In different ways female and male sexuality can act negatively on society if not channeled into acceptable, society-friendly avenues. Women can be dangerous through their polluting effect and men through their powerful libido that can discharge in violence and lawlessness. The need to control and regulate both genders' sexuality accounts for much of the gendered division in Islam. Thus it can be said that a theory of gendered difference, though implied more than overt, underlies Islamic doctrine. It is not so much different from modern scientific viewpoints in its fact-recognition value (about the differential thrust of sexuality, the focus of the emotional range humans as a species are capable of, etc.), but it draws different conclusions—conclusions about how society ought to harness this God-given potential, and contain the dangers it creates, to best possible effect.

I cannot claim to be uninfluenced by the various arguments about gender conditions just outlined. It seems to me the best way to understand (and appreciate) Islamic gender rules is to accept that the Islamic ideal model of gender relations, more implied than made overt, is to create a situation of homosociality: a social ideal which ensconces both genders in their own respective life world. It appears to be based on the perception that a well-functioning society must rest in keeping the genders apart, and restricting and regulating their interaction in ways that are compatible with a quasi scientific view of their innate differences. The resulting inter-gender relationship in social practice is one of capillary power in which power is not exercised unidirectionally (in the classical Marxist sense) from maleness to femaleness, but more diffusely, reversibly, and multidirectionally (as formulated by Foucault).[29] However, the mutuality and multidirectionality of the relationship is not easily discerned as the doctrinal aspects, those that are relatively clearly spelled out seem to underpin male power. Female power is more covert. This is to say, maleness draws on openly formulated and codified power—ceding to it a doctrinally underpinned authority—while femaleness relies on informal, subliminal, and more cryptic skeins of power. (I am not claiming though that seen in this way there is a complete balance of gendered power. Quantifying power is a tricky and unreliable business.) The relationships, which are expressive of power and happen to be amenable to observation, and seem to be of some spectacularity, favor the impression of male dominance and female submission. (The areas of social interaction, which may favor female power, lie more in the privacy sphere and therefore are more obscured to observation.) The greater accessibility and visibility of doctrine and of some social dynamics support the appearance of strong androcentricity and patriarchy. It is then when seen against the modern Western foil that these characteristics are being even further accentuated and create an even stronger impression of unfairness and imbalance.

The diaspora tends to generate new constellations of power relations between the genders. Protection from Western laws, education, capacity to earn income and compete with men in the labor market, and the like, create shifts in gendered power relations and may give women added weight in family affairs as well as in the public domain. Conversely, situations in which women may become victims of traditional forms of male dominance—perhaps by relying too much on the new opportunities (freer socializing, bonding with non-Muslims, etc.)—may increase and the resultant conflict come into sharper focus in a Western context than would happen in a Muslim majority society.

THE DANGER OF POLLUTION MAKES WOMEN STRONG

Apologists of Islamic doctrine argue that the detailed and abundant divine imperatives spelling out correct behavior for women and, in fact, limiting their social responsibility are advantages: this makes it easier for women to find the right way to salvation. In their view it is a compliment that shows that God and the Prophet have given much thought to the women and what behavior behooves them. On the opposite side it has been said that this shows that God and the Prophet thought of women as being weak and, therefore, in need of supervision and strict rules to help them behave correctly and live their lives in accordance with divine expectations. They also seem to need firm guidance from the men who by nature are made of sterner stuff. No matter whether this argument is put forward by defenders who want to underline the benign realizm of the faith, or critics of Islam who wish to point at its sexism, it can hardly be denied that Islam subscribes to the conservative view that men and women are fundamentally different by nature and therefore quite reasonably predestined for different social roles. The obedience to carry them out faithfully needs to be fortified by gender-specific rules. On that presumptive basis it can hardly be disputed that status differences, accompanying different rights and duties, are appropriate.

The benign interpretation by Islamic apologists insists that differential gender roles are for women's protection and constitute positive discrimination. In this view clear boundaries circumscribing female activity, even if narrowing liberty, are for their own good. This is so not only for their physical comfort, but by being observant of religious doctrine and obeying divine command, women enhance their soteriological chances. Being surrounded and guided by many rules of divine invention women find it easier not to stray from the straight path to heaven. (No doubt, some analyzts will interpret this rationale as a male conspiracy.) However, a side effect beneficial for men may be that restrictions on female behavior may be for men's spiritual safety; they may also ward, for instance, against male aggression and thus protect general sociability and social cohesiveness. (This may sound paradoxical, but can also be "rationally" argued on the basis of assumptions about the gender-specific nature of human behavior and proclivities.)

In a culture in which exposure to religion is of vital practical and spiritual importance, it is significant to what extent women are granted access to the sacred sphere. Not surprisingly benevolent viewpoints are seeking to turn gendered restrictions into advantages. When women are not required to observe the regular prayers at the mosque (especially the all-important salat-al-jummah, the Friday midday prayer)—as men are, it does not mean, it is said, they and their prayers are of lesser importance; it is simply more convenient for them to pray at home and thus being able to pay more attention to family matters. When it is ruled that women may not act as imams, it is both to take into account that they are not required to attend mosque services (and only do so on a more voluntary basis than men) and that they are more focused on domestic affairs. Denying women traditionally the role of imam also has to do with the physical postures the praying person is to assume. The physical gender separation in mosques—relegating women to side rooms apart from the main prayer hall—also is to their benefit, as the apologist argument has it. Separation helps to protect their decency and decorum when prostrating themselves. It needs to be remembered that the posture of prostration uncannily resembles female coital positions. Therefore, another reason usually given for gender separation in the sacred sphere is that certain required postures when women perform them may radically distract men from concentrating on their prayers.[30] In a less benign interpretation this may suggest a weakness and lack of spiritual discipline on the part of men, which as a gender characteristic not only reflects poorly on men but should not be used as a reason to bar women from sharing on an equal footing in prayers and in ritual leadership. (One should remember that gender separation in church was not uncommon in the past and in some local communities and in some sects is still practiced today.)

Menstruation is hedged in with taboos and commands. In the Quran the underlying idea of impurity and pollution is justified with references to hygiene,[31] but in the context of other rules surrounding the female period, the wider symbolic significance beyond physical cleanliness is evident. A restriction on femaleness flowing from this is that women in menses are forbidden to touch the Quran or conduct other ritually significant exercises (e.g., observing the fast of Ramadan, entering the mosque, even praying). In fact, in very strict interpretations, menstruating women should not even engage in social intercourse of any kind. In this context one should mention the gender-segregation on public transport, as practiced in some Muslim-majority countries.

I remember well an incident many years ago when as a young and inexperienced traveler I jumped on a suburban train in a Pakistani city. The train was already slowly leaving the station and—it was one of those old-fashioned ones with wagons whose compartment doors opened to the outside—without giving it a second thought I ripped open a door and jumped inside. I found myself faced with a compartment full of giggling women obviously delighted with my faux pas and consequent discomfort. When I hurriedly left at the next stop some men stared in silent disapproval. I wonder what would happen today as fundamentalization prescribing much greater strictness is sweeping the Muslim world.

Such gender separation is not solely practiced for the benefit of women, even though this is the most commonly used rationale, but also to protect men. A closer look reveals that the social gender division, called purdah in South Asia, at least in some of its aspects, can be interpreted not as a symbol of female submission, a caging of the weaker gender for its own protection, but as a symbolic containment of female strength.

Gender segregation in confined public places in a wider sense reduces the risk of illicit contact between unrelated men and women, which would bring shame and danger if not strictly regulated. Arrangements of gender-segregation are not only for women's comfort and protection, avoiding groping and indecent approaches, for instance, facilitated by cramped conditions on trains and buses, but are also meant to protect men. Coming into contact with a menstruating woman during the holy month of Ramadan would spoil the effect of sawm, the fast. The dangerous potential of femaleness, physically manifest in the menstrual secretion, overpowers the sacred status of a man observing the fast: purity is annulled by pollution. Although this physical separatism appears obviously to be designed for women's protection, it is evident that notions of the polluting and dangerous effect of the period, and specifically the menstrual blood, concedes a position of power to women that has to be checked. Although by and large a subliminal notion, it leaves men with an Achilles heel, a ritual weakness, which doctrine and the regulations it imposes in social life try to address.

Beliefs of the dangerous power of menses and menstrual blood are extremely widespread in the world and exist in many cultures. In fact, one may consider this dread a human universal.[32] (Although ubiquitous, in some cultures it is so weakly expressed as to be socially unnoticeable. In contrast, in some cultures beliefs are so acute as to confine menstruating women to certain areas and houses in the village until purity is restored.) The perception of the contagious condition of menstrual blood and its polluting effect can then all too easily and logically be extended to a notion of its defiling effect on sacred matters and result in women having a more restricted access to the sacred sphere.[33] Overlapping the danger of femaleness to maleness with the sacred—profane dichotomy introduces new possibilities of ritual and symbolic configurations.[34] This may apply not only at the time of the period but avoiding the risk of pollution altogether may be extended to a blanket restriction on all women at all times. On a symbolic level this physiological condition may be hyperbolized to the paragon of impurity, a permanent defect endangering purity itself, and in a related vein may be extended to the view of an innate potential risk that femininity poses to masculinity. This, in turn, would justify restrictive rules of gender interaction and limiting women's freedom of movement and choice. It is interesting that the idea of female sexuality and physiology being dangerous to masculinity has cropped up recently again in a new guise of rational scientific hypothesizing. The statistically verifiable lowering of the fertility rate of European men is traced by this hypothesis to the saturation of the environment with waste estrogen. One might suspect this new insight—which is far from being universally accepted in the scientific community—of being a cognitive derivative of ancient gender beliefs.

Paradoxically, this perilous defectiveness of women, who, on the basis of their capacity to pollute, can endanger the sacred and masculine, turns into empowerment. It is not they, the women, who are in danger from pollution; they control it, and alternatively by lack of control, through carelessness or design, can do damage. Reducing and threatening male power, female physiology thus may become a powerful weapon. (Even if its source is decried from a male point of view as a defect!) It is exactly the power inherent in the female condition that makes it necessary to place restrictions on women's activity—regardless of whether this is rationalized as for the protection of maleness, or femaleness, or more encompassing is for the good of society as a whole.

Mernissi argues that the Prophet's intention was to do away with superstitions surrounding female impurity and sexual pollution.[35] However, his mission seems to remain incomplete as the belief in the danger of femininity to male devotion and sacred purity is still intact in Islam. It is not doctrinally spelled out, but can be detected to have an implied presence. Conventionally, the hadith is ascribed to Muhammad that a donkey, a dog, and a woman may not come in between a praying man and the qibla.[36] It is clearly insulting to place women in one rubric with dogs and donkeys, in addition to ascribing to them an anti-sacred presence uncongenial to men carrying out ritual duties. This clearly supports the view, if only at a subliminal level, that maleness is associated with sacredness while femaleness represents the antinomious counterpoint, that of mundaneness. In structuralist types of analyzes it, has been argued this reflects an even wider, cosmic antinomy, that between order and chaos, civilization, and wilderness.

At best this gender dichotomy and its imputations reflect a male-centered world perception, which in all innocence renders a highly gender-biased slant in ontological matters. In other words, it is not malicious but assumes a male point of view is representative for all of humanity. Let us remember that the recognition of the genderedness of ideology and cognition is a very recent insight. Sigmund Freud, who cannot easily be accused of crass misogyny, had a similar, underlying male bias in his psychoanalyzis through a sustained tendency of giving psychotic phenomena and their causes not only a sexual origin but also one lodged predominantly in maleness. (As is the case with his theory of the origins of human society.) Whether in this he is reflecting the common legacy of Middle Eastern monotheism or simply imitates the male-biased slant of his time and society is apt to inspire a fascinating debate.

FEMALE DEFICIENCY

Let us move from a consideration of the strength femaleness to the opposite. Even when the scriptures admonish men to treat women fairly and kindly—for instance Quran 2/231 or the hadith, "I urge you to treat women kindly"—they implicitly speak of the legitimate dominance of men and their authority over women. There are many more scriptural passages that point to the women's dependency on men's ethical goodwill; for example Quran 4/34, which openly refers to men's superiority in saying "men are the protectors and maintainers of women, because Allah has made one of them to excel the other." It continues to point out that women are supported by the means of the men and, therefore, owe a debt of obedience: "Therefore the righteous women are devoutly obedient . . . [to their husbands]."

Among the more spectacular gender-specific restrictions placed on women, as practiced at least in the conservative interpretation of Islam, are those that are based on the belief that women are unsuitable for leadership. As the oft-quoted hadith goes "a people who entrust their affairs to a woman will never prosper." The famous Muslim sociologist Fatima Mernissi[37] makes this hadith the starting point of her investigation into gender inequality. Her mission is to prove that today's Islam's misogynist features are an aberration from the Prophet's divinely inspired intentions. By a thorough isnad[38] as well as using the asbab an-nusul[39] she seeks to demonstrate that at the root of this derogatory adage, so widely quoted and believed in the Islamic world, is a particular historical event and a series of misunderstandings as well as some malice of at least one recorder of this hadith.[40]

For the non-Muslim, historical and sociological analyzt Mernissi's undertaking is doomed to remain unconvincing. What was Islam's original intent and what had the Prophet in mind with specific rulings? How can that ever be convincingly reconstructed and claim historical authenticity beyond the obvious insight that the original Islam shows a preoccupation, if not obsession, with constructing the ideal society. Beyond that the burden of proof is not diminished by even the most sophisticated conjecture. The demand for credibility cannot be fully satisfied when the argument is founded too strongly on blind faith and a subjectivity that is based on the overriding will to believe. As said in the introduction, the undertaking of distilling historical veracity from hearsay, rumor and decades-old memory, and trying to reach back into a past that lies centuries ago, is a very uncertain enterprise. On this basis to construct a picture of the Prophet's innermost intentions, unwavering or not, and considered benign or humanitarian or not, and heartwarming as this speculative exercise may be to the believer, ultimately is no more than wishful thinking. Above all, what casts a big shadow of doubt over Mernissi's argument are Quranic verses that assemble to indicate an argumentative thrust that seems akin to the hadith "women should not be leaders."

This influential maxim that women should not be leading men, which tends to pop up in the political discourse in the Islamic world whenever women compete with men for power, is supported by a Quran verse (4/34) that—despite protestations of gender equality elsewhere—says "men are in charge of the affairs of their women by virtue of that God has favored some over the other";[41] and also in another verse (2/228): "women have rights equal to the rights incumbent on them according to what is equitable: and men have a degree over them." And a hadith says, "I urge you to treat women kindly. . . . They are a trust in your [the men's] hands." As these samples show, men acquiescing under the leadership and control of women would run counter to the spirit of these exhortations. While modern politics show a tendency to sometimes defy these religious recommendations, civil service and competition for higher public positions in Islamic societies are bracing against any changes to achieve greater gender equality. It is necessary, however, to note that the history of Islam shows no consistency in this regard.[42] The beginnings of the Muslim community are especially replete with strong female characters: Khadija, the Prophet's first wife; Aisha, one of his later wives and a particularly free spirit; and Fatima, his daughter. Also the Queen of Sheba is being held up as a shining example of female leadership in the scriptures.[43] Mernissi[44] endeavours in her writings to show that the women under the rule of the Prophet enjoyed freedom; and his women especially did so to a degree allegedly not usual in Arab society at the time. They engaged themselves in the community's political life, and, not slow to express their opinion, were consulted and even were present at battles. However, as Mernissi's argument goes, Muhammad's good intentions were thwarted in the long run by his associates who were of a more conservative bent of mind. Then as now the truism may apply that a few exceptions confirm the rule. While for many Muslims the hadith and related verses of the Quran amount to a straightforward recommendation not to confer political power or other leadership functions and prominent social roles on a woman, it is not always heeded as the outstanding examples of female presidents and prime ministers testify to: above all there is the former presidency of Megawati Sukarnoputri in Indonesia, Benazir Bhutto in Pakistan, and Begum Khaleda Zia, the first female prime minister in Bangladesh.[45] But overall women certainly are severely hampered in gaining leadership and influential public roles in Muslim society.

The reason for such discriminatory assumptions—running counter to feminist tastes and gender-liberationist ideas in today's world—is the traditional, ancient, and very widespread view that women are lacking in emotional and physical stamina. The benchmark is, of course, provided by the generic abilities ascribed to men, regardless of the fact that it is not reached by a goodly portion of that gender. Bad gender essentialization as it may be, this belief has gained universal currency. It may be based on the primitive empiricism that men on average are visibly more endowed with muscle mass and usually can physically overpower women. But further extrapolations from this fact lack in rational corroboration. Nonetheless further conclusions about inferior female abilities and gender-specific weaknesses are made: for instance, that their physically weaker constitution corresponds with weaker courage, less intrepidity and fortitude—requirements for a socially leading position. This may be further exacerbated by the prejudicial view that females are suffering a deficiency in intelligence and maturity, again, when compared with the innate generic abilities males are believed to possess. It is clear that this must have repercussions for a society's structure—leaving uncontested here the chicken and egg debate whether gender ideas came first or whether they are derived from social conditions or whether both sides evolved in a cycle of mutual confirmation. In socially more highly structured societies, women not unusually are given a more childlike image that tends to justify their exclusion from rights and duties that flow from, and are contingent on, social and mental maturity. The more kindly judgment on that point is that women should not be punished through harsh social subjugation for their gender-specific handicap, but need male guidance, kindness, and protection. Understandably, this dubiously premised "chivalry" is repaid by modern feminism with derision and labeling it insufferable male arrogance and sexism.

Verse 2/282 of the Quran, which allocates to a woman the status of a lesser juridical persona (her testimony in court is only half that of a man's; she cannot make herself clear in disputes 43/18), is often commented that it reveals very clearly the perceived deficiency of femaleness. Women lack in degree of intelligence, trustworthiness, and education when compared with men, which makes them less reliable as witnesses.[46] A hadith attributed to the mouth of the Prophet spells it out clearly: "Women are deficient in religion," he is recorded as saying and when asked why, he said, "Is not the witness of a woman equal to half the witness of a man? This is the defect in her intelligence. And when she is ceremonially impure she neither prays nor fasts, this is the defect in her religion." Women being fickle, emotional, and less rational by nature, and confined to the domestic sphere, thus being less world-wise and formally educated, all this militates against total gender equality and justifies social disadvantage—or what may be seen as such today—for women.

It is often remarked by Islamic apologists that the Prophet had the best intentions vis-à-vis women which shows in his insistence that women have inalienable, divinely granted rights—an idea that presumably had not existed previously in pre-Islamic Arab society. The right of their testimony being heard before court, rights of divorce, of inheritance, the right for fair and just treatment and fixing it in law were quite possibly improvements, and certainly are considered by apologists to have been progressive for the times. However, benign as they may have been, they do not exclude the idea that women are slightly inferior in terms of the abilities, responsibilities, and rights men possess and this would necessitate the kind and considerate treatment God and the Prophet demand of men. It can be assumed as a certainty that today's Western ideal of absolute gender equality in all aspects of human existence would have seemed completely preposterous and utterly ludicrous to the Prophet and his contemporaries. The very concept of today's feminism that ascribes to women the same capacities—or perhaps even superior qualities— as men possess, could have had little traction in premodern societies. Bachofen's[47] speculative retrospect of the ancient society and its supposed matrilineality and matriarchy was just that—speculation. It can only be subject of fanciful imagination whether the numerous finds of so-called Venus figurines from Mesolithic to early metal times found in Europe and the Near East are proof of the worship of feminity and female fecundity, represented by a female supreme deity. The apotheosis of femaleness to the status of a supreme mother goddess, or earth mother as some ardent feminists have us believe, takes shameless advantage of today's gynocentrically slanted ideological climate. More plausibly, this art form may represent the veneration of women's child bearing capacity, and in this sense may possibly be connected with ignorance of paternity and a belief in parthenogenesis.[48] It could have represented a metaphorical focus on general nature fertility or even less significantly may simply have been an erotic fashion associated with faintly fertility evocative ideas, but without expressing socially and religiously normative functions. This is completely open to debate. Even if fashioning and keeping such statuettes really was of serious religious significance—an artistic expression of a religious cult—it did not necessarily have a correspondence in matrilineal conditions or a matriarchal social order. Similarly, descriptions of Amazonian societies in classical times were probably no more than figments of an erotic imagination, fanciful and entertaining legends or attention-seeking tall tales of would-be travelers. Amazons and other men-hating and men-devouring female characters that can be found in the legends

of several societies may say something about the imagination of male-domi-
nated societies (deliberately playing with a fantastic image of absurdly inverted social conditions),[49] but in terms of veracity belong in the same category as the mares about fantastic peoples (umbrella footed and double-
headed creatures and the like) inhabiting the periphery of the known world—
but only so in the imagination current at the time of the very early explora-
tions of seafaring Europeans.

In saying this I am fully aware that not all Muslim societies comply with
the stereotypical picture of being patrilineal, patriarchal, and showing a tendency to being androcentric and androcratic to varying degrees of intensity.
Minangkabau tribal society in West-Sumatra, for instance, is both devoutly
Muslim, but at the same time is well known for its matrilineality and matriarchal features.[50] The successful combination of strict adherence to Islamic
doctrine with matri-centered social features is no mean feat—logically and
socially contradictory as it internally must be—and yet it has produced and
inspires a vibrant and proud ethnic group. It is, however, abundantly clear
that to find such societies within the precincts of the so-called Islamic world
is surprising as it runs counter to one of the major doctrinal accents of this
religion.

The notion that androcracy, patriarchy, and other gender-biased features
were post-revelation and post-prophetic additions is on weak grounds, as
such tendencies are clearly contained in the Quran. A woman's alleged immaturity, when compared with a man's legal standing, is reflected in the
presumption that her testimony before a court of law is only worth half that
of a man's; at least this is the most common interpretation of an aya that is
actually not all that clear (Quran 2/282). In a similar vein, a woman's legal
share of an inheritance is less than what a man is entitled to (see Quran 2/
180,240; 4/7-9,12,19,33,176; 5/106-8). The man being the guardian and pro-
vider for women is thought to have a greater need for wealth than the woman
beneficiary. Both basic laws are explicitly contained in the Quran and, therefore, of supreme authority.

Modern hegemonic ideology, spreading through globalization and fashionable gender egalitarian currents, recognizes only physiological gender
distinctions, and even so dismantles the last institutionalized male preserves
(for instance, in the armed forces). Ingrained social gender-discriminatory
conventions, hardened over millennia, will presumably take much longer to
disappear—especially in the non-Western world. In this perspective even the
more moderate Islamic position, inclined to resist such impulses, must seem
suspect. In reverse, the conservative Islamic inclination is to regard the fre-
netic drive towards total gender equality as madness, an ideologically driven
denial of plainly obvious gender differences, and a hostile challenge against
divinely designed human nature.

FEMALE OBEDIENCE AND DEPENDENCY

Being under the supervision as well as provision of the male head of the family, women owe him total obedience (beya). They are subject to his authority and surrender to him the right to punish them for wrongdoing. This right is specifically referred to in the Quran (4/34), though the extent of legitimate physical punishment is not clearly defined. In practice it can range from a symbolic beating with a toothpick, a miswak, to a severe physical assault. However, most, even conservative, Islamic authorities seem to agree that this punishment must not leave visible or lasting injuries. The incident in which an Afghan woman had her nose cut off by male relatives apparently for "insubordination" (fleeing from her husband), as was widely reported by the world media in 2010, is unusual in its excessive cruelty. Thankfully, it is rejected as legitimate punishment by most Muslims, even conservative ones, judging by reactions on the internet. Confined to the "backblocks" of Asia, where a "medievalist" version of sharia is practiced, it provides a stark contrast even to the most conservative Western paradigms of marital discipline. It is interesting to juxtapose this case with the incident in which a Spanish imam writing a learned treatise (entitled *La Mujer en el Islam*, Woman in Islam) recommended effective ways of meting out an exemplary beating to a woman, but with many restrictions and moderations (so as to avoid visible haematomas or scarring of face and hands).[51] I can only speculate that as a devout Muslim the imam's motivation in advising moderation was not primarily to hide the punishment from public view and in wider consequence from Spanish authorities, who then might intervene, but for the sake of implementing the correct version of sharia. Yet, even in this form, it became a celebrated court case as domestic Spanish and European Union laws took a dim view on the matter. Enforcement of obedience through corporeal punishment falls under the rubric of domestic violence, and doctrinal recommendations constitute incitement to violence, both of which Western law seeks to discourage. (Exercising the right of religious freedom tends to come off second best in such cases when physical punishment is inflicted.) Even the underlying ethical paradigm of enforcement of obedience, whether by physical means or psychological intimidation, within a family is abhorrent in the dominant Western social discourse, even when it is not directly proscribed by law.

The sharia gives men legitimate authority over women in familial matters, to the point where in diasporic situations Islamic convention may clash with Western social and juridical ideals. While moderate Islam seeks to compromise by reducing punishment to a symbolic gesture—for instance by using only a miswak, a toothpick, for the "beating"—conservative notions resist what they see as undermining male dominance within the family. Domestic relationships are divinely and naturally unequal and legitimately hierarchi-cal.[52] The divinely ordained duty of obedience for women and the rights of men to punish disobedience expunge in practical family life the malodor of domestic violence. Any such violence can be justified as a man exercising his rights—or may even be regarded as a fardh ayn (an individual duty). Its imposition only establishes and maintains the "rightful order" of social rela-tions within the basic Islamic social unit.

The dependent status of women is expressed in various ways in the scrip-tures, but fundamentally harks back to their natural difference from men. The Mutazilah school guided by its rationalist leanings tries to overcome this conservative and deeply entrenched viewpoint at the root of gender inequal-ity, by arguing that it was defensible in traditional Arab society, when wom-en had little or no access to education and had little experience with the outside world, being cosseted within the home for their own protection. This condition made it natural for men to take the lead in family matters and to have the authority to enforce discipline.[53] Apart from its bland pragmatism that assumes that only a highly disciplined and tightly organized family unit under strict leadership functions effectively, it is based on "old-fashioned" values, which extol the virtues of unilateral authority over democratic con-sultation. However, both impulses, participatory democratic and authoritar-ian, are present in Islamic thinking, and although they create a seemingly irreconcilable ideological paradox, modern conditions make it possible to allow women a greater degree of equality and freedom.

The conservative argument contains a certain chicken-and-egg circular-ity. The women's lack of knowledge and emotional hardiness is supposed to be the result of their being confined to domesticity, while this confinement is thought necessary because of their shortcomings in intellectual and emotion-al stamina. What can break this vicious cycle of social convention and female natural constitution so as to achieve gender equality? The Mutazilah argu-ment goes[54] that nowadays better education can overcome the natural emo-tionality and inexperience of women. Their natural lack of physical stamina can be compensated for by their innate (species-typical) capacity for reason, which was bestowed on all human beings by God. This viewpoint is anathe-ma to the ultra-orthodox interpretation that denies women the right to educa-tion because they are doctrinally destined to perform only domestic duties. In a bizarrely extreme manner this has been globally publicized by the Taleban regime, but it should be remembered that some local communities in various parts of the Islamic world may share this conviction. It has even been re-ported that individual Muslim families in the Western diaspora try to hold fast to this arch-conservative value and resist compulsory education for girls.

The unpleasant intensity of this conservatism has a parallel in the doctri-nal metaphor that women are "the field to which men go when they please." Domesticity and the dependent status of women are also expressed in scriptural references to sexuality. For instance, Quran 2/223 says, "Your wives are a tilth to you, so go to your tilth, when or how you will." This places the sex act under male control and attributes a submissive role to women. (Muslim scholars seem to argue whether or not this implies a permission to have anal intercourse,[55] whether this requires the consent of the woman, and some even insist that this permits anality in homosexual acts.[56]) Be that as it may, the point to be made here is that the agricultural metaphor, whether deliberately or not, objectifies women and reduces them to passivity. Their wishes and needs are secondary, while the scriptural candidness openly panders to the sexual whim of men. On the other hand, it has to be noted that several ahadith also address female preferences and make it incumbent on the man to defer to female sexual needs.

Some of these discriminative rules seemingly prescribed by Islam would have struck a familiar chord in the West of fifty or one hundred years ago, before women's suffrage became a commonplace and an unquestioned right. In fact such attitudes of ancient and modern Arab society would have resonated also in other preindustrial, socially hierarchisized societies. A protective mantle seen as necessary to be wrapped around women had the drawback of lowering their social status (similar to children's). This must be the immediate conclusion unless one does not mind succumbing to a brutal domination theory (lurking in Social Darwinist thinking): human nature and the natural harshness of social conditions combine with the power growing from strength to produce certain authoritarian gendered patterns with unfailing inevitability. In any case I am certain not many Muslims would wholeheartedly agree with either of them, except to accept that male domination may arise from the need to protect females. The Islamic gender rules are ambivalent and allow also for another spin to give them a more positive gloss: protection may not be necessitated by innate female weakness, but may arise from a perception of women's inherent value. This certainly is the benevolent Islamic interpretation in justifying the gender relations that from a Western viewpoint may seem so iniquitous. Objectively seen, female domesticity is a condition that allows quite different interpretations ranging from this being a discriminative, unwarranted restriction on personal freedom to it representing the esteem and special worth with which women are held in Arab society and which justifies keeping them away from the harshness of life outside the family.

In a generalized sense in human society for a woman to be shut away in the privacy of the home and to have little contact with the outside world could be a signal of high status. The comparison with "imprisonment" and unfreedom may be totally inappropriate. In preindustrial and early industrial types of stratified society such a condition symbolized a certain amount of affluence in this family. While lower class women by necessity were involved in the labor process, high-class women experienced the often brutal "outside world" only filtered through the more or less benign screen of a protective home environment more or less lovingly, or dutifully as the case may be, provided and maintained by the male breadwinner. Restricted to the relatively minimal worries of the household—and confined possibly to a solely ceremonial supervision of the domestics or house slaves—female domesticity was a signal of a family's good socioeconomic standing, a sign of good fortune and a matter of pride. It is quite conceivable that an exaggerated result was a certain measure of "unworldliness," naivety, and lack of experience with the harsh reality outside—a proud characteristic of the sheltered women belonging to the affluent classes. In hyperbolic form, Queen Antoinette's naïve comment "If they don't have bread, let them eat cake," revealing her ignorance about living conditions of ordinary Parisians, could plausibly be taken as symptomatic for the level of experience of this kind of women. According to serious historiography, she never said that, but it is a symptom of social relations between the privileged classes and their women—be they pharaohs or European high aristocracy—and the wider society. The women on both sides were living in different worlds, in a manner of speaking. To deduce from this socioeconomic condition an ethical negative is very much a product of modern Western ideology.

The majority of less fortunate women were condemned to toiling in the fields, in menial jobs or on the factory floor shoulder to shoulder with men, thus demonstrating the ambiguity of gender equality. In peasant societies, hunter-gatherer societies, and the peasant milieux in complex societies women participated equally—or sometimes more than equally—thus contributing vitally to the physical existence of the family or group through their labor. In early industrial society the ability of a woman of the proletariat to have a job, poorly paid as it may have been, was seen as a stroke of good fortune as it gave greater financial security to a family. The insistence that women cast off the shackles of domesticity and be able to join in the labor force on a basis of total equality with men—and to see this as a desirable sign of personal freedom, freedom of choice, and gender liberalism—is a relatively recent phenomenon. In a traditional and socially structured society, gender roles were determined in a differential fashion. Add to this the fact that rebellious attitudes and the desire to break out of the mold were not options easily accessible to women and ambitions, such as they were, were normally driven by necessity rather than the fervent ideal of gender equality. To break with traditional gender expectations to achieve public acclaim and outstanding success, in pre- and early modern European or Western society, was a luxury few women achieved. (Usually only those born into the highest classes had the chance to break out of the expected social mold.) Only much later in modern society did it become a normal option. In history the Jean d'arcs and Boadiceas are so rare that they soon acquired mythical status, if they were not mythical figures from the start—figments of the imagination. As always, the real acid test of what constitutes freedom, gender equality and ethical advance does not so much lie in the social conventions and patterns themselves, but in the extent free choice is available to all.

Features of female unfreedom and legal inferiority have been noticeable in Western society until not so long ago—and even today, if we are to believe radical feminism. In more recent times they were not part of canonical law, but a result of secular conservatism. (However, in Christian fringe sects such "conservative" social features may still be rationalized in terms of divine law.) In the United States a "respectable" married woman would refer to herself, or be referred to, as Mrs John Smith attributing the juridically relevant persona of the married couple to her husband and deferring to his legal status. Very conservative couples still do. In New Zealand and Australia (and probably elsewhere too) up to the 1970s, hire purchase agreements for larger items such as washing machines, or cars, had to be signed by the husband to make them legally binding—thus not only recognizing the traditional economic dominance of the husband, but also by implication attributing legal immaturity to the wife. Such social features have tended to disappear only less than forty years ago.

Domestic violence on first sight seems to run counter to the socializing mission of Islam. However, on reflection intrafamilial violence can be seen not as a discrete category of social pathology (which is the common Western perception in this matter), but as the extreme ends of the moral imperatives of female subordination, the need of enforcing social order and discipline, and as the price to secure family cohesiveness. Ethically, it is an extension of the doctrinal obligation of female obedience. Disobedience surrenders the right to the pater familias to enforce discipline.

The juridical concept of domestic violence came into the focus of Western law only since the 1970s[57] when women's rights groups began to pay close attention to familial violence (battery, rape, forced marriage, homicidal aggression). Previously, such incidents had been considered largely private and beyond strict law enforcement. In the Islamic world powerful constituencies still regard curbs on male authority even when its exercise leads to violence as a contravention of the sharia.[58]

Intrafamilial violence is common in all countries even though some Islamic countries seem to have a higher percentage than others.[59] This can only be guesswork as accurate statistics do not exist. Globally seen, most incidents of this kind go unreported because familial violence is commonplace or appears to be religiously sanctioned. It may be given support by the ideology of male supremacy (as integral part of machismo) and may be inextricably associated with respected images of masculinity. As in Islam, meting out punishment within the family sphere to enforce discipline may be seen not only as a male entitlement, but a duty. The sharia does not criminalize intrafamily violence though it can be interpreted to admonish moderation. Routine brutalization and intimidation of women certainly is neither encouraged nor condoned. The ideal is a reasonable acquiescence of both genders in the respective roles commanded by God, thus minimizing the need for violent enforcement and punishment. The ideal pattern is constituted by the un-shirked duty of men to care for their women and provide them with suste-nance and protection, to which women should respond with a loving and grateful recognition of a debt of unquestioned obedience.

HONOR, A DEADLY AFFAIR

Another issue routinely raised to bolster the argument that women are badly treated in Islam is so-called honor killing (izzat). It merits a closer look. The concept of honor killing refers to execution style killings of "wayward" women who do not meet the ethical expectations of their male guardians. It can be seen as the ultimate weapon to control a woman's sexuality and to enforce obedience. In this capacity it is closely related to notions of adultery and its appropriate harsh punishment. And above all it is linked with the important concept of honor. Honor killing has been sarcastically described as deriving from the notion of the "family's honor literally residing between the legs of its women"; or even more graphically expressed, women's sexual organs serving as the "vessel of collective honor." The hadith expresses this notion in a more circumspect, respectful manner: "the best of your women is the one who when her husband looks at her she pleases him; when he beck-ons to her she obeys him; and when he is away from her she continues to have regard for him, protecting his wealth and preserving her honor."

Honor killing, as the name suggests, asserts—by some stretch of moral-ity—that it is to be considered an honorable murder or a homicide committed for the sake of honor. (The notion that an injury to one's honor demands a very strong response is well-nigh universal and certainly was not alien to Western society not so long ago.) In this sense it has a ring of justifiability around it—falsely so in the view of many Muslims and most Westerners. But even so, it is a theme that firmly belongs in the cultural repertory of conser-vative Islam, even if only thematically. It is not carried out physically in all instances and with inevitability when the family honor appears to be in peril.

To the Western mind the concept of honor killing, apart from its brutality, is another strong signifier of the men's condescendingly censorious view of women, which degrades them to the plaything for a man's whims and has strong connotations of the dependent sexual status of a woman. Indeed in the usual understanding, this stricture on female behavior relates primarily to sexual license. However, this is only partly correct in a literal sense, as much less than a sexual liaison may be enough to trigger the perception that the family honor has been violated. Shaming the family takes much less than a sexual dalliance. As past cases reported in the media (mainly in the West) demonstrate, just an innocent friendship, platonic emotional involvement, choice of lifestyle, or even a casual brief acquaintance may be enough to trigger this kind of response. As in the case of female circumcision, honor killing is not confined to Muslims, but is also practiced by Middle Eastern Christians and among Hindus for the same or similar reasons. This suggests that it is a pre-Islamic cultural tradition of this region and is tied in with ancient notions of honor, which have become incorporated in Islamic dogma. Indifference of monotheistic religious doctrines towards this issue, if not through their active encouragement, has allowed this custom to persevere through the centuries.

Honor killing, in some cases, may conflict with the Quranic command that sexual relations between unmarried persons are to be punished with lashing, not death. In this respect the doctrinally prescribed punishments may be at odds with each other, though anecdotally from the Taleban it has been reported that women were first whipped and then put to death.[60] When an honor killing is privately arranged and carried out it seems to have more to do with disobedience, indifference to strict custom, and not necessarily with sexual conduct. Sometimes shadowy sharia courts may clandestinely pronounce a death sentence and delegate its execution to the family.[61] But as far as illicit sexual conduct is concerned, it should be properly considered under sharia provisions, which demand that the accusation be supported by reliable witnesses and not by circumstantial, ambiguous evidence. This does not always seem to be the case.

As the label "honor killing" suggests, it is intimately tied to notions of honor. Violating the code of honor and bringing shame to oneself and one's family requires a determined response. If it is possible to quantify it, honor usually and more strongly attaches to maleness, its code ideally influencing male behavior; it features prominently and explicitly in the worldview of traditionally minded men of most cultures. It is interesting that a female anthropologist (Lila Abu-Lughod) has argued that in Arab society, Muslim women accept and embrace this male concept of honor and make it theirs as a measure of their own worth and self-esteem. This concept is based on masculinity, male dominance, strength of character, single-mindedness, autocracy, and expresses itself in the enforcement of male supremacy not to the exclusion of brutality. Though rough and unmollified by feminist values, devoid of expressions of love and caring devotion, it inspires respect in women. "If a man is a fool [which seems to mean tender and complaisant to his wife] a woman rides him like a donkey"[62] seems to sum up this attitude. Women take pride even in the man's readiness to back up his command with physical brutality. This seems, however, to refer more to the Bedouin ethos, at least in this severity, and where it can be found it is probably linked to the social and educational standard of the respective family. (Similar features could be observed in European families less than a hundred years ago.) It needs to be noted that a man's personal dishonor—for instance by showing character weakness, consuming alcohol or engaging in homosexuality—reflects also on his wife and family.[63] Perhaps a vital gender difference in perceptions of honor is that a man, having brought shame on himself, does not seem to be in danger of being killed.

Family honor has the important dimension that it is contingent on the honor of the constituent parts of the entire social unit (family, clan, or tribe). Personal honor and collective honor are intimately linked. As a man's personal honor reflects on his family and family members can take pride in it, they also contribute to the social unit's collective honor. If they bring shame they do not only shame themselves. The deficit in honor that results has to be addressed and usually it is done so in a violent way. A woman running away from her husband is not only shaming herself, but bringing shame also on her family, her husband, and her parents. Many persons can be "wronged" by an individual act. I have referred before to the case of an Afghan woman whose nose and ears had been cut off by her husband. She had tried to escape from his and her in-laws' bad treatment and had been punished for disobedience. However, the brutal act was probably more than simply punishing an insult or exacting revenge. It may also have been perceived as an act necessary to restore the honor of the husband who had been shamed by her. He was humiliated not because by running away the woman had drawn attention to his brutality and bad treatment of her. The damage was done by her disobeying the religious imperative of absolute female obedience in all matters. She has brought disrepute to his family and besmirched its good name by her disobedience.

With some hyperbole it may be said that this case shows that honor is not to be gained, or regained, by forgiveness. (As mentioned before, the Quran mentions it, but Islam is not known for exaggerating its importance.) Honor in Muslim society is gained primarily by virtuous conduct in strict alignment with doctrinal demands. Criteria, which determine honor and by which, sometimes through a process of accumulation, one builds it as a capital, vary from society to society. In a global context, honor may be gained in various and quite different ways: it may be through bravery and courage in battle, the violent destruction of an adversary (and displaying his head as is done in headhunting societies), it may be through the calculated destruction of a store of valuables (as in the potlatch system) or of food (as in the pig slaughtering festivities of the Melanesian Big Man system). In Islam, honor predominantly is determined—not by wealth or physical prowess, although this may count too—but by the fastidious observance of divinely mandated social and religious rules and conscientiously following doctrinal imperatives.

The murderous rationale behind honor killings is part of a wider philosoph that links individual identities strongly with the collective identity of a social unit—an attitude which has been eliminated to a large extent by Western individualism. A term used in anthropology for this constellation is groupism, which refers to social givens of a particular kind (in which members of a social unit engage in joint activities and derive a sense of satisfaction from doing so) as well as an attitudinal and conceptual way of prioritizing certain forms of human existence. As a socially expressed inclination it refers to the collective ethos that accepts shared responsibility, which makes a member of the social unit co-responsible for other members and thrives on total solidarity through which a member partakes in the honor and shame of the whole group (which may overrule a person's individual or personal merit or deficiency to some extent). This social and spiritual intimacy produces a conjoined identity in which group members emphatically share in each others' identity and are subsumed under the identity of the social group. For an extremely individualistic identity formation, as is common in modern Western culture, it is difficult to empathize with this attitude, but, in fact, it is predominant in traditional societies and cultures. The failure of one member of the group to live up to the standards expected from the group, whether this be honorable and proper conduct, to uphold rules of morality and religiosity, becomes the burden of the whole social entity. The notion of "collective guilt" is deeply ingrained in traditional, tribal, and even more complex legal systems and persists in people's thinking even in modern Western society. In traditional societies such juridical notions of collectively shared identity (and thus also responsibility and culpability) resulted, and in some cases still do, in retribution directed at, and punishment being exacted from, any member of the group to which the miscreant belongs.[64] There is good reason to assume that such ideas are hardwired into the apperceptive ability of humans.[65] Modern jurisprudential reasoning has an uphill battle to set aside such notions.

The idea of collectivism makes it also incumbent on every member of the group to attempt to rectify a situation of moral failing of a group member. In extreme cases this involves the execution of the miscreant at the hand of the in-group. Discharging this responsibility may be considered to expunge the collective guilt. In the case of Islam, what appears to be most objectionable about this "reasoning"—from a Western perspective—is the draconian nature of punishing misconduct and the fact that a misconduct of the kind that would require a woman to be killed, when perpetrated by a man, is not punished in the same way. The fact that it is specifically the moral purity and sexual discretion of the women—and not of the men—that protects the group's collective capital of honor seems unjust. Searching for an answer, the reason may be found in that it has to do with "archetypal" conceptions of the value of the female procreative ability, which needs to be safeguarded in the interest of the whole group. (This aspect will be discussed later.)

Undertones of the strength of group identity, which takes precedence over individual identity and individual volition, have disappeared from Western society. Individuality is much less subjected to the collective good. In con-temporary non-Western societies, however, a collectivist consciousness has remained more intact—despite Western influences through globalization. A longing to belong to a group, rather than seeking meaning in the pursuit of individuality, can lead to some interesting and paradoxical phenomena. [66] Such differences in identity construction have led to devising alternative human rights declarations that place greater emphasis on the collective good over individual entitlement. [67] Awareness of the self is submerged in the collective identity and expected to defer to the greater good and greater need provided by family, clan, group, or state. This clearly has ramifications for the space provided for personal freedom. (In modern times the "groupism" as political ideology has tended to legitimate repressive state powers.) Thus the fundamental human dichotomy of individuality versus collectivism in iden-tity formation and its social consequences in the Asian and conservative Muslim self-understanding produces distinct answers, which are quite differ-ent from what modern Western awareness holds up as ideal.

The case of Muslim honor killing also represents the extreme end of the doctrinally required female duty of obedience: a woman owes obedience to the head of family in return for protection and sustenance. [68] The concept of obedience to the family's male figurehead includes not bringing shame on him as the representative of the social unit. It is important to preserve collec-tive honor by obeying customary religiously defined practices and maintain-ing absolute fidelity to the family head. Wrongdoing damages the collective honor, making it defensible and dutiful for the pater familias to inflict pun-ishment. This is another vital ingredient of Islamic ethics, whose insistence to subject one's whims to the common good of the group may be capable of being appreciated by the Western mind, if it were not for the specific condi-tions which in conservative Islamic perspective bring collective shame and therefore deserve the most severe penalty. Under ultraconservative family conditions the cause for severe punishment could be something as innocent as eye contact, speaking to a stranger and not maintaining a conspicuous reserve, failing to keep a cautious distance to infidels. Anecdotally at least any of these failings may provoke execution. (Exercising this traditional right in practice nowadays is challenged by state law even in the Islamic world, but often is treated with leniency, if not ignored altogether.) In a situation of conflict between ethical demands the pater familias' duty to care for and protect the females under his authority seems to be of lower priority in relation to maintaining the family's collective honor. This ranking, though not explicitly spelled out by doctrine, is certainly not specifically discouraged by it.

GENDERED SEXUALITY AND FEMALE MUTILATION

Female sexuality (as opposed to fecundity), universally taken for granted and in human history hardly ever the subject of benevolent religious attention,[69] has come into the focus of feminism in very recent years. This has accentuated certain aspects of Islam of which the West now believes that in this respect it distinguishes itself significantly from Islamic culture. A closer inspection, however, easily shows that there is considerable complexity involved in this issue defying a facile value judgment. Only ethnocentric naivety can turn this topic into one of simple, contrasting sexual values. Even nowadays in Western society the kind of eroticism, whether it is in so-called "good taste" or in "poor taste," that serves female interests is much more rare than that which caters to male inclinations. Women's liberation has resulted in a recognition that erotic tastes and imagery are highly gendered but has only insufficiently been translated into social life. In advertising and product promotion, for instance, this lack is blatantly obvious—despite the growing awareness that women constitute 50 percent of the market and have gained in financial independence. Although gradually the imbalance is being addressed by moving female sexuality into the focus of attention and removing cultural taboos on expressing eroticism in a manner pleasing to females, equality has not yet been achieved. Taboos surrounding female sexuality though are being dismantled[70] to the extent that by comparison I cannot think of a traditional society, not even so-called matrilineal ones, in which women by law as well as convention enjoy such cultural recognition of their sexuality. Matriarchy, uxori-locality (or matri-locality), matripotestality (authority exercised by mother and mother's-mother) are social mechanisms that grant to women important positions, but appear to have little effect on the power distribution in sexual relations or elevate sexual femininity to exalted cultural status. Machismo may not necessarily be a panhuman trait, but female sexual liberation certainly is not. Sex and power, beyond current erotic stereotypes, are ubiquitously and traditionally located in close embrace and chronically favor the male position.

As in so many other matters relating to human rights, it is Western society that has been pioneering in the matter of taking human sexuality out of the closet and strives towards gender equality in this matter. Feminism no doubt has been an ideological torchbearer, among other things by most loudly demanding that female needs be adequately addressed.

Insistence on female sexual rights and the right to reject male sexual domination are closely related to the possession of the freedom of choice manifest in the absolute right of refusal. It follows that the enforcement of sexual acts is not just ethically deplorable, and is not just to be labeled with the odious term rape, but is to be actively discouraged by punishing the offending party.[71] The redefinition of the concept of enforced sexual contact and tightening its juridical meaning led to the particularly controversial idea that this may include the right of rebuffing the husband and, if not heeded, enforced sexual acts could be considered rape and be treated as a crime. Taking the now prevailing Western perspective as benchmark, conservative Islam sticks out unpleasantly. While Islam frowns on rape, by definition it refers to coercion in matters of sex among persons outside marriage. Within marriage the concept of rape does not apply. A signal feature here is the sharia-based indisputable right of the husband to insist on his "conjugal right." This is not just a privilege that may be granted or withdrawn. Literally, it is considered a right enforceable even against a woman's express wishes. In fact a woman has no legally enshrined right of refusal. A woman has the right to refuse her husband only when she is menstruating, as then intercourse is expressly forbidden by the Quran (verse 2/222). The husband's refusal to accede in this case may even be taken as a reason for divorce. (This harks back to the universal belief that there is harmful potency in menstrual blood.) Under normal circumstances female recalcitrance can legitimately be punished with violence, as it falls under the rubric of female disobedience. The fact that the man has the right to use exactly this strategy—withdrawal from the marital bed—to punish his wife shows clearly Islam's highly gendered attitude to sexuality. As the Quran (4/34) prescribes how to deal with disobedient wives, when admonishing does not appear to help and before the last resort of physical punishment is applied, withdrawal of sexual interest in the offending woman is recommended. The possibility that a man's abstention from sexual demands may be a relief to the woman, does not seem to enter theological thinking.

Most Western juridical perspectives are agreed that a person's aggressive insistence on sexual contact, regardless of marital status, conceptually falls into the jurisdictional rubric of rape.[72] Depending on the particular jurisprudential provisions relating to nonconsensual sex between marriage partners, the offense extends into the area of domestic violence, or rape, or general violence. In any reading of such matters Western judicial systems nowadays tend to assume an unsympathetic stance towards the male perpetrator. ("Rape" by women of male minors, for instance, is both rare and usually not accompanied by violence and thus more readily subsumed under "seduction.")[73] Even in Western society this attitude is relatively new. Previously the wife's marital sexual duty was couched in the recommendation to "close your eyes and think of mother England." However, the advice not to resist was not suggested in law. When the "democratic" government of Afghanistan in 2009 introduced a law making it mandatory on women to accede to their husband's sexual desire, it came as a shock. The Western world was aghast. Voices were raised wondering whether such an administration was worth fighting for. This very act by the Afghan government, more than anything, in the eyes of some seemed to put in question the difference between the supposedly modern, enlightened administration and the Taleban.

Under a Western aesthetic regime this makes for a stunning contrast between male sexual license in marriage and the Islamic taboo on public displays of sexuality and any behavior even faintly akin to it, such as kissing, petting, embracing, sexually suggestive gestures, and "seductive" clothing. Unleashing male libido, legalizing its raw, unsublimated force and, on the other hand, its harsh, uncompromising restraint, breaches of which entail severe punishment, seem to sit uneasily side by side. (Marveling over this legal and aesthetic dichotomy seems to have given rise to a hypothesis on terrorism, as will be mentioned in the last chapter.)[74]

It does not take by surprise that in Western diasporic situations conservative Muslim viewpoints on male sexual prerogatives and female sexual submissiveness not infrequently clash with the host society's legal sensitivities. However, by all indications it is apparent that most cases of domestic rape remain hidden as very few Muslim women seek redress by applying to Western law enforcement. Out of shame and embarrassment, women usually keep quiet as much as from the knowledge that they would receive little sympathy or support from their community. Marital rape usually surfaces as a problem only when through media reporting the public's attention is drawn to the pronouncements of conservative imams who make female submissiveness in sexual matters mandatory and unconditional.

While rape within marriage is a notion unfamiliar to Islam, rape outside marriage is a very serious matter and in a conservative interpretation of the criminal law aspects of sharia is a crime worthy of the death penalty. Despite its seriousness, it is not always the offending male that pays the price. In actual practice the perpetrator frequently escapes legal consequences by claiming the victim had sent out ambiguous or seductive signals. If accepted by the judicial authority (if this be a formal court or a committee of village or tribal elders) as a valid defense, the consequences for the victim could be dire. Even if guilt and innocence is correctly established and the raped woman escapes the stigma of being a seductress or worse, a prostitute, she is considered to have lost her honor. She is usually considered to be unmarriageable and is often ostracized. Because of notions about the intertwinement of personal identities tightly woven into a collective entity, the whole family has been shamed and fearing to be collectively blemished by a severe stigma often victims and their families do not raise accusations.[75] In a few cases, the family even may resort to an "honor killing" to expunge the collective stain.

When approached from a different perspective, untinged by sinister considerations, it may be said that Islam treats human sexuality in a realiztic manner, namely, as the irrepressible force that it is. Being among the strongest and most basic instinctual behaviors freedom to express it requires to be finely balanced with restrictions to avoid what may be considered social damages. Thus chastity and modesty are emphasized as virtues, while sexual intimacy is reserved for marriage. Within the bounds of strict regulations, sexual gratification is considered a sadaqah, a gift or charity from God to be enjoyed (Quran 86/5–7, 2/223). Rather than bashfully denying its importance, Islam presents libido[76] as a God-given gift through which men and women are their mutual "garment" providing comfort for each other. Celibacy is rejected, as is masturbation, although overall the pleasure principle—for both sexes—is emphasized more strongly than the duty to procreate. (A strong hint that sexual intercourse ultimately should serve the purpose of procreation though is given by forbidding masturbation,[77] non-vaginal copulation,[78] and by discouraging homosexuality.)[79] Placing the manifested attitude towards matters sexual in the context of Islam's design plan to create the perfect society, one may surmise that its wisdom lies in the assumption that sexually fulfilled people make better and more committed members of the society, as long as sexuality does not lead to socially disruptive behavior.[80]

The sacred scriptures, in referring, in various contexts, to sexual matters in a fairly straight forward manner, do so in ways that place sexuality and male domination side by side. An indication of hierarchical thinking in gendered sexuality could be seen in that aspects of male sexual dominance are enshrined in the Quran, while female sexual interests can be found advocated only in the Sunna. Even though the Quran contains exhortations to men to treat their wives with dignity and respect, this is overbalanced with absolutist demands for female obedience and subjecting her will to a man's command. This, at least by implication, applies also to sexual matters. Logical contradictions that may emerge in real life between male dominance and the advocacy of female dignity are left unresolved, thus giving broad exegetical opportunity to support one side or the other. However, a power imbalance occurs when a man's sexual interests are presented as a conjugal right, but the pleasure aspect for women is referred to more in terms of a recommendation. Sahih Bukhari is perhaps the exception as he refers to a woman's sexual interest as a right. Addressing men in matters of sexuality he says, "And your wife has a right over you." Several ahadith do, in fact, refer to females' sexual needs and admonish men to take heed of them. For a man to just satisfy himself is doctrinally frowned upon. "It is rude to start sexual intercourse with the wife before foreplay." "When one of you copulates with his wife, let him not rush away from her, having attained his own climax, until she is satisfied." And "Let not any of you fall upon his wife in the manner a male animal suddenly jumps upon his female partner." On a positive note, one should realize that such utterances are akin to the recommendations of modern Western sexology and reveal a viewpoint, which historically has emerged and gained traction in Western society only relatively recently. Yet, from a critical standpoint, it seems that Islam is failing to achieve a doctrinal reconciliation between female preferences and male entitlement. It seems more to appeal to the noble nature of a devout man to accede to the wishes of his wife than to place restrictions on his conduct or to give unambiguous rights to her. As a feminist viewpoint would quickly point out, benign discretion and good will are commendable but arguably do not have the same binding powers as juridical prescriptions.

In the context of highlighting what appears to be female sexual subjugation, it is often pointed to the existence of khafd, female circumcision. (Extreme feminism also uses the epithet of symbolic assault.) This concept may comprise a range of different physical interventions such as introcision, cliterodectomy, and infibulation. Through pseudo-surgical interventions, a range of physical results may be achieved: partial or total removal of the clitoris or of the labia majores or minores, prepuce removal, and stitching together of the outer labia leaving only a narrow passage for urine and menstrual discharge, but preventing full penetration. In some regions (primarily in Africa, but to a lesser extent allegedly also in pockets in Southeast Asia) young girls and women, both Muslim and non-Muslim, are subjected to such painful "genital mutilation" of various kinds.[81] (This shows that this custom is fundamentally detached from Islamic belief and has acquired only the ambiguous tolerance Islam accords to some other pre-Islamic customs.) Operations, usually carried out by backyard practitioners and villagers with little or no medical training, sometimes have a lethal outcome and even when "successful," as credible sources maintain, inflict an inordinate amount of pain and negatively impact on female libido in later life. Pressure on girls to have the operation performed, ironically, is exerted by older women, who use their authority over the younger ones, and, by playing on gender solidarity, make sure this custom is kept alive. Social acceptance, the credit of being a "proper" woman, and marriageability are made out to be entirely dependent on this form of genital alteration. Despite its formal prohibition in law, for instance, in Egypt, it is rumored to be still widely practiced. In fact women's rights groups claim that the custom is on the rise again.[82] This would accord with the fundamentalization observed in other areas of culture.

Islam takes an indifferent position towards this custom, despite admonishing through ahadith that "man should not alter what God has created" (in reference to bodily characteristics).[83] While not advocating it, it condones it, admonishing only in a hadith, "Do not cut severely, as that is better for a woman and more desirable for a husband." It may be said that the same kind of indifference is shown towards female infanticide (wa'd) that appears to have been practiced in Arab society in pre-Islamic times.[84] The Quran in three passages (6/151; 16/58–59; 81/8–9) advises against it, but in a fairly low-key manner hinting at a diffuse divine displeasure. Again the transcendental blueprint of society, even where it is benign vis-à-vis women, does not come out strongly in support of rights (or what is regarded nowadays as such) for them.

The Islamically condoned artificial deformation of the female genitals routinely provokes revulsion in Western society—and also among many Muslims. It is overlooked that cliterodectomy was practiced in Europe in the nineteenth century to "cure" hysteria and habitual masturbation. The medical perspective on both issues has in the meantime fundamentally changed considering operative intervention as totally inappropriate. It must be food for thought, however, that research claims to have shown that cosmetic genital operations among Western women are on the increase. For example, the surgical narrowing of the vaginal passage is meant to enhance sexual pleasure. Other operations altering the appearance of genital organs (usually through labia reductions, but also the reduction of the clitoral hood) follows dominant aesthetic notions, current erotic regimes, and peer pressure. In effect this is not too dissimilar in motivation from customary pressures on Muslim women in some local cultures. In their case it is not solely a religious imperative, but also popular notions of what it means being desirable to men, pandering to their sexual pleasure, and obeying respected customs and aesthetics. In both cases social ideals and norm perceptions are the main drivers for this operation: conventional views of genital beauty, normality, and physical propriety exert domination over practicality and discomfort. Highly artificial notions determine what a desirable woman should look like below the waistline. Peer pressure is often more obvious than male dominance. It is women who exert peer pressure effectively and as far as Muslim practices are concerned, seem to be the more uncompromising defenders of the value of such interventions and the harshest critics of the resistance to it.

One can cast the comparative net even wider to include other bodily enhancements practiced in Western culture, such as breast enlargement, (or breast reductions), genital piercings, and hymen replacements. In all these cases the objectively achieved gain in beauty is highly debatable, and the payoff lies in social approval and peer admiration. Muslim women have been known to seek the help of Western surgeons to be reinfibulated in order to gain "sexual" attractiveness in their community or enhance their marriageability. Notions of social attractiveness through sexual aesthetics can be powerful motivators to accept pain, discomfort, and even diminution of sexual gratification. One difference between the Western and the Muslim practices may be that social sanctions for noncompliance (or failing the virgin test) may be more severe in the Muslims" case, and the motivation on the surface may tend more to compulsion than voluntary beautification. But underlying power relations between the genders are a different matter altogether. In principle, the responsibility for the perpetration of such deformatory (or restorative as in the case of hymenoplasty) interventions rests obviously with the dominant cultural notions, which are shared by men and women. Deformatory genital practices exist in many societies, giving them the tinge of a human universal.[85] To prove that they arose through the exercise of raw power by the opposite gender hinges on totally nonempirical assumptions. In effect this moves the argument into the territory of gender polemics and into current ideological discourses fashionable in the West.

In the feminist understanding female genital mutilation (FGM) is among the strongest and clearest expressions of male domination over female sexuality, an unmistakable sign of male power overruling female self-interest. More than that, for some it has become the hated symbol of universal oppression of women by maleness, a major signal of where human society has universally gone wrong. Some countries have specific anti-FGM laws, while in others, it falls under laws of assault and inflicting bodily harm.[86] This poses an interesting paradox for two reasons. One is juridical: prohibition of this operation contradicts mantras of religious and cultural freedom and violates the principle of gender equality as long as penis deformation for cultural and religious reasons is legal. The other reason is customary. Insofar as all kinds of vaginal alterations for cosmetic purposes (either for beautification or to enhance pleasure, for instance, through vaginal narrowing) are quite legal, where is the line to be drawn between which intervention is legal and which is not, and between custom and shared notions of genital beauty? In particular, one suspects, in the case of the FGM practiced by some Muslims, the operation is seen as a crass expression of male domination characteristic for this religion. This serves then as a rationale for Islamophobic sentiments and allows for the operation's legal suppression. Its absence in "enlightened" Western society, by contrast, is applauded then as an indicator of gender equality. As said before, this achromatic, black-and-white perspective ignores that previously FGM was used as a rational, scientifically respected medical intervention to cure (what was then regarded as) certain ailments and to restore normalcy. And more importantly, it is conveniently overlooked that today in Western society cosmetic alteration of the female sex organ is practiced (only in some cases for medical, curative purposes) and without entailing a social stigma.

There is a common basis underlying such practices: namely, socially accepted ideal images of beauty and desirability and perceptions of sexual normality, which in essence are highly artificial and culturally formed. Now, it may be argued that in one case the alteration of sex organs is based on free choice, while in the other the operation is brutally enforced without the victim's consent. (This of course is not always true. The great detractor of FGM, Ayaan Hirsi Ali, has written about cases where women have demanded to be infibulated so as to be acceptable in their community.) On the surface this sounds convincing, but underlying it and applying to both cultures are the pressures of socioculturally formulated values and notions of physical beauty and normality, beliefs of sexual hygiene, and conventions that exercise a coercive pull on individual motivations. To conceive this as mind control and brainwashing—and to see these women as helpless zombies, the victims of a gender struggle for power—not only sounds far-fetched, but in equal measure and in principle is applicable to all customary culture. Is the formation of human culture universally then highly susceptible to be determined by a gender struggle?

FGM assumes a somewhat different complexion if one considers it in a wider, universal context of body-altering customs. The gender-reverse side of this issue is that men in many cultures are subjected to equally "senseless," scurrilous and torturous interventions dictated by convention and tradition. Islam makes male circumcision mandatory, which is usually done at a relatively early age. It is not commanded by the Quran, but contained in the Sunna. Neonatal circumcision is also part of Judaism, but it is also practiced in some local Christian churches. Leaving aside whether it is actually a violation of human rights to perform the operation on minors, it is of dubious value also in other respects. The rational medical benefits of this operation (in a profilactic sense for the purposes of hygiene, avoiding the risk of infection, and protection against sexually transmitted diseases) are highly disputed (except in pathological cases where the prepuce may restrict urination or obviously cause other health problems). Yet it is among the most widespread customs in human society. Circumcision is traditionally mandated in several religions and cultures. In addition to this form of genital mutilation in some cultures there are additional physical operations mandatory in socialization. Some regional Australian Aboriginal religious systems augmented circumcision with subincision;[87] and there were other physical tortures inflicted usually in the course of youth initiation (such as chest scarification and producing decorative scars, extraction of teeth, piercing of body parts such as the nasal septum and ears, head biting, and other forms of exquisite cruelty), many of them resulting in permanent bodily deformation. Some of these interventions result in making the sex act somewhat less pleasurable or leave other lasting health problems similar to the ones experienced by women who have suffered severe forms of FGM. In Western society, parallel with female cosmetic operations, there is also a wide range of "beauty-enhancing" options available for men, from penis enlargement and piercing to horn implants on the head. To draw a parallel between penis mutilation and FGM, the question—at least in a rhetorical sense—arises whether the artificial deformation of the male sex organ, as well as other torturous procedure that are practiced in many traditional cultures, is amenable to the same explanation, namely, that they are the result of the sadistic power exercised by the opposite gender.

Let us leave this kind of polemical argument, fascinating as it may be. It is reflective of the gynocentric preoccupation of present-day West, which gives rise to such highly argumentative discourses. Setting aside the turbulence of ideologically inspired explanations of culture, it does have its uses to place both male and female genital alteration in a universal context. This custom can be seen as part of a universal syndrome of rites of passage[88] to mark a variety of social and physiological circumstances. Above all, they are signifiers of social maturity. Much of this sociocultural phenomenon is associated with bodily alterations and pseudo-surgical interventions, many of which are painful and to the modern mind appear to be no more than a deliberate torture.

A particular form of initiation rite has received the blessing of some forms of Middle Eastern monotheism, being seen there as a token of the covenant between the chosen and God.[89] Much could be said about this topic, but I shall confine myself to only a few comments. The vast majority of human societies have puberty rites, religious initiation rituals, and youth induction rites of some kind. In some societies such rites are based on the appearance of physiological phenomena, which signify the arrival of an individual at social maturity; in others social status depends more on procedures combined with religious tuition and induction into esoteric secrets. Revelatory education then is sealed and made visible by bodily deformations.[90] In some societies the process of familiarizing a person with esoteric contents, considered vital for the survival of the group, can take years as the individual climbs a religious hierarchy enhancing their personal status and increasing responsibility for the welfare of the group. Most of these procedures, leading to and marking the new status, in a rite of passage, involve physical operations: from hair cutting to penis splitting. Some tribal societies excelled in inflicting excruciating pain on the novices, perhaps as a symbolic sacrifice or to make them earn their new social status. Through my own fieldwork among Australian Aboriginal groups, I could still observe the results of such traditional customs and at several occasions could even participate in the requisite rituals and operations. (As mentioned before, Aborigines traditionally had various initiation operations, such as evulsion of incisor teeth, nose piercing, chest scarification, hair plucking, scalp biting, finger nail extraction, circumcision, subincision, and introcision. Several have ceased through the postcolonial reformulation and reconstitution of traditional culture. Others persist or have been reinstituted in the course of cultural revivalism.) Traditional initiation rights in some Papuan societies involved beating the neophytes with nettles and forcing them to eat dog feces—in comparison to which the drinking of human semen, which was ritually practiced by some Papuan groups, seems almost benign. The exquisite range of torture is seemingly endless. Not surprisingly, speculations in anthropology abound about the meaning of initiation: from Freud's interpretation of circumcision as symbolic—but nonetheless pretty graphic—emasculation,[91] fired up by the Oedipus complex, to sacrificial (sacrificing part of one's body for social status or bringing one's pain as a sacrificial offering) and other symbolic meanings (such as subincision of the opened-up and bleeding penis for instance being an imitation of female sexual and physiological phenomena,[92] drinking of semen to imbibe male strength and strengthen virility in an act of sympathetic magic), to perceptions of pure and deep-seated sadism as driving force. Whichever way such ritual procedures and mutilations may be rationalized by the practicing society, being aware of their existence puts a certain complexion on the FGM practiced by some Muslims.

The feminist assertion that female genital mutilation is a form of male aggression to subjugate and brutalize women can be considered to be in the same league as the Freudian hypothesis that male circumcision is a symbolic form of castration inflicted by the "archetypal" father on his sons.[93] Yet, at least superficially, such explanations make some sense of rather pointless, bizarre customs, which are so widespread as to nullify the view that they are nothing but random psychopathic aberrations. It is comforting to know that they at least have some symbolic meaning that lifts them from the quagmire of mental illness and the absurd behavior insanity can produce.

As a parting thought in this matter, one should consider the following situation: the desire to enhance and beautify one's appearance, of face as well as body, can take many forms. Its history is as old as humankind and even older than the existence of homo sapiens sapiens. (The use of cosmetics and ornaments such as red ochre, body paint, shell necklaces, etc., to improve one's appearance, according to some experts, goes back 250,000 to 300,000 years.)[94] Human history and culture can offer hundreds of examples of strategies of physical beautification, of "improving on God's creation." Islam is sparing in its approval of such tactics, exhorting believers to be thankful of God's natural gifts. Vanity is discouraged and its expression in the use of wigs, "nose jobs," breast enhancements, and the like, is strongly discouraged. However, makeup, or traditionally the use of kohl[95] (even for men) is widely considered acceptable.

The West has no such qualms and cosmetic enhancement is set no limits. Interestingly, among such beautification operations, one finds increasingly genital surgery to reshape and reaestheticize this area. Penises shaped to order and designer vaginas appear to be becoming fashionable.[96] By seeing labiaplasty and reshaping the sexual orifice in a wider, panhuman (if not species-typical) context, it is unnecessary to take recourse to the alleged "pornification" of modern Western culture, as some have argued (i.e., blaming the increased contact people have with pornographic imagery for the growing wish to have fashionable-looking genitalia). Nor is it necessary to blame it on the debilitating mental condition of body dysmorphic disorder. It seems rather expressive of an innate human tendency to direct excessive attention—beyond their functional reproductive importance—to the symbolic and aesthetic aspect of sexual organs. In this sense female circumcision is in the same rubric as modern, painless interventions for intimate surgical enhancement. This is not to underrate the question of freedom of choice: clearly the force of custom, tradition, and religious edict is different from the freedom to choose a bodily alteration—but in various ways such interventions express a deep-seated human fascination with sexuality, and enriching it with symbolic meaning.

HOMOSEXUALITY: A CONUNDRUM

Islam utterly condemns homosexuality (usually referred to as sodomy, al fahishah; Quran 29/28–29) as zina and fawahish (42/37), which interchangeably refers to illicit sex and worst sin. The Quran verse 7/81 spells out God's disgust: "Verily, you practice your lust on men instead of women." Exemplary divine judgment passed on homosexuality is mainly elucidated through the myth of Lot (Lut). It provides a salutary moral lesson through divine punishment of the debauchery rampant in the cities of Sodom and Gomorrah.[97] The strong doctrinal condemnation Islam expresses through the medium of mythology for this sexual orientation is by no means universally shared. While decriminalization of homosexuality, the acceptance of "gay culture," lifestyle and marriage is a growing trend in Western societies, signifying a mounting moral liberalization, some societies traditionally do not ostracize homosexuals and stigmatize homosexuality. Such societies do not consider homosexual practices as a waste of procreative potential and an abomination, nor as an unwelcome factor of disturbance in the basic, socially desirable mechanism of marital life.

   Today, only a very conservative interpretation of sharia insists still on punishing homosexuality with death. Traditionally, harsh views on this topic emanate mainly from the Hanbali school, while Hanafism takes a more liberal stance, yet still does not tolerate it and prescribes some form of punishment. Shi'a Iran is known to execute even minors convicted of homosexual activity by hanging.[98] This strict attitude hides a crass social paradox. Such harsh condemnation and punishment are handed out, despite the claim made by some that because of strict intergender avoidance, homosexuality among Muslim men is widespread and in some cases even institutionalized.[99] Not surprisingly, no statistics are available and one has to rely on intuitive and casual observations.

Islam is strong and unambiguous in its condemnation of homosexuality, bisexuality, and transgenderism—forms of sexuality that obscure God's creation of two genders. They constitute abominations as they diffuse and mix up clear gender boundaries. Homosexual prostitution and transsexuality for hire[100] may have been traditional and openly practiced in some Muslim regions, but can now only exist in the underground where pre-Islamic customs may persist. In particular, with the strengthening of fundamentalism they are bound sooner or later to become extinct as customary institutions. In Afghanistan in pre-Taleban days, I could observe young men taking the role of women—and wearing women's clothing as well as female makeup—in traditional dancing at certain festivities. (This is enforced by the conservative gender division, which forbids unrelated men and women celebrating together and women performing in front of men.) Whether this has greater depth and casts a diffuse light on culturally institutionalized homosexual inclinations or is just a variation of the trope of sexual teasing is open to interpretation. In any case, the Taleban regime of course was quick to forbid such lewd entertainment.[101]

The existence of homosexuality seems almost logical in Muslim society given that sexuality is considered a social and personal good, yet its fulfilment is not only confined to heterosexuality but also socially strictly limited to formal marriage. Casual sex, sexual experimentation, sexual adventurism, and "one-night-stands" among non-married adults (of different gender) are not only ethically discouraged but heavily penalized if they come to light. For men and women it means loss of honor, shame, diminished marriageability, danger of being considered a rapist, lashing, and even death (though it would appear that the degree and severity of punishment is also gender-differentiated). Illicit sexual activity, especially when associated with matrimonial infidelity, may even invoke the harshest form of punishment reserved for adultery: stoning. Prostitution, similarly, is subject to moral discouragement and interdiction on pain of severe punishment. An alternative form of libidinous release may become desirable under such circumstances—although this, too, is not without dangers. Usually labeled sodomy, homosexual activity, if not homosexual tendencies themselves, are subject to heavy penalties. Under Iranian jurisdiction, for instance, not only adultery but also homosexual activity is usually punished with death. Saudi Arabia and Sudan have this punishment at least in the statute books. The Taleban regime had demonstrably little sympathy for this activity and in more liberally minded Muslim countries it entails lengthy terms of imprisonment. The blossoming of "gay culture" and legalizing or at least decriminalizing male homosexuality and lesbianism in the West is widely derided by Muslims as proof of its decadence and moral decline.

The stigmatization of homosexuality is a curious feature. In classical civilizations at the time of Islam's emergence and also earlier on, bisexuality was not unusual and never perceived as a punishable perversion. Both Greeks and Romans passed no active moral judgment on carnal love among men and boys and even idealized it in covert form or passed it over considering it "pseudo-Platonic" in nature. (Pictorial representations of fellatio among men on Greek vases seem to have been an aesthetically acceptable image.) Whatever indifference or liberalism classical civilizations had for homosexuality, sexual puritanism that places the emphasis on the procreative role of sexuality was introduced as a divine law by monotheism. A heterosexual preference was also extant among the northern "barbarian" tribes in Europe. Their attitude was praised by Tacitus for its moral fortitude. However, one cannot be certain whether he had that on good evidence or used "poetic license" and made it up to use it to underscore his diatribe against Roman debauchery. (Absolute truthfulness was not a professional imperative for classical Roman historiography.) On the other hand, many tribal customs, if not manifestly homosexual, show elements of a sexual nature among men. Penis mutilation in youth-initiation ceremonies, ritual masturbation, ceremonial semen drinking, penis holding rituals, and the like, can quite plausibly be interpreted as phenomenologically containing aspects of homophilia, if not homosexuality.

Sami Zubaida, following Khaled El-Rouayhib's classification,[102] distinguishes homosexuality from homoeroticism. This distinction permits the denial of widespread homosexuality in Islamic culture. Traditionally, it was not uncommon for a man, who was also married to one or more women and who may also have had concubines, to maintain a sexual relationship with a "beardless boy." This was apparently not considered homosexual and, therefore, not in conflict with Islamic doctrine. The boy assumed the female, "penetrated" part of the relationship, thus, one might say, adding to the man's harem. It is clearly just sophistry not to classify this relationship as pederasty and its consummation homosexuality. Allegedly, in this relationship the ingredient of love was absent. One might infer, then, in the absence of the relevant emotion, it was no more than a reflex-like mechanical satisfaction of sexual urges—comparable to men using masturbation boards in some cultures. Pivoting this classificatory distinction between illicit homosexuality and homoeroticism on "love," its presence or absence, is a dubious enterprise. Islamic custom does not elevate "love" to such an exalted position in the relationship between man and woman as Western culture does. How could the concept of love play a crucial role in the sexual relationship between man and woman when marriage ideally and routinely was of the arranged type, where the sexual partners had no prior experience with each other, initially probably had little feeling for each other, and at least in the beginning presumably entered the marital bed to perform only a duty?

MARRIAGE, DIVORCE, AND A MOST MARVELOUS GIFT

At the basis of an ordered society, in the traditional view of Islam as well as in conservative Western viewpoints, is the controlled marriage and its product, the firm and stable family unit. Where nowadays in the West state law in the name of gender protection and liberalization of family composition intervenes, setting aside divine imperatives, it is feared that a catastrophic breakdown of the family structure will occur and ultimately damage the whole society. The conservative Muslim viewpoint in this matter agrees, and with more or less satisfaction, foresees the imminent disintegration of Western society, citing as evidence the erosion of family cohesion and the disappearance of the nuclear, heterosexual family structure. This is the vile nature of jahiliya breaking through and destroying the West from within. One of the first signs of this anticipated ruinous condition is the high divorce rate, and the emergence of a-traditional and "unnatural" family patterns (one parent families, same sex parenting, etc.), which are considered unwholesome and indicative of social pathology. The strictly monogamous, heterosexual unit in the West is increasingly being eroded not only by permissiveness and changing moral imperatives, but by alternative family structures, the secularized state legitimates in various ways. This development results in a loss of social esteem for the traditional family unit that previously had been looked at as the unquestioned and unshakable bastion of a strong, healthy society. Apocalyptic visions foretell the disappearance of the family as the "breeding unit" designed to perpetuate society and guarantee the future of national culture. Marriage is increasingly replaced by a notion of a partnership based on short-lived emotional mutuality, economic self-interestedness, and sexual gratification. In condemning modern trends affecting the family composition, conservative Islam, superficially seen, meets with conservative Christianity. While the latter denounces this as a slide into ungodliness and contrary to divine planning, the former sees it as just deserts for the West's mounting decadence and the return of jahiliya.

It is interesting that at present Iran, too, as variously reported in the press, seems to be getting increasingly concerned about the high and growing divorce rate among its citizenry. It is uncertain whether this has to do with an increase in the traditional concept of limited, contractual marriage mut'a, which is tolerated in Shi'ism but rejected by Sunnism, or is of a different kind.

While conservative Islam regards the West's apparent moral deterioration with quiet satisfaction, in the West the Islamic custom of polygamy comes under heavy criticism from both religious and secular positions. The gynocentric perspective, despite welcoming the softening of the traditionally rigid family structure in the West, regards the Islamic polygynous marriage arrangement as an insult to womanhood and as another testimony of Islam's oppressive androcracy. It is not only insulting that a man may legally have more than one wife (while the reverse is not possible), equally objectionable is the marital bond's flexibility and the apparent ease with which the man can dissolve it. Even Muslim women are reported to speak out about their unhappiness with polygyny.[103] In diasporic conditions, critics, more concerned about the pragmatics of the welfare society than religious ethics, scorn it specifically with regard to the millions of Muslims who have migrated to the West and now openly or by subterfuge seek legitimation of their polygamous family arrangements. If successful they will derive unfair pecuniary advantages, it is feared. Adding to the cacophony, Muslim voices have been raised, tentatively at first, about their human rights to adhere to their religiously sanctioned polygamy even in the Western diaspora. In some Western countries, Muslim organizations have asked that Islamic family and marriage laws be recognized. In response, some Western countries, which under a regime of multiculturalist policies try to accommodate to Islamic requirements, strain juridical flexibility to satisfy their Muslim minorities at least in matters of private law and family law. In this way Islamic marriage comes under critical scrutiny from several sides.

Islam stipulates a maximum number of four wives (Quran 4/3), even though the Prophet had a greater number of wives simultaneously. In his case, one may surmise it was predominantly for political reasons. His charismatic persona also demands a certain privileged exception. (Interestingly, modern cult leaders tend to justify their libidinal concupiscence by claiming special charismatic privileges. It is not unusual for this type of spiritual leader to have more than one wife or require the personal freedom of open promiscuity. Some practice multiple concubinate. Even when their cults are heavily drawing on Christian dogma, Christ's celibacy seems far less attractive.) In Islam the right to have multiple spouses is made dependent on the ability of proper maintenance of the women's requirements and to guarantee an emotional equity (Quran 4/3). Muslim sources make it clear that permission of polygamy was not only given to sanction a hallowed Arab custom, but also was originally sanctioned for practical reasons. The many deaths in battle in the original Muslim community necessitated an effective welfare system to look after the widows.

The idea of securing procreative potential must have been prominent at the early stages of the Muslim community's formation. In the small Muslim group, forced to fight for survival, there clearly arose the ethical need that widows be cared for, but also encouraged Muslims to focus on the procreative aspect of marrying women. Caring for widows had the practical dimension of recognizing the fact that many of them still possessed their socially valuable child-bearing potential.[104] Utilizing this physiological potential made practical sense.

Underlying many doctrinal regulations, there appears to be the motivation that family structure, stable marriage, and sexually productive family life have to be secured and fostered. Achieving this would be beneficial for the formation and maintenance of a strong, integrated, and vibrant community of believers. Islam's preoccupation with establishing a well-ordered, family-based society shows also in the thorough and numerous scriptural reflections on divorce, talaq (Quran 2/228–232, 236, 237, 241; 4/35; 65/1–7; etc.). Marital break-up multiplied many times can have a very disruptive effect on society as a whole. Even though many traditional societies allow a considerable fluidity in sexual unions, far from making it an indissoluble sacrament, other societies prefer more stable arrangements, placing greater emphasis on durability.

Exiting a legal marriage union in the Islamic scriptural traditions is described as hateful to God[105] but allowed. (In special cases it may even be prescribed.)[106] Rules around adultery do show a pro-family bias and the implicit value placed in stability. It is one of the capital crimes unequivocally punishable with death (willful homicide, apostasy, heresy, and blasphemy). Presumably reflecting a male bias extant in Arab society's legal perspectives of that time, it is customarily made much easier for male partners to dissolve a marriage than for wives. It can be done simply by repudiation—although Islamic law does make it more difficult than the Western stereotype holds. Rapidly uttering three times the formula "I divorce thee" does not satisfy the procedural requirements. Women are also given the right of initiating divorce, though they are not encouraged to do so. It is more difficult for them as they have to cite factual reasons (infidelity of husband, lack of financial support, cruelty, even lack of sexual interest, etc.) and may have to bring witnesses and adduce evidence. The point I am making here is that much attention is doctrinally given to the dissolution of a marriage. In a roundabout way this indicates the significance attributed to the stability of the family unit. By clearly defining the rightful manner of dissolving marriage and by prescribing an orderly process the separation can be achieved with minimal disruption. Equally important to this end is to regulate the splitting of the property and the financial settlement.

If sexuality contained in social relations is to be closely regulated, both entering into a union (with the subsequent legitimation of sexual conduct) and its dissolution have to occur in a lawful manner (to avoid protracted conflict). If a marriage constitutes a procreative unit, not only its beginning, to mark the lawful condition in which the marriage may be consummated, has to be signaled but also the cessation of sexual relationship has to be clearly terminated. In this way paternity with all its legal consequences (of property, inheritance, descent, name, etc.) is regulated. This leads to the requirement that a certain period has to elapse to show whether the woman to be divorced is with child before the responsibilities of the potential father are extinguished and the woman can entertain thoughts of remarriage.

Before divorce becomes legal and final, certain ritual requirements have to be met—some of them designed to encourage reconsidering the separation. Also the division of property and the division of wealth have to be settled. The dowry remains the property of the woman. The father usually retains financial responsibility for the offspring and the right of care. The rationale behind all this seems obvious: by following orderly process, obeying the clear and firm rules commanded by divine authority, festering disputes and wider social disruption can be avoided.

In looking at Islam's preferred marriage arrangements (arranged and enforced marriage, child marriage, child betrothal, etc.), an important question emerges. Is emotional suppression in partner choice and the absence of deep affection as the mainspring of marital choice an aberrant phenomenon—as it would seem from a modern Western perspective? Are marriage rules, as promoted by Islam, deeply injurious to natural human rights, a violation of personal liberty, and a foolish denial of human sentimental nature?

In achieving an ordered society, controlling female fecundity is a major cornerstone. Calculated and strictly regulated marriage arrangements, strategic partner choice by third parties, and controlled sexuality are important ingredients. Social prudence leaves little room for inordinate expressions of emotions, romanticism, and individual, whimsical freedom of choice. Order requires discipline, control, and even a certain measure of coercion—a constellation that all-too easily can degenerate to the treatment of women as chattel, in enforced betrothal and in underage marriage for strategic purposes that serve the interests of others. The scriptures, directly and indirectly, give tacit or open support to such "abuses," but are parsimonious, to say the least, in extolling the virtue of loving attraction and affection in partner choice. The Quran (30/21) does advocate peaceful and harmonious marital relationships as a preferred condition—although this is not to the exclusion of the de jure right under sharia law for the husband to enforce the "harmony." The exemplary marriage is squarely based on wifely obedience and submissiveness to male authority and reinforced with doctrinally sanctioned physical punishment.

Islamic unions, like traditional forms of arriving at matrimonial arrangements in other cultures, are not based on free and emotive choice. Romance and attraction through discovering love leading in due course to marriage is a trope iconisized in modern Western culture, popularized by films, and celebrated in novels. Its paramoucy in the Western emotional repertoire and especially as the most important factor in marriage partner selection historically is a very recent phenomenon. It has come to be considered the "normal" prelude to marriage (most recently not only for heterosexual unions). In the less romantic reality of universal mechanisms of pair bonding and formation of connubial-type unions arranged, enforced, controlled, and underage partnerships are overwhelmingly the norm. While in arranged marriages both partners may be excluded from the decision, the lack of choice generally affects women more often than men. Men are more readily granted some influence in partner selection than women, can initiate a marriage proposal (especially so when the prospective husband is much older than the bride or of higher social status), although the reverse (the marriage proposal emanating from the bride) may occur in some cultures. Bride abduction, either real or symbolic, is a strong expression of male discretion in the matter. In some regional customs brides are offered, given, and received to expunge debts or settle feuds, and betrothals may be made for financial or political advantage. These arrangements accentuate the image of women being commodities at the disposal of their family to be bartered and traded for gain. Islamic culture traditionally condones all forms of controlled marriage arrangements in preference to free choice of marriage partners. [107]

The grim reality is that in many traditional cultures the attempt to choose freely traditionally is punished severely, especially if this is in conflict with existing marriage rules, whatever these may have been (for instance, violating exogamy or endogamy rules, invoking the danger of incest, etc.). Again, in my experience, Australian Aboriginal society sticks out from among humanity by the complexity of its traditional marriage rules, their sinuous betrothal mechanisms, and by the cruelty through which offenses against these rules were punished. As in many tribal societies, the onslaught of colonial conquest has brought about changes, among them the hegemony-inspired romantic admiration for love and free partner choice.

Behind such moral considerations clothed in traditional social rules, there seems to lurk the universal brutal rationality that the men of the group are empowered to control the sexuality and fecundity of female group members for the common good. Every basic social unit—be it family, clan, tribe, or totemic group—in a society exercises some customary control over its women and their procreative capacity. Sigmund Freud [108] constructed around this theme an hypothesis on the origins of civilized society. (More appropriately, it may be called a narrative or a creation myth.) The beginnings of ordered human society, in his mind, lies in sexual discipline. Chaotic relations arising from immediate sexual gratification have to be eliminated by activating the Oedipus complex, deeply anchored in the human psyche. This happened in the Urhorde (the primordial horde—or should that be archetypal social construct?—at the beginning of hominid existence). By restraining the sex urge continuing parricide, anarchy and brutal sexual competition among the men is avoided. In order to stifle unbridled sexual urges, which threaten to destroy sociability, totemic arrangements are devised, whose function it is to construct "fake" kin relations. This makes in-group sexual relations illicit and

incestuous, thus freeing the group's women from in-group sexual demands.[109] Peaceful and ordered sociability has been established. Freud's
flight of imagination about how human society has come into existence can
be extended further to explain how marriage rules have arisen. Through
establishing the extended incest taboo, the women born into the group are
available now for strategic purposes. Sexually thwarted males of the original
human society now have a "bargaining chip" to compensate for their loss.
The women are preserved for outsiders to receive them in marriage. This
plays on another theme, hardwired into human beings: that of reciprocity.[110]
Giving women as "gifts" may be regarded as a commodification and, in a
Western perception, insulting to womanhood, but from a standpoint of societal "rationality," it activates in the receiving group a sense of their indebted-
ness and the perception of a need to reciprocate. Women being given and
received between social groups has the advantage of creating bonds and
cementing cooperation and loyalty. The force of reciprocity tends to create
bonds that lead to political alliances, sharing of resources, cooperation, joint
defense, and appropriate responses in terms of surrendering women in return—or at the very least secures some peace. Claude Levi-Strauss developed these basic ideas into an intriguing theory, which by an ingenious stroke
seemed to explain much of human social arrangements in creating social
bonds. The anthropologist Edward Tylor, before him, is credited with the
wise remark that "man can either marry out or die out." (The "sexist" wording may simply reflect the nineteenth century use or may have been a deliberate reference to the fact that males usually are the controlling agents in this
game.) That in clipped wording says that he recognized that practical survival value lies in forming sexual and marriage unions outside the group to
establish cooperative relationships with neighbours and outsiders. There is a
universal social rationality at work, which inspires people to give women to
others in marriage rather than for a group selfishly to keep them for itself and
thus isolating itself. Abstention from sexual consummation by the in-group is
important. Aided by the strength of the incest taboo, it preserves a precious
aspect of the gift: its virginity; or to phrase this argument in somewhat
distasteful clarity, it means preservation of a woman's pristine procreational
potential for outsiders to enjoy. To couch the idea even further in crude
material terms, it is easy to understand that a gift in "mint condition" is more
valuable than an already used one. Secondhand clothing, despite calling it
"pre-loved," for a good reason is much cheaper than brand-new stuff.

Europe's aristocracy, and especially royalty in centuries past, have espoused this universal trope of strategic marriage openly and spectacularly in
the service of raison d'etat. Using marriage quite blatantly as a device to
forge political alliances to secure the political advantage of the nation, to
enhance its powers, or for other pragmatic reasons, the political map was
constantly redrawn. Australian Aborigines created elaborate totemic systems

based on the implicit subliminal notion of reciprocity. By exogamous rules tabooing the women of clans and other social units, as well as avoidance relationships, rules of licit marriage, and so on, these systems served the ultimate purpose of freeing women from in-group sexual demands and thus allows them to be used as gifts that could be handed over to other social units for some benefit. To make this system work, individual choice has to be eliminated (by threatening to punish illicit dalliances, willful sexual inter-course, and technically "wrong" marriages with death). Such complex ar-rangements, backed by a strict "criminal law code" that punished violations of rules harshly, are able to create complex clusters of allied social units. Most importantly, they shared resources and were internally linked by tight mutuality and responsibilities. In this way resource security was vitally en-hanced with much improved chances of long-term survival for the social groups and for the individuals involved. This emotion-denying model of social rationality is clearly extensible to Arab society, which was not blessed with extremely favorable environmental conditions and, therefore, marriage had a vital strategic function to perform. Islam by insisting on a paternalistic and strictly marriage-controlled society offered a rational survival chance of a kind, which a society based on free choice may not have done.

The same practical rationality may also govern other social relations. Using women as gifts to forge alliances and cement loyalty between social groups regulates social interaction on a wider level and through complex exchange relations creates a more restrained sociability in which the unsubli-mated sex drive is no longer the prime mover of human action. To a certain extent women do have to be commodified to enable them to perform this vital function. On this basis it is conceivable why the Prophet thought that women were precious, a "mata," an asset more precious than perfume—though not as precious as prayer—and why his inspiration led to the strict control of sexual relations. Classical Arab society attracted by this social rationality developed a preference for cross-cousin marriage, which through lasting exchange relationships tends to link different patrilineally orientated clans whose members otherwise might remain hostile to each other.

This explanation seems to suggest that marriage customs ultimately are expressions of male power. Female sexuality and procreative potential ap-pear to be totally under the control of men: first of the men of the parental group, especially the father, the genitor or pater familias, who makes the decision and marries off a daughter. And later it is the husband and his in-group who exercise control over the woman and may even terminate the arrangement. Thus marriage appears to be clearly a social mechanism out-wardly expressing androcracy par excellence. What is overlooked in this interpretation is that such arrangements usually serve the interests of the whole kin group, both consanguinal and affinal. The advantages may be in terms of facilitating reconciliation between hostile groups, or avoiding violence, or by creating alliances enhancing mutual security, or bringing economic advantages from which all group members would benefit. Thus, rather than male domination, such arrangements can be seen more in the light of securing collective interests at the expense of sacrificing individual liberty. It is only in the light of cherished assumptions of personal freedom and the value of romantic love, a value so highly prized nowadays in Western society that arranged marriage systems (and especially underage marriage and so-called enforced marriage) seem repulsive and in contravention of basic human rights.

Women in societies with arranged marriage systems are often the strictest disciplinarians, supervising duties and enforcing ethical demands on younger female members of the family or group. It has been observed in various societies that older women, especially by their social functions, become "honorary men" by siding with what appear to be the interests of the men. Older female relatives often perform the circumcision on girls, supervise the performance of household chores, mete out punishment on behalf of the men, act as informers, and the like. They demand as much obedience of younger female kin group members as men expect generally from women. Gender solidarity seems to be an extremely rare occurrence. If cases in which the women of a group bandied together to oppose the pater familias have existed, I have yet to find them described in the ethnographic literature.

Some observers, in crass hyperbole, have spoken of women being used as chattel in the power games of men. Despite its sloganistic appeal, this sentiment ignores the fundamental social reasons lodged in the human condition. However, it ought to be recognized that such critical views emerge from the conditions in modern Western society, which has lost the ability to empathize with the social rationality that drives premodern societies. Social survival mechanisms relating to procreation, security, and alliance have retreated completely into the background. The strategic value of marriage has almost completely disappeared, retaining only a precarious toehold here and there in enclaves. It dwindles even in urban Muslim society, and when it appears in the Muslim diaspora, it only helps to revive Western prejudices against Islam.[111]

IS THE SHARIA MORAL?

Islam is a highly structured belief system with an incisively this-worldly agenda that is more concerned with social rules to determine the believer's actions (for the sake of creating the perfect society) than with the individual freedom to choose vague principles of morality as the pathway in life (which creates much uncertainty in the resulting sociability). Consequently, rules and regulations, prescribed social mechanisms, and the corresponding ethical demands surrounding marriage and sexuality arise from the intent, inscribed in Islam, of creating a smoothly functioning and vibrant society. These rules are meant to enable perfect sociability where otherwise, it is feared, selfish interest, gratification of instincts, and violence would reign supreme. Islam seeks to strike a perfect balance by hedging sexuality in tightly, without disavowing it, and regulating highly desirable procreation through controlled marriage.

Islamic gendered rules show very clearly a preoccupation with a well-ordered, family-based society, recognizing that unregulated gender relations driven by sexuality and given the "natures" of men and women make for a chaotic, inefficient, and ultimately weak society. Order is to be established by controlling sexuality and by regulating power relations. In the formative years of Islam and at the time of the original Muslim community, it must have been of eminent concern to create and accept rules (whether divinely inspired or not) that have a socially strengthening effect, rather than weakening the collectivity by emphasizing individual freedoms. Family, when accepted as the basic building block of a well-functioning society, has to be fostered in its cohesiveness so as to avoid disturbing stresses that undermine the whole society. It involves also a power theory that implicitly holds that by centralizing absolute authority within a family, a more cohesive unit is created. This presumption, in turn, rests on a perception of what the natural, raw conditions of the two genders are, which makes them quite different and makes one the natural authority. Left to themselves, the natural proclivities would militate against forming a cohesive, strong, integrated society.

Because of the perception of the gendered natural differences (female natural pliability and domesticity accentuating her child-rearing ability, and male strength, aggressiveness, and need for assertion), homosociality is a social solution that both overcomes and embraces such differences and itself is close to being "natural." Because of these differences the genders are to some extent kept separate in social life, and the areas in which the genders necessarily socially interact and overlap have to be governed by strong rules, which, however, do take natural proclivities into account.

The sharia shows two regulative tendencies: a theological and a social. One is to regulate the believers' relationship with the divine. This is done mainly by ritual precepts and a few transcendental speculations: prayer, fasting, pilgrimage, rules about blasphemy, and apostasy. Here the basic principle is a hierarchical one between God and humankind and an egalitarian relationship among people. Hence a frequent repetition in the scriptures of the mantra that men and women are equal before God. (Human differences logically pale into insignificance before the exaltedness of "the Almighty.") Some of the rules, other than being metaphysical speculations, also have additional social functions: communal prayer, the hardship of fasting for everybody at the same time, and the pilgrimage are apt to instill a sense of solidarity and contribute to a society's integration. Quite in the Durkheimian sense, ritual communality enhances and heightens not only a personal sense of the religious—giving a deep and personal experience of the numinous—but through being a shared experience establishes bonds among the participants. The joint physical act of prostration in rows of believers, shoulder to shoulder faintly touching each other in this way, through its physicality, is apt to establish a deeper bond than could be achieved by cerebral reflection on the common good and the advantages of cooperation.

The other main tendency of the sharia is clearly a socially regulative one. Among the five pillars of Islam, the demand for zakat (alms), although showing some ritualist features, very clearly has a social dimension. And then there are myriad rules, commands, and edicts relating to human social interaction—either by direct command or indirectly commanded, requiring exegesis and interpretation; and ranging from the very general—such as that gentleness in social relations is mandated[112]—to the very specific (e.g., that unripe dates may not be sold because it may lead to quarrel[113]). As is well known, the sharia directly or indirectly is capable of spanning the whole range of human sociality and experience.

Islamic gender relations and overt and implied notions of human sexuality throw up a host of ethical issues. Given the proposition that Islam and the sharia, being this-worldly in their orientation, are socio-regulative in their primary intent, one would logically expect that in such a system morality is subordinated to social reason. The question, whether Islam is more concerned with ontologically pragmatic issues or places greater emphasis on the provision of transcendental ethical rules regardless of their impact on socialization, hinges on several assumptions whose universalism is by no means assured. Most prominently, this assessment rests on whether the two options (whether normative functions are exercised to a greater extent by moral principles or by requirements of sociability) are mutually exclusive and are sufficiently disjunctive so that they can be seen in isolation from each other. In other words, is that which is considered ethical not always in one form or another useful to society in a practical sense in that the obedience to such norms—artificial as they may be—enhances social cohesion? For instance, scriptural Islam condemns, and acts with harshness against, "lewdness" (luwat) in any form—its definition totally rejects not only sodomy, but also pornography, exaggerated eroticism, and by further extension condemns contents that in Western culture would come under the rubric of art or would be tolerated as freedom of expression. The question arises: is that socially useful morality?

Basically, the question about ethics in Islam, and whether it can be credited with a high standard of morality, rests on a modern understanding of the parameters of ethicality. Benson and Stangroom, in their interesting book

Does God hate women?[114] point out that the Prophet is taken by Muslims to have set an example of ever-lasting validity and through his behavior to have set eternal standards of propriety and goodness. If he is seen then, for example, to have been highly gender-inegalitarian it makes him liable, when looked at through today's ethical prism, to be condemned as having acted unethically and thus having put his stamp of a rather pernicious kind on Islam per se. The authors provide an impressive example: the Prophet's marriage as a forty-something-old man to a nine-year-old girl. The fact that he has apparently consummated the marriage at that girl's age—she became his favorite wife Aisha—thus is to be labeled pedophilic.[115] There are other "sins" in today's Western terms that are commonly attributed to him. The views on women attributable to him—though clearly not misogynist or gynophobic—were certainly patriarchal in flavor, if not downright condescending. Several of the ahadith are infused with a bias of male superiority. Modernist Islamic interpretations willing to shoulder the burden of being dangerously close to heresy would claim that such attitudes and forms of behavior as espoused by the Prophet are simply culture and time specific, characteristic for classical Arab society, and do not represent divinely sanctioned behavior or divine inspiration. As a person, Muhammad was programmed by the ethic paradigms of his time and social environment, as well as operating under the constraint to propound a message that could be assimilated by his Arab compatriots. While radical in some respects, his message had to fit certain cultural and ideological parameters valid at the time and understood by this society—a common problem for all charismatic personages. A person making a claim to an extraordinary, charismatic status, and articulating a revolutionary message that is totally outside the comprehension, the value system, and ideological field of a society, has little chance of being accepted and succeeding in making a social impact. There has to be an affinity between the cultural matrix, socioeconomic conditions (Realinteressen), basic cognitive and moral paradigms extant in the society, and the articulated ideology, ethics and social program. If no such affinity between the charismatic pretension and the sociocultural conditions exists, the prophet's or charismatic pretender's efforts have no chance to resonate with their society.

The Prophet Muhammad may have been infused with a sense of humaneness, a basic goodness and compassion in trying to lift the status of women from ambiguity to benign firmness in divine law. But could he have been more radical by insisting on total gender equality, on abolishing slavery and betrothal of underage girls, and the like? Had he attempted to do that, his message would have run the risk of being refused as too bizarre. Rather than issuing strict prohibitionary edicts or articulate an unambiguous condemnation, he admonished that female genital mutilation should not be too incisive, that slave women be treated with a modicum of kindness, that female infanticide should not be practiced. However, citing culture specificity as responsible for the specific forms of religious doctrine, to the conservative mind subtracts from the message's divine value and infuses it with an ingredient of utility that denies, or at least undermines, the autonomy, eternal validity, and authenticity of the revelation. In this vein, when Tariq Ramadan proposes that a modern version of Islamic doctrine—and moral instruction as part of it—should be distilled from the essence of scriptural literality, he is crossing swords with conservatism.

Moral relativity is applicable in several ways. Benson and Stangroom, like most harsh critics of Islam, apply today's ethical instrumentary in judging, and condemning, the Prophet's exemplarism[116] and, by extension, the moral acceptability of Islam as a whole. Doing so seems justified to them as the patterns established by the Prophet and by his message are considered to have binding and timeless validity. However, this argument relies on an ethical instrumentary that is of very recent provenance. It is of doubtful value in applying it retrospectively to times long past. In history writing this is a recurring problem: it is all too tempting to judge past ideas, actions and behavior by the moral standards of today as if these were of eternal value and immutable relevance. Are there eternal ethical principles that justify this kind of judgment? Radical feminism seems to think so when it comes to gender issues. This stance is corroborated by the existence of a universal human rights charter. Befitting its sweeping globalized status, it has self-aggrandizing tendencies in implicitly claiming that the views, standards, criteria, and regulations propounded in it have eternal validity. Its laudable ethical spirit seems to overlook that, like all legislation, it has a limited shelf-life. Despite universalist aspirations, its eventual redundancy is already pre-determined. A judgmental assessment of its ethical and juridical merits a few hundred years from now would no doubt consider it remarkable in its shortcomings; perhaps infused with good intentions, but lacking in legal sophistication and certainly deficient in addressing the pressing issues of the day.

Accepting that there are no truly eternistic cosmic ethics in existence[117] —or if they are, they are not recognizable by humans in an empirical manner—it leads to the question: is it justified that religious law claims that its ethical standards, its morality principles, are of eternal and cosmic validity, and, therefore, its juridical regulations are unchanging and everlasting? Regardless of how one may want to answer this question, it always remains a question for some of humankind. Certainly Islam tends to singularize the two, melding law and ethics, and considering one identical with the other.

Is judgment of religious traditions, their ethics and regulations, practically necessary in a globalized world? It obviously runs counter to cultural relativism and a newfound tolerance of cultural Otherness—but the latter is a luxury increasingly pressed into the defensive as the need mounts to share an ever-shrinking planet, and by the enforced interpenetration and cohabitation of societies through commerce, strategic militarism, migration, communication, and environmental crises. Thus the need arises for commonly agreed-upon and respected rules and ethical norms regulating human interaction and behavior without significant exceptions.

WHAT SHOULD MUSLIM WOMEN DO?

On the question of gendered freedom of choice, defenders of the Islamic gender relations have pointed out that Western modernity for women conveys simply the freedom of seduction, the right to choose to be a sex object, and to expose oneself to sexual harassment. Though provoking it in the first place, women then are forced to find cunning ways to avoid the pitfalls of falling victim to male sexual predation. Islam and its gender rules offer protection as the higher public good than the freedom in which natural gender proclivities can openly and aggressively be expressed.

In particular in non-Muslim, Western perception, the social status of Muslim women seems very dubious and the public appearance of Muslim women becomes a highly contested topic. Concern with only dimly comprehended symbolisms often exceeds understanding of substantive issues. Politics of the veil, because of its signal effect, are often more eye-catching and are given more attention than issues of real disadvantage for Muslim women (such as the absence of active and passive vote in some Muslim countries or Saudi women not being allowed to drive cars). Indeed, the image of the veil has become a negative cliché exploited by detractors of Islam when more significant issues slumber unattended. In fact one may suspect that such sartorial issues are serving as a smoke screen for other problems. What are the underlying issues defining these clashing images of Western modernity and Islamic tradition? When in France (since April 2011) Muslimas dressing in facial veils get arrested and fined 150 Euros under a policy that claims to strike a blow for women's equality; it is widely speculated that the real reason is for the governing party to curry favor with right-leaning voters and thus lure them away from the anti-immigration and anti-Muslim Front National. Only a few hundred women—at the most two thousand by some accounts—are reportedly wearing a burqa or niqab, out of a Muslim population of up to 6 million. What is anthropologically of particular interest in this matter is the fact that a largely symbolic gesture may be a tactic of strategic importance: it can potentially have a wide-ranging political effect and is calculated to do so. However, on a philosophical level it is disputable that the freedom of Muslim women does vitally hinge on whether they hide their faces. One wonders where the difference in freedom lies between being beholden to a tradition, or perhaps to a supposed religious edict, that dictates that one's face be hidden, or being coerced by law under threat of a fine to reveal it. (This is perhaps even more glaring in the case of converts, making use of civil liberty by freely choosing to embrace Islam and its strictest form of dress, but then being forced by law to abandon the religious rules they have chosen to obey.) Inherent in this is the fundamental paradox that proscribing freedom of choice in matters sartorial is supposed to enhance freedom in general. It may be expected that the European Human Rights Court will shortly be busied with this oxymoron.

It needs to be emphasized again: sartorial issues lie only at the surface of much deeper issues. As the democratization movement sweeping through the Arabic world in 2011 shows, female participation in the protests is welcomed but does not easily translate into lasting political gains of gender equality in sociopolitical matters. Afghanistan has shown similar mixed results. Surely, such developments are of infinitely greater concern.

The French and Belgian problem is no more than a sideshow in comparison to the issues facing Muslim women on a global level. What preoccupies Muslim women as they form their identities and structure their lives as professionals and citizens of modern nations in an increasingly transnational age? Is it possible to even discuss "women and Islam" without evoking clichés, defensiveness, Occidentalism, vested ossified interests, and ideological disputation? What road should women choose in societies suspended between a traditional Islamic order and a Western world that simultaneously attracts, repels, and intrigues? Are the women who try to be heard in their societies and in the world really representative? The debate may be elitist, involving only the better-educated women, and by shutting out the views of the less educated may inexorably slant whatever consensus may be reached.

Often, Muslim women's organizations—such as SIS (Sisters in Islam) and WLUML (Women Living under Muslim Laws)—are exposed to the critique that they have a Western influenced ideological agenda that is anti-Islamic and designed to attack Islam from within. A book[118] published in 2005 by SIS, shortly afterwards, in 2008, was banned by the Malaysian government. The Home Ministry had charged the publication of eight essays with undermining people's faith and disrupting public order. According to a letter from the ministry to SIS, the book went too far, among other things, in questioning whether Islamic family laws discriminate against women in issues of polygamy and divorce. In 2010 the Malaysian High Court, however, ruled that the book did not pose a threat and its distribution was allowed. This event clearly shows that Islamic conservatism can be as problematic, if not more so, to women's interests than Western non-comprehension, ideological meddling, and sneering condescension.

Contemporary conversations about women and Islam are marked by deep polarization, intellectual acrimony, and competing agendas. The subject seems almost immediately to generate Western accusations and Muslim apologetics, if not counter-accusations about the West's decadence and immorality. With the formation of vibrant transnational networks among Muslim women, from diverse locales and espousing different worldviews, new and more authentic conversations are emerging. These women, despite their sociological, cultural, and ideological diversity, espouse new forms of meaning of religious femininity, gender solidarity, and belonging. Their aspirations may not yet have become mainstream, yet their conversations and affinities may overcome in practical reality the severest dissonance between Western secular views and conservative Islamic doctrinal imperatives.[119]

In the face of polarization of positions and the absence of Muslim unity through external pressures and internal disagreement, increasing numbers of Muslim women are uniting in organizations to explore their social position and to engage in feminist transnational dialogue. The increasing ability to cross boundaries transnationally so as to engage in exploratory debate in itself is a mark of mounting liberalization. However, recognizing one's marginal status in society is still a long way from empowering oneself. Amidst the din of geopolitical and religiocultural conflict the women's voices are not clearly heard, and most often ignored in their own society or countered with threats. As these opinion- and meaning-making women claim, the reality is that female self-empowerment works only with glacial speed and Muslim women, although they represent 50 percent of Muslimhood, are still an undervalued, often precarious "minority."

NOTES

1. According to the Quran 24/2 both men and women should suffer the same punishment. However, it seems more often than not only the woman of an offending couple is subjected to this harsh treatment. Adultery is not only committed in an illicit relationship between men and women who are married (not to each other) at the time of the "crime," but is also committed when either or both have been married before. Only persons who have never been married escape the draconian punishment of stoning and are to be flogged instead (according to the Quran with one hundred lashings).

2. This prohibition is not a law, but a religious edict. Religiously sanctioned moral standards are enforceable by the religious police beyond the letter of the law.

3. Poulter, "Multiculturalism and Human Rights for Muslim Families in English Law." In *God's Law versus State Law*, M. King (ed.). London: Grey Seal, 1995; p. 84.

4. Hassan, "Rights of Women within Islamic Communities." In *Religious Human Rights in Global Perspectives*, J.Witte and J. van der Vyvwer (eds.). The Hague: Nijhoff, 1996.

5. Riffat Hassan, "Rights of Women. . . ." ; pp. 380–381.

6. Robert Hoyland, *Arabia and the Arabs: From the Bronze Age to the Coming of Islam.* London, New York: Routledge, 2001; pp. 129–134.

7. Riffat Hassan, "Rights of Women . . . " ; p. 368.

8. Lila Abu-Lughod, Do Muslim Women Really Need Saving?, *American Anthropologist* 104/3 (2002): 783–790.

9. Afghan President Hamid Karzai seems to have a clearer notion of the reason why Americans are fighting. "They are here for their own purposes," he said, "and they're using our soil for that." Fighting for ten years was not for some quixotic quest to raise the status of Afghan women.

10. To further speculate on the symbolic fascination with the mysterious female facial beauty is tempting and may lead to the contention that, deeply buried in the subconscious, it underlies the urge to unveil the hidden faces of Muslimas in niqab. Equally, the emphatically faceless appearance of the Venus of Willendorf can lead one into an extended speculative discourse on the semiotic qualities of such ancient representations that seem to indicate the exact opposite to the facial cult surrounding the Mona Lisa.

11. *The Making of Great Men: Male Domination and Power Among the New Guinea Baruya*. New York, Cambridge: Cambridge University Press, 1986 (French orig. 1982).

12. In Antonio Gramsci's *The Prison Notebooks* (various editions) such analytical viewpoints are anticipated.

13. There is a considerable body of anthropological literature on this topic. Maurice Bloch, "The Political Implications of Religious Experience." In *Symbolic Textures: Studies in Cultural Meaning*, G. Aijmer (ed.). Göteborg: Acta Universitatis Gothoburgensis, 1987; Jürgen Habermas, *Technik und Wissenschaft als "ideologie."* Frankfurt a.M.: Suhrkamp, 1969; Roger Keesing, "Creating the Past: Custom and Identity in the Contemporary Pacific." *The Contemporary Pacific* 1/1-2 (1989):19–42; esp. p. 23; Allan Hanson, "The Making of the Maori: Culture Invention and Its Logic." *American Anthropologist* 91/4 (1989): 890–902.

14. See Jürgen Habermas, *Technik und Wissenschaft.* . . .

15. See, e.g., Fatima Mernissi's various writings, Irshad Manji (*The Trouble with Islam Today*), Hirsi Ayaan Ali (*The Caged Virgin, Infidel*), Amina Wadud's literary output; and in the German language area, Seyran Ates (*Der Multi-Kulti-Irrtum.* Berlin: Ullstein, 2007, 3rd ed.), innumerable blog sites, Muslim feminist organizations, and so forth.

16. Her name is variously spelled as Fatema, Fatimah, and so on. She has published several books (e.g., *Beyond the Veil, Women and Islam*, etc.) dealing with and critiquing gender relations and the position of women in Muslim society. See Raja Rhouni, *Secular and Islamic Feminist Critiques in the Work of Fatima Mernissi*. Leiden: Brill, 2010 (ebook).

17. Mernissi, *Beyond the Veil*. Cambridge: Cambridge University Press, 1975; p. 103.

18. Most strongly in her book *Le Harem Politique; The Political Harem*. The edition referred to here is the translation into the German: Fatema Mernissi, *Der politische Harem*. Freiburg, Basel, Wien: Herder, 1992.

19. Fatema Mernissi, *Der politische Harem*; pp. 188–193, 206–214.

20. This does not only apply to married persons, but also to those who had previously been married. Only persons who have never been married escape the death penalty, but are to be punished by whipping.

21. Allegedly Iran not infrequently sentences women to stoning for adultery and prostitution. But usually the execution is deferred and in any case the rest of the world usually remains ignorant. As someone pointed out to me, it is a sign of Islamic justice's gender equality that female criminals are treated with the same harshness as males, but only females attract so much attention in the West.

22. Summarized in the Cairo Declaration of Human Rights in Islam, 1990.

23. Ophelia Benson and Jeremy Stangroom, *Does God Hate Women?* London, New York: Continuum, 2009; p. 115.

24. There is also the nurture school of thought, which argues that differences between the genders are not hard-wired at birth but are the result of later training, expectations, and experiences. However, physiologically and anatomically at least there can be no dispute.

25. Muhammad Abdul-Rauf, *The Islamic View of Women and Family*. New York: Speller and Sons, 1977.

26. Francesca Merlan, "Gender in Aboriginal Social Life." In *Social Anthropology and Australian Aboriginal Studies*. Canberra: Aboriginal Studies Press, 1988.

27. This question is also closely associated with the dominant ideology theory derived from Karl Marx's sociology: how ideological dominance can be maintained against observational reason. See, e.g., Nicholas Abercrombie, Stephen Hill, and Bryan Turner, *The Dominant Ideology Thesis*. London, Boston: Allen & Unwin, 1980.

28. Rare exceptions tend to come from Muslim researchers. For instance, Lila Abu-Lughod, *Veiled Sentiments: Honor and Poetry in a Bedouin Society*. Berkeley: University of California Press, 1986.

29. For instance, Michel Foucault, *Power/Knowledge*. Brighton: Harvester Press, 1980.

30. It may be well to bear in mind that gender segregation in churches was not unusual in the past and is still practiced in some rural areas and in some fundamentalist congregations. The rationale given also may be based around sexual distraction.

31. See, e.g., Quran 2/222.

32. The gender dichotomy does not necessarily result in a dread of pollution through female physiology. As in Yin and Yang, for instance, it can be conceived in ways that emphasize different attributes of the male-female division and yet imply a hostile and dangerous oppositionality between male and female principle.

33. See, e.g., Mary Douglas, *Purity and Danger: Analyzis of the Concepts of Pollution and Taboo*. London: Routledge & Kegan, 1966.

34. The connex of the dichotomy sacred and profane with that of masculine and feminine has already been pointed out by Emile Durkheim many years ago.

35. Fatema Mernissi, *Der politische Harem*; p. 101. According to her, these were pre-Islamic sentiments. But as she also hints at the existence of pre-Islamic matriarchal and matrilineal features in Arab society, the concept of excessively strong female pollution does not sit well. It is possible, but unlikely.

36. Mernissi (*Der politische Harem*; p. 95) argues that this hadith is based on a misunderstanding.

37. References here are to the edition Fatema Mernissi, *Der politische Harem*; esp. pp. 67–84.

38. Tracing of ahadith by checking the credibility and succession of sources back to their origin.

39. Literature on the speculative historical circumstances in which revelations were received and sayings were formulated.

40. The chronology is somewhat confusing. If this opinion was uttered following the battle at Basra (the "battle of the camel" in 657 AD) in which the losing party was led by Aisha, the Prophet's widow, it could not have been uttered by Muhammad (who died in 632 AD). However, there are also other interpretations and sources making the origins highly debatable.

41. This is a slightly different translation from the one used before, which makes the assertion that women are unsuitable for leadership roles more explicit.

42. This theme has been taken up by Fatima Mernissi, *The Forgotten Queens of Islam.* Cambridge: Polity Press, 1993.

43. Quran 27/23–44. Although the Queen of Sheba starts out as a non-Muslim, she later converts (ayat 44). What later became the Islamic core region is replete with female characters of considerable political stature: from Cleopatra to Carthage's mythical queen Dido, and Palmyra's queen Zenobia (or Bat-Zabbai) who in the third century led her people in revolt against Rome. The later Islamic period also has sultanas and other leading female figures.

44. *Der politische Harem*; esp. p. 218.

45. Fatima Mernissi advances the theory that in classical times women could still hold influential positions in society as sultanas and malikas, and hold secular power (mulk), but this ability has disappeared over the history of Islam. See her book *The Forgotten Queens of Islam*.

46. The right of women to give valid testimony in a court of law in European judicial systems was patchy at best until very recent times. Especially canonical law tended to dismiss woman as unreliable and untrustworthy, tainted by the role of temptress and seductor of the Old Testament.

47. Johann Jakob Bachofen, *Das Mutterrecht* (orig. 1861, various editions and translations).

48. Apparent ignorance of the importance of insemination among Australian Aborigines has been the object of heated argument at one time. See Edmund Leach, "Virgin Birth." In *Genesis as Myth and Other Essays*. London: Cape, 1969.

49. For example there is a type of mythology among Australian Aborigines that ascribes social and religious predominance in precontemporary society to women. The original conditions of female dominance were eventually reversed by men outsmarting the women. There is no archaeological evidence that this reflects an actual diachronic chronology.

50. Joel Kahn, *Constituting the Minangkabau: Peasants, Culture, and Modernity in Colonial Indonesia*. Oxford, Providence: Berg, 1993. Inheritance of name and property occurs matrilineally; the matriarch controls land, property, and family matters. Young men have to go elsewhere to make their fortune before they are allowed to return and marry.

51. Described by Peter Madsen, "Rebellious Women—Discourses and Texts." In *Shari'a as Discourse*, J. Nielsen and L. Christoffersen (eds.). Farnham: Ashgate, 2010; pp. 226–231.

52. Lynn Welchman (ed.), *Women's Rights and Islamic Family Law: Perspectives on Reform*. London, New York: Zed Books, 2004; p. 239.

53. As mentioned before, there is a certain contradiction in the Sunna as Mernissi (*Der politische Harem;* p. 218) analyzes it. The Prophet's women who are acknowledged by Muslims as examples seem to have participated in the political discourse and even physically took part in the community's political life.

54. I am referring here to the published work of Nurcholish Madjid and interviews I had with Harun Nasution in Indonesia. So-called Neo-Modernist Islam in Indonesia may be considered on the cutting edge of the endeavour of "modernizing" Islam.

55. The English translation of the official Saudi version in a footnote remarks, "Have intercourse with your wife in any manner as long as it is in the vagina and not in the anus."

56. While homosexuality allegedly is widely practiced in the Islamic world (presumably) due to the strict gender separation and the legal unavailability of women outside marriage, the doctrinal position (not only in Islam) is that homosexuality is a sin, luwat, zina (sodomy), and in "Biblical" times led to the divine destruction of Lot's people.

57. According to Welchman, *Women's Rights and Islamic Family Law;* p.236.

58. Welchman, *Women's Rights and Islamic Family Law*; p. 237.

59. Welchman, *Women's Rights and Islamic Family Law;* p. 241.

60. It is impossible to say whether this is a vicious rumor designed to slander the Taleban or has a basis in fact.

61. Unsubstantiated rumors make claims of this kind under diasporic conditions.

62. Lila Abu-Lughod, *Veiled Sentiments*; p. 95.

63. Gabriele Marranci, *The Anthropology of Islam*. Oxford, New York: Berg, 2008; pp. 129–131.

64. The concept of vendetta, blood revenge, practiced in many societies (and criminal organizations) even today is based on this principle. A plethora of superstitions and prejudices, even in modern Western society, have come about on the basis of implied, barely conscious notions of collective guilt.

65. In other words, in the cognitive process of internalising the external world, the formation of classificatory schemes based on generalizations is necessary for ease and speed of apperception (to wit, recognizing and ordering the phenomena of the world to allow efficient responses and to do so with speed). This process shows a tendency to link the categorization with issues of causality (as in homeopathic thinking, which assumes that the members of a classificatory category share a causal intimacy that extends into the area of co-responsibility.) Translated into the realm of human society, through categorization of social units individual members are seen and treated not only as alike, but in some respects as the same.

66. For example, large amateur choirs in Japan singing Beethoven's "Ode to Joy" for the sake of collective harmony. See Eddie Chang, Ode to "Personal Challenge": Reconsidering Japanese groupism. In *Identity in Crossroad Civilizations: Ethnicity, Nationalism and Globalism in Asia*, E. Kolig, V. Angeles, and S. Wong (eds.). Amsterdam: Amsterdam University Press, 2009.

67. Elena Asciutti, "Asia and the Global World: Identities, Values, Rights." In *Identity in Crossroad Civilizations* . . . E. Kolig, V. Angeles, and S. Wong (eds.). Amsterdam: Amsterdam University Press, 2009.

68. According to Lynn Welchman (*Women's Rights and Islamic Family Law;* p. 244) the aya 4/34 referring to this duty has a complex origin.

69. The assertion that the female "Venus" figurines of Europe (and other female representations of the Near East) dating back to Meso– and Neolithic times represent some form of veneration of female fecundity and reproductive ability, or in a wider sense signify a recognition of the sexual nature of femininity, is just extremely speculative.

70. The "cougar" syndrome, for instance, is beginning to catch up with the "sugar daddy" phenomenon as a sociological topic.

71. Serial rape has been recognized as a vicious war strategy and is considered a war crime by the Human Rights Court.

72. I do not go into definitial details as to whether rape means enforced penetration or in a wider sense violation of a woman's sexual integrity. When the reporter Lara Lohan claimed she had been "gang raped" at Cairo's Tahrir square during the democratization demonstrations on February 11, 2011, it appears she was not referring to penetration by male sex organs, but rather to a sexually motivated physical assault.

73. Rape carried out by females on males in some cultures has ritual undertones and is carried out traditionally at certain times in which social norms are inverted.

74. To the structuralistically inclined mind this leads into a series of antinomies, such as male power sexually expressed versus female sexual submissiveness, public versus private spheres to which different laws and aesthetics apply, and the like.

75. It has been widely claimed that during the Balkan wars in the 1990s, captured Bosnian Muslim women were serially raped by Serbs because the perpetrators were aware of the severe social consequences for the victims in their own communities. Following these atrocities the Human Rights arm of the UN declared these rapes a "war crime."

76. I am deliberately using Sigmund Freud's terminology as a reminder that elevating it to centrality in his psychoanalytical insights brought him in direct conflict with the Catholic hierarchy of his time. Conservative Christianity by comparison has a more circumspect approach to human sexuality.

77. Although it is not mentioned in the Quran, both Sunni and Shi'a madhahib reject it more or less strongly.

78. Quran 2/223.

79. Called lewd acts (4/16) that are sinful and should be punished. But if the persons involved repent, they should be left alone.

80. Prostitution may be sexually gratifying, but has the potential to be socially disruptive and is discouraged (Quran 24/3). It is forbidden in the Bukhari ahadith.

81. In the literature often the acronym FGM (female genital mutilation) is used and terminologically expresses disapproval.

82. See, e.g., Hoda Rouhana (ed.), "Women Living under Muslim Laws (WLUML) Network's Understanding of Religious Fundamentalism." In *Muslim Women and the Challenge of Islamic Extremism*, N. Othman (ed.). Selangor, Malaysia: Sisters in Islam, 2005; p. 183.

83. Alfred Guillaume, *The Traditions of Islam: An Introduction to the Study of the Hadith Literature*. Beirut: Khayats, 1966; p. 130. This seems to refer more to the beautification of bodily features and nowadays is applied to cosmetic surgery. Khafd does not seem to fall in this rubric.

84. Quran 6/151, 16/58–59, 42/49–50, 81/8–9 refers to it. While this custom most likely has to do with low esteem for female children, verse 6/151 mentions poverty as a reason. Mernissi, *Der politische Harem*; p. 255 doubts that infanticide was connected with ideas of female inferiority. It was rather meant as a sacrifice and forbidden by the Prophet in the course of suppressing polytheism. This explanation that perceives a ritual value in killing female babies, possibly for the sake of appeasing female deities, seems unlikely in the light of the fact that other societies with patrilineal and androcratic patterns also condoned the killing of female babies and expressed preference for male babies in various ways. Certainly, Islamic custom today places greater value on the birth of a male child.

85. See, for instance, Mircea Eliade, *Rites and Symbols of Initiation*. New York: Harper, 1958. Jean La Fontaine, *Initiation*. Harmondsworth: Penguin, 1985.

86. In some Muslim countries and in most Western countries this operation is criminalized and persons involved in any capacity (surgeon, responsible adult in case of minors, etc.) are liable for criminal prosecution. The UK has a specific FGM law, but France does not, but criminalizes this operation in other ways (as assault). New Zealand law forbids FGM and criminalizes accessories and anyone involved or implicated in the execution of the operation, even if it is performed overseas. (See, e.g., Erich Kolig, *New Zealand's Muslims and Multiculturalism*. Leiden: Brill, 2010; pp. 185–186.)

87. It had been practiced traditionally as a form of religious initiation by some groups in the interior of Australia. The operation involves the splitting open of the penis lengthwise down to the urethra and in these groups was considered an indispensable prerequisite of manhood. At ritual occasions in later life men would open the subincision wound to let the blood flow. Regarding the symbolic meaning of this mutilation anthropological opinions are divided.

88. Arnold van Gennep, *Rites de Passage/ Rites of Passage* (several editions and translations).

89. This, most probably, is a reinterpretation of an older initiation custom.

90. Especially in societies in which nudity is the norm, such bodily changes are important signals of changed social status.

91. Dehymenation in this interpretation is the female counterpart.

92. Les Hiatt, "Secret Pseudo-Procreation Rites among Australian Aborigines." In *Anthropology in Oceania*, L.R.Hiatt and J. Jaywardena (eds.). Sydney: Angus and Robertson, 1971. John Cawte, Why We Slight the Penis. In *The Psychology of Aboriginal Australians*. G. E. Kaerney, P. R. De Lacy and G. R. Davidson (eds.). Sydney: John Wiley, 1973.

93. Sigmund Freud's hypothesis of the "urhorde" and its sexual dynamics is too well known to require elaboration here. (See his *Totem und Tabu*, translated into many languages and issued many times in edited form.)

94. Chris Knight, "The Origins of Symbolic Culture." In *Homo Novus—Humans without Illusions*, U. Frey, C. Störmer, K. Willführ (eds.). Berlin-Heidelberg: Springer, 2010. A recent report in the journal *Science* records the discovery of an ochre paint "factory" in South Africa dated to 100,000 years ago.

95. Kohl, kol, or kuhl, a mascara to highlight the eyes, is widely used in the Middle East, Africa, and South Asia by women as well as men and children. It variously has magical, medicinal as well as aesthetic purposes. It was used, together with ochre oil lipsticks, as far back as ancient Egypt (3500 BC) by the aristocracy.

96. This increase in such operations was reported (in March 2011) for the UK by the *Observer* and *Guardian News and Media*.

97. Quran mainly 7/80–82, 11/77–83, 15/61–77.

98. Some Muslim thinkers argue that a difference be made between homosexual proclivities and homosexual acts. Only the latter should be punished.

99. Unni Wikan, *Behind the Veil in Arabia: Women in Oman*. Baltimore: John Hopkins University Press, 1982.

100. Unni Wikan, "Man Becomes Woman: Transsexualism in Oman as a Key to Gender Roles." *Man* 12/2 (1977): 304–319.

101. Interestingly, both film and book *The Kite Runner* refer to the Taleban using boys to dance and perform a female role. It is difficult to doubt the authenticity of the narrative description of Taleban custom. Perhaps the author's intention was to point to the hypocrisy of the Taleban.

102. Sami Zubaida, *Beyond Islam: A New Understanding of the Middle East*. London, New York: Tauris, 2011; pp. 20–21. Khaled El-Rouayhib, *Before Homosexuality in the Arab-Islamic World*. Chicago: Chicago University Press, 2005.

103. Austrian press (July 2010) reported on a survey of the Malaysian organization "Sisters in Islam." Malaysian men may marry up to four wives, but must seek a sharia court's approval. First wives were reported to suffer psychologically through subsequent marriages of their husbands. Seventy percent of first wives are against polygamy. Sixty-five percent claimed they were not consulted by their husband about further marriage plans.

104. The mixture of ethics and pragmatics can be detected also in Islamic pronouncements on female infanticide. It seems to have been (widely?) practiced in Arab society at the Prophet's time, placing pride in maleness above procreative potential. The Quran does not clearly prohibit it, but seeks to discourage it (6/151, 16/58–59, 42/49–50, 81/8–9).

105. Alfred Guilkaume, *The Traditions of Islam. . . .*; pp. 102–103.

106. In some Islamic countries hisba (intervention, verification, control of observance of Islamic principles) allows state-enforced divorce for apostasy of one partner.

107. In June 2011 the world press reported that Saudi Arabia has introduced a law that bans child marriage and enforces a minimum age of seventeen for girls. Traditionally girls as young as eight years of age could be given in marriage.

108. Freud, *Totem and Taboo* (various editions).

109. This requires a rethinking of the concept of incest, shifting the accent from genetic relationship to the field of cryptic social rationality. Indeed, the concept of incest as understood and applied in several societies has little to do with issues of blood relationship or genetics, but is based on terminological kinship relations.

110. See Marcel Mauss's classical work *Le Don* (*The Gift*), (various editions).

111. See, e.g., Unni Wikan, "Citizenship on Trial: Nadia's Case." In *Engaging Cultural Differences: The Multicultural Challenge in Liberal Democracies,* R. Shweder, M. Minow, and H. R. Markus (eds). New York: Russell Sage Foundation, 2002; p. 128; Unni Wikan, *Generous Betrayal: Politics of Culture in the New Europe.* Chicago: University of Chicago Press, 2002.

112. Alfred Guillaume, *The Tradition of Islam*; p. 99.

113. Alfred Guillaume, *The Tradition of Islam*; p. 101.

114. Ophelia Benson and Jeremy Stangroom, *Does God Hate Women?*

115. Ophelia Benson and Jeremy Stangroom, *Does God Hate Women?*; pp. 37–38.

116. The Quran clearly refers to the Prophet as a role model, an exemplar of leading a God-pleasing life to be emulated by the believers. See, e.g., 33/21.

117. As mentioned before, the Frankfurt School of Social Research was concerned among other things with the question of whether ethics can be scientifically corroborated. Max Horkheimer, the director of the institute, is reported as regretfully commenting on the relativity of ethics that arguing that one ethical system is better than another is like saying that milk is better than an egg or red is better than blue. (H. Gumnior and R. Ringguth, *Max Horkheimer.* Hamburg: Rowohlt, 1973; p. 103. Max Horkheimer, *Zur Kritik der instrumentellen Vernunft.* A. Schmidt (ed.). Franfurt a M: Suhrkamp, 1967; p. 33.)

118. Norani Othman (ed.), *Muslim Women and the Challenge of Islamic Extremism.* Selangor, Malaysia: Sisters in Islam, 2005.

119. Some published books give reason for hope: Fatima Mernissi's *Beyond the Veil* (1990) and *The Veil and the Male Elite* (1991); Sherifa Zuhur's *Revealing Reveiling* (1992); Lila Abu-Lughod's *Veiled Sentiments* (2000); and Erqun Mehmet Carter's *Voices behind the Veil* (2003). Other voices, such as Halleh Gorashi's and Amina Wadud's, are beginning to be heard internationally.

Chapter Five

Sartorial Conundrums

THE VICTORY MARCH OF HEADSCARVES

Muslim women, in the eyes of outsiders, not unusually are essentially reduced to their wardrobe. Their sartorial appearance seems to encapsulate their social and psychological—in other words, their essential—being. Beyond the manner in which they are dressed, there seems little worthy of analysis and interest, nothing that can bring about a revelation of what it is to be a woman in Islam—as though from their dress one can deduce their existential circumstances, their being a social and cultural phenomenon, and the sum total of their Muslimness. By a further small stretch of the imagination their dress seems to allow some, usually negative, inferences about the nature of Islam and its prescriptions of gender relations.

The public appearance of Muslim women indeed often seems extraordinary from a conventional Western viewpoint. Sometimes heavily veiled, but almost always at least covered by voluminous clothing and a head cloth, the hijab, Muslimas provide a striking image in most Western contexts. Leaving aside "emancipated" and "secularized" women (baraza) who refuse to cover their heads with even a token piece of fabric, the variety of garments for the devout or tradition-minded stretches from a thin gauze-like head scarf, a symbolic bow towards Islamic piety, to the heavy cloak covering a woman from head to toe, the burqa.[1] While some women prefer fashionable hijabs in gay colors and modish dresses, others of a more conservative bent wrap themselves in shapeless, ungainly, and dull gray, blue, or black cloaks. This is usually combined with a heavy hijab that leaves only the face bare. There are also regionally valid, customary differences. In the Middle East head coverings and female dress are preferably of dull, dark colors, while Southeast Asian women generally prefer light and gay colors.

Among the very conservative modes of dress there is the shapeless, baggy jilbab and abaya, a wide mantle that clearly has not been touched by a fashion designer for centuries. (From Saudi Arabia it is reported that young women know how to add a few subtle modish flourishes without attracting the attention of the religious police, the mutaween.) There is the concealing khimar, a knee-length shirt usually combined with a bulky headcovering. The Iranian chador, made from one large piece of material, allows the wearer to either draw it across the lower part of the face or leave it uncovered as the situation demands, thus serving the double purpose of headscarf and veil. Shapes and styles of headdresses and clothes, and the names referring to them, provide a sheer endless variety. While the pious attitude prescribes a body-shape-concealing garment, more modern-minded Muslimas know how to combine a pretty hijab with more fashionable garments such as clinging trousers or even tight blue jeans. Someone once told me he had seen a young woman combining a hijab with a miniskirt—but I cannot vouch for this information.

In the West, it is the face veil that creates the most controversy. It has not only stimulated much debate, but most recently also legislation. On the extreme end of garments there is the heavy tent-like burqa—a type of clothing that provides only a small opening for the eyes to allow some vision. This slit is usually covered over with fine netting to hide even the woman's gaze from the public. Another similarly privacy-affording dress style is the niqab, a face veil, covering balaclava-like the lower part of the face from the eyes down, and usually combined with a very long and loose fitting abaya. Sometimes the niqab is suspended like a little curtain below the eyes and held in place by an uncomfortable looking metal ring around the head. This type of clothing—in particular the face veil that does not even reveal the wearer's eyes—represents an individualized purdah,[2] a gender separation, made sometimes even more impenetrable with gloves to hide even the skin of the hands. In the ultra-orthodox sense of propriety, the burqa's all-protecting embrace may be only broken by a view of gloves and shoes, perhaps a glimpse of an ankle—even though under the Taleban's strict etiquette showing too much of wrist or ankle may have earned a woman a hiding from the religious police. Popular Western perception of this garment is reflected in calling it a female jail, a coffin, a body bag for women and other unflattering, graphic terms. In accordance with the saying "you are what you wear," the wearers are often seen as Islamic extremists, fanatics, or as hapless victims of oppression being under the thumb of their jealous and ultraconservative men folk. The way they dress is supposed to give clues to their psychology and intimate social circumstances. There are indications that even for those who wear it by choice, it is an uncomfortable garment. Some say they are wearing it as a kind of sacrifice, a sacrifice especially new converts in the West are prepared to make in order to show their devotion. One French woman hoped that for concealing her beauty and preserving it only for her husband, she would be rewarded in heaven. In the case of those who prefer the full facial veil so as to reserve their facial features solely for their husbands to contemplate, one wonders why they have adopted the view that to see their face and enjoy its visual aesthetics is the prerogative of their husbands; it does not seem to bother them that this attitude comes close to the unfriendly stereotype that veiling is tantamount to regarding a woman's body as her husband's property. Obviously strong religious convictions overrule possible scruples and even a desire for bodily comfort. A friend of mine, a university teacher (at a European university) specialized in Turkish language and history, had two or three such heavily veiled women in her class who bitterly complained about the heat when the room temperature rose in summer. However, my friend's suggestion that they need not wear this type of garment was met with loud protests and complaints about the lecturer's lack of understanding. Leaving aside the fanatical insistence of the Taleban swathing women by law in this ungainly outfit, not always, perhaps only for a few, wearing this garment is truly a demand of canonical law that outweighs everything else. The appearance of burqa and niqab in Western society in particular amounts to a statement in which fundamentalization and the search for personal spiritual integrity collide heavily with the West's female fashion sense, sartorial symbolism as well as the pragmatics of convenience.

In the late 1960s, when I did field work in Afghanistan, there were few burqas to be seen—both in urban areas and in the countryside. It was my clear impression that it was not the most popular form of female dress, worn only by ultraconservatives. In Kabul, especially around the university, young women were dressed in fashionable Western clothes; no headscarfs, or only the occasional token flimsy one, was to be seen. The emergent middle class had totally abandoned the uncomfortable cloaking garment. In the Hindukush villages, where I also carried out research, it was not too different, although the women were quick to draw their head cloth across the face when a stranger approached. Wearing a burqa would have been a dangerous handicap by limiting the wearer's vision on the narrow, stony, and uneven mountain tracks. I cannot imagine how these mountain women later coped with the Talebanic edict.

Concessions are possible. A modern creation, the so-called burkini—an all-covering swimsuit, perhaps an expression of Islamic frivolity and barely tolerated only by the most liberal Islamic authorities, is a concession to the barest convenience and to a Western lifestyle for the bravest of diasporic women. It has been developed in the West in recent years to allow young Muslim women the pleasure of bathing in a semi-public environment and yet remain completely covered. The clinginess of wet fabric—usually quite revealing of body contours—has been overcome by using a liberal quantity of the material.

There is a growing feminist movement of a rebellious bent of mind—even among devout Muslim women—which may target, among other things, the gender-distinct dress code. Most probably influenced by Western perceptions of the meaning of veils and headscarfs, and bravely resisting the vilification as closet lesbians by conservative Muslim circles, they are fighting an unequal ideological battle against Islamic fundamentalization. The global momentum seems to be firmly on the conservative side. Setting aside the reality that in many regional Muslim cultures the traditional female dress continues to be an indispensable sartorial necessity, making it virtually impossible for women to reject it, it has been observed by social scientists and journalists that there is a worldwide tendency for increasing numbers of women opting to wear the hijab, even when there is no discernible pressure from long-standing tradition or male guardians.

A heavy and near-total cover is customary and traditionally expected of women in some regional cultures, and in some countries may be demanded by state law. Some Muslim countries (like Iran, Saudi Arabia and the erstwhile Taleban regime) have stringent and uncompromising sartorial rules, usually enforced by a religious police punishing even seemingly slight violations with great harshness. Among the most disturbing cases of this kind is that of fourteen girls dying (from burns and asphyxiation) in a fire at their school in Macca in March 2002. They had been prevented from leaving the burning building by the religious police, the mutaween, because they were not properly dressed.[3] In Afghanistan it has been observed that even though the legal requirement to wear the burqa has disappeared under the Karzai regime, many women continue to wear it. The reason seems to be the precautionary consideration that if the Taleban should regain power, which does not seem unlikely, the wearers would be on the safe side. However, especially in the Western diaspora, this is clearly not the case and such reasons do not apply. Even when in some families pressure is exerted on women, the dominant society and its sartorial tastes and mantras of freedom, one would expect, provide a sufficient counterweight. And yet, the Islamic covering for women seems to be on the increase. There are no statistics on this issue, but it seems that the wish to wear a head covering, even a face veil, is common among otherwise well-adjusted women and is preferred even by Western converts when there is no pressure from tradition or family. Quite clearly, the simple headscarf enjoys increasing popularity. In Muslim majority countries—as for instance Indonesia and Malaysia—in which the traditional covering only a few years ago seemed to retreat from urban areas into more rural ones, more recently clear signs of revival can be observed. This can only be explained by connecting it with a global process of fundamentalization resulting in a resurgence of personal conservatism.

The seeming victory march of the hijab has raised questions as to the likely causes, especially as it seems to be a reversal of a process widely held to be inevitable and unstoppable: a process of liberalization of Islamic doctrine in which the headscarf was seen to be the flag bearer of conservatism and its disappearance was welcomed as a sign of progress and modernity. This has obviously not happened. Clearly a sign of commitment to a religion and of devotion to its commands, wearing a head covering, beyond being a personal choice, also has deeper sociocultural reasons. A plausible explanation is that the headscarf has to do more prosaically with establishing and displaying a personal identity. In the search for a strong and defining identity in a sea of offerings in the modern world, women may take confidence and security from openly declaring their Muslimness. In a broader, but closely related, sense, it may also be one of the many expressions of "cultural closure"[4] —the attempt to protect "indigenous" culture and its attendant identity against the seemingly unstoppable juggernaut of cultural homogenization driven by the West-dominated globalization. In this connection, the hijab may be subject to cultural valorization[5] —or even more strongly, iconization, a process in which a traditional cultural element is becoming the marker of a particular desirable collective identity and is regarded as a mark of distinction like a "brand." This may be the foremost reason why an increasing number of modern, well-educated young women opt for this garment despite the absence of family pressure or local cultural tradition.

However, a return to head covering and face veiling and their religious meaning is also amenable to the explanation that it is the result of a process of re-religionization of the world in the postmodern era, as some social analysts believe they are observing.[6] This hypothesis places causative emphasis on the diminishing sense of existential meaning and growing epistemological uncertainty modernity and rationalism have supposedly inflicted on humanity, and the consequent search for spiritual certainties.[7]

Putting a slightly different, but related, emphasis on the situation, the hijab and the veil may be interpreted as representing a search for stricter and unambiguous ethics in a morally lax and permissive world. Not unusually from this perspective, the process of moral "decline" would be seen to emanate from cultural homogenization driven by globalization and to be an integral part of Western hegemony. As decadence and amorality are believed to spread, some women may take pride in declaring in this way their moral staunchness. (And in an indirect manner express disapproval of globalization, which harbors the danger of moral decline.) Especially diasporic conditions for Muslims, encapsulated as a minority in Western society, may provide an impulse to demonstrate moral resistance in this way. Thus, rather than signifying an anachronistic religious passion, the hijab represents an anchor of moral personhood for those modern women. But still, cases where women choose to wear conservative Islamic clothing simply for practical reasons, such as to escape molestation—as it has been reported from the French banlieues, seem to be rather rare.

In some cases the hijab may be expressive of culture-political concerns. The motivation in affirming personal Muslimness may have specific ideological undertones of antagonism vis-à-vis Western culture as a whole, but this may not necessarily be so in a majority of cases. It would be wrong to jump to the conclusion, as is often done in the West, that wearing traditional Islamic costume—especially the face veil—points to a hostile attitude towards the West, its liberal democratic system and its core values. Concealing the face with a veil does not mean revealing an extremist inclination in a political sense. (The burqa and the niqab are not the equivalent of the terrorist's balaclava, although they may be misused for this purpose in rare instances.)

It seems to me more likely that on a deeper level of understanding, the mounting popularity of the hijab is related to globalization and the perceived slide towards cultural indistinctiveness, which drives people into the arms of traditionalism and causes them to adopt distinctive cultural markers. Part of this may be a declaration of adherence to strict moral standards and an implied rejection of cultural Westernism. However, by and large, to deduce from it an extremist attitude is a step too far.

The West perceives this development with some alarm. The hijab's popularity does not fit into expectations of increasing global secularization and in a Western context, conservative Islamic dress is seen as a clear sign of maladjustment and discontent. Western countries rally their legal and ideological forces—often hypocritically so—in a concerted onslaught on a symbol they consider to be implacably opposed to its values: female equality and personal freedom of choice. In particular the all-covering burqa and the niqab come in for heavy condemnation. Cases in which veiled women are accosted or refused service seem to be mounting.[8] In fact going vastly beyond personal distaste, some local and regional authorities in Europe have restricted wearing these garments through by-laws and some countries have enacted, or have considered, or are currently considering, national legislation to ban them altogether from the public domain. France and Belgium are in the forefront by having enacted legislation to this effect, but also some Muslim majority countries are in the process or have already banned the total veil.[9] Worldwide, the legal situation is confused, to say the least, with a plethora of divergent national and local regulations, and specific rules that apply to employment and the particular public circumstances. Some countries have engaged in internal debates through the media whether bans should be legislated but have not yet done so or have refused to enact laws. New Zealand, Denmark, and Austria, for instance, have discussed the issue but declined to legislate so as to implement a blanket ban. In some countries veiling is prohibited in the public education system, in others even wearing a headscarf falls under the prohibition; in some instances this ban applies to teachers and in others to pupils. Such bans may also apply in other specified public spaces such as offices. Some banks in Western countries have introduced house-rules that prohibit women wearing a veil from entering for security reasons. Some police forces have expressed concern about women drivers wearing the face veil, as it impedes peripheral vision, and also have raised questions on how to perform identity checks on women apparently exercising their relig-ious freedom by concealing their faces. From the point of view of public security objections have also been raised as some female suicide bombers have used this voluminous garb to conceal explosives. However, it is clear that it is highly prejudicial to link this garment with criminal intent: suicide vests and weapons can be concealed even under less conspicuous garments. In some debates on the burqa, to support banning it, it has been pointed out that the odd robbery in France and Australia has been committed with the perpetrators (presumably men) being disguised in this way. Yet, for criminals there are better, less cumbersome ways of concealing their identity. Banning the burqa will not stop criminals from using other disguises such as balacla-vas, hoods or face masks. One suspects that imposing restrictions on conceal-ing dress is less of practical value and rather pitched at the symbolic level, namely, a show of suppressing manifestations of what is believed to be anti-Western attitudes, objections to Western core values, and a hostile insistence on cultural Otherness.

BURQA—POSTER EXEMPLAR OF FEMALE OPPRESSION

France (which has already banned the hijab in the public education system)[10] and Belgium are banning the total face veil in public places.[11] In France the law has been in force since April 2011; it allows for arrest and a fine of 150 Euro[12] for contravening it by covering the face entirely. Generally, conceal-ing the face by whatever means will be treated as an offense unless done in the context of a masquerade or carnival festivities. A penalty would even be exacted from men who force their wives or daughters to wear face veils. The debate had been raging across France for some time previously, with Presi-dent Nicolas Sarkozy heavily weighing in and describing the Islamic veil as "unwelcome" in France. The debate saw politicians, opponents, and advo-cates of the face veil using the terms burqa and niqab interchangeably, de-spite the fact they describe very different types of Islamic dress. The burqa (the all-enveloping cloak with a woven grill over the eye slit) is rarely seen in

France. More frequent, in line with the North African origin of most French Muslim women, is the niqab, a garment that conceals much of the face but leaves the eyes uncovered.

Arguments politicians used were "We can measure the modernity of a society by the way it treats and respects women"—implying that the face veil signals female subjugation and its absence signals a progressive, liberated society. And "Wearing the full body veil is about extremists who want to test the republic"—which assumes sinister political-ideological reasons behind this custom, used by fanatics to push the envelope. Some politicians warned that the law would be difficult to enforce and, in that it violates provisions of religious freedom, would probably face a challenge in the European Human Rights Court. Critics also argued that a specific law enacted to ban the full veil would be tantamount to using a sledgehammer to swat a fly. As Muslim community leaders pointed out this contentious form of dress remains a rare exception among France's Muslims, the biggest Muslim minority in Europe. In France it is estimated that fewer than 2,000 women wear the total veil out of a female Muslim population of between 2 to 3 million.[13]

Banning the all-covering body veil by law in a Western liberal democracy contravenes cherished and popular values of personal liberties, ignores mantras of religious freedom, and may even violate human rights laws. The inherent contradiction between allegedly liberating women by restricting their choice of garment provides a rich paradox. For the proponents of the ban this Islamic garment symbolizes female oppression, anti-democracy, religious intolerance, and male tyranny—all of which is believed to have congealed into a repulsive religiocultural custom. Thus the enforcement of European—or rather French—values is justified; the virtues of modern French citizenship of liberty, freedom of choice, and gender equality have to be inculcated if necessary by compulsion. For France also the preservation of laïcité, a vital ingredient of French national identity, is at stake. Laïcité, secularity, is enshrined in law and gives a legal basis for suppressing the ostentatious display of religious contents in the public sphere.[14] Thus the enforcement of laïcité gives secularization, an "inevitable process" anyway, a helping hand, but more importantly makes the acceptance of the specific national French identity compulsory. In addition to legal and identity issues, and only harmlessly hinting at religious commitment, the face-concealing dress has been suspected to indicate the wearer's dangerous religious fanaticism. By suppressing the dress, a signal blow is meant to be struck also for the public's liberation from such undesirable, politically dangerous demonstrations of religious fanaticism.

The idea to fight oppression with what amounts to unfreedom, or at least reduced freedom, is worthy of further comment. By imposing a ban on these garments, women are to be liberated from the shackles of tradition—or gynocentrically put, from male domination. Public prejudice and radical feminism meet each other in harmony. With less partisanship it may be said that this enforced emancipation eliminates the "enemy image" from the street scene, but does little in terms of demonstrating in real life the principle of personal liberty. It nullifies exactly the ideals and values the West prides itself on— and likes to distinguish itself from the Muslim world: creating a polity based on a maximum of personal freedom and using legal proscription sparingly, and only for the purpose of suppressing behavior considered harmful to the collectivity. (Self-harm may also be subject to legal restrictions.) Especially liberal democracies—which predominate in the West—set themselves off against other political systems by allowing their citizens considerable liberties in matters of personal lifestyle. The veiling prohibition removes the right of women to dress as they please in public and confines it to the private domain. In doing that it replicates Islamic conceptions, which also seek to limit sartorial freedom in the public area, yet corrupts them in another respect. For the prohibition amounts to a total reversal of what the veil is meant to achieve, namely, to preserve a woman's complete privacy in public and to reveal the very personal only in private. Bizarrely, it also perverts Western protestations of personal freedom and in doing so falls in line with a recent and disturbing trend. The restriction belongs into the wider category of paradoxical developments in Western free democracies: to continue to have free and liberal political systems and institutions, and to live in societies enjoying a maximum of personal freedom, some liberties, so it is argued, have to be surrendered now. A reduction of civil liberties is necessary through the state's enhanced, and still growing, legal ability for surveillance, detention, and the like, designed officially to secure the state's ability to thwart acts of terrorism. While the state's responsibility, legally and morally, for national security is certainly an important factor, a general and diffuse mistrust of Islam, deeply lodged in the West's collective subconscious, is at the root of anti-terrorist strategies. By attributing various and numerous negative aspects to Islam, a range of proscriptive measures appear to be justified and become palatable to a polity otherwise vitally concerned about its civil rights.

The main official excuse is that these minor sartorial restrictions are protecting the secularizt nature of the public sphere and promote core values of a free society. This view can only have arisen from the poorly grounded perception that this Islamic garment is an embodiment of female oppression. Has anyone asked Muslim women? In fact some Muslimas did express an opinion, as well as Muslim men, in favor of a ban.[15] When Muslims express such views, they are based on the proposition that wearing the face veil is not essential to being a Muslim and a ban does not cut to the core of Islam; hence the prohibition does not infringe on religious freedom.

What about the reasoning that a prohibition of the veil is liberating women, as was vociferously claimed by the advocates of the new law? Yet, if Muslim women en bloc are not asking to be "liberated," such a law limiting the choice of garment is clearly a net loss of freedom from a Western point of view and presumes to tell Muslim women what is good for them. The argument that the removal of choice is beneficial for the person concerned shares ethical kinship, though admittedly somewhat distant, with burning witches and heretics in the past with the rationale that this would liberate their souls and through earthly penance they may incur God's forgiveness. As the veil debate has pointed out, forcing something on someone under the pretext that this is for their own good is a morally dubious undertaking.

As always, there is a counterargument: the actual life world, even in the most liberal of democracies, abounds with boundaries and conventions setting limitations to personal choice. Sociability comes at a price. It is only through renunciation of liberties that human society is possible. It may also be argued, and indeed it has, that in this case, pitching the two major ingredients of a liberal democracy against each other, democratic principles (i.e., the will of the majority) outweigh personal liberties—against which another viewpoint holds up the concept of "majoritarian terror," which a truly enlightened, liberal society should avoid. The debate reposes in irresolution.

In one sense or another, the Islamic dress certainly has a strong signaling effect, both visually and symbolically, and as such is apt to arouse passion. The Western host society as well as Muslims themselves acknowledge, though for different reasons, that it sends a strong signal in everyday life, even though it addresses quite different and contradictory values. There is no easy answer why some Muslim women, some of them well educated and socially emancipated, and fully conscious of the effects of their choice of garment, out of their free will wish to send this strong signal. Especially in situations in which revealing their identity as overly committed Muslims may stir hostility and discrimination one must wonder about their reasons. The answer Muslim women themselves provide vary widely. For many the reason simply is their conviction that it is religiously commanded or that covering oneself is customary and that this custom is doctrinally required. As such this is a right and on purely ethical grounds should be fully protected by the assurance of freedom of religion in both belief and practice. This, however, is no more than a clumsy, deceptive gloss on the much less glamorous fact that all humans are constrained and limited in their choices, by culture, convention, and tradition. Total freedom in behavior, values, belief, and thought is a myth. The iconic freedom of choice is in tune with hegemonic discourses of personal freedom of expression and of cultural freedom, but when analyzed under the sociological magnifying glass, in many respects turns out to be illusory. Just that fraction of personal freedom or discretion, left by normative perceptions, social conventions, and cultural traditions, may be rejected by some women (by submitting to a coercive, intolerant religious dictate), while paradoxically at the same time claiming the newfangled notion of personal liberty to do so. The juridical and philosophical entanglement seems to be endless. No matter whether veiling is a choice made for reasons of identity based on rejection of the cultural homogenization that globalization in general,[16] and diaspora in the West in particular, seems to threaten, or because it is seen as a religious imperative and an open confession of faith, should find strong support from the global discourse on legal and ideological personal freedom, but fails to be realiztic about the fact that total freedom is not possible. What is to be debated, though, is where to draw the line and where to compromise. In any case, it is the interpretation of the signaling effect of these garments, which is of particular interest here. Not only are cultural systems of aesthetics quite different, but as the burqa and niqab demonstrate, the perceptions of the underlying symbolic message are also quite diverse.

THE DOCTRINE OF VEILING

The exact origin of the face veil is unknown.[17] Covering the face, some scholars surmise, started in the Byzantine Empire from where it diffused into the expanding Islamic realm. Others argue that it was present already in classical Greece and in Persia. According to another hypothesis, it has originated 2 millennia BC in Arab culture and from there spread throughout the Middle East and the classical Mediterranean civilizations. Another argument connects its origin with dusty desert conditions, the strength of the sun, and the wish to retain a youthful and light-skinned appearance. These advantages were also recognized then by women in less harsh environments. Partial veils were also used in early medieval Europe apparently to protect the delicate complexion of high-born ladies. For very similar reasons well-to-do women dwelling in the hot Australian climate in earlier decades (Victorian and Edwardian times) used broad brimmed hats and elegant shawls loosely slung around the head and covering part of the face to protect their fashionably pale tint against the rigors of sun, heat, dust, and flies.

Historically more factual is that ancient Arabic pictorial representations do not show women with full facial cover, while a cloth loosely thrown over the top of the head can be made out. (It may have been used to draw across the face at times.) In this context it should be noted that before Islam forbade the representation of the human form and thus from then on there is little visual evidence one way or another, older depictions of people show that the typical Bedouin dress of flowing robes and headdress does not seem to have existed. Instead a loincloth for men and ihram clothing for females (one large piece of fabric covering the whole body) appears to have been worn.[18] Exaggeratedly "modest," demure forms of clothing for women certainly seem conspicuously absent in ancient pictures. Frescoes and other pictures, and written descriptions, show women entertaining at male wine feasts, singing and playing instruments, and wearing revealing and alluring garments. Even under Islam in its classical period palace, households continued the tradition of being entertained by lightly clad dancing girls. Today's belly dancing—while some dancers may be hiding their faces behind a niqab—is a faint afterglow of this tradition. Western society certainly developed a romantic appreciation for this tradition and it became an object of fascination in the classical Orientalist conception of Islamic culture, which seems to have run parallel with a religious disdain for "Mohammedanism."

Ultimately, it remains mysterious where the inspiration for face veiling in Islam has come from, while the headscarf seems to have long antecedents and certainly makes sense in the climatic conditions of the Middle East. Almost equally mysterious is its religious connection with notions of modesty and chastity.[19] Both face veil and head scarf, as well as the sartorial ideal of body concealing clothing, are expressions of the same virtue: female modesty.

The doctrinal requirements on which the traditional Islamic sartorial code relies are, superficially seen, relatively straightforward, but hide some considerable complexity below the surface. Among several verses that refer to sartorial rules (leaving aside other relevant verses in the Quran such as 7/26, 33/59) there are in particular three Quranic ayas (24/31 and 33/53, 55) that are usually cited as the guide to correct clothing of the female body to preserve the degree of "modesty" desired in females. No reference, however, is physically precise in its directive, beyond a general ethical command to preserve female modesty by "covering" and "concealing." The display of naked skin is strongly discouraged by notions of propriety and, in a very general sense, should be kept to a minimum. The lack of specificity allows for multiple interpretations as to what exactly must be covered and how to achieve the prescribed degree of modesty. And, of course, concealment is gender targeted: women are not required to hide their bodies vis-à-vis other women as strictly as is demanded vis-à-vis men, excepting husbands.

One Quranic reference (24/31) in particular relates to female modesty, the ethically prescribed need to cover the body. It also gives a precise list of the male kin categories who are allowed to see more of a female's body. Verse 33/55 repeats the kin groups that may see a woman "unveiled."[20] This again can be taken as an exhortation that women should be veiled when in public and may be uncovered only when in the company of other women or the male relatives so named.

Verse 24/31 contains the main ambiguity that continues to lie at the crux of face veiling:

> And tell the believing women to lower their gaze . . . and protect their private parts . . . and not to show off their adornment except only that which is apparent . . . and to draw their garment all over juyubihinna . . .

Concepts like adornment (whether this is hair or other physical attributes) and private parts (certainly more than just the genitals) can be interpreted quite differently. One of the crucial issues here is the interpretation of the Arabic word juyub (ihinna), which needs to be covered, and whether its semantic meaning of "body" refers also to the face. The authoritative English-language, official Saudi version of the Quran in a footnote specifically defines it as body including face, neck, and bosom; and specifies the parts that may be publicly seen as the eyes, outer palms [sic] of hands. It also seems to recommend gloves to conceal even the hands. This is an interpretation that goes beyond the wording of the Quranic text. Other definitions of "awra (or aura), the parts a woman needs to conceal, exclude hands, face, and feet. The reference to "adornments" presumably refers to body parts that are considered in traditional Arab culture as particularly erotic or sexually attractive—other than the primary sexual characteristics of femaleness—such as hair and neckline.

The interpretation which insists on total veiling, including the face, takes as the precedent a hadith,[21] that records that when this verse, which exhorts the women to draw their garments over their bodies, was revealed to them by the Prophet, on hearing it, they tore their clothes and covered their faces. This seems paradoxical, as this action was likely to uncover even more of their bodies.

The other textual reference that is usually interpreted in favor of the demand for an even more complete covering that includes the face and possibly the hands is Quran verse 33/53 (and to some extent 54 and 55). However, it refers stricto sensu to the approach Muslims should take to the Prophet's wives and how they should behave in the Prophet's home: "And when you ask [the Prophet's wives] for anything you want, ask them from behind a screen." In one interpretation this divine imperative refers to the requirement that in the home a curtain or screen should separate the private sphere from the more public domain where visitors may enter. The directive given is gender-ambiguous as it contains behavior rules for the Prophet's wives and for visitors most of whom would have been men. Yet, it is predominantly interpreted as an imperative that is intended for women to stay hidden. The conduct required refers more to a physical separation rather than a particular type of clothing. It is only by extrapolation that the gender distance is translated into a movable screen to be worn by women. This would form the rationale for a total veiling including the face. In another important interpretation, it is a requirement that was meant only for the Prophet's household and not meant for ordinary people. The Prophet's house was a semi-public place where visitors, petitioners, supplicants, and friends were coming and going virtually all the time. Under the circumstances preserving a degree of privacy was highly desirable and required some rules of conduct. Thus possibly the demand for a separation—only implicitly referring to gender—was not meant to be extended to other Muslims, their households, or their wives. However, this argument is countered by the school of thought that takes the Prophet as the exemplar of God-pleasing standards that should be emulated by all Muslims. Therefore the Prophet's private rules are public demands. They are inspirational for all Muslims and, in this case, command the total covering of all women when they are in a public space. The question of what constitutes the public domain and what meets the requirements of privacy where veiling is not required constitutes another rich field of contestation and debate. Interestingly, during the haj women are forbidden to cover their faces, despite the fact that they are very visible to the public. This may indicate that too fine-grained a search in the scriptures for logic and consistency may be ill-placed.

Mernissi[22] argues that the way in which the verse on the Prophet's women is interpreted now is based on a misunderstanding. Apart from the fact that the verse relates to a very personal concern the Prophet had, it was meant to refer to a curtain, sitr, not a veil, to divide the private from the public sphere. Use of curtains for the purpose of maintaining personal privacy was later made by princes and caliphs to remove themselves from public gaze. Mernissi believes curtains are also to distinguish the sacred from the profane. There are several verses in the Quran[23] that refer to screens as dividing walls between the divine sphere and humans. However, it may be said that when defenders of total veiling argue that it is a transportable screen, or a movable extension of the concept of a dividing curtain, there is a difficulty in reconciling this with the dichotomy of sacred and profane. It would mean the woman in the burqa or under the niqab represents the sacred, and the outside world in relation to her the profane. Equating women with the sacred and by extension men and everything else as profane seems far-fetched and not quite in tune with Islamic conceptions.

It is in particular the two Quranic verses 33/53 and 55 that inspire some Muslims to insist on the tent-like dress, notoriously known now even in the West as the burqa. It affords an individualized privacy no other garment can offer. Especially in Western countries, this garb makes for striking images in the urban landscape. The image of the burqa-clad or niqab-wearing woman has been used time and time again as representing Islamic fundamentalism, even extremism. One suspects it is the ninja-warrior impression that black niqabs are creating which makes them look sinister and thus establishes an easy affinity with danger. If niqabs consisted of white gauze, reminiscent of bridal veils, it would make them much more acceptable—at least in the West where cultural perceptions routinely associate white with goodness and black with evil. In cartoons the dark, full veil personifies the evils of religious fanaticism. (It is not surprising that the Darth Vader figure in the Star Wars film series has a distinct resemblance with the black burqa.) Even for most Muslims the full face-concealing garb exemplifies extreme religious devotion and in their view is not necessarily and expressly commanded by doctrine.

While total veiling is customary in some regions, state law in Muslim countries does not actually require it. (Saudi Arabia encourages it but does not enforce it by religious edict.) The majority of Muslim scholars seems to be agreed that a woman is not obliged by the Quran to wear the face veil. Liberal Muslim interpretations recommend that it be left to a woman to decide whether to take on the veil or not. Either decision should be respected. By and large, fundamental Islamic doctrine commands that the female body should be covered except "what is apparent," which is also translated as "what is usually seen thereof." This allows for several interpretations. Strictly speaking, not even the hijab is expressly commanded and is an obligatory part of the religious sartorial code.

The headscarf is a token acknowledgement of the religious requirement to avoid flaunting female beauty, as much as the whole body should not be an incitement to immoral behavior. Fundamental orthodoxy demands explicitly a garb that is concealing of body shapes and contours and covers as much skin as possible in order to satisfy the demand for modesty. In other words, beyond this doctrinal demand, to what extent clothing may hug the body or may be suggestive of its shape is open to debate. Usually tight-fitting trousers, such as blue jeans, may be discouraged—or even forbidden by local or state ordinance. In the province of Aceh, Indonesia, the religious police are given the power to cut off the offending garment with scissors on a woman and replace it with a more suitable covering. Elsewhere imprisonment and lashing may be imposed for "indecent" clothing.

THE CONCEPT OF MODESTY

In the Islamic understanding of female attire, its appropriateness, or otherwise, relates to an important female virtue: namely, modesty. A complete cover expresses a woman's respectability and decency, and in this way demands respect, in particular from the believing Muslim. Muslimas living in banlieue-type ghettos and other disreputable neighbourhoods in Western cities are reported to have said they wear conservative Islamic dress to escape being raped by fellow Muslim men. Conversely, the absence of this type of dress seems to convey (at least to some Muslim men) a woman's sexual availability. (Indeed this is a claim—spurious as it is—occasionally made by

Muslim rapists of Western women.) Mernissi[24] argues that slave women going about "unveiled" in Madina at the Prophet's time were considered easy prey for rape. In fact this was encouraged by slave owners, so she argues, who forced female slaves into prostitution as the children they would give birth to were also slaves and could be sold.[25] A covering dress seems to have been evidence of a free woman who may not be molested.[26] (It is uncertain whether this would have applied in the literal sense of concealing the face or refers simply to a head cover or to other forms of being covered to avoid enforced intercourse.)

On the basis of this doctrinally exemplified situation, a lasting subliminal perception is insinuated to Muslims. A woman being "uncovered" or only lightly dressed signals sexual availability as well as low social status. This can lead to misunderstandings, just as much as when veiling is interpreted as a sign of oppression. Australia experienced a scandal in 2006 when a Sydney imam—and allegedly the mufti for all of Australia—in a khutba scathingly criticized the liberal dress sense of Australian women. Comparing scantily dressed women to unpackaged meat, he argued this would invite men to rape them, just as cats are lured to uncovered meat. Just as they cannot be blamed for their instinctive greed, the rapists cannot be held morally responsible.[27] As one might expect, this did not go down well in the host society, where a benign climate and a relaxed dress sense combine to produce sartorial conditions that almost any monotheistic orthodoxy would place into the rubric of loose morality. It seems almost logical that in the eyes of conservative Muslims, this disqualifies women from being considered respectable and likely to be judged responsible for their own misfortune if they get raped. Regardless of any truth value, however, when articulated in this tactless way this proposition is thoroughly unacceptable to Western moral notions, while within an Islamic context it has been fair comment. In a Muslim social environment, for a woman to flaunt her body openly and to draw attention to her physical attributes goes well beyond harmless eroticism, teasing or freedom of expression. It invites severe trouble. According to Mernissi,[28] the hijab and proper bodily cover for that reason became customary among respectable free Muslim women first in the Madina exile and later becoming a doctrinal requirement. The purpose was for the original Muslim women to distinguish themselves not only from infidels but also from female slaves who—at least in Mernissi's interpretation—could be molested with impunity and forced to have sexual intercourse by anyone encountering them in the streets. While this appears to be somewhat of a historical exaggeration, modern examples do show that partial or total veiling does seem to give some protection, not only among Muslims. The implied message of respectability, sexual disinclination, and religious devotion is normally understood. In contrast a greater state of uncover—unless in a situation of sports or recreation—signals a more careless and sexually inviting posture. Even a liberal Western perspective might be inclined to interpret scant dress as an erotic invitation, although not perhaps to the same alarming degree of sexual licentiousness and promiscuity as a conservative Muslim one would. As will be discussed later, the degree of cover traditionally may also send a subliminal message about a woman's social and socioeconomic standing, to the extent to which Muslim societies allow some latitude in the way women may dress. When the Taleban enforced wearing the burqa of a standard design regardless of social rank, it was the quality of the fabric, not the style or completeness of cover that offered some clues to the socioeconomic circumstances of the wearer.

Apart from feminine contours, especially hair, eyes, and neckline are considered by Muslim aesthetics to exercise erotic attraction. From a very conservative viewpoint even showing an ankle may arouse irresistible passions in a man. As a hadith says, "A woman is a sweet creature and can easily be seductive." It may seem unfair that the men's (presumed) lack of self-control—or their excessively libido-driven nature—should force women into an existence of perpetual concealment in public. The strongly suggestive nature of the female form, and especially some of its parts, beyond being merely tantalizingly erotic, through its mesmerizing ability is credited with unleashing unrestrainable passion in men. The resulting asocial behavior must be kept in check—already at the source—so as to allow a well-ordered and peaceful society. Strictly regulated sexual relationships in which nothing is left to spontaneous libidinal urges are at the core of the Islam's intent. Hence there is an abundance of stringent rules, to be broken or circumvented only under threat of terrible punishment, relating to marital conduct, fornication, adultery, and even the proper conduct of the sex act itself. It also entails among other things that partner choice become a tactical and controlled matter to be arranged ideally by third parties who are dispassionate enough to make rational decisions. While the passionate nature of men can be an impediment, under any circumstance female choice has to be eliminated on account of the emotional and highly excitable nature of women and their reduced rational ability. For both genders it is more wholesome and beneficial that male attention be focused on the qualities of a woman other than her body. In other words, Islam's laws and social rules relating to issues of sex, dress, gender relations, and restraint were not whimsical or the prudish fantasy product of a charismatic person, but were grounded in a quasi "scientific" understanding of human nature current at that time. Being a divine creation and the product of unfathomable divine wisdom, sexuality and human behavior relating to it were vastly beyond a rational argument about how to correct them. (An argument about "nature versus nurture" would have been pointless.) They were axiomatic and outside human capacity to change them; they could only be channeled along the lines of divine command.

Another argument usually provided by Muslim men is that something as precious as a woman should not be offered openly, quasi on a platter, to others to view and enjoy. Underlying this view is the belief that concealment is a natural response to high value. Indeed it appears to be a universal tendency that something of high and rare value should not be freely accessible. The precious tends to be kept hidden and secret. Offering it openly to unrestricted public viewing would cheapen it. It should be preserved for the appreciation by only a select few or accessible only at special occasions accompanied by some decorum. Veiling of sacred contents and objects, keeping them hidden and surrounding them with great secrecy, is a universal feature, present in virtually all cultures. Images of gods (being kept covered or clothed), shrines (the Ka'aba is shrouded in cloth), ritual manipulations (the sacramental metamorphosis of the Eucharist happens under cover), sacred objects (the veiled tabernacle), and living persons of exalted status (hiding behind curtains) are all examples of secrecy, shrouding of special contents, keeping them hidden from the everyday, public, mundane sphere, and revealing them and granting access happens only under ceremonial, special circumstances. The list of cultural examples can be extended ad infinitum.

This condition relates to the intrinsic nature of so-called esoteric secrets and as the terminology suggests shielding them from public, indiscriminate access. It is an observable universal in human society that things, information, or knowledge held to be of enormous value tends to be treated in a restrictive, secretive manner. Regardless of the objective or practical value of the information or material thing, the esteem for it is expressed in sharing it only sparingly, making it subject to restrictions and ceremonializing access to it. The gate keepers derive benefits from their privileged status as guardians of the secret and the controllers of access.

In traditional or tribal societies practical empirical knowledge, vital for physical survival, usually is freely shared and handed on from generation to generation, while especially that of a religious, non-practical kind is hedged in with restrictions, taboos, and secrecy. Religious and ritual knowledge is given the status of a life-giving, world-maintaining power or attributed with other important functions (such as magically securing fertility, health, good fortune, etc.). Fredrik Barth[29] describes this notion, which he encountered in New Guinea, with the following words:

> The value of information seemed to be regarded as inversely proportional to how many share it. From this it would follow that if you seek to create highly valued information . . . you must seek to arrange worship . . . so that [only] a few persons gain access to these truths.

Boundaries of mystique and secrecy are erected around select things, as they are removed from ordinary access. To gain access and become the beneficiary of revelation—a special privilege that has to be earned or paid for—has to be marked in a special way. It may require a ritual of some form, a religious initiation for which, in order to be admitted to it, a sacrifice of some sort is required: this may be of a pecuniary kind, or a payment in pain or blood, or something else of some value. Before admission is formally granted or earned in some way, the cordon of secrecy is not to be breached by unveiling the item. This is the usual constellation in esoteric matters where the value of the valuable content is artificially inflated, secrecy and inaccessibility being means and end at the same time.

Veiling (in a literal, physical sense, or through hiding and restriction of access) and ceremonial unveiling become important functions to mark high symbolic value. In some cases this is also clearly connected with notions of power. The greater the intrinsic power of the precious information or object, the greater the secrecy and the fewer those who are privileged to know it. A common proverb goes: power told, is power lost. Hence in initiation procedures the most powerful secrets (in terms of information and sacred objects) are kept for the final stages open only to the most worthy candidates. It is not far-fetched to assume that the notion of the preciousness of women and esoteric value of information have a common hard-wired root—a species-typical tendency—that links the degree of worth of something with the desire to keep it secret, or at least control its dissemination. This leads to various expressions of secretive behavior and concealment of precious things. The associated symbolism can be found in the treatment of women in some cultures. (Rudimentary traces may be detected in the lifting of the bride's veil in traditional wedding ceremonies.)

The argument of the precious nature of women goes back to the sacred hadith texts relating the Prophet's attitude in this matter. The Prophet is said to have enjoyed the company of women, ranking them highly on a par with perfume, though lower than prayer. He is said to have referred to women—more precisely the pious ones—as "mata," a prized possession, something precious and of great value.[30] This utterance admits to some ambiguity. It is both a compliment, in its abstract sense, and an insult through commodifying women when understanding the Prophet's comment in material terms. In either case, however, holding something as precious explains removing it from public gaze and knowledge, while openly displaying it would send a message of worthlessness.

This basic inclination to "cover up" something that is considered of great value can be seen to extend into several areas of human behavior and can metamorphose into several cultural guises. As the next example shows,[31] a "decent" cover also relates to aesthetic notions of style, elegance, and superiority of appearance. Applying this benchmark to Western liberal attitudes in matters of female dress, its usual state of "undress" or "under-dress" seems rather gauche and contemptible, signaling worthlessness and low self-esteem. An observation of some Muslim men is rather revealing:

> While out for dinner last week with colleagues, we sat beside three 20-something women. There was the usual posing and glances exchange, and as they paid their bill two Muslim women entered and sat nearby. Whispers were quickly exchanged and we could hear, "Why do they wear those things anyway?" . . . "I feel sorry for them" . . . and so on.
>
> As they filed out of the restaurant, we noticed they sported a mixed collection of the following: skin-tight pants, short skirts, exposed midriffs, push-up bras, high heels, jewelry, see-through or plunging tops, piercings, lipstick and makeup, and one had breast implants for certain. We observed the two Muslim women as they were engaged in close conversation over coffee.
>
> Their graceful features complimented [*sic*] their dark headscarves and warm eyes. Their natural gestures were flirty without even trying—revealing natural beauty. And their clothes, while conservative, brought forth the hidden potential of something wonderful and truly feminine.
>
> The idea of dressing modestly terrifies some western women—but why? Perhaps it would trample their "right" to show off. Would their self-esteem fall along with their hemlines?
>
> After some debates, we identified the cost of the western "right" to flaunt. The Muslim women were free from the fashion trap—free to "just be" without posing, comparing, dieting and spending for the approval of men and each other

The—supposedly Muslim—men making these observations came to the conclusion that Western women were exhibitionists, desperate to perform sexual displays, and in their zeal revealing their enslavement to unwholesome values. The gaudiness of display rather than being a declaration of freedom to these men expressed the exact contrary. Interesting here is the underlying connection being made between visual restriction, and freedom. The observers seem to have unconsciously hinted at the Islamic triangle perception of restriction of access, high worth of that which is subject to restriction, and this constellation expressing not lack of freedom but its opposite. The description of this encounter lends itself also to another interpretation, plausible not only to Muslim conservatives. In actual social discourse competing in an arena of vacuous vanity, where appearance defines a person, is so ingrained in Western culture that modesty has come to be seen as regressive to the point where a virtue has become a stigma.

THE SLAVERY OF VEILING

In her article cited previously, Abu-Lughod[32] focuses on the veil, specifically the burqa, the all-covering tent-like cloak that was forced on women during the Taleban regime. She rightly points out that for the West this is the symbol par excellence of gender discrimination and misogyny. This garment's forced disappearance may easily be mistaken as a gain in liberty for females. For the social status and public appearance of Muslim women are intricately connected issues in the Western mind. Indeed in a critical stance towards Islam and the status of women in it, veiling in general is usually taken as a foremost symbol of female unfreedom, as incontrovertible hard evidence of the lowly status of women in Muslim society. A priori it is not immediately clear why this connection so readily suggests itself. What are the underlying images and concepts that so hastily establish a causal connection between concealment of the body, and especially the head and face, and a person's social situation? Does the covered or uncovered condition of the human body really indicate conditions of liberty or unfreedom?

What seems to be the Islamic obsession with concealing the female form has been an object of fascination and derision in Western society for some time. In the common Western perception, this female dress code signifies subordination to male whim, submissiveness to gendered domination. This negative verdict is based on the implicit assumption that "normal" women if allowed free choice, would not dress in this way. Their choice freely made would be different not only for reasons of convenience and corporeal comfort, but also because of the symbolic meaning of veiling. Attached to the veil is an odor of subservience and degradation. It smells of an absence of power, the wearer's enslavement to someone else's will. Even if it is the impersonal force of tradition and not the whimsicality of male power that compels women to hide their hair, faces, and bodies, it must be a tradition devised by men and somehow serving the interest of a patriarchal society. Whatever the case may be, in this perspective, it signifies the absence of free choice through the exercise of one-sided power, and symbolizes gendered inequality. However, while questions of liberty and power are certainly tied up in the female sartorial code and its enforcement—be it either by tradition or heavy-handed "law-enforcement" by male guardians or religious police— other symbolisms relating to social power are of equal importance and have contributed to the origin and continuation of this tradition. As explained in the previous section, this issue conceals not only faces and body shapes in the empirical world, but also contains cryptic symbolisms conditioned by culture-specific concepts of respectability, status, individuality, and eroticism.

The question imposes itself: why is female veiling evidence of male domination, even when it is not enforced by law or custom or family tradition in patriarchal societies? It is not an a priori convincing argument insofar as exercising this kind of control over women's sartorial code does not bring any immediately obvious advantages to men. This was highlighted to me through a bizarre event reported in the *Gulf News* in February 2010. In the United Arab Emirates, a diplomatic envoy reportedly called off his engagement to a woman just after the marriage contract had been signed. They had met a few times previously when the woman always had her face covered by a niqab. As it was reported, when he attempted to kiss her and lifted her veil, he discovered that she was cross-eyed and had facial hair. This is a tragic turn of event for both sides, but its bizarre newsworthiness aside, it is probably symptomatic for many marriages of this type. When they are arranged by third parties or for other reasons, a physical appraisal of the future partner's features is not possible, surprises are inevitable in a certain percentage of marriages. Feelings of indifference, physical incompatability, or even revulsion may arise and have to be overcome in the interest of establishing at least of modicum of harmony. The diplomatic envoy in breaking off the engagement may be accused of not acting in accordance with Islamic values that recommend that a woman be judged and appreciated for her inner beauty, her piety, and her loyalty. Conservative Muslims will readily emphasize that one of the functions of veiling is to empower women by forcing people to pay attention to a woman's personality, her character, her mental persona, and not judge her by her physical form. It is typical of Western superficiality to focus on the body of a woman, her sexual attributes, and the attractiveness of her face. As Muslims will argue, this means treating women as sex objects. While this certainly sounds like a high-minded, commendable perspective, the example from the UAM shows physical attraction is not unimportant in partner selection, and if this is denied it is certain that a large percentage of unhappy, disharmonious marriages will occur. Against this Muslims will claim, quite reasonably, that the search for statistical proof is motivated by the Western bias that physical attraction and romantic love are indispensable. Partners of an arranged marriage can and will grow to like or respect each other over time and develop a fondness for each other. Certainly from this angle, rising divorce rates in the West, despite free partner choice and the liberties of physical "inspection," are not good advertising for the Western viewpoint.

Physicality—together with the concept of physical beauty and the romantic concept of love—for Muslims is overvalued in modern Western society. Some have spoken of "a cult of the body" that venerates physical perfection over other possible, more socially valuable attributes. Where identity of self is primarily lodged in one's bodily appearance and a person is judged by criteria of physical aesthetics, notions of self-worth and self-respect are intricately tied in with "body." To possess naturally physical presence and beauty ennobles a person and makes it easier to gain respect and affection than it is for someone of unremarkable or repulsive physique. A Quasimodo can hardly be expected to be an admired, popular figure. On this topic, can one imagine an American president under five foot, bald, and paunchy, although endowed with an IQ of 180 and two PhDs? Such a person's electability would approach zero in a society that places as much emphasis on physical appearance as contemporary American society does. (Europe is probably now not far behind.) Clearly on this attitudinal basis and combined with the excessive value placed on romantic "love," a more or less arranged marriage to a veiled woman would seem a recipe for disaster. Unpacking the bride by lifting her veil may be a romantic gesture in highly ceremonialized weddings, but actual social and aesthetic conventions have totally eliminated the surprise element—and with it the initiation aspect of lifting suddenly the veil of secrecy surrounding the precious object. It may be said that the obsession with corporeal beauty in Western society, that makes attraction contingent on it, has had a profound influence in altering and sidelining what is actually a culturally more entrenched expression of "natural" inclinations (namely the fascination with the obscured, the secret, the hidden).

A QUESTION OF FREEDOM AND SYMBOLIC MEANING

Indonesia as a country, by and large, is reasonably liberal in matters of gender and dress. Although the most populous Muslim nation with roughly 220 million Muslims, it also has significant minorities of Christians, Hindus, and adherents of pre-Islamic and tribal religious forms (agama adat) who abide by widely different dress conventions. A majority of Muslims are only nominally so (so-called Muslim statistik), others are abangan, syncretistic Muslims who mix Islam with pre-Islamic beliefs. The more devout and purist Muslim sector, the santri, in proportion has been growing steeply in recent years due to a general trend of re-Islamization. In particular, the region of Aceh at the northern tip of Sumatra has always been well known for its staunch Islamic commitment. Historically, the people of this province have claimed a special status as the purest Muslims in the country. Now, as a province Aceh enjoys semi-autonomy, and its legal system recognizes the sharia to a greater extent than does national Indonesian law.

A current affairs website from Indonesia describes the situation of sharpening the sartorial code for women under provisions of sharia law.[33]

The West Aceh (a semi-autonomous province of Indonesia) Regent Ramli M.S, based in Meulaboh, has issued a regulation that women found wearing tight trousers such as jeans will have them cut by sharia police and forced to wear loose-fitting attire as of January 1st 2010. (The Jakarta Post 28.10.09). He will also attempt to enforce that vendors cannot sell jeans or slacks.

Ladies can, of course, still wear jeans and slacks in other regencies or provinces, which could necessitate a ring of religious police road-blocks around the regency, with changing rooms at twenty-four hour border gates.

It is not clear if these restrictions apply to persons of uncertain gender who traditionally play a significant role in Aceh social life, since they are really men who look like ladies. This is a difficult theological point and there may be no underlying grounds for restricting the tightness of their jeans, even if they look quite immoral, or at least very happy about it.

But since their customers are usually men, this should not involve any women, so no female immorality is involved, although the religious police may sometimes have to look into it.

The Regent has also issued a regulation prohibiting government agencies from serving members of the public wearing "un-Islamic" clothing such as tight jeans and slacks when visiting government offices.

This could be unconstitutional since it is unlikely that any official has the right to withdraw Indonesian central government services from its citizens on such grounds. However, Ramli M.S is a practical man and has reportedly set up a contract to produce 7,000 long skirts, which he will provide free to those stripped of their trousers.

In the same vein, though slightly less humorously, the Human Rights Watch website in early 2011 reported that Chechenya's Kremlin-installed strong-man Ramzan Kadyrov has ordered Chechen women to wear "modest attire" and sent out vigilantes to attack women considered violating this edict with paintball guns.[34] This at least is less brutal than the Sudanese solution to enforce certain dress standards. As the world media reported in August 2009, women who dared to wear trousers in public in Khartoum were sentenced to flogging. By enforcing an Islamic dress code Sudanese women are meant to be weaned from immoral Western tastes, Western hegemony deflected and Islamic honor restored. Leaving aside the brutality of punishment, on a basis of principle one must wonder whether this sartorial suppression cannot reasonably be compared with initiatives in the West to ban the burqa and niqab in the public sphere and to fine disobeying women. Ironically, in both cases the motif is that in enforcing a certain dress code a blow is struck for the liberation of Muslim women. And in both the French and the Sudanese case, it remains unclear how this is achieved by restricting individual freedom of choice.

Coming from opposite sides of the attitudinal spectrum, the West and the Islamic world are approaching each other in an uncomfortable accord by making female dress a highly symbolic and politicized marker. For the West—or at least those agencies that press for outlawing the total veil—the burqa symbolizes not personal religious devotion that requires respect, but presents an image of hostility and unfreedom. It is suspected of expressing anti-democratic sentiments, religious intolerance, and female oppression. But how blunt suppression of this garb does not signal exactly the same negative values has remained unexplained. Approaching from the other side, Islamic authorities may well argue that with their brutal prohibition on some types of female dress (considered un-Islamic) they are applying an effective means of liberating women from the oppressive demands of Western fashion hegemony. While the West is rallying its legal forces against a symbol considered to be irreconcilable with its values, the Islamic world may come to similar conclusions. Each side sees their own restrictions in the same didactic light of women needing forceful encouragement through law (both in the restrictive and punitive sense) to liberate themselves.

Islamic dress is treated by the West as an essentialized, even cathartic, expression of Islam's antagonism to Western culture, while vice versa in a Muslim context, Western dress is seen in the same light of being oppositional and assertive of cultural dominance. Both sides rival each other in elevating female dress to new heights of political symbolism. The reactions of both sides reveal the political potency of female dress and how its perceived symbolism fits smoothly into the respective register of cultural and political prejudices.

The octruization of dress codes by authorities, be they provincial or of the state, Western or Islamic, may defy the ideal of personal freedom—so cherished by law and popular perception in the West. However, in actual fact individual freedom—not only in sartorial matters—is circumscribed and curtailed even in a free society in so many ways: the dictates of tradition and convention, of so-called good taste and decency, pose no less stringent confines. Even fashion trends tend to restrict free choice. Contravening such rules may entail consequences from alienation, ostracision and ridicule to expulsion, arrest and imprisonment, even in the most liberal and open-minded of societies. For instance, wearing gang insignia (signaling "patched" membership to certain "criminal" gangs), even if the gangs themselves are not outlawed, Nazi paraphernalia or Ku Klux Clan coverings will spark immediate arrest and prosecution in many countries. Helmets for certain sports and for riding motorcycle or even bicycles are mandatory in many countries; balaclavas and similar head coverings are subject to legal restrictions. Just tying a handkerchief around the lower part of one's face will draw the attention of the police. Informal dress rules seeking to hem in the lax dress sense of visitors also apply in the Vatican, in important ecclesiastical precincts, in official offices, even in some prisons, at certain functions, and the like. Some local authorities of popular holiday spots have even drawn up rules to curb the irritating semi-nudity of tourists. Demanding a certain decorum in a person's attire because of its symbolic capacity to express respect or its opposite is related to notions of the prestige and importance of the place. Even bars, nightclubs, and country pubs enforce certain sartorial standards presumably in the dimly understood assumption that dress has some influence on the wearer's behavior. A good dress standard tends to generate a respectful attitude to the environment that enforces it and in this way exercises influence over a person's conduct. The amazing degree of cultural concern clothing can generate, the iconic centrality it is capable of assuming, though apparently bizarre and rationally groundless, in fact draws on a cryptic connectedness between clothes, their semiotic message, and the belief that they are revealing of the wearer's intention and motivation.

The Western presumption is that unrevealing dress reveals a lack of choice. It presupposes women are constrained by Islamic law or the conservatism of their male relatives to cover up. If women could exercise free choice, they would tend to show off their facial features and flaunt their bodies. Would they? There certainly is a grain of truth in that some women, if they could choose, would dress differently: dispense with the hijab, the uncomfortable cloak, the bulky chador, the stifling-hot burqa; but by force of law, custom, tradition, and the threat of violence from their male guardians, this possibility is taken from them. Many Afghan women, against their will, were forced by the Taleban to adopt an archaic dress sense to hide under heavy burqas when in public. Poorer families could afford only one for several family members, thus enabling only one of them to venture out into the streets at a time. Iranian youngsters show their dislike of the drab chador, although they have to be careful not to violate the dress laws too openly. Iran, like other Muslim countries, seems to have problems with young women attracted to pop culture who like to show off their fashionable make-up and do not like to wear the heavy head cloth, much to the chagrin of the religious police and the Revolutionary Guard. Many women if permitted would undoubtedly shed unwieldy Islamic clothes for fashionable items—which means accepting fashion dictates normally reflecting the Western dress sense—or something simply more comfortable.

To bring the question to a point: in the final analysis, are Western, non-Muslim women completely free to dress as they like? Are they not subject to constraints of law, concepts of decency, and tradition? The short answer is, yes, of course limitations to freedom of choice do apply. Many of these constraints are so ingrained that they do not seem to be constraining to the average person. Through the force of socialization, dress rules seem sensible, plausible, even rational.

In defense of the veil let us explore the symbolism of clothing and especially female dress in some greater detail. It is immediately clear that there is a great deal of complexity far beyond the pragmatic simplicity of wrapping up for warmth or to protect the skin. Cloaking the body, especially that of females, is done either for reasons of appropriate modesty or religiously dictated propriety. In other words, it may be a desirable virtue not to flaunt bodily beauty. Concealing body and face may even reveal a highly gendered access to power and an appalling degree of submissiveness of women. And in an even broader sense it broaches questions of civil liberties in law and philosophical issues of personal freedom.

Much of this complexity has to do with historical experiences and with semiotic functions of clothing in the past. In particular, the Western interpretation of the headscarf is largely shaped by historical experience. In previous centuries, up until most recent times, a woman's head covering in Western (or European) society was considered both a status symbol as well as signal of juridical unfreedom. This symbolic ambiguity stems from two sources: getting married moved a woman from immaturity and social incompleteness to fulfilment of her womanhood and to a status of a adult person, while at the same time coming under a husband's jurisdiction. This was usually understood quite literally so that marriage in fact continued a condition of a female's legal dependency. The transition to a new social status was signaled by starting to wear a bonnet and containing the hair under it. Hence the German language idiomatic expression "unter die Haube kommen" (getting under the bonnet) for a woman getting married. Nuns with their heavy clerical habits declared their status as "brides of Jesus." Only a few decades ago it was still customary for "decent" married women showing off their social worth by wearing some kind of fashionable hat (in urban areas) or head scarf (more popular in rural areas). Especially modish hats of the early twentieth century were festooned with tiny fishnet veils, often only a few square centimeters, as a residual mark of the veil. At least since early medieval times, free-flowing hair was regarded as a sign of a wild spirit as yet untamed by marriage. In a grown woman it signaled asociality; it symbolized untamed chaos over social order and civilization. Traditional costumes in Europe's rural areas delighted, and still do, in cultivating the most fanciful bonnets with rich embroidery and elaborate shapes (even though nowadays even unmarried women are allowed to wear them). Religious sects as well as orders of nuns prescribe bonnets for females. Even most early suffragettes, despite rebelling against ingrained gender traditions (and supposedly male domination), were keen on showing their social respectability by wearing a hat. By rejecting this head gear later, however, it was taken to be a symbol of submission and a sad reminder of women's subjugation under the male yoke. Feminism then extrapolated from the specific European experience and made universal assumptions including the Islamic head cover.

Covering head, face, and hair, if not for protective reasons, part of a uniform or traditional costume (worn for ceremonial reasons), has many meanings. None of that is reducible to one single symbolic root. Even when seen solely within the context of Western culture, this gesture can be attributed with several semiotic functions. But especially when it is traced to a human behavioral universal can it be recognized as being capable of conveying quite diverse messages.[35] There is an enormous multivocality in the act of concealment. Covering one's face can plausibly be understood as a universal expression of reducing interpersonal communicability (as most communication value resides in the face). In this sense this gesture tends to relate to extraordinary emotional states. Severing social contact by hiding the face can be for reasons of shame, mourning and grief, penitence, but can also signal pride and deliberate social distance. Partially hiding one's face (for instance, behind a fan) and seeking eye contact at the same time can be flirtatious, which in a coquettish sense seeks to establish a communication. That is to say, removing the face or part of it from public gaze has a certain theatrical effect that rarely fails to impress, but can convey quite different meanings.

Hooding, probably normal in Europe in medieval times, is now associated with a rebellious youth subculture—and the music styles of rapping and hip-hop—that thrives on a mental state of chronic excitement and in some cases also a real association with criminality. Hooding may be part of a dubious secret society (like the Ku Klux Klan) or of pure religious devotion at ceremonial occasions (at Easter processions in Spain, for instance, in the semana segrada). A headscarf in European pictorial art for instance in representations of Biblical female figures, is the traditional attire meant to signify humility and noble melancholy—a tradition continued into modern times. In any of these circumstances, concealing part or all of the head and face signals an anomalous, extraordinary condition. It is more than just the search for anonymity—which in itself would be a suspect motif. It is inviting negative imputations, especially in a society that is torn in between the imperative to preserve privacy (in relation to the onslaught of state supervision) and the maniacal drive to "put oneself out there" through internet, Facebook, texting, tweeting, and incessant use of the cellphone.

THE SHAME OF UNDRESS AND THE POWER OF NUDITY[36]

It is probably correct to say that in matters of clothing and wrapping the body, Western society may have reached, if not a climax of liberty, then certainly historically unprecedented heights. The right to clothe oneself in various states of dress or undress has benefitted much from the general discourse of individual freedom and human rights. Even though they were intended primarily to refer to freedom of discrimination relating to race, religion, ethnicity, and gender, sartorial issues also tend to be subsumed under the rubric of liberties to which everyone is entitled. It may be well to remind us that sartorial freedom has its limitations and whatever tolerance Western culture is prepared to evince (for instance, in relation to public nudity) is a relatively recent phenomenon. Even after women had achieved universal suffrage and had become more frequent visitors to the beach, special inspectors measured the length of garments in Australia and New Zealand up to the 1950s. Bikinis were not tolerated long after their invention, just as total nudity is frowned upon now and bare-breasted women are ordered off most popular beaches. G-strings straddle the boundary of acceptability even nowadays. On the other hand, the pin-up girls in swim suits whose pictures gave much joy to soldiers in World War II, considered almost pornographic then, would seem totally insipid today. And Playboy's centerfold, moving on the fringes of publishing liberties in its heyday, in the degree of daring is outdone now by the most timid pornography. The imperative to hide the body for the sake of respectability and decency is fading away fast.

Much depends on the situation to determine whether the liberty of scanty dress or even undress can be used in public with impunity and when it would invoke ridicule, insult, or even some form of punishment. A daring show of "flesh"—cleavage, buttocks, thighs, butt crack, midriff—may be completely acceptable in some circumstances, while others—such as a funeral, being in a sacred precinct like a church, or the British queen's garden party—demand a more perfect cover and careful decorum. Church services usually attract a well-dressed gathering and some communities obey a strict sartorial regime for this occasion. Unwritten codes make that clear to everyone bar the most dim-witted. Streaking at sports and other public events attracts the unfavorable attention of police and officials, but the public accepts it usually with good humor. It results in arrest, if the offender can be apprehended—but it could be argued it is not the lack of dress but the disruption that causes such behavior to be ruled out of order. Despite increasing tolerance of nudity and semi-nudity, it is far from being allowed everywhere. In official places, such as a court of law, public offices, and especially at official events, a stricter code of cover applies. However, on the other hand, nudity, semi-nudity, and various degrees of undress at certain events are tolerated in public as long as genitals are not ostentatiously displayed. Gay and carnival parades replete with sexually suggestive themes and the display of female breasts at similar occasions are gaining in popularity and become "decriminalized" and destigmatized, even though there still is a section of public opinion that adheres to the view that this is a public nuisance and a demonstration of modern immorality. This is in striking contrast to attempts to suppress a more total cover of the body as dictated by the Islamic dress sense. Incidents of discrimination against the all-too-concealing Islamic dress are frequently reported in the media from many Western countries almost on a daily basis: for example, a burqini clad woman being evicted from a French public swimming pool—presumably for dubious reasons of hygiene; cases of hijab- and burqa- wearing women being evicted from courtrooms in various Western countries, and the like—while Catholic nuns are not suffering the same treatment. All this is clear evidence that so-called sartorial freedoms in the West are far from being total, logical, coherent, or even uniform.

As mentioned before, in September 2006, a Sydney imam and (then) Australian mufti, Shaykh Taj el Din al Hilali, in a sermon at the mosque referred to Australian women in their scant clothing as unpackaged meat inciting men to rape them. Like cats attracted to meat cannot be blamed for helping themselves, rapists are also naturally drawn to what seems to be freely, though perhaps unwittingly, offered. As may have been predicted by everybody—though obviously with the exception of the mufti—once made public by the media, this comment roused a storm of protest against this chauvinistic statement in particular and Islamic gender attitudes in general. [37] Al Hilali publically apologized in January the following year, claiming that he was misunderstood and meant no offense, but then continued his tirade rather dishonestly when he returned to Egypt. Nahid Kabir, who observed from close quarters, opines that Hilali wished to "preserve women's honor," but this clearly is an apologizt's argument. For everyone else it sounded like an undiplomatically moralizing condemnation of the female Western dress sense. Taken as the self-righteous homily of a Muslim misogynist, it was not only deplorable, but believed to be symptomatic for Islam's gender attitude. It was able to confirm the worst prejudices extant in the wider Australian society. Scant dress in most parts of Australia is encouraged by a benign climate and supported by rather liberal attitudes; and as critics of the mufti pointed out, it is part of the Australian way of life to freely choose one's clothing. Somewhat incongruously, some of the proponents of this view, fiercely defending Australian liberalism, were arguing at the same time for the banishment of the hijab.

In northern Australia, ironically, I could observe over a period of two decades (from the 1970s to the 1990s) a remarkable transformation in dress codes. While "whites" in public life were shedding more and more fabric in line with the increasing liberalization of notions of dress propriety, to the point of sporting semi-nakedness—which, one might say, is quite sensible in a hot climate, Aborigines were embarked on the opposite trajectory: leaving behind their traditional nakedness and dressing up more and more in obvious imitation of an attitudinal dress sense that was disappearing in the culture they tried to emulate. If it was done to earn respectability in this manner, it failed, as the dominant culture had moved on. (Dressing up as a status symbol may still have worked within Aboriginal society though.) The outfits favored by Aborigines of ten gallon hats or woolen caps, high-heeled cowboy boots, heavy long-sleeved shirts, and thick blue jeans formed a strange contrast to the super-short pants, singlets, and "thongs" of the "white" folk of both genders. In this context, and by relativizing the relationship, one might say that semi-nudity was more indicative of social power, while complete cover was rather indicative of relative powerlessness.

The lack of clothing deemed appropriate in a certain public context can have a strong signaling function, which is not always welcome. Openly displayed nakedness (or semi-nudity or an excessively risqué dress sense) can be taken as an assault on someone's sense of decency, an offense against appropriate decorum and a deliberate denial of the moral standards applying in the particular environment. The case of Western tourists in various states of undress bothering the sense of decorum of Third World people (or Vatican clerics) is well known. Wearing what may be called "the holiday uniform" may simply spring from the desire to be comfortable in hot weather, but to a more formalist mind it signals lack of respect. In a third-world context, the modern Western sense of expressing in this way personal liberty may be taken as a gross demonstration of Western hegemony and a superiorist attitude that cares little for other people's sensitivity in matters of dignity and politeness. (In the Vatican's case it may be taken as an insufferable demonstration of the hegemony of secularization in Western society.) Just such an anecdotal case from Egypt has been described in the ethnographic literature by a well-known author on matters of Islam:

> I myself once watched, with fascinated embarrassment, as a tall young woman, possibly American, bra-less and clad in a sleeveless shirt, wearing shorts which exposed the upper portions of her thighs, purchased some mangoes from a stallholder, a dignified young peasant clad in the traditional galabiya. This woman—I reflected—is sexually assaulting the man, though she may not realize it. Her garb was a systematic violation of all the sartorial codes governing male-female relations in traditional Islamic society. Only the extreme boorishness of super-power arrogance could produce such a display as this.[38]

That such sensitivity towards semi-nudity is not unique to Islamic culture was brought home to me in a celebrated and controversial case in New Zealand in 2001. A high-ranking female civil servant of stunning appearance and controversial fashion sense was dismissed from her contract and in the ensuing court case was accused by her superior of sartorial extravagance. Calling her outfit "indecent and offensive," he claimed that through the exaggerated display of her female sexual attributes he felt very uncomfortable.[39] He seemed to have no problem in drawing a clear line between decency and lack of it: for him being shown an "embarrassing amount of breast" was clearly stepping over the line. Her large earrings were a "come on," her short skirts offensive, and her long bare legs had proved a distraction for a visiting foreign dignitary, he said. Her audacious dress sense seems to have been at least a contributing factor in her dismissal. While the squeamish tastes of this male bureaucrat may be open to ridicule, apparently this was taken seriously enough to be discussed at length in open court. Even though the sartorial code of the higher echelons of New Zealand's public service may be regarded as somewhat antiquated, it does reflect a subliminal dress sense that seems to have wider, perhaps even universal, currency. Uncomfortably coexisting with more recent attitudinal developments in the wider Western society that accept now more latitude and flamboyance in clothing, it adds to the bewildering symbolic complexity surrounding female clothing.

The body is not just a biological and physiological apparatus enabling motion, digestion, and procreation. It is equally important as a site of various expressions of power and a medium of communication. Covering or uncovering, as the case may be, sends important messages relative to the particular culture in which they occur, and even relative to the context. Especially the type and extent of cover on a woman's body, or its absence, can act like a flag signaling personal intentions, proclivities, and attitudes, but may also reflect social and economic status. And bewilderingly, it may be the site from which significant confusion and misunderstandings arise.

Covering up can be a status symbol, a sign of social superiority, a signal of a particular social standing. Only in relatively egalitarian tribal societies, everybody shares in a condition of nakedness or near nakedness. Status differences may be expressed with body decorations, the size of penis sheaths or other bodily insignia; they may be incised in the skin, painted on, or show, in artificial deformations. In more highly differentiated and hierarchisized traditional societies, higher status tends to be signaled with body covering, its elaborateness and style pointing in a fairly precise manner to social conditions. Status may become measurable by the amount and length of fabric. Covering not only the body completely, but also the face thus logically, it would follow, signals the highest status. The peasant woman toiling in the fields traditionally is less lavishly covered and elaborately decked out than a woman of high class, rich in pecuniary means and leisure. Indeed, the history of face veiling in the Mediterranean and Middle Eastern ancient societies does point at its origin in the highest social classes. In Tuareg society traditionally, free men are heavily veiled, and to some extent also free women, while slaves of both genders are rather less elaborately covered. The same is recorded in relation to women from the emergent Muslim community in Madina.

In pre-Islamic, pre-historic Arabia due to climatic conditions for a relatively lightly pigmented people protecting the body including the face against the ferocity of the sun held both a physical advantage and implications of social status. Skin tone, as a vector of hierarchy—which is the case even today, is connected with notions of physical beauty as well as social position and rank. Possessing a lighter skin tone is considered desirable both as a physical attribute of beauty and an indicator of social position. Both are causally connected. A dark tan is associated with physical labor, poverty and lower social status. Apart from purely aesthetic considerations, the skin tone of the face also has strongly religious overtones in its symbolic valuation. In Quran 3/106 it says that on the day of resurrection, the righteous will have white faces, the unbelievers black faces. This quite clearly points to the value attributed to the pigmentation of the face, which provides an incentive to influence natural skin conditions to retain a lighter skin tone by keeping the face and hands covered when outdoors. Interestingly, it has been suggested that in diaspora situations when Muslim women who prefer to be fully veiled are living in cold northern climate zones it can lead to a health disadvantage. Covering up may lead to vitamin D deficiencies.[40] The desire to remain covered in public may even be exacerbated by living conditions in the West, especially in urban areas where most people live in flats or apartments. In the absence of inner courtyards or secluded backyards, where women traditionally may safely be able to dispense with the veil, the ultra-orthodox sartorial style by preventing exposure to a healthy dose of sunlight may represent a health hazard.

Covering clothes send a strong hint of social distance. The wearer of a face veil in particular is physically removing herself from public gaze and thus from ogling and the demeaning judgment by the public of her physical appearance. In a non-physical sense, at the same time and on a higher level of sociability, she removes herself from ordinary interaction.[41] Erecting a visually protective barrier in social intercourse suggests social distance as well as intimating nobility and absence of ordinariness. When the face veil appeared in the classical civilizations of the Mediterranean region, it was reserved for the upper classes and slaves were forbidden to wear it. In Greece and Rome, upper class women used it when among the public, and later in the Byzantine empire it became fashionable for aristocratic women not to show themselves without it. In some parts of the early Muslim empire it became obligatory. The veil is also mentioned in the Bible, both the Old and New Testament.[42]

In medieval Europe and into modern times in south-European societies, a light veil half drawn over the lower part of the face or hiding behind an elegant fan was the mark of ladylike behavior. Partially hiding the face was coquettish and expertly handled, accompanied by meaningful glances; it was apt to express erotic connotations in a stylish manner. Yet despite this coquetry, the communication retains an element of distance and condescension: by keeping part of the face covered, the pretension of a social gap between the "high status" woman and the "socially lower" male is upheld. Similarly, the religious habit of nuns is not just a form of sartorial tradition harking back to ancient forms of Oriental dress, but has considerable symbolic value: hiding hair and body form indicates social distance, social exaltedness (not necessarily humility), and the social and sexual unavailability of the wearer.

Following this line of symbolic thinking, the face-concealing niqab may be recognized to have yet another communicative significance. Facial expression is an important part of body language. Normally in direct social intercourse and face-to-face communication, it accompanies all verbal and even nonverbal communication, giving important clues helpful in interpreting the message. Facial expression can add emphasis to verbal communication, underline particular parts of speech in terms of sincerity, express doubt and uncertainty, or can even negate the spoken message by revealing the speaker's true intentions or feelings. Even the proverbial poker face contains a modicum of communicative value: it shows intent of detachment, studied unemotionality, and the desire not to communicate an inner state. Face veiling removes all of these possibilities. In this respect, face concealment may have an advantage in eliminating body language totally from social interaction, thus leaving the receiving party deprived of vital clues in interpreting the verbal message. As part of the communication by which to evaluate the contents of the communicated is removed, it places the receiver in a position of slight disadvantage. Concomitantly, it supplies power to the veil wearer, who may capitalize on the other's uncertainty. Not surprisingly, many Muslims emphasize the empowerment of women through their concealing dress.[43]

Interpretations, symbolisms, and values may change drastically over time, and even within one and the same cultural context. The cultural or social feature seen as an advantage or elevation in one interpretation may come to be seen as a disadvantage and an insult in another. Ultimately, a symbol, by ignoring its multivocality and its ability to express a paradox, may come to invoke both derision and admiration, and in an analytical sense admit to endless speculations what its essential message may be and what the purpose of the intended communication may once have been. It is obvious that veiling for women has undergone a profound change of meaning: from signaling high status and preciousness—in a culture in which swaddling in woven fabric was a mark of distinction and wealth—to a stigma expressive of subservience and powerlessness, attracting derision and rejection.

In a society where women go out in public without enough fabric to cover their "indecency"—and are not even being wolf-whistled at—certain values appear to be dominant, which are not only diametrically opposed to traditional Islamic ones, but negate and reverse the symbolic messages just outlined. A relative absence of body cover and the freedom to make this choice signals a positive value. Scant dress in modern Western society is a measure of liberty, the freedom to choose whether to cover or uncover; it represents the empowerment to defy a tradition that is so hollowed out that it has been rendered meaningless. This was a tradition that had regarded proper and often excessive body cover as a status symbol; the size of fabric being the gauge for decency, prestige, and wealth.

Scanty dress—which from an Islamic viewpoint equals semi-nudity and signals indecency—because it is quintessentially expressive of freedom in modern Western understanding, has become not only acceptable but also respectable. In a Western sense, shedding clothes means shedding the shackles of tradition, gaining the freedom of self-expression, exercising a liberty that has no need for keeping privacy private and strictly to oneself—it can be openly revealed to the public without fear of retribution or ridicule; a freedom by which a person is legally entitled to be literally herself. Not so long ago in Western history, nudity was taken to be expressive of primitiveness, cultural retardation, or undesirable eccentricity. Now "showing body" liberates. (Or, as the opposing school of thought wants to have it, is a desperate signal of sexual availability or insufferable narcissism. However, even if this is true it might be said that to be able to send this signal without fear of social repercussion is a sign of freedom.)

There is no clear univocalism in this value. This freedom sends out quite mixed signals. The fashion industry reflects this confusion with sartorial ambivalence: semi-nude, barely clothed models bestride the runway together with others almost suffocating under a heavy burden of cloth. Sometimes both variations are combined on the same model: hiding head and face under hoods and bulky shawls, while exposing slender legs up to the buttocks. The exposed midriff for women's fashion has been commonplace a few years ago, finding its equivalent in men's wear of long baggy pants worn low on the hips to expose the upper part of the buttocks.

Nudity, or absence of cover, may have another important signaling function in the modern world. It may not just convey a sense of liberation and a celebration of the human form as the Western "cult of the body" purports to do. The body can directly become a medium of communication, a canvas on which a message may be inscribed: this can be done most notably through decoration, for instance, decorative cicatrices (as tribal or status markers), painting on the bare skin (henna painting in the Islamic world is widely practiced for beautification and to mark festive occasions), or tattooing. Tattooing is forbidden in Islam yet practiced without religious sanction in some traditionally orientated communities. In Western and Pacific societies, over recent years, it has become increasingly popular. Once confined to the criminal underworld, sailors, and other marginalized sectors of society, today tattooing (of the more subtle kind) has conquered the highest echelons of modern society. All kinds of motives may be found on human bodies: from very artful to the crude, tribal patterns with traditional meanings, to the simple message "do not resuscitate." Body decoration is able to convey messages of personal identity, of cultural or tribal affiliation,[44] and thus becomes a mark of cultural pride and gives a sense of belonging and personhood. Using the skin as a canvas to beautify it or to send social messages is tightly circumscribed in Islam. Doing so assails the spirit of Islam where it says cursed are those that "alter what God has created."[45] The Prophet forbade women to tattoo their bodies or to use wigs to change their exterior,[46] presumably because believers should humbly accept the looks God gave them. Yet coloring beards and hair bright red with henna seems to attract no religious sanction. Dentures and eyeglasses are allowed, because they do not serve vanity. While body piercings—being done not for practical reasons—are subject to prohibition, somewhat incongruously, genital mutilation for both men and women is not only allowed, but for men even prescribed. Tattooing on the other hand manifests a kind of control over one's body that presumably God had not intended. It manifests an illicit perfection of divine creation, as do other body altering practices, which are forbidden in conservative Islam. Cosmetic surgery, sex change and transgendering, bulimia, body building, and using steroids are all expressions of humans taking control of their flesh and trying to augment their God-given assets beyond the normal duty of taking good care of this gift.[47] The Western culture of body dissatisfaction resulting in the desire to change, enhance, and beautify one's body according to aesthetic standards knows no bounds—and is complete anathema to Islamic restrictions.

Exposing the body to public gaze can create other problems when freedom turns into its opposite. In the arena of sports Muslim women have a handicap. The concealing dress of Muslim sports, women not infrequently gives rise to disharmony in international competitions dominated by Western conventions, and in effect bars them from participation in many disciplines. Similarly, Muslim women seeking to use public swimming pools encounter difficulties. They are sometimes barred because they refuse to uncover to the prescribed "skimpy" state of bathing suits. Making the body an object of public scrutiny, if enforced, can provoke resistance, even among Westerners. The right to keep one's body private has led to furious reactions against full body scanning at airports. It is not only a problem for Muslims. Invasion of privacy, the possibility of offering indecency to those scanned in this way and other issues are vehemently raised, often blotting out the pragmatic reasons of ensuring the safety of travelers. It will be interesting to observe how Muslims, especially the orthodox and women, will react when the requirement of unveiling for face recognition to check a woman's ID is already a problem for some.[48] As reactions in the West already indicate, body scanning that produces images of the naked body elicits serious questions regarding the deep invasiveness for nonmedical reasons amounting to an infringement on personhood. Even assurances that images will not be stored and will be slightly blurred by computer software and the like do not allay everybody's concerns.[49] In this context, when nudity is enforced by the state, liberty alarmingly is diminished. Suddenly the ideological distance between the hegemonic West and the Islamic world shrinks.

The crux of the matter is that the condition of liberty in a universal sense is not a priori signaled by the public display of a person's body, or alternatively by covering it up. It is also not universally expressed by the extent or manner of cover. Thus the hijab may signal enforced female subordination under male domination, while in another context it can mean liberation from Western dress convention and the insidious dictates of corporeal beauty. Even wearing the burqa is highly ambiguous: in some context it may truly express lack of choice and the woman's unfreedom; while in another, being able to wear it contrary to dress conventions, tradition, and fashion may signal a high degree of personal liberty. Alternatively, both men and women can be unfree by being victims of tradition: the man enforcing a particular type of clothing on a woman may feel himself to be constrained by custom, good taste, a common and shared sense of decency, and the like. The argument that male dominance is inherently and cryptically present in culture or certain features becomes tenuous and a matter of biased interpretational preference. What may seem like an exercise in raw social power in sartorial matters may be the force of tradition, customary, and habitual standards, which may have developed a long time ago and, in fact, may have conferred practical advantages and represented a different kind of symbolism and value system. In other words, total freedom of choice in matters of covering the body does not exist in any society—despite the fact that the range of permitted choice granted in modern Western society is historically probably unsurpassed. This includes the right to keep the body concealed from public gaze or to offer it for viewing in public—with the notable exception that in some countries the liberty of Muslimas to choose to cover their faces in public is being challenged.

As Islamic culture in a globalized world meets Western culture, a discord of mutual noncomprehension arising out of different readings of symbolic meanings is bound to arise. The globalized discourse—articulated in the human rights ideology—has begun to center around the notion of personal freedom. Although there is (as yet) no binding consensus that conditions precisely constitute it, it will be interesting to see how clothing will fit into this agenda. At the moment human rights laws have yet to be tested to determine what juridical and practical impact they might have on the dress code both in the West and in the Islamic world.

A MALE AFTERTHOUGHT

It is often overlooked, and therefore worth noting, that rules of decent clothing also extend to Muslim men. A short comparison with the male Islamic dress code may be useful. While men enjoy much more liberty in the way they dress, they are also required to dress modestly. Unless engaged in hot sweaty work, a man is expected to cover his body appropriately and at a minimum from the level of the navel to the knee. This makes it barely possible to wear so-called Bermuda shorts, but certainly nothing much shorter or revealing than that. For the devout showing their bronzed and muscular bodies off at the beach in skimpy bathing trunks is hardly possible. On the other hand, men's trousers should not be too long either. Any length below the ankles is for the devil, as the hadith goes. [50] In a conservative understanding, men should also not wear gold and enhance their appearance with wigs and other beauty accoutrements. Vanity is neither encouraged nor promoted, but tradition has much less to say than about the rules of modesty to which women are subjected. In a hegemonic Western view, the fact that more stern attention is paid to female modesty, hedging women's desire for beauty in with many rules and preventing them from flaunting their physical attributes, fewer restrictions circumscribe male behavior.

Traditional Islamic dress for men has recently gained in symbolic value— not so as to make a fashion statement, but rather to underline an Islamic identity in highly politicized situations. While Arab shaykhs and Saudi princes have almost always made a point of appearing in the West in traditional Arab flowing robes and characteristic head cloth, most Muslims visiting the West have usually preferred Western clothes. Muslim politicians and businessmen—in tacit and unconscious deference to Western hegemony— usually wear Western dress when in the West. This may be simply for convenience or for the sake of blending in and facilitating social intercourse. In some situations this, conspicuously, is not the case and Islamic garb ostentatiously worn is meant to send a different message. In diasporic conditions it has become fashionable among the very devout to wear Islamic dress, and if it is not for the important Friday salat al jummah at the mosque, it is indeed meant to make a statement. (At the occasion for the doctrinally mandated Friday midday prayer, wearing Islamic dress can be compared with the churchgoers wearing their Sunday best and means no more than showing respect for the event.) Since men are not religiously constrained—to the same extent as women are—to stick to characteristic Islamic garb, preferring it over Western-type clothing is indeed a symbolic act. It manifests a conservative inclination and in a diaspora context may even signal a deliberate, conscious rejection of assimilation. In such circumstances male dress does assume a symbolic significance.

Video clips showing Muslims readying themselves for suicide missions and offering their farewells to friends and family—saying their "morituri te salutant"—almost always show the men in traditional garb. This clearly reinforces the religious, almost festive character of their mission; perhaps even reassures the candidates for martyrdom that they as good Muslims will reap the promised rewards in paradise. (It is part of preparing a mental context in which their impending action assumes heightened meaning and which seeks to shut out disturbing, contradictory influences.) Similarly, Muslim extremists appearing before Western courts—and also in Muslim countries—demonstratively don an unmistakably Islamic garb: long white shirt, baggy trousers, skullcap. Their Muslimness is often even further underlined with a full beard. This is meant to send an unmistakable, clear signal of the wearer's Islamic identity and intentionally puts a certain light on the accused's actions, which brought him before the court. It becomes clear that whatever act was perpetrated, or intended to be carried out, it was meant to be the idealistic act of the believer in defense of his faith. The festive dress points to the purity of motive. Another interpretation is also possible. An unintended side effect may be that wearing this special clothing ennobles the court of law and dignifies the proceedings by giving them equality, through the religious dress code, with attendance at the mosque. Doing so is probably not intended nor is it meant to appease the court's sense of its own importance and respectability—on the contrary. It expresses antagonism to the jurisdiction, which in passing judgment on the devout jihadi has disqualified itself from being Islamic. Emphasizing their Muslim identity through their clothes means hyperbolizing the moral and idealist political stance they wish to impress on the world. I remember vividly the pictures of the Bali bombers in court, for instance, dressed in impeccable long, white shirts and skull caps—punctuating their appearance with occasional shouts of "allahu Akbar," and eventually walking to their deaths in celebratory gear. There are also the many images showing other extremists before Western courts in flowing robes and caps. Thus Islamic dress through its expressive multivocality becomes another weapon in the armory of what is essentially an ideological battle.

NOTES

1. In parts of Afghanistan and Pakistan it is also called chaderi.
2. Purdah is a word used by South Asians for the gender division. Arabic speakers do not use it.
3. According to news reports, the police were unapologetic afterwards. The religious police are an official organ of the Committee for the Promotion of Virtue and the Prevention of Vice, a state body in Saudi Arabia.
4. Simon Harrison, "Cultural Boundaries." *Anthropology Today* 15/5 (1999): 10–13.
5. Nicholas Thomas, "The Inversion of Tradition." *American Anthropologist* 19/2 (1992): 213–232; p. 219.
6. There is a vast literature on the re-spiritualization through the New Age, NRMs (New Religious Movements), and other phenomena (revival of tribal ritual and beliefs associated with the revitalization of indigeneity) that seem to be a reaction to rationalism and secularization.
7. I cannot cite the numerous literature here; I can only mention Peter Berger, Brigitte Berger, and Hansfried Kellner, *The Homeless Mind*. New York: Random, 1973; and Paul Heelas, *The New Age Movement*. Cambridge MA.: Blackwell, 1996.

8. Two cases in which niqab-clad women were refused entry to a bus by the driver occurred in July 2011 in the city of Auckland, New Zealand. A short time later a similar case occurred in the capital, Wellington. Being very unusual in the multicultural and usually tolerant country, the incidents were widely reported by the media and the drivers heavily criticized. In defense of the bus drivers, the company argued they suffer from maskophobia (fear of masks) and would be undergoing psychological counseling. It remains to be seen whether this new psychological concept will gain in universal acceptance to justify rejection of veiled women; a behavior which otherwise would be classed as Islamophobic.

9. Syria seems to have such a law, but it is unclear whether it is enforced.

10. The law came into force on September 2, 2004, and bans all religious symbols in the public education system. For a fuller description of the French foulard controversy see Joan W. Scott, *The Politics of the Veil*. Princeton, Oxford: Princeton University Press, 2007. Even though it is often confused, terminologically there is a difference between foulard, headscarf, and voile, veil.

11. Apart from France and Belgium and some regional authorities, which have enacted a ban on total veiling (as has Syria), other countries have considered it (Spain, Austria, Netherlands, Switzerland, Bosnia, etc.) but for the time being rejected enacting legislation. Italy was still pondering the issue in late 2010. Interestingly, the press reports that gendered surveys show that non-Muslim women are more in favor of a ban than non-Muslim men. This would support the supposition that demands for a ban are feminist driven.

12. The fine can be replaced with lessons in citizenship. The police does not force the person to remove the veil but escort them to a station for identification. Belgium has passed the law but does not seem to enforce it.

13. Approximately 9 to 10 percent of the French population are Muslim, i.e.,, around 5 to 6 million. Precise statistics on religious affiliation are not available.

14. Olivier Roy, *Secularism Confronts Islam*. New York: Columbia University Press, 2007 (original in French 2005).

15. For instance, Ayaan Hirsi Ali's website www.ahafoundation.org (accessed August 2010) reports that two prominent Australian Muslims demanded that the country legislate a ban of the burqa.

16. Jocelyne Cesari, Islam in the West: Modernity and Globalization Revisited. In *Globalization and the Muslim World*, B. Schaebler and L. Stenberg. New York: Syracuse University Press, 2004. Jonathan Friedman, *Cultual Identity and Global Process*. London: Sage, 1994. Simon Harrison, Cultural Boundaries.

17. Some contributions to the volume *The Veil* (Jennifer Heath (ed.). Berkeley: University of California Press, 2008) offer some explanations.

18. Jan Retsö, *The Arabs in Antiquity: Their History from the Assyrians to the Umayyads*. London, New York: Routledge Curzon, 2003; p. 583.

19. Jennifer Heath in her article "What is Subordinated, Dominates" (In *The Veil*) connects veiling with face masks. If one extends veiling conceptually into the area of masking, there is hardly a culture that would fall outside the framework. However, this connection is semiotically tenuous insofar as veiling serves the purpose of concealing personal identity, whereas masking—whether for ritual purposes or for fun—means assuming and displaying another identity. It indicates a hyrophonous change of identity, not its obliteration.

20. This is the interpretation of the official Saudi translation, which is missing from other versions.

21. Sahih al-Bukhari vol. 6, hadith no. 282. Footnote to verse 24/31 in the official Saudi version of the Quran.

22. Fatema Mernissi, *Der politische Harem*. Freiburg, Basel, Wien: Herder, 1992; pp. 114–115, 125–126.

23. Quran 19/17, 7/46, 42/51, 41/5. The dividing wall may also metaphorically refer to humans not seeing or finding God.

24. *Der politische Harem*; pp. 206–214.

25. Quran 24/33 seems to refer to this situation, though obliquely.

26. Quran 33/59, which leaves it unclear whether molestation is to be avoided because they are to be respected as women, or because they are not slaves, or because they are Muslimas. See Mohja Kahf, "From Her Royal Body the Robe was Removed." In *The Veil*, J. Heath (ed.). Berkeley: University of California Press, 2008; p.29.

27. See Erich Kolig and Nahid Kabir, "Not Friend, Not Foe: The Rocky Road of Enfranchisement of Muslims into Multicultural Nationhood in Australia and New Zealand." *Immigrants and Minorities* 26/3 (2008): 266–300.

28. *Der politische Harem*; pp. 240–252.

29. *Ritual and Knowledge among the Baktaman of New Guinea*. Oslo: Universitetsforlaget; New Haven: Yale University Press, 1975.

30. Alfred Guillaume, *The Traditions of Islam: An Introduction to the study of the Hadith Literature*. Beirut: Khayats, 1966; p. 124.

31. This is taken from a Muslim friend's email communication, but appears to have been an article in the *Toronto Star* of January 23, 2002. I am unsure whether this is a verbatim or modified version.

32. Abu-Lughod, "Do Muslim Women Really Need Saving?" *American Anthropologist* 104/3 (2002): 783–791.

33. This example is taken from www.albawa.com (accessed March 2010), referred to by the NZDawa eNewsletter.

34. Despite official federal Russian law applying in Chechenya, in reality some elements of sharia are brought to bear surreptitiously.

35. I am taking some cues here from Irenäeus Eibl-Eibesfelt's work in ethnobiology. (For instance, *Menschenforschung auf neuen Wegen*. Wien, München, Zürich: Molden, 1976; and *Der vorprogrammierte Mensch*. Wien, München, Zürich: Molden, 1973.)

36. In referring to a state of undress, I do not make a strict semantic distinction between nakedness and nudity, although one refers to a physical de facto condition while the other relates rather to an abstracted image or perhaps an idealized conception.

37. The case is described in some detail in Nahid Afrose Kabir, "The Media is One-sided in Australia," *Journal of Children and Media* 2/3 (2008): 267–281. The mufti acquired a reputation for advocating arch-conservative views of an anti-Semitic, anti-Western, and anti-gay kind, but also tried to secure the release of an Australian hostage in Iraq under the Saddam Hussein regime.

38. The anecdote is related by the Islamicist Malise Ruthven. Quoted in Daniel Easterman, *New Jerusalems: Reflections on Islam, Fundamentalism and the Rushdie Affair*. London: Grafton, 1992; p. 27.

39. See Erich Kolig, *New Zealand's Muslims and Multiculturalism*. Leiden: Brill, 2010; pp. 191–192.

40. I have found this suggested in a column written by the social and political commentator Gwynne Dyer in August 2011.

41. I am leaving aside here the issue of disfiguring sicknesses that also encourage people to resort to concealing their faces.

42. Genesis 24/65; 1 Korinth 11/4 and 11/6.

43. Not being a psychologist, I cannot judge whether the unease this creates lies at the root of maskophobia, a concept that has lately been used to explain some non-Muslims' behavior in discriminating against veiled women.

44. See the strong resurgence of the tattoo or moko in New Zealand and generally in Western society. Needless to say that tattooing has a very different connotation when it is forcibly done, like to concentration camp inmates or even the SS elite (noting the soldier's blood type), even though in this context also it bears a message.

45. Alfred Guillaume, *The Traditions of Islam*; p. 130.

46. Alfred Guillaume, *The Traditions of Islam*; p. 130.

47. As discussed before, male and female circumcision, as a body-altering procedure, somewhat illogically falls outside this framework.

48. Official portrait photos for passports and other documents in some countries, e.g., the European Union, are subject to strict rules in every detail. Normally they prohibit any kind of head covering or concealment of face or hair. (However, in July 2011 Austrian media reported

a case of a man being granted an exemption on religious grounds allowing him to wear a headcovering in his image on a driver's licence. Absurdly, his religion is Pastafarianism and his religious headcover is a noodle sieve.) Some countries allow veiled women the dignity of having their identity checked by female officials.

49. To some extent these concerns have meanwhile been allayed by using generic imaging, which makes the procedure more impersonal and somewhat less intrusive.

50. Alfred Guillaume, *The Traditions of Islam*; p. 128. The relevant hadith says, "The portion of the drawers below the ankles is hell fire."

Chapter Six

The Intellectual Ingredient of Freedom and Levity

BLASPHEMY AND THE POWER OF LAUGHTER

English language news media in March and April 2010 carried the story of a bizarre stoush involving an American comedian, the nation of Australia, and the U.S. federal state of Alabama, both political entities represented by the highest level of civil administration. On an American talk show (David Letterman), Hollywood star and "funny man" Robin Williams, just returned from a trip to Australia, used the throw away line that "Australians are basically English red-necks." He seemed to have enjoyed his sojourn in Australia and the intent of his remark, as suggested by this context of light-hearted banter, was humorous and not meant to give offense. Amazingly, this remark was picked up by the (then) Australian prime minister Kevin Rudd who in a radio interview angrily retorted that Williams should not look further than Alabama for rednecks. This, in turn, infuriated some good people of Alabama, including its governor, who demanded an apology from Rudd. Good humor had quickly given way to offensiveness and escalated to nastiness and mutual recriminations. Some of the comments thrown about were, for example, that if it had not been for Alabamans fighting in the war, Australians today would be speaking Japanese; and another one, using, in the circumstances, a more appropriate humorous slant, promised he would go to the zoo and punch a kangaroo in the nose.

Apart from its obvious silliness and appalling lack of sense of humor, courtesy, and diplomacy on all parts, this episode shows very clearly that mockery has the uncanny ability to offend deeply. In defiance of the children's rhyme "sticks and stones . . . ," it arouses passions and emotions that appear to be disproportionate to the words and means used to compose the satire. Even supposedly level-headed, rational people, as one must suppose the prime minister of Australia to be, react in a highly emotionally charged manner that may quickly get out of hand. The prime minister of Australia would most probably not respond by flinging a death fatwa against Williams and Alabama will not declare jihad against the Australians. But some damage, temporary as it may be, to international harmony and goodwill has undoubtedly been done.

Devout Muslims regard Islam as an instrument of moderation and wisdom, which uses jocularity only sparingly and carefully. Although Islam is not totally devoid of a sense of humor, it prescribes strict limitations in accord with its fundamental socializing function. Not permitted is anything uproariously funny, titillating, and against a person's natural dignity. Joking is permitted under the condition that it be moderate, not hurtful or insulting, or against the truth, nor must it distract from religious duty. As it says in the Sunna, "joking appropriately is permissible, for the Prophet [. . .] joked, but he only said what is true." Not surprisingly, jokes attributed by tradition to the Prophet and his companions would seem today from a Western perspective rather insipid. The most hurtful joke the Prophet seems to have ever uttered, according to the tradition, is to say to an old woman, who anxiously inquired whether she could go to heaven, that only young girls can enter. As the Sunna relates, afterwards he instructed his companions to tell the distraught woman that righteous old women would become young again before entering paradise.

Socially, gentle joking is encouraged—especially after prayers—to create an atmosphere of friendliness in the circle of family members and children, but also with guests to entertain and to relax. But as so often doctrine issuing multivocal commands is not unambiguous. Some jurist-scholars, on the basis of some ahadith, have seen fit to prohibit all joking. Their source of inspiration in particular is one tradition that attributes to the Prophet the saying, "Everything has a beginning and hostility begins with joking." Other warnings found in the Sunna are: "Beware of joking for it causes embarrassment"; "Joking shows foolishness and arrogance"; and "Joking causes offenses, spite and malice between people." These sayings betray a good psychological insight, but by the same token eliminated a useful release valve, which at times is able to lessen tension, from the social discourse

Even though it evidently is a matter of interpretation, Islam, by generally placing by far the greater emphasis on seriousness, has a narrowly circumscribed sense of what is permissible humor. By their very nature mockery and satire not only exaggerate, caricature, and distort and thus defy the rule of truthfulness, but also are designed to annoy and offend and thus may become a source for social conflict. Like most aspects of social interaction referred to in the scriptures, levity is considered in a social context and what effects it may have on the integrity of the social fabric. Seen in this light, joking, whether careless or calculated, is a social hazard. It contains a social volatility that requires great care.

Despite recognizing mockery as a psychologically dangerous instrument and a source of social trouble, the scriptures do not advocate its use against an adversary. Used judiciously it may become a potent weapon for the subversive effect it may have on the morale of an enemy, and concomitantly, it may enhance the mocker's own sense of empowerment by belittling the opponent. In the doctrinal view the negative reflection on the user's character outweighs any tactical advantages that may be gained. No exception is made even for the just fight, the jihad, against an enemy of Islam. Taunting the enemy, for instance, provoking him into headless fury with ridicule was a useful battle strategy of the ancients as well as some tribal societies. Before joining battle, a not-so-gentle "ribbing" may have been exchanged among the "contestants" to build up their own morale as much as putting down the adversary. Yet, Islam, despite its history of belligerent expansion, seems totally adverse to the idea. From that one can draw the conclusion that the Iranian government's reaction to the *Jyllands-Posten's* cartoons, inviting insulting cartoons on the Holocaust and Zionism, is without religious precedent and lacks doctrinal encouragement.

As may be expected, the gravest and most pernicious form of mockery is that directed against Islam itself. Any religion is not a fit subject for satire, but especially so Islam. Not only does doctrine rule itself out as a legitimate subject for satire, fun poked at religious matters of any kind quickly assumes the proportion of intolerable blasphemy. An insult of this magnitude requires a very firm rebuttal; in fact more than that: a deterrent that prevents further insults. However, Islamic doctrine and shariatic views, are far from presenting a united front in terms of jurisprudence, ethical views, and proper response to insult and inappropriate humor directed against Islam. The Quran (6/68, 9/65–66, 15/95) refers to the sin of mocking Islam and to how Muslims should react. Surprisingly, it suggests a fairly mild-mannered response. It even recommends ignoring the insult and avoiding the company of the mockers: "And when you see those engaged in conversation mocking our revelations, stay away from them until they turn to another topic . . . and sit not in the company of the zalimun (wrong-doers)."[1] Here mockery, though despised and irritating, is treated rather lightly. The "hypocrites" are promised their punishment in hellfire.[2] The point at which teasing that can be ignored turns into infuriating mockery, or when it assumes the shape of unacceptable blasphemy, is left unclear. The Quran does not define the condition and nature of the blasphemous insult that would necessitate a more deadly answer, nor does it even intimate an active punishment for the provocateur. The Sunna and subsequent Islamic history, however, give many examples of the harsh reaction to blasphemous injury—a reaction that was clearly absent during the time of the early revelations and is not recommended in the Quran, not even the later revelations. It seems, only later on, from a position of strength, did Islam develop a disinclination to tolerate even the slightest insult. For much of its history Muslim authorities have reacted with deadly force to any perceived slight against the religion.

By and large, the concept of mocking Islam, thus intentionally or accidentally committing blasphemy, is not clearly separated from apostasy and heresy, and they are often addressed in the same terms. They tend to be treated as equal offenses, are often terminologically referred to interchangeably, and practically responded to with the same severity. They are one in showing disrespect to God's word and, therefore, are all crimes committed directly against God. Given the gravity of the crime, the appropriate punishment is death. The Quran characteristically does not terminologically or conceptually distinguish between sinner and criminal (mujrimun), and the two concepts merge in the sharia. Religious misdemeanor, verbal attack against religious substance, and disregard for social rules become one conceptually as all logically are offenses against divine authority and bear a connotation of rebellion.

The part of the sharia that constitutes criminal law and penal justice is not entirely clear on the subject of blasphemy as several interpretations exist. With few exceptions, however, the jurists of all Sunni and Shi'a schools demand the severest penalty for blasphemers. The punishment deemed appropriate for blasphemy (ridda, kufr) is more or less aligned with notions of what the sharia prescribes in cases of apostasy (irtidad, ridda) and sedition or heresy (bida, kufr). In terms of judicial seriousness, they are considered to be among the worst crimes according to the Islamic sense of law and justice, and occupy a higher rank than unjustified homicide. While murder may be forgiven by the bereaved family, religious crimes are unpardonable. Saudi law, which among the contemporary legal systems in Muslim states conforms probably most closely to the edicts and practices of classical sharia and represents its spirit most faithfully, prescribes the death penalty for the religious criminal murtadd. This system of law considers beheading the most appropriate punishment, while other forms of execution such as hanging, stoning, and death by shooting are being practiced elsewhere. The only mitigation that can be claimed to escape execution is insanity, which entails imprisonment until natural death or spiritual rehabilitation in some form such as by recantation.

As one can imagine, satirizing core doctrines of Islam or even "inappropriate" reference to them would easily fall within the parameters of capital crime. Few escape routes are open to the blasphemer. To claim temporary addling of the brain and for the offender to throw themselves on the mercy of the religious authorities may perhaps help in an official sharia court but is no guarantee against extra-judicial assassination. (In 2011, a Pakistani government minister who wanted to change blasphemy laws became a blasphemer himself in the eyes of the pious and was assassinated by his own bodyguard.) A simple apology—as Salman Rushdie issued over the furor he caused with his novel *The Satanic Verses*—will not suffice. Reconfirming his faith in Islam, as he did, if not the wrong move entirely, was unhelpful. Radicalized Islam, not given to charitable forgiveness, unsurprisingly adheres to the strictest principles in such matters and holds even the infidel world to the standards of Islamic justice. It believes it has a divine mandate, in fact a religious duty that applies to all Muslims individually, to bring "criminals" offending against Islam to Islamic justice. This may involve a declaration of a death sentence through a fatwa (as Khomeini issued against Rushdie), or in severe cases may provoke a (small-scale) campaign of jihad (as some would-be assassins of the Danish cartoonists insisted they were carrying out). Blasphemy requires a strong response regardless of whether this is embedded in a context of official jihad or justice is done through individual initiative. Some recent verbal and juridical clashes between the Islamic world and the West—ranging from *The Satanic Verses* to cartoons—have their origin in this religiously prescribed reaction.

Present-day interpretations by Muslim experts are divided on the issue of mocking Islam through humorous portrayal. Some modernizts recommend showing forgiveness, clemency, or simply ignoring the insult, but by far the more prominent position, preferred by fundamentalists and conservatives, is to consider mockery a form of blasphemy and to respond with fierceness. Pointing out that the Prophet has not recommended turning the other cheek, this attitude insists on exacting the severest penalty. In so doing, the concept of what constitutes sacrilege and punishable mockery is usually drawn very widely, including, for instance, even what may seem to be relatively innocuous, "inoffensive" representations of the Prophet. Websites designed for the enlightenment of believers as well as non-believers render long lists of what may be regarded as blasphemous insults in Islam and from which one should wisely stay away. Joking in religious matters always and in any context risks injuring religious sensitivities and provokes charges of blasphemy. There is no provision for acceptable satirization in any form as divine dictate does not allow for the slightest hilarity in religious matters. Especially the religious trend of fundamentalization seems to be moving Islam towards a purism that disavows humor altogether, even if entirely "secular," as ungodly. Wahhabism, radicalized forms of Islam and those belonging to the Salafya in particular show a distinct rejection of humor no matter what the subject matter or what or who becomes the target of ridicule. Overall, in an intuitive assessment, it seems there is a shrinking tolerance of humor in the Islamic world, at least a stagnation of liberalizing impulses, which may have signaled advancing secularization.

In Muslim majority countries, the arts have to be careful not to infringe on the religious dictate in matters of jocularity. Cartoonists, for instance, have to be very much aware of this if they value their lives. Satirical comedy, ever conscious of trespassing on religious territory, is a sparse art form. Stand-up comedy is virtually unknown, and where it can be found nowadays, it marks a recent and rather timid incursion of Western cultural influence.[3]

Rare as it may be, moving the contemplation of religious contents outside the conventional sacred context and its hallowed decorum is readily open to charges of sacrilege and blasphemy. The dramatization of religious contents through theatre play moves on contested grounds. While Shi'a Islam allows and appreciates passion play relating to the suffering and martyrdom of its early imams, especially the Wahhabi purism, which globally is gaining much traction in recent times, shuns and condemns it. Research in Indonesia has taught me much about the position of the arts—although by comparison with Iran or Saudi Arabia it is far less precarious. (Much of Indonesia's traditional artistic repertory is taken from the pre-Islamic Hindu past.) Nonetheless, devout Indonesian Muslims (santri) complain about too much levity in television and theatre, and generally too much social emphasis on entertainment and not enough edifying religious instruction. Indonesian performing art forms, for instance, in theatre, puppetry, television plays, and film frequently do draw on the figure of the jester, the clown, and the comical monster, but never in a context that could be construed as relating to Islam or Islamic values.

In the course of research in Indonesia, I have briefly enquired into an art form known as wayang sadat.[4] It is a kind of puppet play, wayang kulit (shadow puppetry), which enacts Islamic religious themes and does so, one should emphasize, in a very respectful manner. Its intention is to educate, not satirize. While the representation of religiously important figures with "cute," little shadow puppets does have an element of mild caricature, one should have thought that because of the expressed intent of this art form as dawah (or dakwa in Bahasa Indonesia), religious instruction, it would enjoy some tolerance. Yet, this kind of Islamic theatre is fiercely opposed by exponents of conservative Islam, especially by those inclining towards Islam aliran garis keras, the stern, radical brand of Islam. It considers portraying religious contents with the means of puppetry not only frivolous but even sacrilegious, even when it is clearly not humorous and obviously not intended to mock but rather to enlighten and to draw people towards Islam. (In addition, however, the puppetry's means of representation, based on the human form, are another reason for conservative Islam to view it with much skepticism. This will be briefly explained later.) Even when this artistry, with the blessing of moderate Islamic authorities, is shown on national television and is meant to enliven the religious spirit of festivities, puppeteers, the dhalang, of wayang sadat often receive threats from fanatics.

In a wider anthropological perspective, joking, appreciation of that which is considered funny and responsive laughter—despite Islamic strictures—are clearly behaviors recognizable as universal. The actual contents of what may be considered funny are very culture-specific, making cross-cultural humor difficult. (In complex societies, what is considered humorous may depend on social and educational differences.) In very general terms, a fully developed sense of humor is a human characteristic, although some primatologists would argue that the highest animal primates also possess a sense of the bizarre and absurd and when confronted with it show some distinctive reaction. Researchers insist that animal primate behavior shows the embryous phylogeny of laughter as a response to something considered funny. Some keen observers of primate behavior even believe that chimpanzees can actually laugh in appreciation of the amusing.

Regardless of whether a sense of levity meets a need anchored in human nature, humor clearly shows ambiguous features. It does not solely entertain, its product is not simply and harmlessly funny, and it does not necessarily invoke laughter or harmless mirth. But when does a joke stop being a joke? In the form of satire, irony, parody, sarcasm, and mockery the humorous and the comical transcends the primary purpose of being "fun." It succeeds in exercising a degree of power that would not exist otherwise in serious consideration. Joking about something reduces it in status, and in belittling the object of mirth, a relative relationship between commentator and the commented-on is established. The active part elevates itself and arrogates authority of judgment to itself over the object of derision, which in terms of social relationship may be anathema to the appropriately termed "butt" of the joke. The result is that joking is rarely totally harmless, devoid of barbs, or inconsequential in a social respect. The power of humor is such that, especially in the strongly satirizing form of mockery, it can be hurtful and insulting, vastly in excess of its apparent surface meaning. A gibe can express a powerful derision that is difficult to ignore or pass over as inconsequential. In fact intelligent satire is not only intended to entertain and provoke harmless laughter, but to stimulate reflection, to make a serious point and in attempting to do so may deliberately wish to offend in order to press home this purpose. Cabaret can perform as an effective medium of social critique and skillful farce lampooning the "powers that be" and can carry some considerable political clout. Cartoons in performing similar functions can offend vastly beyond their artistic and imaginative merits. The most artless graffiti may carry a satirical value incommensurate with its physical location in a lavatory or under a bridge. Not unusually, dictatorial regimes grumpily frown upon being mocked by satirical art forms and react violently. The higher the prestige and status of the content that is being mocked, the greater the offense. Lese majesty and blasphemy, ridiculing the highest authority in a state or offending divinity, are traditionally considered insults of the highest order and demanding of the most severe punishment. But as can be expected in a highly secularized society such as the West as a whole, Christian contents enjoy little practical protection by law. Although relevant laws in many Western countries are still on the law books, today they are rarely, if ever, invoked. Thus no drastically effective defense exists in highly secularized societies against religious insult, despite the existence of blasphemy laws, because pressing them into service very likely would make such a case a cause célèbre of absurdity. The juridical firewall against insults protecting Christian contents is only slightly higher than that for other religions. In general, royalty still seems somewhat better protected against disrespectful jest.[5] Legal conditions aside, public disapproval, rules of good taste, decency, and civil values also have a powerful role to play in setting boundaries to the use of satire and mockery. For instance, satirizing the Holocaust may not fall under criminal law provisions, but would seriously discredit the satirizt and their product. Linking British royalty with obscenity, humorous as it may seem, would be unthinkable for any reputable publication. Such examples show that freedom of expression, even in Western society where this is considered a high public good, is not limitless and the legitimate use of humor to mock has its boundaries no matter whether they are set by laws or dictated by taste and convention.

The West's much-vaunted freedom of the press, the media in general, and artistic expression, unbeknownst to many, is hedged in by a string of strict laws.[6] Add to this aesthetic conventions, majority tastes, and values and the so-called freedom of expression turns out to be largely imaginary. In the fluid world of morality, graffiti "art" as much as art forms considered pornographic or in some way injurious to legal norms operate in the shadows of this freedom. Media freedoms are controlled in several respects—not even considering defamation laws: for instance, contents of a sexually more explicit nature must not be screened on public television before a certain time in the evening, material judged obscene, pedophilic, or grossly pornographic falls under strict censorship laws, and even the general presentation of nudity and sexual activity also has limitations both in terms of laws and a sense of what is aesthetically acceptable in a public situation. Even the private sphere is not immune to legal constraints and controls—even in the most liberal Western democracies. Aesthetic and legal regimes vary in finer details from country to country. The exact boundaries dividing the harmlessly smutty and indelicate from the unacceptably foul and dirty vary, but the general principles of what is legally and aesthetically acceptable and what is not are fairly uniform in the Western world. In individual cases, political influence and other social dynamics may set such boundaries rather whimsically and in blatant contravention of the mantras of personal or artistic freedom of expression. Some years ago, a New Zealand cartoonist lost his contract with a newspaper following a complaint by the Jewish lobby over a provocative drawing that likened Israel's policies towards Palestinians with apartheid. Apple Inc. in 2009 and 2010 refused repeatedly sexual and satirical material for the app store in iPhone and iPad—in the case of "public persons" being satirized presumably on grounds of defamation laws being applied against it. (Some material was admitted only after massive electronic protest.) The list of satirical material being prevented from being aired in public or arousing serious dispute and anger could be enlarged ad infinitum. Overall, the unhindered and unlimited promulgation of any content, material or idea, funny or serious, turns out at closer inspection to be a cherished myth or an unattainable ideal far from being emulated even in the most liberal democracies of the West.[7] It is important to bear this in mind when evaluating Islamic strictures on the dissemination and treatment of religious items.

Another aspect is the perceived injury to the dignity of a content by placing it in the "wrong" context. Sensitivities surrounding cultural items, especially those of iconic value, can be found in many contexts and are far from being confined to Islam. In New Zealand, for instance, moves are afoot to hand to Maori (the indigenous people or tangata whenua) controlling rights of their treasured cultural contents (taonga), whether material or immaterial. The aim is to make sure that their treasures are not abused or used in an inappropriate way. This happened, for instance, when a sacred dance (the haka, which is reserved for men) was mockingly performed in a television commercial by Italian women for a car advertisement. Also offensive to Maori is when sacred facial tattoos (moko) are used arbitrarily and without formal permission by entertainers or sportspersons who are not Maori. (This is not only a breach of cultural copyright, but has been inappropriately lifted from its sacred cultural context.) The more subtle points cannot be discussed here as to whether such controlling rights over cultural matters—not only Maori but other indigenous people as well wish to possess—refer to ownership or guardianship (kaitiaki), whether they are total or can be called upon only when the use and the context in which the cherished item is placed are cheapening it or are insulting to the item's cultural dignity. Indigenous people clearly wish for a culturally protective mechanism that transcends in its formal firmness the conventions and so-called good taste of the hegemon. Often it seems that while there is considerable sympathy for the protection of indigenous cultures and their dignity, Islamic culture remains "fair game." And while so-called "political correctness" in matters of aesthetics has spread a protective mantle about traditional Third World cultures, Islam continues to be buffeted by the winds of undisguised sarcasm.

The Islamic world draws a much harsher line to protect treasured sacred contents. By law or tacit convention, this line divides sharply between respect and apparent disrespect shown towards important cultural items. Consequently, the Gordian knot tying together in awkward conflict hilarity and sacrilegious insult, religious restraint and freedom, in some respects is much tighter than in the West. Here, laughter has to tread lightly, as the line between acceptable humor and mockery is easily overstepped. The droll, the comic, and the laughable have an application different from the West's and the division between harmless jest and insult is differently located in the social discourse—as is the notion of the personal freedom to blur the line sometimes. In most Muslim countries laws protect secular powers of state and personages of state and government from gross satire in line with a more authoritarian understanding of official administration, its functions and the inviolability of public persons. Humour used in this connection usually has the deliberate purpose of insulting, and if the barbs are directed against the powers that be, such satirical efforts are confined to the political underground.

Above all, religious (Islamic) content is sacrosanct. Humour considered blasphemous falls under much stricter prohibitions than in the West, even when the particular country's state law is not directly based on the sharia. Muslim society, having avoided secularization to the same extent as the Western world, is still much more inclined to consider mockery of the religious a heinous crime. Responses today may vary in severity but still reflect the principles of a traditional religious value system. If state law is secularized to the extent that it does not apply capital punishment in such cases, religiously inspired vigilante justice is never far from being meted out.

The ructions caused by Salman Rushdie's "transgression," more recently have been surpassed by the cartoons published in the Danish paper *Jyllands-Posten*. In fact several times in recent years, European cartoonists—not only those publishing their works in the *Jyllands-Posten*—have caused grievous offense through their art. Because of their mockery of Islamic contents, they have become targets of Muslim fanatics' wrath. As a consequence they had to take extraordinary security measures to escape assassination. So far, several attacks have been successfully thwarted by police.[8] For the need of taking precautions and keeping always alert, the Dutch filmmaker Theo van Gogh's fate serves as the horrible example.

Muslims have delivered in recent years many demonstrations of how fervent believers react to what they see as the crime of blasphemy couched in illicit humor. In the course of venting their anger, they have succeeded in making themselves even more vulnerable, by provoking further deliberate attempts to insult their religious sensitivities. Clearly, the cause célèbre in this matter was the *Jyllands-Posten* cartoon affair. This affair is too well known to need description here.[9] It was not the first and not the last case of deliberately or unknowingly giving offense to Muslim sensitivities in this manner. Explanations and interpretations as to the motive of organizing the publication of the cartoons have varied widely: from encouraging serious discussion of multiculturalism in Denmark to deliberate "Muslim baiting." Since it roused such controversy some cartoonists have followed suit, their engagement in copycat acts not so innocent any more. While the *Jyllands-Posten* newspaper may have still argued with some convincing that it was their wish to initiate a debate on Islam in Denmark, and not having realized just how offensive their strategy was, subsequent cartoon publications had slightly different objectives. Of those the noblest and most principled motif was to underline the freedom of press and art, and exercising it provocatively perhaps to "push the envelope." Some artists and publishers may have wished to demonstrate their fearlessness in the face of Muslim outrage; while for others it obviously was a chance to vent their Islamophobia and by taking pleasure in Muslims' discomfiture to unmask Muslims' violent fanaticism— and perhaps even to promote the contention that Islam per se is a "backward" and violent religion.

Among the most infamous cartoons is the image of a bearded man, obviously representing the Prophet, with a bomb in his turban, a lit fuse sticking out of it, and flanked by two heavily veiled women. (Ironically, a suicide attack in Afghanistan has since been made by using this method.) Epigones have produced similarly insulting images: the Prophet depicted as a dog or with the features of a pig. In these cases it is difficult even from a secularized Western viewpoint to distinguish between artful satire and the calculated insult designed to provoke outrage. It stretches the imagination to discern a higher purpose relating to art and freedom despite protestations of the artists and their apologists that there is a principled point to be made. It seems more reminiscent of the kind of enemy baiting before the spears are thrown in tribal battle.

Pictures and portraits of people in general are a contentious issue in Islamic doctrine and in a conservative interpretation are subject to severe restrictions. Even though only Wahhabism has a history of extreme iconoclasm (and under its influence, the Taleban regime),[10] Islam in general is adverse to the realiztic representation of the human form. In a very general sense the aversion to realiztic pictorial representation of all living things is expressed in the hadith: "Angels will not enter a house containing a dog or pictures."[11] Punishment awaits the artists in the afterlife when they will be asked to bring their pictures to life, and they will fail as they must. They have brazenly tried to arrogate the act of creation to themselves, ignoring God's monopoly on it. Only inanimate objects (containing no spirit) may be drawn and painted without committing a sin.[12]

This interdiction applies even more strongly to sacred personages and above all most strongly to the Prophet's image.[13] The Hollywood film *The Message*, which relates the story of the Prophet and his struggle to establish the original Muslim community, pointedly respects this doctrine. The figure of the Prophet, although he is the protagonist around whom the story unfolds, in deference to Islamic requirements does not feature in the film. He remains totally unseen and unheard even though the character is cleverly drawn into action and dialogue. Because Islamic sensitivities have been respected, the film has apparently been endorsed by Muslim authorities. Manufacturing representations of holy or otherwise exalted personages, and especially of the Prophet, is not only considered blasphemous but also seen to invite, or come dangerously close to, idolatry, a major sin. In severity it represents shirk, that is undermining tawhid, the oneness of God, and ignoring the prohibition of connecting God with another entity or elevating it to an object of adoration. The Prophet, despite his exalted position in Islamic hagiography, is no exception.

Having said this, one must add that in Muslim society such rules are not always completely obeyed. I have it on reliable authority that occasionally an imaginative artistic portrait of the Prophet Muhammad can be found, although I cannot recall having ever seen one myself.[14] Photographic images of people are not considered to be human creations; they are natural reflections of reality—although the Taleban had a more restrictive notion on this topic and forbade all pictorial representations of people. Apart from photographs, which are usually considered not to fall under the regime of illicit "creation," pictures of reigning monarchs, statesmen, leading clerics, and the like, can be found in offices and schools and may be carried in processions. They may be displayed in a reverential manner without raising suspicions of idolatry. Especially, Schi'ism appears by and large to follow a more liberal interpretation in this matter. Oversized images of Khomeini and the current spiritual leader Khamenei can be seen on almost every street corner in Tehe-ran. Pictorial representations of saintly men, above all of imam Ali and Hussein, are carried prominently in processions at Ashura and at other cele-bratory occasions. However, even at such occasions of heightened religious fervor displaying a (necessarily fictitious) picture of the Prophet would be unthinkable. The very strict prohibition observed nowadays on portraying him is probably due to the rising strength of Wahhabi iconoclastic purism.

In recent years cartoons depicting the Prophet as dog or pig have appeared in Nordic newspapers[15] sparking vigorous protest and even assassination attempts. It can easily be understood that this is a particularly explosive combination of two taboos. It does not require much cultural sensitivity to comprehend that connecting the image of the Prophet with pigs and dogs is extremely insulting. Especially injurious to the dignity of this exalted figure is the lack of esteem in Islamic belief of these animals. Dogs and pigs are among the lowliest of creatures, considered "unclean" (najis) in a sense less to do with hygiene than with ungodliness[16] —a conception that runs through all Abrahamic religions, though it is far from being so strongly expressed in Christianity[17] as in Judaism and Islam. In the Islamic hierarchy of things, pigs and dogs are ranked with urine, feces, semen, corpses, blood, alcohol, and sweat of animals that eat carrion or refuse. The flesh of pigs and dogs is strictly haram (Quran 5/3), not fit for human consumption, except in situations of utter starvation when eating it makes the difference between life and death. Islamic doctrine prescribes that dogs not be kept as pets or companions, although they are acceptable for farming purposes, shepherding, security and hunting.[18] Prey brought down by trained hounds is permissible to be consumed, but a bismillah has to be spoken over it to purify it (Quran 5/3). Bedouins enjoy certain exemptions so that they can keep dogs in their tents without breaking Islamic rules. That more than hygiene is at stake is evidenced by the rule that plates and utensils that a dog has licked have to be washed seven times (including once with sand and water) to make them clean again for human use.

The *South Park* cartoon series with a track record of irreverence towards religious contents not surprisingly also ran foul of devout Muslims. Given its socio-critical mission of lampooning socially sensitive contents, it was only a matter of time before Islam would somehow feature in it. *South Park* having learned a lesson from the fate of other cartoonists, did not openly satirize Islam or the Prophet. Accepting the prohibition on pictorial representations of the Prophet and recognizing how easy it is to give offense in this way, the creators of *South Park* chose to dress the Prophet in a bear suit. However, this tactic of circumventing the prohibition, and bleeping out part of the dialogue did not seem to have the desired effect. The producers of the series were still subjected to threats—or warnings, as it was put—on the internet that they could "end up like the Dutch filmmaker."

Monotheistic religions—in contrast to Hinduism, archaic, and so-called tribal or totemic religions—seem to have a tendency to regard the close association with animals as violating the sacrosanctity of religious contents. There is no reason here to enter into a theological argument, but cursorily put, this aversion may have something to do with the proud perception that human beings are the pinnacle of creation and associating them too closely with lower forms of the creation hierarchy is a loss of status and an insult. Christianity in particular speaks of man having been created in God's image and also cryptically keeps alive the idea of the Great Chain of Being. Although the Quran refers to camels and horses in appreciative terms, (and Christianity exhibits some warmth towards donkeys and sheep), hierarchical ideas about the structure of creation imply a dragging down and diminution of the highest contents by linking them in intimate connection with the lower aspects of the created universe. The resultant dichotomous division into the realm of human beings and that of nature and animals is quite different from totemistic thinking of many other cultures, which, lacking in this hierarchical conception of creation, in one form or another establishes a close relationship between humans and nature.[19] Similar objections relate to a connection of sacred contents with sexuality. One cartoon of the *Jyllands-Posten*, also considered highly offensive by Muslims, at least implicitly established this connection by referring to the promise of a number of virgins—sometimes thought to be seventy-two, though this can vary—for martyrs to enjoy in paradise.

Religious folk of the monotheistic persuasion more often than not turn out to be seriously deficient in a sense of humor when their beliefs are subjected to irreverent mirth, especially when it has sexual connotations. A clerically inspired satire in early 2010, in the New Zealand city of Auckland comes to mind. Shortly before Easter in that year, an Anglican church publicly displayed a large poster that showed a distraught-looking Joseph in bed with Mary looking longingly up to heaven. The caption read, "Poor Joseph. God is a hard act to follow." No sooner was it up, it was defaced by devout Christians. The same fate befell subsequent replacements. Poking fun at the Christian conception story, as a priest explained, was meant to remind people of the true meaning of Easter. The intent certainly was not to offer an insult to the religious sentiments of Auckland's Christians, but rather to inspire reflection through satire.

Satirizing Christian belief contents is happening on a daily basis all over the world (though not usually by church circles) and certainly is condoned in the ex-Christian secularized West. Not all of it is good-humored and relatively gentle such as the example above. Some years ago, New Zealand's national museum Te Papa Tongarewa in the capital Wellington hosted a traveling art display. Among its exhibits was a replica picture of Leonardo da Vinci's *Last Supper* in which the image of Jesus Christ was replaced by a nude woman. But even greater offense was offered by a small commercial statue of the Madonna covered by a condom.[20] It caused a serious uproar among the Catholic community—a minority in the country, who was supported in their loud protests by fundamentalist Protestants and Muslims. Demonstrations and prayer meetings were held and even a bomb threat made, but it did not sway the museum management, which pointed out that in a secularized society, the freedom of the arts is paramount. The offending item was not removed from display and the exhibition ran its full course. As in other cases when art seriously offends, the artist defended herself saying she wanted to stimulate intellectual debate on important issues: in this case she meant to generate a discussion within Catholicism on female rights, contraception, and abortion. Needless to say, she did succeed in unleashing a rather heated debate, but it was focused on artistic licence and the need to impose limits. Her assurances that her intention was not to offend were simply not believed. Compare that with Muslim anger about satirical representations of the Prophet and not much difference will be discerned. Caricatures of the Prophet as a pig or dog, or as a bomb-carrying terrorist may rather cryptically be intended to make a point about artistic freedom and freedom of expression, or to express the artist's in-your-face courage to defy the brutal threat of a death fatwa almost in the nature of the inveterate thrill seeker and adrenalin junky.

Believers of the religious contents that are brutally satirized will find it very difficult to accept that there was a laudable point of higher principle involved beyond simply offering a gratuitous and calculated insult. Offense is especially great, when the religious content of iconic value is associated with something that in the respective culture has particularly negative connotations. It is more than just a little risqué to establish a close association, both physically and conceptually, of a highly revered sacred content—namely "the mother of God"—with the overly profane object of a condom, connected as it is with the idea of lewdness and being the receptacle of excreted bodily fluid. Despite its life-giving potential, in these circumstances it represents a waste product and stands for utter profanity—all of which marks a condom out as antithetical to sacredness and anathema to adoration. It is difficult to interpret such a combination of socially well-understood, but in their meaning antinomious, symbols as anything less than offensive. In Islam's case the intimate juxtaposition of pigs and dogs with its iconic founder does not fail to have the same effect. The capacity of these associations to insult is clearly understood not only by the respective religionists, but in a globalized world the satirical and insulting intent can be grasped even across cultural boundaries, although perhaps not in the same severity.

It may appear that respect for religious content and humor, and especially irony, may be highly antithetical to each other to the point of irreconcilability. On the surface, this may seem to be a universal trait of humanity, only abandoned now by the West either because it has advanced beyond such "primitive" sentiments or because it is so decadent that it has lost every sense of respect for higher values. Which of the two it is, is open to interpretation. But species-typical seems to be that laughter and reverence exclude each other in the religious discourse to the point of being considered an emotional and intellectual dichotomy. This, however, turns out to be a mistaken assumption.

Religious conduct, in order to appreciate the spiritual significance of belief contents, does not necessarily require seriousness. Respect does not exclude humor. Nor is a sense of overwhelming awe[21] vis-à-vis religious content necessarily a panhuman, species-typical response. While this is certainly a very prominent feature of religious belief and ceremony that can be found in all religions, a feeling of religious reverence may not always be to the total exclusion of a sense of mirth. The most reverential ceremony may not necessarily preclude laughter. Belief contents may even be designed to stimulate a response of hilarity and fun. Examples of this kind were delivered through my own experience with Australian Aboriginal religiosity in which attendance to sacred religious matters did not at times preclude hilarity. Some religious occasions, which routinely provoked uproarious laughter, stood in marked contrast to others that had to be treated with utmost seriousness and included an acute sense of numinous danger. The causes of mirth usually were references in mythical narratives to comical situations arising out of mishaps and the divine agencies' all-too-human clumsiness or stupidity. Schadenfreude (joy about damage or injury to the actor inflicted as a consequence) quite clearly also played a role in eliciting this reaction. Other satirical references such as relating to flatus and sexuality when embedded in a sacred mythical or ritual context could also serve as sources of amusement.

It is impossible to give here even a highly sketchy picture of Australian Aboriginal religion, usually considered a paragon of a totemic religion, because of its inherent complexity. Suffice it to say that the majority of religious contents have to do with events in a primordial epoch—the so-called Dreamtime or the Dreaming, a sacred period of creation in which prehuman exemplars lived very much like humans later did, hunting and gathering, fighting and loving, experiencing joy and sadness, being ethical or lawless, and basically displaying humanlike needs and wants. However, they had the superhuman potency to be creative through their acts, both by exemplifying culture and physically by transforming the landscape. (The anthropomorphization of the divine sphere is not unlike the medieval Christian conception of divinity and classical Mediterranean religions in which the pantheon also displays very humanlike traits).[22] Their deeds impressed themselves on the physiographic and natural features of the land, as well as setting sociocultural precedents, which became binding on their human successors. In keeping with the totemistic character of this religion, the divine exemplars were zoomorphic, a few botanomorphic, and some of unspecified shape, but all of them possessing human attributes through which they espoused sociocultural patterns not unlike the ones Australian Aborigines lived by until recent history when colonization began to have an impact in various ways and eventually destroyed or irrevocably altered traditional society and culture. The narratives about the totemic exemplars' deeds are properly rendered in song form, in which key words relate more or less obliquely to specific events and activities.[23] Such sacred mythical records of the Dreamtime and its beings are reenacted—or from a believer's viewpoint, re-lived—either ritually and in highly choreographed form, or in more informal sessions may be sung without physical dramatization. Some ritual performances demand utter seriousness, some even specifically prohibiting expressions of mirth or jest as they are believed to contain a sacred potency of great destructive force that better not be provoked. Yet, others have no such prohibitions and even seemed to encourage a rather bawdy sense of humor.

At the occasions when men gathered to sing the myth songs, there could be, depending on the general mood, much teasing and hilarity about the exploits of the totemic beings, their misfortune, or their clumsiness. This is so despite the fact that singing and performing these myths is not done simply for entertainment, but as a religious duty, which when executed properly entails a beneficent efficacy. Among the adventures of a group of myth-beings, recorded in a song cycle popular with the men among whom I was conducting my research in the 1970s, was a particular event relating to mythic beings who had gathered edible grass seed, as Aboriginal women had done in precontact times. The collected seeds then have to be ground between rough-textured stones to produce flour, which then can be baked into flat loafs of so-called damper. However, finding that they had no flat stones to grind the seeds, the mythic beings were reduced to using their testicles for the job. Whenever the song cycle came to this point, the men were hooting with laughter, obviously hugely enjoying the none-too-subtle humor. Their imagination never seemed to tire of this topic. Another mythic occasion, which elicited similar hilarity, related to a man who extended his penis underground surreptitiously burrowing its way to penetrate a woman squatting on the ground in some distance. Another myth was about a white giant who would sneak up on other Dreamtime beings at night and, unplugging his anus, would poison them with his intestinal gases. His murderous antics must have been prolific, as the bodies of his victims were manifested in the numerous anthills in the area. When the reverential singing had progressed to such events, the usual decorum would erupt in great hilarity, yet demonstrating unambiguously that seeming profanity does not necessarily destroy respect for the sacred.

On other occasions when highly secret-sacred objects were ceremonially viewed, sung over and ritually attended to, usually an atmosphere of deep reverence, awe, and sometimes even electric tension prevailed. To understand this, the situation must be placed in the wider cultural context in which such objects are embedded: they are traditionally treated with the highest of reverence and unauthorized access and manipulation in precontact times attracted the death penalty and even today may be subject to heavy forms of "tribal" punishment. A facile comparison may liken the act of ceremonious manipulation of such objects to the handling of a very significant sacred relic, religious icons of high prestige, or even, perhaps slightly hyperbolically expressed, to the ritual act of the Eucharist. Such sessions may end with people rubbing their hands over the objects to imbue themselves with the sacred potency—a notion, which in James Frazer's taxonomy may be described as "contact magic." Sometimes men would then rub the particles of grease and ochre with which the objects are coated over their own bodies and faces—an act not unusual in other religious forms in which believers wish to absorb some of the numinous powers by touching the sacred objects. At one such occasion a man rubbed his hands over an especially large, highly prestigious and potent object and then stroked his hand over the mouth of the man sitting next to him. This was a very respected elder known for his sarcastic eloquence. "This will cure you of your big mouth," was the explanation given while the men present, including the one who had received this attention, broke into loud laughter.

The behavior of these devotees of the Dreamtime, undoubtedly sincere in their religious beliefs, demonstrated to me that expressions of worship may not be to the exclusion of laughter, humor, jocularity, irony, and satire—some of it in Western estimation quite coarse and far from subtle. The Abrahamic religions in particular appear to have banned laughter from worship, elevating its exclusion to the indispensable requirement to show appropriate respect and awe. The required solemnity treats humor as anathema to religious content and contemplation. However, the brief examples described demonstrate that worship of the divine, respect for important ceremony, and belief in supernatural efficacy can be combined with humorous levity without loss of reverence and without degrading the sacred.

Muslims have delivered in recent years many fine examples of the exact opposite attitude. The rejection of humor in religious matters is exacerbated to enormous sensitivity towards critical satire. Having thus delivered the power of mockery into the hands of its enemies and detractors, Muslims continue to darkly utter threats and make attempts on the lives of blasphemers—which in turn confirms the contempt of Islamophobes and provides welcome sustenance for further satire. Whether Muslims will learn to ignore disrespectful jibes at their beliefs or Western cartoon art acquires a more respectful attitude, remains to be seen. The prospect of protection of Islamic contents through blasphemy laws remains negligible in the West, even though there is now a (non-binding) resolution on "defamation of religion" by the United Nations. Proposed and supported by Muslim nations, it is clearly designed to shield Islam against negative attitudes emanating from the West, although since its first drafting it has meanwhile been extended to go beyond Islamophobic utterances and cover also Judeophobia and Christianophobia. (This is probably to conceal its true intention to protect the dignity of Islam.) How this can be reconciled with provisions of freedom of thought, consciousness, opinion, and expression contained in articles 18, 19, and 20 of the Human Rights Charter, which at least implicitly comprises also the right to humor, provides an interesting conundrum.

The notion of what are precious cultural contents and the conception of what constitutes a slight or insult are culture-specific. In the West the idea of blasphemy being a crime, the gravity of offering an insult to Christian contents has been watered down and although in many countries it may still be on the law books and be considered an offense, it is rarely acted upon nowadays. Should blasphemy against Christian contents occur, a small community of believers will be vociferously outraged, but there is no wider social stigma for the perpetrator attached to it. Certain tropes are off-limits to religious satirization such as attributing a digestive tract or sexual desires to God, but if it does occur, the "miscreant" does not have to fear for his life. Connecting the divine with flatus and sex, even if done in a light-hearted vein (such as in the Auckland case mentioned before), is considered more than just a little risqué. Traditionally even the God-Son relationship and its procreative innuendo has been de-sexed through the intervention of the Holy Ghost, even at the time when God was still predominantly perceived in patriarchal, anthropomorphic terms. That this trope of sexuality is not necessarily a taboo in other religions is well known from classical Greek and Roman mythology, it is an integral part of Hinduism and can be impressively demonstrated with Australian Aboriginal material. Islam has probably the strongest taboo on the sexualization and even the physicality of Godness. Islamic doctrine makes no mention of humans being created in the likeness of God or refers to the maleness of God. The traditional Islamic social ideal is of a sentient culture, not a sensate culture. Thus anthropomorphising Islamic contents is bound to be blasphemous.

Rather than legislating to preserve Islam's dignity, the solution may lie in the development of new tacit conventions based on tolerance and courtesy on the one side and a certain degree of openness and indifference to perceived slights on the other. While globalization requires of the Islamic side to adopt a more secularized "thicker skin," the Western sense of the humorous and what is a legitimate target of mockery has to be adapted to new global realities of cultural interlinking. Today's information highway of electronic communication, instant information sharing, and language-independent cultural connectedness no longer enables cultural productions to hide behind geographic distance and barriers of language and cultural communicability. New, hitherto unexperienced cultural sensitivities have to be developed in an increasingly complex and interconnected world. Western museum culture has taken decisive strides in this direction. Pains are taken with the proper storage and display of cultural artifacts, human remains, art works, and the like, not to give offense to the culture from which the objects originate. Many items, previously carelessly exhibited or randomly kept in dark, cavernous storage basements, are being repatriated, locked away under the control of the relevant cultural guardians, or displayed with great sensitivity and newfound respect. Traditional, culture-specific forms of decorum, even rules of secrecy and gender differentiation imposing important restrictions on display and viewing, are being increasingly observed. All this heralds a new respect for cultural difference and although confined at this time to the "intercultural" elite, there is no reason why this attitude, through wider education, cannot be extended more widely.

BOOK BURNING: THE SACRILEGIOUS POWER OF SYMBOLIC ACTION

Among the most heinous religious crimes in Islam is the deliberate mishandling of "the holy book," the "Noble Quran" as it is called by believers. For them it contains God's revealed message word for word, and through this message, each copy assumes the quality of a sacred object. In Muslim households a place of honor is reserved for this book; it is always handled with reverence and, at least in theory, ritually impure persons (such as menstruating women) should not touch it at all. Beyond the book's content of containing a most sacred message, the physical manifestation itself, the paper, print, binding, and gold-impressed cover all embody the most exalted sacredness. Instances in recent years in which the book supposedly was placed in demeaning situations or damaged, and thus its inviolability compromised, have infuriated Muslims, repeatedly spurring them to aggressive protests and bloody reprisals. For instance, accusations that copies of the Quran had been used in a deliberately insulting and blasphemous manner—by placing it in a context with human waste—in the Guantanamo prison led to violent demonstrations with loss of life. [24]

On the international level, through the internationalization of information, news about religious offenses quickly spread; when canonical law, which demands a severe penalty, is not implemented by state law some violent action is likely to follow. Mockery of religious contents, whether deliberate or accidental, is answered with severe protest action and even assassination. Religious offense may be offered even by seemingly innocuous occasions— from a Western standpoint—such as naming a teddy bear Muhammad[25] or decorating fast food containers and dresses with Quranic verses. [26] Muslim majority societies and their official judicial processes usually react severely to such offenses when they fall in their jurisdiction. Western nations may have blasphemy laws on the books, but do not employ them in the defense of Islam. Secularised society generally shows little sympathy for expressions considered religious zealotry. Another reason is that a charge of blasphemy likely would come up against the weighty claim of exercising the freedom of expression or other civil liberties. However, even though in the West the offender against Islamic sensitivity does not run the risk of being punished by order of state authority following orderly process of jurisprudence, they may fall victim to, or have to fear, extrajudicial vigilante action. As the Anglo-Indian author Salman Rushdie and some cartoonists experienced, the offender may become the subject of a fatwa, a ruling, by a religious authority, making them a legitimate target for the believer trying to execute the religious warrant.

Considered in this light, demonstrative book burning was one of the milder forms of public protest against the publication of the *Satanic Verses*. However, in itself this action represents an interesting topic of great symbolic value. What are the reasons, on a deeper level, for incinerating books in a quasi ritual fashion? If the target of book burning should be Islam's holy book, the Quran, the symbolic meaning of the act is magnified to pure sacrilege and becomes a crime worthy of the most severe punishment.

Human history contains a long and shameful catalogue of events in which books have been burned ceremoniously and deliberately.[27] The reasons range from the attempt to practically contain the dissemination of information to pure symbolism expressing derision, insult, or purification. (I will leave aside events in which whole libraries have been incinerated seemingly by accident, by an act of war and general destruction, or sheer incidental aggressive vandalism.)[28] Interestingly, not only dictatorial and strongly authoritarian regimes engage in this practice, but also occasionally democratic societies, though in these cases this is not done by the state itself or condoned by normal legal process. (In such cases, when official censorship appears to be called for in the form of the purposeful destruction of written material, it is achieved by means other than public and demonstrative action. Shredding or pulping are the preferred methods in such cases, for instance, when the published material is considered seditious or pornographic. In modern days, censorship of the internet constitutes a practically more effective method of containing, or at least restricting, the spread of information or views considered unacceptable.)

The incineration of Alexandria's library has assumed almost mythical proportions but remains shrouded in mystery as to the purpose and even the exact time. There are many more examples of book burning ranging from medieval incineration of heretical literature, to Nazi efforts to eradicate Jewish literary and scientific products.[29] In the same category of cultural vandalism and symbolic censorship, we find the burning of records and souvenirs relating to the Beatles in 1967 in America organized by church organizations and conservative, "patriotic" circles.[30] Among the latest incidents of this nature is the ceremonial burning, in 2001, of J. K. Rowling's Harry Potter novels. This event was instigated by conservative Christians who objected to the glorification of magic. In some cases, the effort to suppress unacceptable or rival knowledge has been sadly effective and done irreparable damage: for instance, the thorough destruction of Mayan codices in the fifteenth and sixteenth century by the Spanish conquistadores and Catholic priests, which has left precious few remains allowing today only a few tantalizing glimpses of these fascinating pre-Columbian records. Even though Christendom and the West stick out in terms of the number of demonstrative book burnings, it does not have a monopoly. Other cultures also avail themselves, or have done so, of this tactic for various reasons. The efforts of the Chinese Emperor

Quin Shi Huang[31] in the third century BC to expunge all traces of certain forms of knowledge, combining for good measure the incineration of written records with killing the scholars, the living repositories of this information, have also left gaps in humankind's history of ideas. In such cases laissez-faire vandalism merges seamlessly with tactical attempts at culturecide and thought control.

By and large, however, history shows that such demonstrations of disapproval—sometimes termed with high-sounding labels such as libricide or biblioclasm—have rarely worked as an efficient means of censorship. Much more effective is the act's symbolic value: the symbolic element of purification by fire, expunging a wrong through total incineration, or simply to offer an insult through desacralization. (It stretches the imagination too far to interpret such acts as a form of immolation by fire.) The symbolic multivocality of book burning does not easily lend itself to be analyzed with regard to its cryptic magical connotations, that is to say, the underlying, subliminal cause-effect calculation. The act of destruction by fire (unless intended as a straightforward, quasi-rational means of censorship) may be imitative in establishing a supernatural, causally effective parallel between symbolism and empirical reality. As the destruction by fire of an effigy is expected to have an effect on the real person or thing, burning a book is meant to make its message disappear by mysterious causation. Burning politicians in effigy or national flags, as is frequently the case when Muslims protest Western personages or actions, is not simply a token of outrage, an emotional outlet, but contains vestiges of this kind of magical thinking. It may be rightly seen as an expression of homeopathic thinking premised on the paradigm of like affects like.

The paradigmatic belief in a correlation between ritualistic and symbolic acts and utterances on the one hand, and certain events in the real world on the other, is open to quite diverse anthropological speculative explanations. But what seems beyond doubt is that on a subconscious level of the human psyche, some causative expectations are locked in and anticipated to be mysteriously effective in the empirical domain. The symbolic act is supposed to be instrumental—in other words, is intended to be more than metonymy or metaphor.[32] The destruction or humiliation of a sacred book in this sense has a deeper expectation beyond its surface meaning of insult, derision, or injury to pride and sensitivity. Most theories of magic have assumed its instrumental nature as a given—regardless, whether this was premised on the assumption of a premodern or prelogical form of thinking (as Lucien Levy-Bruhl did) or on the idea of activating wishful thinking (as Bronislaw Malinowski argued) or ascribing magic to early scientific or prescientific intellectual forms (Edward Tylor, James Frazer).[33] In any case, there is a cryptic causal expectation at play in the instrumentalization of magical acts, even though in modern society this may be rarely the motivation on the level of fully conscious awareness.

In September 2010, Pastor Terry Jones, leader of an obscure Florida church with reportedly a congregation of twenty-five to fifty, came to global notoriety through his announcement that he would burn two hundred copies of the Quran. The act—its intended effect combining the impact of sheer quantity with the enormity of extreme sacrilege—was to commemorate the anniversary of the 9/11 attack. The threat to publicly incinerate hundreds of copies of the Quran found a strongly disapproving echo in the highest circles of the U.S. government and throughout the world. Muslims threatened retaliation, the U.S. military leadership in Afghanistan predicted increased casualties among the troops, and Christian missionaries worldwide were warned to be mindful of reprisals. Joining in the chorus of universal condemnation U.S. President Barack Obama called the act a bonanza recruitment drive for al-Qaeda. Others, remembering the burning of Rushdie's *Satanic Verses* by enraged Muslims, called it a descent into the darkness of medievalism. After initial resistance the pastor eventually seemed to relent under pressure presumably from the U.S. administration. However, in March 2011, despite earlier promises to desist, Jones did organize the ceremonial burning of a copy of the Quran with the direct consequence of several persons (among them seven Westerners working for the UN in Afghanistan) losing their lives and dozens being injured in subsequent protests.[34] This was not unexpected and the pastor had been warned that his act would cost innocent lives. Apart from such pragmatic considerations, the symbolic act constituted a breach of a tacit strategy of official Christianity not to vilify or deliberately insult another religious creed but instead treat them with dignity and, at least outwardly, with respect.[35] The world does not expect Islam to return the favour, well realizing that this concession, unreciprocated by fanatical Muslims, is the result of secularization processes that have affected Christian religion profoundly. Relativization of belief, rationalism, and multicultural realities have played a role in this as much as the realization that symbolic acts of this sacrilegious nature are just that: highly symbolic, likely to inflame emotions, but in a practical sense achieving little. Whatever expectation of a practical, empirical effect through magical causality symbolic acts of this kind may once have had has long since evaporated. Witches have been burned to purify and even save their souls; bodily excreta, finger nail clippings and hair, or personal representations (such as dolls or images) or belongings intimately associated with a person (such as underpants and bras) may up until recent times have been burned in "tribal" societies to kill and damage a person—but beliefs in such magical causation have retreated to a few recesses of the

modern globalized mind-set. What has remained strong in modern humanity's awareness is the symbolic impact and its message of insult and blasphemy through the act of incineration.

Terry Jones' act of defiance, which led to the death of some people, poses
an interesting legal question: to what extent should religious and intellectual
leaders in general be held responsible for their teaching, including their exemplary symbolic action. In Jones' case there can be little doubt that his
spiteful act had a predictable consequence. Several innocent persons were
killed in direct and provable causal connection with his enactment of a universally understood symbolism. Western jurisprudence since very recent
times inclines towards holding radical Islamic clerics and imams responsible
when they exhort their followers to engage in murderous jihad or, on a lesser
scale of severity, encourage the physical disciplining of wives.[36] In several
cases arrests, court indictments, and convictions have followed. Some such
radical preachers, being considered responsible for terror attacks in terms of
intellectual authorship, have ended up in detention, some of them at Guantanamo, and one having moved from the United States apparently resident in
Yemen at the time when he was killed in a drone attack. The preaching
activities of the radical Islamic cleric Abu Bakar Ba'asyir in Indonesia have
earned him frequent court appearances and lengthy terms of imprisonment.[37]
He has not been absolved of responsibility, at least in part, for the Bali
bombing even though it could not be proved that he actually was the leader
of Jemaa Islamiya, the terrorist organization behind the attack. If Joseph
Goebbels had been caught alive, no doubt he would have been indicted at the
Nuremberg trial simply for his role as the head ideologue of the Nazi regime.
In early May 2011 a prime example was constituted for holding an ideologue
responsible for actions perpetrated by others. Osama bin Laden, the emblematic figure of al-Qaeda, was shot and killed in a raid on his secret compound in Abbottabad, Pakistan.[38] In a very negative sense, bin Laden and his
message of a jihad against "crusaders and Jews" had shaped the beginning of
the twenty-first century. In some other cases even cherished, fundamental
liberties such as academic freedom were infringed on for the sake of suppressing the dissemination of "dangerous" ideas. Perhaps in this context the
most conspicuous case was the denial of a work permit for the eminent
scholar Tariq Ramadan by the U.S. administration, preventing him from
taking up a teaching post at Notre Dame University in 2004.[39] But let us also
remember that the social philosophers whose teachings have inspired—
though in some cases in a very roundabout way—the youth revolt of the
1970s and 1980s in the West have never been officially indicted for the
formation of extremist groups such as Baader Meinhof, the Red Brigade, the
Weather Underground, and the like. In some cases it appears the connection
between teaching and action is too opaque to allow legal process easily to
spring into action. Equally important, such charges relating to intellectual

responsibility may raise serious issues around academic freedom and the freedom of expression. Here I cannot engage in a full discussion of the problematic of intellectual accountability and ethical responsibilities of this kind. Suffice it to say that the line between acceptable freedom of intellectual and religious teaching, action and social influence that may accrue from it, and criminality is ill-defined, porous, and diffuse. Not surprisingly to Muslims it appears, when inconsistencies appear in the interpretation of civil and academic liberties and freedom of opinion, as though Western law applies more restrictive stringency to Muslims while conceding greater latitude to non-Islamic and anti-Islamic expressions.

In 2009, the United Nations Human Rights Council urged countries to legislate against defamation of religion, and especially Islam.[40] As I have mentioned before, not surprisingly, the agenda had been advanced strongly by Muslim-majority nations represented on the council, aiming at what to detractors would amount to the dead hand of censorship not only on outright mockery but on all critical enquiry, art, drama, literature, humor and comment that someone might find offensive on religious grounds. While this resolution is not binding and practically will change little, it does encourage a consideration of the relationship between faith, satire, and critical enquiry. Unhappily, it conjures up shades of the tense relationship of church and the budding sciences a very few centuries ago in Europe.

FAITH AND REASON: NEVER THE TWAIN

To say Islam is not opposed to reason makes for a good opening statement on this topic. However, there is much underlying complexity to this relationship. While it is an open question whether an explicit and systematically worked out Islamic epistemology exists, it is undeniable that various relevant issues have been discussed in Islamic philosophy. Ultimately, this endeavour was carried forward with an orientation distinctly different from that of modern Western epistemology. Today attempts are being made to understand the basic epistemological issues still in terms of that orientation, but with some reference also to intellectual modernity. This may take the shape of uncompromising rejection or some cautious rapprochement, barely sufficient to integrate Islam with the modern world. To couch the conservative stance, which extends over both extremes, in sloganistic phraseology: islah (licit religious reform) may accrue cautiously from tafsir (exegesis), but not from an unshackled falsafa (rationalism).

Knowledge (ilm, in the sense of legitimate knowledge) in the traditional Islamic use, unsurprisingly, has not exactly the same semantic meaning as in Western languages. It refers to knowledge that is not in conflict with theology. The term and concept of "knowledge" in the West is also used in quite different meanings. There is a fundamental semantic difference between the usual, everyday use of the term, which is reflected also in scientific epistemology, and a "sociological" use. The former understands "knowledge" to be a collection of well-founded, rationally derived, empirically reconciled, legitimate intellectual products, as opposed to intellectual content, which is not valid and therefore does not qualify as knowledge. In the colloquial sense, and in somewhat rough approximation, this division is represented by science and religious belief (to which one might add, superstition). The sociological understanding differs in that it subsumes all intellectual and mental products, belief as much as science, rational or irrational, well-founded or not, under the category "knowledge." In this context, in order to illuminate the interplay between the scientific knowledge production and religious belief, it is necessary to follow the more general usage of epistemology. However, at times, and depending on the context, "knowledge" will also be used in the more encompassing sense.

Islam, and the religio-philosophical reflections it has inspired contain countless arguments on "knowledge," the accumulation and validity of it, and the relationship between faith and reason. For its sheer volume and complexity this literature cannot be discussed or replicated here even in outlines. Al-Gazali, for instance, distinguished between useful and useless types of reason, the former possessing a religious flavor, absent from the latter. Abu'l-Wahid Ibn Rushd, better known in the West as Averroes, attempted to incorporate ancient classical Greek knowledge into Islamic thinking to give it the seal of religious approval. Mutazilite epistemology stresses wujub al nazar, the obligation to use speculative reasoning to attain ontological truths, but reasons must not be misused for the purpose of "disproving" Islamic belief. Shi'a jurisprudence uses aql (intellect, reason, or logic) to deduce law from doctrine, or in other words to illuminate and extend belief with reason (but certainly not use reason to challenge doctrine), and so on. There is in Islamic literature a sheer endless variety of reflections on human intellectual ability, its uses as augmentation to revelation (wahi), and its aberrations (bida, jahl). Yet, one fundamental principle prevails: reason may not become a legitimate tool to challenge, control, and undermine belief. Herein lies the difficulty of conservative Islam with modernity and the processes of globalization.

Mutazilah is the epistemic strand of Islam that emphasizes the coequality of faith and reason.[41] Reason is God's gift to man and is there to be used, as Harun Nasution,[42] Indonesia's leading Mutazilah theologist in the last century, explained to me. Only 8 percent of the Quran's contents are creed, refer to rituals and social ethics and rules. The rest is redundancy, repetitive formulae, and poetry that gives little guidance. Much that is important to human existence has to be made up by reason and must be made to convene with the times. This is perhaps a very radical view on the importance of reason, even for Mutazilah. But even so, it holds that faith and reason are supposed to give to each other support in a relationship, which puts the larger onus on reason in its supporting role. Their purpose is not to contradict each other as did happen in Christianity's history as fledgling science emancipated to become a major opponent. At best, reason can be used to reinterpret and gently modify ingrained doctrinal views, to make them sit more easily in the modern world. And in a wider sense the careful application of rational critique can bring about a synergy between faith and reason. Although not influential enough to decisively and globally recalibrate Islam to the modern world, Mutazilah provides a useful stimulus for reinterpreting Islamic laws and rules—for instance on the gender division, on family planning—to modernize and rationalize mainstream Indonesian society to a certain extent. However, even in this modest enterprise—which still concedes supremacy to faith—Mutazilah is opposed by more conservative Islamic currents.

The question is: if contradictions between faith and reason occur, how is this being resolved in the Islamic way? And what influence does this have on the social discourse? How are the products of intellectual modernity assimilated into Islam? Christianity, in the time before it parted company with science, considered reason as an ally supporting the case of God, much as the progressive-conservative version of Islam still does. Science with its methods founded on the human capacity for reason and honed to methods of rationality, as long as it supported articles of faith and was working in the service of the church, was more than welcome. Its findings were thought to be subservient to revelation, assist in understanding creation, and ultimately of Godness itself. The crisis came when reason assumed a trajectory that contradicted faith and pointed in a direction anathema to the church, as it seemed to undermine its epistemological domination and hence erode its social authority. In very short time, both became fierce contestants not only for epistemological supremacy, but for social control as well.

By and large, Islam is taking a stance similar to that of the church in the past. Islam as a whole, to varying degrees of doctrinal importance, recognizes reason specifically as God's gift and as a source of valid knowledge. However, its relationship with faith is still chiefly one of subordination as a supporter and not as a controlling agent that is authorized to critique or censor faith. In conjunction with faith, ijma, and tafsir it is meant to lead to valid—that is, religiously approved—knowledge; it enhances revelation, corroborates licit knowledge of the religious kind, and sharpens and extends the range of theologically approved epistemology. This is not too different from the official Christian attitude in Western society. The recent Regensburg address of Pope Benedict XVI in this respect—although used to criticize Islam for its lack of reason—revealed him as an heir to the legacy of Thomas of Aquinas. Official Christian viewpoints still regard "scientific" reason as the junior partner of religious "reason," while the socially dominant, secular-ized view attributes to religious belief only a "client" role. It tends to relegate the religious intellect in the epistemological hierarchy to secondary impor-tance, a tolerable situation as long as religion is adaptable enough and does not strive towards openly exercising social control. As a social anthropolo-gist, my emphasis has to lie on how discrepancies between the two sides become effective in the social discourse (and the social roots of this relation-ship) rather than on a purely philosophical or theological contemplation of epistemology. What is of interest here lies in the degree of social influence the two sides, faith and reason, are able to exert respectively and in the social treatment of logical irreconcilabilities that arise between their intellectual products.

Mockery, its power and its violent rejection in Islam, I believe, point to the social consequences of this epistemological issue. Islamic knowledge theory and knowledge appreciation, taken as a hypothetical entity, deviate significantly from the Western understanding in which the religious agenda has been so socially weakened that religious targets of mockery pass with impunity. They may injure convention or good taste, but hardly provoke punitive reaction. As this secularized attitude has become globally hegemon-ic, differences with the Islamic world have grown in significance. The West-ern epistemology informs modernity and, pushing along globalization, seems poised to become universally dominant, excepting, that is, the viscous resis-tance put up by the Islamic world. Bassam Tibi[43] has articulated the heart of the issue concisely: Muslims must not only accept the fruit of the West's advances (the technology, the material lifestyle, the medical advances, the practical science), but must embrace the intellectual culture and epistemolog-ical conditions that have produced them. Therein lies the problem. Doing so means assuming a critical stance towards all knowledge (in the wider sense) and treating none as untouchable, axiomatic, and beyond human appraisal. It includes the eternal questioning, dogma-skeptical irreverence that drives ad-vances, as philosophers of science and knowledge (such as Karl Popper) have argued. In the rationality-driven "growth" of knowledge relentless skepticism towards knowledge monopoly, rejection of blind obedience vis-à-vis knowledge authority, and the refusal to accept received wisdom unques-tioned are indispensable. While this model of knowledge improvement is open to philosophical attack on all sides, from a sociological perspective it offers a useful insight. The rational method, fundamentally instrumental in bringing about what has been called modern, scientific knowledge, has total-ly relied on the fundamental disrespect towards revealed and received knowl-edge and, on a personal level, its defenders. Even philosophers of science (such as Paul Feyerabend and Thomas Kuhn),[44] who have been highly skep-tical of Popper's idea of the teleological function of the rational method as the steady motor of knowledge growth, seem agreed that even in non-goal directed paradigm change the fundamental openness of knowledge to revision is vital. An intellectual "no-holds-barred" approach is characteristic for the Western knowledge enterprise. Critical reasoning is not just reliance on method, but equally importantly the acceptance of a fundamental attitude of skepticism towards "received wisdom." Intellectual irreverence, anti-authoritarianism, are as important as the application of the finest rationality.

Critical rationalism means—as Karl Popper[45] has convincingly argued—holding all knowledge routinely and unreservedly open to scrutiny and critique and rejecting axiomatic knowledge, which is dogmatically closed to the intrusions of empirical analysis, critical scrutiny, and the free exchange of ideas. Among the requisite attitudes of skepticism, to which nothing is untouchable, "sacrosanct," or taboo, is not only chronic doubt, but also irony and sarcasm. In the process of shifting the goal posts of truth, irreverence towards it, be it revealed or received or the product of scientific labor, is essential. In applying close scrutiny, important weapons in the amory used against dogmatic bulwarks are irony and sarcasm. Even downright ridicule may serve a purpose as useful as the method of criticism itself. Even if intellectually weak, if nothing else, sarcasm, irony, and satire are symbolic markers for the absence of obsequious respect towards social and knowledge authority. The satirical treatment of dogma forms a very effective means of undermining the automatic, hardened credibility of any paradigm, be it religious or scientific. From a strong rationalist perspective, there must be no dogmatic sanctuaries that can spread intellectual rigor mortis to a whole society. While Western society adheres to this creed only imperfectly, and there are many boundaries that are not easily crossed and taboos that will take courage to tear down, doing so is not at the risk of life and limb. And while Herbert Marcuse[46] some time ago made the pronouncement that "the idea of Reason has been superseded by the idea of happiness," it still has an iconic place in Western society and exerts considerable influence—an influence greater than in the Islamic world.

It is not difficult to understand that the functions of the critical approach to knowledge have sociopolitical ramifications. Undoubtedly, certain technological advances (a vital boost was Gutenberg's printing press), together with opening religious doctrine linguistically and ritually to general inspection (e.g., through Luther's Bible translation) aided the budding libertarian spirit of knowledge production. These developments were instrumental and even foundational in the eventual emergence of the Enlightenment, which facilitated further sociopolitical developments. Growing literacy undoubtedly played a role in the process of "democratization" of knowledge and its skeptical spirit. Effectively demolishing the church's rigid monopoly on the preservation and maintenance of knowledge, it allowed a much wider intellectual enterprise with enormous consequences in setting in motion social reform. Not only did it lead to a wave of dissemination of information and news reporting through the avalanche of published information and discussion, it also stimulated and popularized critical viewpoints. The second wave of democratization happened through the information highway and the digital revolution and eventually discharged into the super-abundant electronic exchange of ideas and news on the Internet, Facebook, blogging, Twitter, and other modes of information sharing. The resulting information networking and electronic interaction makes it difficult to retain a controlling influence on knowledge and information production. Investigative, anti-authoritarian journalism, academic freedom of research and teaching, or simply social critique are aided considerably now by the electronic media from the global web to cell phone picture transmission. WikiLeaks is no less an important result of this development than Wikipedia contributing to this incessant information and opinion flow which governments, intelligence services, and net controllers have great difficulty in hemming in. Some experts warn that there is no one-to-one relationship between the new technology and its beneficial effects for humanity. While knowledge democratization (in the sociological sense) has certainly benefitted through the lightning speed of information sharing, on the other hand, the quality of information has not. The risk in terms of the continuing possibility of spreading the most appalling prejudices, distortions, and lies has not necessarily been summarily eliminated as the quality controls operating in print-published material have to a considerable extent been sidelined. Again, this hints at a shift in the authority exercised in knowledge production. Although the massive availability of information in itself does not determine the truth value, it does tend to undermine the traditionally axiomatic, privileged status of some forms of knowledge. The official, privileged status of such views and information is difficult to maintain and enforce when a wealth of alternative and contradictory forms are offered and distributed.

In the Islamic world the printed information did not spark the profound intellectual development that it did in Europe. Doctrinally axiomatic knowledge was rarely challenged by open scrutiny, let alone critique—or only so at serious personal risk requiring a person to be equipped with death-defying courage. As far as the impact of the electronic revolution on Islam is concerned the long-term effects are still unclear. Does plugging into the electronic "global babble" stimulate the profound rethinking of the global umma; will it encourage a wholesale revision of Islam fortified with new paradigms and epistemes; will it lead to a redefinition of the relationship between knowledge received from the past and the intellectually processual endeavour of modernity?[47]

What does appear to be manifest in the meantime is that electronic capabilities have led to social reform. They have contributed massively to the "democratization wave" that sweeps the Arab world since the early months of 2010. (At the time of writing its eventual outcome is still very inconclusive and in the long run the effects may yet have to prove that the label "democratization movement" was not a misnomer.) Organizing protest rallies, disseminating cell phone pictures of violent action by the authorities, spreading propaganda material and ideological ideas to the extent shown by these events make it obvious that the masses can be effectively galvanized by electronic means, social momentum harnessed and guided towards concerted political action. While this obviously has the capacity to change Muslim society in a sociopolitical sense, one must not make the mistake to consider this as a clear sign that Islam per se has been "democratized" (i.e., modernized or revised and opened up to critique); nor, as some events have demonstrated, has gender equality, tolerance, or religious harmony been significantly advanced.[48] Political outcomes of the digital revolution and the democratization of information may remain confined to such issues as regime change, but may not necessarily be paralleled by a profound change in worldview.

However, in other respects, the power of critical reason and disrespectful quirkiness obviously does have consequences in the Islamic intellectual discourse. The Muslim diaspora in the West is exposed to it as much as Muslims everywhere in a globalized world are affected by it. From a juridical position Rex Ahdar[49] spells it out candidly for Western society: "If people want to live in a liberal democracy enjoying religious and other liberties they have to accept the liberty of others to criticize and even ridicule them." In other words, if Muslims demand and expect freedom of belief, worship, and religious expression, they have to respect the freedom of open, critical intellectual discourse—as open and free as the Western standards that are involved in the globalizing process at the moment allow. And if they want to take their place in a freely "chattering" world and a democratized cyber space, they have to accept the consequences. This applies also in the global terms in which knowledge, freedom, and law are intricately interwoven. In a world in which universal human rights have currency and the freedom of expression of intellect becomes an increasingly universal public good, Muslims can only rely on a general sense of courtesy and voluntary respect for their religious sensitivity but not on a sharia-regulated juridical regime to protect their tabooed doctrinal fields.

ISLAM'S PERCEPTION OF KNOWLEDGE AND ITS SOCIAL CONSEQUENCES

Let us examine Islam's doctrinal attitude to knowledge, its enhancement and promulgation. Muslims, even of the meanest education, are rightly proud that according to their comprehension of history, they were the transmitters of valuable knowledge to the West. Muslims formed the vital bridge between the knowledge produced by the classical Mediterranean civilizations—which themselves stood on the shoulders of earlier Middle Eastern cultures—and the Europe of the Middle Ages when it was ready, after the "dark ages," to open itself to this intellectual harvest. Especially Moorish Spain was a vital point of seminal contact for a while. The consciousness of Muslims having been the torchbearers of civilization and knowledge is proudly expressed by a Muslim author, Munawar Ahmed Anees, with the following words: "The floodgates of knowledge unlocked in Muslim Spain left their lasting imprints on every conceivable domain of Western society."[50]

It is a cliché that in history as much as in personal life one cannot rest on one's laurels for too long. Nor is there a lasting gratitude for services once rendered. The West by and large does not acknowledge a debt to the Islamic world; on the contrary, it conceives this region as underdeveloped, deficient in advanced knowledge, science and technology, modern morality, and attitudes congenial to modern scientifically infused times. The West's cultural politics stress opposition and contrasts to Islamic culture—have always done so, as Edward Said[51] did not fail to criticize—rather than acknowledge its knowledge roots and the lasting legacy of Islam.

Muslims bemoan the fact that their once leading position in the production and maintenance of cutting-edge knowledge has become so eroded to the point that they are now not only socioeconomically, but also intellectually part of the Third World. Deprived of the leading position, Islam has stood aside to watch from the sidelines the divorce of reason from religion, and reason crashing ahead shedding all pretense to be in the service of faith. Once close allies, reason and religion in Western thinking have irreversibly separated to form now opposites of rationality and blind faith. In the political sphere in cases of conflict between the two, reason—unless overruled by pragmatism, opportunism, or complacency—almost invariably prevails. Secularization has wrested the controlling powers, both socially and intellectually, from religion and religious institutions and surrendered normative functions to secular agencies. For the most part science, with its rational method and grounded in empiricism, claims a monopoly on the truth and its formulation, and on the dispensation of this-worldly blessings. The Islamic world has not followed the new epistemology its religious dominance has never been challenged by an intellectual revolution similar to the Enlightenment.[52] Although the dogmatic view is that Islam is science friendly, in conflict situations social conventions make sure that the dominance of Islamic doctrine may not be openly challenged. Scientific insights are not supposed to discredit religious assumptions. It has been argued that scientific paradigms of very recent provenance with regard to evolution, human ontogenesis, cosmology, and astronomy, have been anticipated in the Islamic revelations.[53] Where there is no convergence, science must be at fault or must be deficient.

Islam's traditional protestation about its appreciation of knowledge is based on the strict requirement that reason complement, correspond with, and explicate revelation.

The debate in the Muslim world today is indeed between ideologically extremely conservative interpretations of the scriptures, and more flexible ones. Tentatively even courageous questions of the status of the revelation itself are being raised, though very timidly. Doctrinal modernization that places the rational method (aql) higher than hallowed tradition (taqlid) let alone revelation (wahi), still sails close to the wind of heresy (bida). Even when it is careful to remain within widely acceptable doctrinal confines it risks being derided as utter heresy (bida) by the prevailing conservatism and to fall victim to severe sanctions—or worse. The core doctrine is the Quranic verse 2/239 which says, "He [God] has taught you, which you knew not (before)." This clearly places revelation in the supreme position and relegates other intellectual forms to a derivative nature. In relation to the truth quality of revealed knowledge, all else is of dubious status.

This points to an inherent contradiction within Islam with regard to the value attributed to "knowledge." Doctrine seems to value the search for knowledge, but what is its value if all it can do is prop up belief? Why search for it in the first place? Why is there a need to corroborate revelation?

Islamic epistemology has always been doctrinally respectful of knowledge, not only of a religious kind, but also of an empirical kind. Islam usually points proudly to some edifying exhortations contained in the Sunna "seek knowledge from cradle to grave," "the search for knowledge is like prayer to God"; and equally clearly, "the pen of the scholar is more valuable than the blood of the martyr." The full gravity of the latter pronouncement can only be appreciated by knowing that the martyr (shahid) making the supreme sacrifice in the defense of Islam fulfills one of the most highly valued missions. While in this hadith the scholar referred to may be a conservative jurist-scholar, and in the first two, knowledge may refer simply to the ability to recite the Quran (becoming a hafiz), another hadith makes it clear that Islam has respect for nonreligious knowledge. It says, "seek knowledge even if you have to go to China"—in other words, in the search of knowledge spare no effort and if necessary go to the end of the world. Clearly, it must refer to non-Islamic knowledge as for the sake of acquiring Islamic knowledge one would not go to China. These ahadith are often interpreted to mean that the acquisition of knowledge is an obligation, not an option. A modernizt inference from this is that education is a duty for Muslims (even without gender distinction). The Taleban obviously had a very narrow interpretation of education, reducing it to religious instruction. However, in case one may doubt whether nonreligious knowledge is primarily meant, another hadith makes it clear that what the scriptures refer to is knowledge of the world. "Receive knowledge even from the mouth of an infidel" means valuing the information coming forth from non-Muslims and, therefore, being without a basis in Islam. It makes it quite clear how much knowledge of any kind is appreciated for its own sake. However, there is always the proviso, tacitly and darkly looming in the background: such knowledge may not challenge religious truths.

The meaning of this restriction was demonstrated to an absurd, hyper-conservative level by the Taleban. Though calling themselves students of religion, they—like modern-day luddites—became the enemies of education, science, and technology. With an extremely narrow conception of what religiously allowed and worthwhile knowledge is, they clearly did not adhere to the knowledge-friendly and liberal-sounding sentiments of the hadith, in fact violated them grossly. Women were excluded from even the most basic education, even though the scriptures do not specifically exclude them from the acquisition of knowledge. The pursuit of knowledge, referred to in the ahadith is not reserved for men. It is only by extension of the doctrinal view that women should be focused on matters of family and household that some feeble justification could be deduced. It may have been for financial rather than doctrinal reasons, that higher education even for men was woefully inadequate and neglected. Education in the Taleban version was at best one-sided, emphasizing religious instruction over modern, scientifically based information. Many conservative madrassas also fulfil the mission of disseminating a fuller repertory of up-to-date knowledge very incompletely. Quite clearly, the Taleban's medievalist, extreme Salafist Weltanschauung can be blamed for leading to an acute paucity of adequate understanding of the world, which in this intensity is unusual even for radical Islam. In their interpretation the desired return to the Prophet's example was not conceived only in a moral, spiritual, and devotional sense, but also in terms of lifestyle, material availability, and information of worldly realities. Modern technology—with the notable exception of advanced armaments—by and large was rejected resulting in broad prohibitions on the use and enjoyment of devices considered frivolous and serving hedonistic, un-Islamic entertainment. Such things as computers, movies, tape recordings of music, television, and the like, were regarded as serving frivolous purposes of enjoyment and contrary to the Spartan lifestyle prescribed by Talebanic rules. (Interestingly, Taleban leadership did use laptops.) Technological prohibitions merged seamlessly with restrictions of other forms of hedonism, such as kite-flying—considered a waste of time, which should be used for religious instruction. (An exception was made for cricket despite its odious repute of being of Western origin.) It is difficult to avoid sensing in all this an uncanny parallel with other fanatically Puritanical utopian and anti-intellectualist movements, with perhaps the most horrible example of Cambodia's Khmer Rouge.

Traces of selective anti-modernizt Puritanism can be found also in other arch-conservative features throughout the Islamic world, even though the main target of criticism is not so much the technological modernism as such, but its misuse for un-Islamic purposes. Egyptian conservatives complain about the (allegedly) abundant quantity of belly dancing shown on television when this medium should be used for pious instruction. Similar complaints I have heard in Indonesia about the frequency of homemade sitcoms being offered on television when compared with the infrequency of Islamic lessons. In this conservative view, modern electronic media as a whole, despite their wholesome potential as means for dawa (proselytization), in actual fact disgorge only filth and vulgarity. This uncanny connection in some cases leads to the wholesale condemnation of all things modern. The desperate search for entertainment of the hedonistic modern world is alien to the stern piety and morality of religious conservatism. Perhaps not surprisingly, not only aesthetic pleasures are constrained by limitations, but licit knowledge advance is also set within strict boundaries. The Islamic viewpoint—common to ultra-conservative views of all religious brands—has difficulty reconciling itself with radical innovations in the field of genetics, medicine, and biology. Cloning and genetic manipulation are seen as forms of arrogation of divine powers of creation. Genetic screening is also rejected, not because of a rejection of eugenics, but because it constitutes an interference with God's will. Contraception, xeno-transplants and even blood transfusions and organ transplants from human donors are considered equally unacceptable. And so are cosmetic alterations, as they arrogantly try to improve on God's creation. In these respects conservative Islam meets with the conservatism harbored in other religions.

In the conservative use of the Arabic language, bida refers to heresy, religious error, illicit doctrinal innovation, conditions that are strictly to be rejected and should be severely punished. But beyond that understanding of the word, it may also refer to social and technical innovation, "modernization," the social revolution, and new economics that came with petro-Dollars and Westernization. It is easy to understand how through this synonimous use new developments in social, political, ideological, economic, and technological circumstances can assume the malodorous flavor of being against God's religion, leading Muslims away from the right path and into the wilderness of immorality, jahiliya, and godlessness. It creates a basic conservatism of outlook and a deep, hard-to-overcome suspicion of sociocultural change. If modernity, its values, irreverent reason, and freedoms is bida, it is difficult to entrench the opposite view of its beneficence. Thus the concept of bida encapsulates the paradigmatic conservatism of Islamic socioculture.

The lack of openness to intellectual innovation on a level of social discourse shows many and diverse results. The social significance to which Islam elevates some conservative values—culminating in the deadly gravity attributed to blasphemous attack, on the substance of belief—sticks out in the flow and ebb of globalization. The passion aroused by perceived insults to Islam and transgression against its doctrine is within the normal register of human emotions. To feel irate, annoyed, and incensed about insults offered to something one holds dear is far from unusual. When something precious becomes the target of attack, many feel provoked to exact harsh revenge. (In recognition of flawed human nature, some legal systems acknowledge provocation as a mitigating circumstance in criminal prosecutions.) In reverse, the tabooization of certain overly sensitive tropes, iconization of values and cultural features, giving them immunity from revision and criticism, satirical or otherwise, sacrosanctity granted to certain social and cultural issues, all that is common in all societies and cultures. When such boundaries are transgressed, conventions demand retribution. Across most cultures, traditionally at least, religious contents rank highly on the list of sensitivities and are insulted only in rare cases when doing so is a deliberately hostile strategy. But only Muslims en bloc insist nowadays that a perceived insult to their treasured religious contents can only be expunged by putting the miscreant to death; and in doing so refer to the doctrines, traditions, and current values of their religion that would constrain them to respond to misdeeds with lethal force. Attacking sacred issues and persons, mishandling the holy book of the Quran (as, for instance, was alleged to have happened at Guantanamo Bay as a deliberate insult to Muslim prisoners, perhaps to demoralize them and break down their resistance), even trying to alter sacred sociocultural traditions and the like count among the most heinous crimes. The hierarchy of cultural iconization is still determined by revelation, not reason.

The West—even in countries where the death penalty is inflicted for certain crimes (such as unjustified homicide and high treason)—fails to comprehend the gravity with which Muslimhood considers religious transgressions. (And bear in mind that in conservative Islam the notion of "religious" extends well into a life sphere that in the Western conception may be purely sociocultural in a secular sense.) It is easily forgotten, or overlooked, that within the range of human cultures such attitudes traditionally are not uncommon. However, as tribal or indigenous societies are concerned, insofar as their traditional conventions have survived the onslaught of colonialism, their sensitivities and reactions to violations are either ignored or suppressed by the respective dominant society or have been discarded together with the detritus of broken cultural traditions. Australian Aboriginal society traditionally was not inclined to generously overlook religious faux pas. Even innovation meant to improve on sacred traditions was not welcome. A seeming bagatelle could cost someone's life. This is no longer the case, although at times surreptitious methods of punishment may be adopted to avoid the attention of the official law. So-called tribal killings, despite multiculturalist policies and attempts to accommodate culturally distinct values, are still being discouraged by the official authorities.

Legal pluralism has become a contentious issue, especially in the area in which the West and the Islamic world intersect and where peaceful interaction is required. In multicultural societies and nations it is a very topical and fascinating subject, but in a practical sense remains underdeveloped. In the globalized world, the West's apparent disrespect towards the values and sensitivities of Islam becomes a source of chronic conflict. Episodically, friction erupts in spectacular incidents—and news spreads quickly. Modern communication mediums, direct social interaction, and mass migration have all contributed to exacerbating the conflict, magnifying it sometimes to global proportions. A problem somewhere has the potential to become enormously distanciated, leading to the death of people in another, faraway country and resulting in repercussions that reverberate throughout the world. The Danish cartoons, published at first in a local paper of modest distribution, led to people being killed in Asia, embassies being torched in the Middle East, and trade sanctions affecting producers and consumers in many countries.

Muslims do not fail to notice that Buddhism and Hinduism are not subject to such sustained scrutiny and scornful criticism as Islam is in the West. Judaism enjoys exemption for various reasons, and the remnants of tribal religions on the whole are looked upon with some condescending, but friendly tolerance and nostalgia (with some exceptions like cannibalism, headhunting, slavery, and the like) "Political correctness" has seen to it that cartoons showing people "of color" cooking missionaries in big cauldrons, and black rag dolls called gollywogs, widely seen as demeaning black people, have virtually disappeared. Tribal decorum expressed in rituals and myths is received with respect bordering on reverence, and room for tribal dance and ceremony is now often made in official state functions. Muslims, on the other hand, have to resort to international law to protect their faith against slander and indignities.

Muslims are not facilely inclined towards cultural relativity in religious and moral matters. Islamic standards are considered universal, even of cosmological relevance. At best, some condescending latitude is given to jahiliya, the amorality, ignorance, and chaos of the West; yet iconic values of Islam are expected to be respected, even by the mushrikun and kafirun (polytheists and infidels). (Not the slightest largesse of this kind is offered to offending Muslims.) Evident disrespect, whether deliberately or accidentally shown by religionists of "inferior" faiths, is not likely to be met only with resignation or laissez-faire indignation. Especially Muslims who have migrated to the West are likely to feel acutely aggrieved, as they are sometimes directly confronted with the West's disrespect. They feel that as citizens or legal residents their beliefs and attitudes are entitled to be respected and protected by law, and should at least have legal parity with Christianity and its traditions. Instead Western Muslims find that they are victimized insofar as their faith generally is frequently derided, singled out for acerbic criticism, and not even accorded the same benign indifference that other religions enjoy.

THE DANGEROUS PATH OF RATIONALIZATION AND MODERNIZATION

It is sometimes argued that the Islamic world is "less developed" in an intellectual sense because it had no Enlightenment. While Europe was propelled forward by this new epistemology and the revolution in world perception it produced, creating in the process its openness to "progress"—a momentum relentlessly and incessantly propelling society away from its present position—Islam either ignored or resisted it. Against this view, it may be said that it is not crucial that the history of the Islamic world has not been formed—or convulsed—by a spurt of Enlightenment in which reason broke away from the tutelage of faith and emancipated from its controlling domination. Neither had Japan, India, or China, and yet they have embarked on a rapid development based on the best of modern science and technology. They have assumed their position at the very front line, so much so that the global economic epicenter has steadily shifted eastward, increasingly decentring the West. Is there hope for Islamic socioculture to follow suit by embarking on a similar trajectory?

Max Weber, though skeptical of this process and whereto it leads humanity, made a bold prediction of the increasing Entzauberung (demystification) of the world. Through the strengthening of instrumental rationality (or practical reason) as primary motivation, other forms such as value rational, but especially affective and habitual motivations, are more and more pushed into the background. Magical and religious paradigms also dwindle and disappear, at least as collective social motivators. But as far as specifically Islam was concerned Weber seems to have had little hope for its further rationalization. He ascribed to it only a limited rationalization potential quite unlike Protestantism, which impacted on Europe and directed it onto a new pathway of intellect. This may seem surprising insofar as Islamic dogma contains relatively few "irrational," magical ingredients.[54] Its dogmatic narrative—beyond its central divine revelation—is not strewn with miracles and miraculous events as Christianity's is. Only insofar as Islam in a respectful gesture towards Judaism and Christianity superficially accepts (at least does not reject) Old and New Testament's supernatural and charismatic events, does it deviate significantly from practical reason. Islam accepts specifically more or less only the revelation of the Quran as a major miracle—representing God's avatar in the form of the archangel Jibril. A miracle of a minor order, not unanimously recognized by all Muslims, is the supposed hoof print of Muhammad's horse at al Aqsa in Jerusalem, which was impressed in the course of the Prophet's ascent into heaven.

Max Weber is probably best known for his theory of how modern capitalist society emerged in the West,[55] giving Adam Smith a leg-up so to speak. Fundamental to it is a specific form of acquisitiveness that is economically prudent and quite different from booty capitalism of pirates and Vikings, the prestige buying through potlatch of Northwest American Indians and the Big-Man status acquisition through pig festivals of some Pacific societies. Of particular interest is the connection Weber made between Christianity—and its fundamentalization—and the emergence of the mercantile ethos and system that became such a characteristic political and socioeconomic force of global reach in the last one hundred years. Global hegemony nowadays is unmistakably based on this system and despite profound secularization still bears many features that betray their Christian provenance. Cloaking its complexity with a rough sketch, Weber's theory established causal linkages between religion, science, freedom, political system, and through his concept of elective affinity drawing idealism and Marxist materialism into one fundamental, causally interconnected sociological system. Important is the connection he made between religious fundamentalization and rationalism. Paradoxically, there is, as he argued, a close linkage, at least as far as Christianity is concerned. Religious fervor and piety led to a desire for greater analytical understanding of the world and in further consequence unleashed an intellectual process that in the end turned against religion. In setting in train an overwhelming ideological force, secularization; it paved the way for the triumph of rationality over belief.

Weber's theory wisely did not make a claim of universal validity. He left it unclear whether he intended to imply that Christianity bestrode a path that other religions would follow sooner or later, or whether he wanted to emphasize the cultural specificity and uniqueness of this historical development. It now seems clear that religious fundamentalism does not inevitably entail a momentum towards rationalization, neither in societal terms (rationalization of institutions) nor in the intellectual terms that lead to the dominance of intellectual rationalism (as methodological instrument) over obedient faith. Certainly Islam and its fundamentalization show no inclination to espouse this pattern of development that Christianity demonstrated according to Weber. One of the more spectacular versions of Islamic fundamentalism results in Salafiya, striving for the more or less faithful return to the example of the early beginnings of Islam and its doctrinal, social, and cultural purity. Protestant Christianity was motivated by a similar desire, yet this guided it into quite different pathways. Extreme Salafism, as the Taleban demonstrated, has the unhappy tendency to lead back to a "flat-earth" worldview.

Islamic fundamentalism lacks one important ingredient that fundamentalist Christianity (especially of the Calvinist kind) seems to have had in abundance: the intent to achieve material, empirically verifiable success on an individual basis; and in achieving this, it needed to value rational control over the created world. Visible success being originally taken as a token of God's grace became an end in itself. Sociopolitical potency could also be seen as an expression of collective success and its divine approval. In Islam there is a different connection between faith and success. Success means, and arises from, the minute adherence to the articles of faith and realizing this in one's lifestyle. A pure form of faith and applying it in the social discourse is the avenue and assurance of collective and individual worldly success, as well as being the way to redemption in the afterlife. The rational comprehension of the empirical workings of the world through scientific enterprise is of secondary importance—and important only to the extent that it does not contradict faith. Modern fundamentalist Islam—unlike classical liberal Islam—has chosen the former path in search of a comprehensive empowerment, guaranteed through a return to the simplicity and purity of unquestioned and unshakeable faith. In Salafism this is magnified to the search for complete authenticity of the kind propounded and practiced by the Prophet himself and his companions. What is to be inferred from this? If intellectual modernization of the Islamic world cannot be achieved through fundamentalization from within, can it be achieved by force of the global hegemon?

Islam prides itself on being in tune with science and its findings. Cryptically even the most modern scientific insights are supposed to be contained in articles of faith, ranging from cosmology to biological processes, from evolution to human ontogenesis. If there are still some discrepancies, it is only that science is not as yet advanced enough to recognize the scriptural truth. Unlike Christianity, Islam has not lost its claim of total inerrancy and literalism of the scriptures and was spared the need of having to symbolize important articles of faith to preserve their relevance in some shape. No internal revolution has shaken Islam to the core, questioning its dispensation of truth.

The fact that Islamic authority is skeptical and disapproving of several modern scientific achievements fits well with the conservative nature of all modern world religions. Weighing the ethical and moral consequences of new scientific findings and technical abilities (such as cloning, gene manipulation, sex transformation, designer fertilization controlled pregnancy, etc.) and reconciling them with theological doctrine is after all part of their traditional function, even though in some cases the social impact of religious reaction is very much lessened through the all-pervading processes of secularization. In the Islamic world this is not the case: Islam still carries out social control to a considerable extent.

Logically, this begs the question: is there an Islamic science? And in what respect does it differ from secularized Western science? Easterman[56] takes a dim view: Islamic science . . . may in time become synonymous with stagnation, acceptance of authority, and imitation—exactly as happened to Islamic philosophy and science generally, after about the twelfth century. Should that prove to be the case, it is hard to see how Muslims are ever to break free of their current dilemma." The current dilemma is that Muslims are consumers of science and its fruits—as Bassam Tibi has argued—but themselves are not significant producers, despite immense financial and human resources.

The prognostication is even bleaker in the social sciences. The conservative theological view holds that religion can explain science, but not the other way round. The Greek parable that if horses had religion their gods would look and act like horses—that is to say, the conception of the divine follows the horizon of comprehension and limits of understanding of a particular society at a particular time—sounds like pure blasphemy to Islam. Easterman,[57] quoting a Muslim author, points to a tense relationship between social science disciplines and Islam: "Western treatment of history, anthropology, political science, philosophy, psychology, sociology and economics has done more damage to the Islamic identity and character of Muslim society than other science." This unmistakeably expresses the verdict: an Islamic social science that is religious and unshackled is hardly conceivable on the basis of a relationship in which religion has the upper hand.

The absence of glaring epistemic contradictions has surrendered so far ideological safety to Islam and eased the pressure for reformation. Its major challenge does not come from pedestrian scientific innovations, but comes from modern, globalized, West-driven sociopolitical patterns and the hegemonic power of a different culture. It also may come from a new global cosmology.

IS THERE A FUTURE FOR ISLAM?[58]

It is often assumed that theoretical physics—as the pinnacle of scientific cosmological thinking—has developed a hostile relationship with the God-idea. It is better described as ambiguous, but not necessarily hostile. Some leading scientists are known to have been, and still are, religious believers. This supports the view that science and religion are not in direct competition as to their purpose and somehow can be combined without producing a disastrous intellectual disharmony. Religion and science, though competing with each other in epistemological fringe areas, in their essential thrust are directed to different existential issues. One deals with the explanation and control of the real, empirical world, the other is meant to give humans a meaningful framework of their existence.[59] However, there are important areas of overlap where religious and secular epistemologies are facing off against each other, with the (Christian) religious side nowadays largely ceding center stage to the sciences in modern Western society. This somewhat one-sided rapport, that avoids open conflict, has not been achieved in Islam.

A quick sketch can illustrate the situation. The idea of a basic divine creation of sorts is conceivably combinable with physical cosmogony. Some seem to think that if Cern's Large Hadron Collider produces the expected results, it will disprove the existence of God. However, even when successful an act of faith can still be sustained without the need to accept a fundamental paradox. If in the Cern experiment mass can be created out of energy this, by a small adjustment of the God picture, would neither confirm nor deny the existence of an "intelligent designer" or seriously undermine the notion of a divine "creatio ex nihilo." Mainstream Christianity has answered the competing claims of science, after initially fighting back furiously, by largely abandoning the idea of the Bible's literalism and strict inerrancy, symbolizing belief contents, retooling doctrines as metaphors and parables designed to give believers moral and existential guidelines, but no strict rules and no final answers about the empirical world. Mainstream Islam has not followed suit. In Quran 55/27 it says "the face of your Lord will endure forever." Avicenna (Ibn Sina, 980–1037) had already proclaimed that descriptions of the divine are to be taken only as metaphors or signs to enable humans—because of their limited perceptiveness and ability to conceptualize—to have an image of the divine. However, the process of understanding "God's speech" as a narrative of symbols, not a series of literal commands, has not progressed since. In fact Islam prides itself on its doctrines being entirely consistent with modern scientific views, having even foreshadowed scientific knowledge and where doctrine is not compatible with science the reason is that science is not yet advanced enough. Such insistence on inerrancy must produce difficulties arising from what once was called "cognitive disharmony" (but meanwhile sadly has lost its currency in the anthropological instrumentary). Conceivably, the difficulty now lies in the concept of an all-too-personal God who objects to pork eating and anal sex, demands that women cover up, and wishes to punish extramarital dalliances. Such indecipherable, seemingly whimsical and petty commandments sit uneasily in a scientific world view, in which humanlike whimsicality and puzzling mysteriousness shown by a personalized divinity are replaced as agens movens on the cosmic level with the strict order of laws, difficult to comprehend as they may be at the moment. The notion that "God has not played with dice" (to modify Albert Einstein's dictum) has led to cutting edge theoretical physics that is already going beyond relativity and subatomic quantum physics (such as the Higgs boson), speculating about multidimensional universes, quantum consciousness, string and entanglement theories, uses random event generators, positron colliders, and explores the complex relationship of noesis with physical reality. Astrophysics searches for dark matter and predictably finding it and understanding it will profoundly influence science's understanding of cosmogony. In a universe of almost inconceivable laws of physics of unimaginable consequences, it leaves the uncomfortable question: where is that God that issues commands in poetic Arabic to cut off the thief's hand, avoid intoxicating drink, and prohibits contact among unrelated men and women— difficult to maintain in a world population that rapidly moves toward 10 billion. As any anthropologist knows, social rules, normative concepts, and ethics can be arbitrary and seemingly bizarre to say the least. Most however are very useful in engendering a cohesive, functioning society, although when such systems are put side by side they rarely harmonize—as political systems of multiculturalism have found out. Yet, modern science and the cosmology it produces offer the irritating invitation that religious systems, undergirding and interwoven with social systems, be reevaluated and enter a dialogue. It will be interesting to see in what manner Islam will grasp the challenge: whether it will be Talebanic, with a firm view on the past, or looking in the opposite direction, with a keen forward vision that encompasses modern science and allocates to humans a meaningful place in the new order of things.

Elsewhere[60] I have speculated about the global meaning of the Talebanization of Islam, that is to say, the development of a version of Islam that at the moment is represented par excellence by the Taleban movement in Pakistan and Afghanistan, but not solely confined to it. This brand of aggressive, ultraconservative form of Islam, medievalist in its world perception, can also be observed in movements in Somalia, northern Nigeria, Yemen, Bangladesh, and possibly also elsewhere. It forms the odious pinnacle of the fundamentalization of Islam, confined to certain groups of Muslims. This raises an important question: what are the longer term prospects for the world at large given the current violent reinvigoration of Islamic ultraconservatism. Some analysts of modern Islam have elevated what seems to be a crisis in Islam to the position of harbinger of a new global era; an indicator of the end of globalizing rationalization; foreshadowing the death of modernity at the hands of the re-religionising post-Modernity; and a declaration of war to the Enlightenment-spawned intellectual globalization.[61] No modern or postmodern trend expresses this in greater and more frightening accent than the Talebanization of Islam. Modernity, infused with the spirit of Enlightenment, in its globalizing mission, though still burdened with the stigma of colonialism, promised to embrace the world in a joint ideology of moderation, tolerance, and humanism. However, encouraged by the shrill tones of the "awakening" of Islam (sahwa Islamiyah), some now are inclined to see this era coming to a close and a return to the dominance of religious thinking.

> Choosing the medievalist certainty religious fanaticism offers, over intellectual insecurity and chronic doubt reason offers, is a great temptation. But it can only be a temporary, very short-lived solution to the epistemological and ontological problems humanity faces. While at this point no one can be certain, I think, this is not an epoch-making dynamic. While Islamic aggressive fundamentalism may be an attempt towards de-Westernization of dominant worldviews and its socializing mission, it is unlikely to succeed in bringing in a new global era. Neither in the traditional Muslim world nor in the tolerant West is it likely to succeed. [62]

Pope Benedict's Regensburg lecture, though in diplomatic terms ill-advised in its sweeping negative essentialization of Islam, [63] was a call on Islam to reason. Although it may seem anachronistic for Catholicism to act as defender and torchbearer of reason, in a broad sense his address was informed by the same nagging question whether Islam as a whole inclines towards uncompromising rejection of adaptability and choosing violence in the defense of its religious paradigms. Bassam Tibi strikes a more optimistic note. He does not see Islamic radicalization as a lasting global and destructive challenge to what he[64] calls the "Verweltgesellschaftlichung des Zivilizationsprozesses"—untranslatable in its literal sense of contorted German, but roughly meaning this: extending the civilizational process to embrace the formation of a global society. Islamic radicalizm and ultra-fundamentalization are not the victorious expression of the globalization process of postmodernism which demolishes the dominance of reason; they are not tailored for Muslims' consumption by reducing them to the spiritual needs of a pre-Enlightenment society. The resultant Islamic exceptionalism may be a culturally reactive force, similar to Western post-modernism, antagonistic to the civilizational mission of modernity and holding up the false promise of offering the solutions to all social and intellectual problems, but it does not have the power to put an end to modernizing globalization. Elevating religious revival to the beginnings of a new phase of the same magnitude as the European Enlightenment means seriously overvaluing it. The product of such a development—the return to an era of religious fervor and intolerance, the clashing of mutually exclusivist belligerent ideologies and transcendentally fixated world views—seems completely out of step with global needs. The globalization of social, economic, and medical problems demands a collective and concerted strategy based on the best of the rational methodologies and not a retreat into the darkest medievalism.

Is there hope for the emergence of a broad front of modernization of Islam to bring it in line with the modern scientific world view and perhaps precipitate a wave of secularization and the concomitant removal of many social and intellectual restrictions similar as it happened in the West and with Christianity? At the present time the cutting-edge scientific cosmology is intellectually too far removed from popular grasp to have a strong impact. Yet, anthropocentricity and theocentricity do exclude each other even though their contrasting pull may be only dimly perceived in real life. As pointed out before, the relationship between empirical science and religious belief is not a simple one of logic compatibility. It is true that the assumed geocentricity in the religious cosmology and the creation belief were chiefly responsible for the major split between faith and reason and the church's eventual loss of social dominance. Yet, in practical life even scientists can be religious devotees and theologians do not necessarily have nightmares about science, secure in the knowledge that religion and science in the final analysis have different directions and objectives. However, there are indeed overlaps of contested ground where contradictions do occur between them. As experience shows, human beings have an amazing capacity to comfortably live with cognitive disharmony. On a societal level such conundrums tend to be resolved only with a glacial speed. There is also another reason, closely related to what was said before, why Islam is not in imminent danger of colliding with the modern scientific world view and why the major impulse for change does not come from a scientific world perception, despite its seemingly petty prescriptions of human life patterns in which the idea of the grandiose nature of an immeasurably vast and complex universe seems to be totally missing. It seems to lie within the human intellectual comfort zone to adopt the firm belief in divine providence and regulative authority, which is aware of the minutest detail of human existence. Individual behavior is warmly covered by the security blanket of divinity maintaining guiding responsibility. Obeying divine prescriptions, even if they appear pointless and whimsical, equips this intellectual propensity with certainty in actual life, a moral compass and a warm feeling of being on the "straight path."

NOTES

1. Quran 6/68.
2. Quran 9/65-68.
3. I am uncertain about the role of court jester, for instance, at a sultan's court—whether, if it existed, it provides a recognized precedent or how much latitude such a person had.
4. Erich Kolig, "Radical Islam, Dakwah and Democracy in Indonesia." In *Understanding Indonesia*, S. Epstein (ed.). Wellington: Asian Studies Institute, Victoria University of Wellington, 2006.

Chapter 6

5. In recent years, according to press reports, a Spanish court of law did punish a cartoonist for lampooning a relative of the reigning monarch.

6. Without going into legal details, usually defamation laws set fairly strict boundaries but also considerations of treason, commercial sensitivities, prejudicing a sub judice case, and the like.

7. The huge WikiLeaks scandal towards the end of the year 2010 is still reverberating around the globe.

8. Especially Kurt Westergaard, one of the Danish cartoonists, has become a prime target. But also others are now under protective police surveillance. In December 2010, Stockholm experienced a partially failed car bombing, which appeared, as the media reported, to be a reprisal for a cartoon by the Swedish artist Lars Vilks, which had depicted the Prophet with the body of a dog. Not long afterwards, a plot was uncovered in Denmark. Over several years since publication, several individuals have been apprehended and accused of planning revenge attacks against these Scandinavian artists.

9. Jytte Klausen (*The Cartoons That Shook the World*. New Haven, London: Yale University Press, 2009) has analyzed the case extensively. However, her finding that the case is an interweaving of personal political agendas glosses over the fact that it represents a fundamental cultural clash. In order to exploit the cartoons for political purposes, it required underlying cultural reasons (different types of sensitivities and understandings of freedom) to be effective.

10. The Taleban's iconomachy culminated in the frenzied destruction of the Bamiyan Buddha figures. Attempts to destroy them had previously already been made several times and had resulted mainly in some partial defacement and other damages.

11. Alfred Guillaume, *The Traditions of Islam*. Beirut: Khayats, 1966; p. 128.

12. Alfred Guillaume, *The Traditions . . .* ; p. 129.

13. For fundamentalist Muslims it hints at an illicit apotheosis. It is considered important not to lose sight that, despite much adoration for the Prophet, he was only human and an instrument of God. On this basis, Muslims object to the use of the word Mohammedan as it gives too much credit to "the Messenger" as if he were the founder of a religion. It reminds of the wrongful deification of Jesus Christ (which is shirk). The West has largely obeyed and the words Mohammedan and Mohammedanism have all but disappeared from the literate discourse.

14. A commentator on a symposium of experts at Vienna University mentions the existence of Islamic post cards, issued in a context of pilgrimage, which show the Prophet's portrait. Sir Peter Ustinov Institut (ed.), *Der Westen und die Islamische Welt*. Wien (Vienna): Braumüller, 2006; p. 66. No further details are given.

15. At the time of writing, the most recent was a caricature in Oslo's *Dagbladet* of February 12, 2010. In 2007 a Swedish paper published an equally insulting portrayal of the Prophet.

16. The pig and pork taboo has been discussed in the section on Islamic commensality. Speculative reasons have been extensively discussed in the anthropological literature. See Mary Douglas, *Purity and Danger*. New York: Praeger, 1966; and *Natural Symbols*. Harmondsworth: Penguin, 1973; Paul Diener and Eugene Robkin, "Ecology, Evolution, and the Search for Cultural Origins: The Question of Islamic Pig Prohibition." *Current Anthropology* 19/3 (1978): 493–540.

17. Yet, in Western society where pork is generally appreciated as fine food and dogs are considered "man's best friend," to call someone a pig or a dog is a grave insult. In some cultures not only pigs but dogs also are considered "food" and may be kept for exactly that purpose (in some ethnic Chinese cuisines, in the Pacific, in Southeast Asia among non-Muslims, etc.)

18. In June 2010, the press reported that a leading Iranian cleric had issued a fatwa against keeping dogs as pets. Dogs are "unclean" he decreed and keeping them as pets blindly imitates a Western custom. People carrying dogs in cars or taking them to public parks should be fined. However, working dogs (for sheep herding or guarding) are acceptable. This reflects precisely classical Islamic doctrine regarding canines.

19. As a hugely fashionable topic of study over many years, an enormous body of anthropological literature has accumulated on the subject of totemism. I cannot discuss here the principal difference in anthropological studies of totemism that lies in whether the human-animal connection is seen in terms of a kinship and descent relationship or in terms of a conceptual

272

device to order the perception of the world. Another significant point of argument within anthropology was in terms of a cognitive differentiation between totemism as a kind of alternative logic or as a form of prelogical, hence primitive thinking. Lucien Lévy-Bruhl's work (*How Natives Think.* New York: Knopf, 1925; more recently, C. R. Hallpike, *The Foundation of Primitive Thought.* Oxford: Clarendon; New York: Oxford University Press, 1979) represents this perspective, which draws an in-principle division between ancient and modern forms of cognitive ability. Claude Levi-Strauss' oevre (*La Pensée Sauvage.* Paris: Plon, 1962 *The Savage Mind.* Chicago: Chicago University Press, 1966), and several other important published volumes), exemplifying the generic binary logic of all human thinking, has, at least for the time being, put the final seal on this topic.

20. See Erich Kolig, "Of Condoms, Biculturalism and Political Correctness." *Paideuma* 46 (2000): 231–252.

21. As Wilhelm Otto posited, as the matrix from which all religion sprang.

22. Examples are, above all, the divine cosmological hierarchy reflecting human social conditions of a distinctly vertically structured society; the image of God and his maleness as a patriarchal figure; the concept of "man as the likeness of God" or "man having been created in the image of God," and the like, all of which establishes a bond of physicality with the divine. Islam shows similarities in its somewhat "earthy" conception of paradise, but not in the concept of the nature of God, which is deemed unfathomable and incomprehensible to the human intellect.

23. One of the best and most sensitive ethnographic portrayals of this religious art form can be found in T.G.H. Strehlow's voluminous tome *Songs of Central Australia.* Sydney: Angus & Robertson, 1971.

24. This desecration of the Quran was alleged to have happened in 2005. In subsequent anti-American protests sixteen Afghans were killed and more than one hundred hurt. Afghan President Hamid Karzai and Muslim organizations demanded that the culprits be severely punished.

25. In 2007 an English teacher in Sudan was arrested for allowing her pupils to name a teddy bear Muhammad. The maximum sentence that could have been imposed could have been six months in jail, forty lashes, and a fine. Instead she was deported after intervention of the British government and presumably also President Omar al-Bashir.

26. The media reported in 1994 that Muslims took offense at the Chanel fashion house embroidering low-cut dresses with Quranic verses. In the same year McDonalds similarly gave offense by printing such verses on throw-away hamburger bags.

27. See, e.g., Rebecca Knuth, *Libricide.* Westport CT: Praeger, 2003; and *Burning Books and Levelling Libraries.* Westport CT: Praeger, 2006.

28. The destruction through a conflagration of the vast library at Alexandria constitutes a lasting mystery. In one interpretation the burning down of the library in the seventh century was an act of deliberate, ideologically inspired vandalism by the conquering Muslim army. It was allegedly done on orders of caliph Umar (634–644) with the purpose of destroying un-Islamic literature. But other interpretations attribute the library's destruction to other causes such as an accident caused earlier by Julius Caesar or even Christian fanatics in the fourth century AD.

29. The most "grandiose" event of this kind was the burning of twenty-five thousand books at the Opernplatz in Berlin on May 10, 1933, which Goebbels called "the intellectual garbage of the past." Imitations of this event occurred in other places at that time.

30. This was in response to John Lennon's stance in matters of the Vietnam War, when his songs were considered seditious and seminal in the protest movement.

31. He is considered the first Emperor of a unified China, the instigator of the first version of the Great Wall and builder of the mausoleum with the terracotta army.

32. This school of thought undervalues the causative expectations that motivate ritual or magic acts.

33. I will not try to allot book burning firmly to any of the many magical categories devised by theorists: such as sympathetic, contagious, homeopathic, imitative, etc. Nor is it my purpose to argue the fallacy of magical thinking.

34. Expressions of Hindu nationalism in India have also occasionally made a point of burning copies of the Quran in recent years, but Muslim reaction specifically to such events is obscured by the frequency of vicious squabbling between the two sides.

35. The rare exception by official Christian church authorities was Pope Benedict XVI's 2006 Regensburg address in which he hinted at Islam's violence and lack of reason – which was followed by lengthy explanations that the intention was not to give offense.

36. There are numerous cases of this kind reported in the media. Perhaps the best known is that of the imam Abu Hamza al-Masri of the Finsbury Park mosque in London. "Incitement to racial hatred," for which he was sentenced, seems however an ill-fitting indictment for religious fanaticism.

37. He is held at least partly responsible for the first Bali bombing. However, culpability could not be established so clearly as to allow a lengthy jail term. At the time of writing he languishes in prison again for trying to set up a radical Islamic group in the province of Aceh, Northern Sumatra.

38. The raid was carried out by U.S. military personnel, thus in a sense making good on the promise of at least two American presidents (George W. Bush and Barack Obama) "to bring Osama bin Laden to justice." It seems "justice" was meted out in this case in a Biblical sense, rather than in a spirit of modern "civilized" justice through the courts.

39. Ramadan, after having obtained a visa from the State Department, was barred by Homeland Security under the Patriot Act, which denies entry to the United States to persons who "endorse or espouse terrorist activity."

40. UN General Assembly report A/HCR/10/L11 (see pp.78–83), with regard to resolution 10/22 of the Human Rights Council (of March 26, 2009), on "combating defamation of religion."

41. Richard C. Martin, Mark Woodward and Dwi Atmaja, *Defenders of Reason in Islam: Mu'tazilism from Medieval School to Modern Symbol*. Oxford: One World, 1997.

42. Saiful Muzani, Mu'tazilah Theology and the Modernization of the Indonesian Muslim Community. *Studia Islamika* 1/1/ (1994): 91–131.

43. Bassam Tibi, *Islamischer Fundamentalismus, moderne Wissenschaft und Technologie*. Frankfurt a.M.: Suhrkamp, 1992; 94–103.

44. Paul Feyerabend, *Against Method*. (1 ed. 1975, various editions); Thomas Kuhn, *The Structure of Scientific Revolution*. (1 ed. 1962, various editions).

45. E.g., *Conjecture and Refutation: The Growth of Scientific Knowledge*. London: Routledge, 1963.

46. *Reason and Revolution: Hegel and the Rise of Social Theory*. London, New York, Toronto: Allen Lane Penguin, 1941.

47. Peter Mandaville (Reimagining the Ummah? Information technology and the changing boundaries of political Islam. In *Political Islam: A Critical Reader*, F. Volpi [ed.] London, New York: Routledge, 2011) has addressed in particular the issue of orientating the umma in a globalized world interconnected within itself and with distanciated sources through cyber space.

48. Events in Egypt, for instance, subsequent to the fall of Hosni Mubarak's regime, have shown that political success has not basically altered gender relations (i.e., conservative views on the social role of women persist) nor have attitudes towards the Coptic Christian minority improved with the removal of authoritarian controls.

49. Rex Ahdar, "The Right to Protection of Religious Feelings." *Otago Law Review* 11/4 (2008):629–656; p. 656.

50. *New Perspectives Quarterly* 19/1 (2002); backcover.

51. Edward Said, *Orientalism*. (Various editions).

52. Haykel points to an argument of a German Islamicist, Reinhard Schulze, that ascribes an Enlightenment to Islam in the eighteenth century. (Bernard Haykel, *Revival and Reform in Islam*. Cambridge: Cambridge University Press, 2003; p. 12) The argument was severely criticized for its speculative basis and rejected. Islam shows none of the features commonly ascribed to European Enlightenment.

53. See, e.g., Maurice Bucaille, *The Bible, the Qur'an and Science*. Kuala Lumpur: A.S. Nordeen, 1989.

54. In a limited sense Ernest Gellner's distinction between High and Low Islam may be useful in this respect. While High Islam for the most part rejects magical beliefs, Low or Folk Islam draws widely on thaumaturgical practices: from the curative powers of Quranic writing to miraculous interventions of saints.

55. Weber, *The Protestant Work Ethic and the Spirit of Capitalism*. (Various editions and translations).

56. Daniel Easterman, *New Jerusalems: Reflections on Islam, Fundamentalism and the Rushdie Affair*. London: Grafton, 1992; pp. 41–42.

57. Easterman, *New Jerusalems*; p. 38; quoting S.M. Zaman, "Islamization and Strategies for Change." In *Today's Problems, Tomorrow's Solutions*, A. O. Naseef (ed.). London, New York: Marsell, 1988; p. 64.

58. Bassam Tibi also examines the future of Islam in a recent book (*Islam's Predicament with Modernity: Religious Reform and Cultural Change*. London: Routledge, 2009) and also argues that reason is at the heart of modernity. If Islam wants to integrate with modernity, it has to elvate reason beyond its current status. Connected with this is the necessity to place the emphasis on the depoliticization Islam as its political dimension is invalid in the modern world.

59. An important debate has been going on about this for some considerable time, the outcome being still far from decided. Here is not the place to enter more deeply into this debate or even hint at the subtleties of the argument. Karl Popper's work (see, e.g., *Objective Knowledge: An Evolutionary Approach*. Oxford: Clarendon, 1972) can be seen as representative of the school of thought that regards all knowledge forms as instruments of survival in the real world; hence religions and their myths are useful, but flawed explanations of empirical, observable reality. Much of the anthropological enterprise takes the alternative, anti-positivist view that religion and science are differently specialised fields of knowledge. (For an example see Edmund Leach, *Genesis as Myth and Other Essays*. London: Cape, 1969. He argues that because empirical knowledge and religious belief are differently focused, total cognitive incompatibilities can persist side by side.)

60. Erich Kolig, "De-Talebanising Islam and Creating Intercultural Spaces." Colloquium on the Study of Islam in Universities, Otago University, July 2009.

61. See Bassam Tibi, "Islamischer Fundamentalismus als Antwort auf die doppelte Krise." In *Die Krise des modernen Islams*. Frankfurt a. M.: Suhrkamp, 1991; p.203. Fouad Allam, *Der Islam in einer globalen Welt*. Berlin: Wagenbach, 2004 (Ital. ed. 2002) ; pp. 26–27. Jocelyne Cesari, "Islam in the West." In *Globalization and the Muslim World: Culture, Religion, Modernity*, B. Schaefler and L. Stenberg. Syracuse: Syracuse University Press, 2004; p. 81.

62. . This is an excerpt of my conference paper "De-Talebanising Islam . . ."

63. See Erich Kolig, *New Zealand's Muslims*; pp. 174–177.

64. Bassam Tibi, "Islamischer Fundamentalismus . . ."; p. 203.

Chapter Seven

Islamic Politics and Leadership

A PASTICHE OF POWERS AND IDEOLOGIES

Among its fundamental doctrines, Islam propounds the virtue of Muslim solidarity, the indissoluble cohesion among the umma. One of the many exhortations reinforcing this binding commitment is, for instance, contained in the hadith that says it is sinful for Muslims to insult each other and unbelief to fight each other. The Quran verse (23/52) expresses similar sentiments, though in a more indirect manner, in emphasizing that Islam is "one religion." In a similar vein, scriptural emphasis is placed on the social ideal of total equality—in other words, a total refutation of any division that might separate Muslims from each other. A prominent hadith states unambiguously that there is no difference between black and white, Arab and non-Arab, and men and women   only in terms of devotion do people merit a distinction. A virtuous, pious Muslim has merits above a bad one and will surely be rewarded for it. Tacitly there is the ever-present yawning chasm between believers and infidels. By and large, the scriptures extol in various forms the virtue of a community of believers, the umma-al-munimin, united by a bond of belief and equality among themselves and a fervent devotion to God. This sets them apart in a quality of life, which is antinomious to the infidel world in every conceivable way. Yet, despite this being doctrinally mandated, Muslim reality defies it.

A Muslim identity does not automatically produce practical Muslim solidarity beyond lip service, just as Islamic transnationalism, being religious in nature, does not produce a coherent political entity or a common concerted action by the so-called Islamic world. Political initiatives to produce a degree of unity among Muslim nations have so far been denied a resounding success. The Organization of Islamic Conference, which represents the prime organization of Islamic unity, hardly ever acts in concert, its member nations representing widely divergent and often mutually opposing political viewpoints and ambitions.[1] (Though possessing the potential of taking a leading role, outside the political elite it is openly derided by fellow Muslims as a club of self-serving hypocrites.) Feeble synthesizing attempts in the past, for instance between Egypt and Syria (1958–1961), Egypt, Syria, and Iraq (1963), Libya and Egypt (1973), and Syria and Iraq (1979) lasted only months, rather than years. Not to mention the ill-fated and ill-judged incorporation of Kuwait into Iraq (in 1990), which split the Islamic world into two opposing camps.[2] The concepts of umma and pan-Arabism were not strong enough to succeed against nationalism despite the nationalist idea having been imposed only recently through colonialist insistence. The prevailing Muslim particularism can be observed in numerous contexts. Solidarity with the fate of the Palestinians, for instance, procures some considerable funds from rich Muslim nations but no articulated unison beyond empty rhetoric and half-hearted political proposals on how to solve the problem. The Ottoman empire, despite its claim to represent the khilafa, at the end of World War I was torn apart as much by the centrifugal force of ethnic particularism as by the allied powers' military intervention.

Going back over a thousand years, there are chronic frictions between Sunni and Shi'i on an international and intra-nation level, simmering conflicts between Arabs and Iranians, the violent divorce between Pakistan and Bangladesh, black Muslims of Darfur pitted against the fundamentalist Arabic-language central government in Khartoum and its allies, the Afghan and Somali civil wars in which extreme fundamentalists fight with less extreme, but no less belligerent Muslims; and South-East Asia where "relaxed" Muslims and so-called syncretists (abangan) are despised by both santri (devout Muslims) and devotees of Islam aliran garis keras (radical Islam). Al-Qaeda appeals to Muslim identity, proclaiming world jihad as a religious fardh (duty) to reclaim former Muslim lands and wrest world domination from the infidels.[3] Its appeal to pan-Muslim solidarity has little resounding success, although it attracts disaffected individuals in sufficient numbers to keep up the fight. The appeal to common Muslimhood and a political unification, whether under a traditional khilafa or any other arrangement, has consistently failed in the face of widely divergent economic, political, sectarian, and ideological interests, and the strength of the nationalist concept.[4] When arguing the existence of a Muslim society, which undoubtedly shares many social features in the global domain, one has to recognize the political limitations of this theoretical construct.

In the present-day Islamic world, especially in the Middle East and North Africa tribalism, ethnicity, sectarianism, and statehood unhappily coexist. Tribal and ethnic identity—together with sectarian divisions—continue to rival a national awareness and in further consequence clash with the identification with universal Muslimness. While it is often assumed that statehood can only succeed after the destruction of tribalism,[5] this mission has remained spectacularly incomplete in much of the Islamic world. Ethnicity and tribalism as subnational entities are not even necessarily contained within national boundaries; they often cut across and go beyond in a way that sweeps aside the modern state's bounded integrity and questions its sovereignty. (The Kurds are probably the best known example in this respect.) Globalization also aids the reemergence of subnational identities and groupings and their reasserting themselves against the nation-state. To compare the sociopolitical reality of this geographic region with a patchwork quilt would be an enormous understatement, especially as it would ignore the multidimensionality of the situation in which identities overlap and intersect, conflict with each other, and retreat or dominate according to circumstances.

What is immediately obvious, even by the most superficial gaze, is that the political reality in the Islamic world starkly contradicts Samuel Huntington's thesis[6] of a coherent Islamic "civilization" united in implacable antagonism towards the Western "civilization." This would only be conceivable if politics of the Islamic world—at least on the level of nation-states—were homogenous and internally integrated. For this to happen it would collectively need to be extremely firmly grounded in the foundational spirit of Islamic doctrine. This might conjure up the exclusive notion of a global umma, a united and spiritually close-knit community of believers, which then might infuse the Islamic world with the necessary sense of solidarity and spur it on to act in concert. Far from that, this "civilization" is very much fragmented in many different ways. Overall, its dominant geopolitical processes are rarely infused by the flavor of Islamic tenets and cannot be profoundly distinguished from those of the rest of the world. World politics produce their own atmosphere where high-sounding, religiously endorsed values like liberty, justice, pursuit of human rights, moral canons like compassion with less fortunate nations, being one's "brother's keeper," and other such edifying maxims are usually no more than a pretext to justify self-interested pragmatic action devoid of laudable ideals. Religious principles and sanctimony, insofar as they ever played a role in the so-called Islamic world's geopolitical dynamism, have long ago given way to real political demands and the lure of power for power's sake. The bland instrumental rationality, self-interestedness, and opportunist pragmatism as the motives underlying political action usually are not even thinly veiled by religious sanction. Rulers who regarded themselves the commander of the faithful (amir al-munimin), "defenders of the faith," or "the sword of Islam" (saif al-Islam) have made way for self-interested elites with few religious pretensions. Where such labels still exist, they are but empty words. When religion does play a role its sectarian dimension acts rather as a dividing force than a uniting one. Given the classic dichotomy between Dar-al-Islam and Dar-al-Harb and its implicit notion of condescension and hostility towards non-Muslims, the cynical wisdom is that the lack of Muslim unity may be for the better as far as the rest of the world is concerned.

Secularization has left its impress on today's political reality, which shows little evidence of a truly Islamic politics being pursued by any established political system or form of governance. In this sense Islam does not inspire international politics to a noticeable extent; it does not even provide the cement strong enough to bind the so-called Islamic world together in the moderate solidarity to form even nominally the "civilization" that in Huntington's scheme supposedly opposes the West. The Organization of Islamic Conference purporting to speak for the Islamic world with one voice does present a façade of Muslim solidarity but the reality of it practically is no more than a bland formality, which never proceeds beyond mere rhetoric. The political antagonism between Muslim majority states is usually greater than their combined differences to the West. WikiLeaks disclosures in early 2011 have again made that abundantly clear. Saudi Arabia's animosity towards Iran, for example, has been known before, though perhaps not in this intensity. [7] Bahrain's Sunni elite's crackdown on its Shi'ite majority—with Saudi help—in July 2011 reflects this tension by proxy. The mix of sectarian and political-ideological differences accounts for most of the tension in the Middle East. Economic problems and boundary disputes are another contributive factor. The pan-Muslim solidarity shown by extremist organizations may at times lead to strange "marriages"—as, for instance, between Baathists and al-Qaeda in Iraq to oppose the American invasion or the internationalization of jihadism against the Soviet occupation in Afghanistan—but is usually only of a temporary nature. [8] Much play may be made of the doctrine of umma, the global community of believers being called up to fight the infidels, but it does not resonate deeply enough to rally the masses. Mass demonstrations of Muslims seemingly united in condemning (usually) the United States do happen routinely in Iran, Pakistan, and some other countries but as yet have failed to generate a concerted effort embracing the whole of Muslimhood. [9]

Not only is the so-called Islamic world not en bloc arraigned against the West in unanimous antagonism and by a concerted action pursuing the West's destruction, it is divided by a plethora of different political systems forming an open, confusingly multifaceted field rent by competing claims to power and governed by political systems of widely divergent ideologies. The Islamic world is a political pastiche in which self-aggrandizing regimes, autocracy, tyranny, real and pseudo-democracy, religious fervor and secularism, pro- and anti-Westernism, satrapism to the West, and relentless hostility towards it coexist more or less unhappily. Jostling for power and influence among themselves, they also have to keep at bay ideologies that internally challenge their authority. Islam can attach itself to any of these competing

forces. As often has been claimed, Islam can coexist with any political system as long as decisions are made in an Islamic spirit and at least faintly in
accord with Islamic doctrine. Only in a few cases has Islam achieved globally noticeable political primacy.

The Islamic Republic of Iran may lay claim to being Islamic, and likes to
mix high politics with theology, yet this is hardly recognized as authentically
Islamic by others, such as Saudi Arabia, which makes similar claims. Applying values and ideas supposedly Islamic in origin in the political sphere
produces widely different results. Sudan, Afghanistan, Pakistan, Turkey,
Gaza and so on—as well as movements involved in the so-called Arab
Spring—may pursue initiatives to move the respective country in the direction of greater compliance with Islamic values, but are hardly agreed in what
exactly that means. Islamization, whether as a diffuse trend to bolster Islamic
values and way of life against advancing secularization and Westernization
or to redesign society more radically as Islamism tries to do can result in
quite different visions and strategies. This is to say, the judgment, what is
specifically Islamic about methods, systems, and ends in the political sphere
is never unanimous or unambiguous, if at all distinct. Here I will concentrate
on those political phenomena that do have a discernible Islamic aroma. In
exactly this point there is little unanimity. While from a Western point of
view, a particular phenomenon may possess this intangible quality of being
"Islamic," this may be denied by Muslims and derided as essentially un-
Islamic. It is not uncommon, for example, that moderate Muslims utterly
condemn the methods, goals, and the spirit of Islamic extremism, which itself
claims to pursue a quintessentially Islamic agenda.

In various ways, the Islamic world through its volatility has come to
demand considerable attention. The anticipated gradual process of modernization and Westernization leading to a modern and acquiescent Islamic
world has not come to pass. Even though much of this course was either
stimulated or enforced and steered by the West through various types of
intervention, it has not taken the deep roots as was expected. Consequently,
globalization—West-dominated as it is—has encountered considerable opposition in the Islamic world. Much of the West's concern, fearing for its
hegemonic position, has focused on the emergence of a diffuse and multifaceted process that may be summed up as re-Islamization. In the past, authoritarian regimes undertook the task of suppressing Islamization movements
with more or less success. Egypt's Nasser and later Sadat imprisoned and
executed Islamists (among them Sayyid Qutb); Hosni Mubarak continued
this legacy though with slightly less cruelty. Syria's president Hafez al-Assad
goes down in history as having sent troops into Hama in 1982 and shelling it
to crush an Islamist-led uprising in the city, with a loss of life of allegedly up
to thirty thousand. The events in Syria of 2011 show shades of this history.
Iran's shah followed the same route but in the end failed. Algeria is still

struggling with this phenomenon. Almost everywhere Islam has reemerged as a significant player in the internal national political process. Although Islamic grassroot movements are often divided against themselves and each other, as a broad sweep re-Islamization has emerged as a force to be reckoned with.

As the wave of what has somewhat prematurely been called "democratization" washes over the Arab world in the early months of the year 2011, it still remains highly unclear what the long-term result of this sociopolitical fomentation will be. It may yet turn out to be no more than a revolt against political and economic stagnation and the status quo, devoid of any further ideological goals. In some cases it may usher in a process of re-Islamization. Regimes, that only a short while ago seemed solidified in familiar patterns, are crumbling, some succumbing to popular uprising, others resorting to brutal violence to maintain the status quo of power for a while longer. It requires more than a large crystal ball to predict the political realities of tomorrow.

It is highly unclear what exactly the uprisings' major motivations are beyond the obvious wish for regime change: economic and social issues are apparent while the involvement of religion as a significant causal factor is much less obvious. Islamic interests may wisely be held back so as not to arouse suspicion and bide their time. Al-Qaeda as well as other radical Islamist groups have cautiously welcomed this development, obviously hoping the tide will turn in their favor. In Egypt democratization has allowed the Muslim Brotherhood to emerge as a political force, but also Salafist groups, such as Gama'a al Islamiya, which seem to have played little role in the overthrow of Mubarak's regime. (Now reports are surfacing of Salafist groups having started to threaten Coptic Christians and Sufis. Previously in Iraq in the post-Saddam era, attacks on Christians had increased, together with an upsurge of sectarian feuding.) Some political pundits have suggested that this is mainly a secularist eruption, others that it is a youth movement driven by the younger generations unhappy with their lack of political participation and lack of economic opportunity. What can be said though with some certainty, as the rest of the world watches in bemusement, is that two seemingly contradictory ideological forces provide the dominant sociopolitical narratives and cast their long shadows now in the political landscape of the Islamic world. They are similar in terms of providing the dynamics of change. One force is expressing itself by the so-called democratization initiative that apparently seeks to remove entrenched autocratic and authoritarian regimes and may have secularist leanings. The other is a re-Islamization trend (sawah Islamiya, awakening of Islam) that had begun to make itself felt in Muslim societies already earlier on by agitating for changes to move society and politics closer to an Islamic ideal. The relationship between the two forces, fickle and unstable as always, remains unclear at this point in time. As earlier events in Iran, Afghanistan, and Indonesia have shown, the two can operate simultaneously, even cooperatively, to effectively oppose oppressive political systems and overthrow them. Sharing a goal for a while, they eventually turn on each other. Iran, after overthrowing the Shah's rule, has taken an autocratic-theocratic turn, which has been opposed by a budding democratization attempt very recently. Indonesia, since removing the dictator Suharto from power, at least for the time being, has moved decisively closer to an open democratic, secular system and now has to keep at bay the radical Muslim fringe.

Taking a wide-angle view, what can be said is that in the last few decades, the Islamic world has been in the process of rediscovering Islam. This has given rise to a patchy dynamic of fundamentalization by which some elements not only seek to reinvigorate social life with Islamic values but some also breathe what they think is a distinctly Islamic spirit into political thought and action. In the process Salafist fervor reaching back for inspiration to premodern conservative doctrine and even endeavoring to reestablish the caliphate, has risen from the ashes of apathy. While religious fanaticism, generally speaking, had seemed to wane in the Islamic world before the latter half of the twentieth century, it has since flared up in various ways conspicuously infusing some political events again with a religious fragrance. In this form it has come to exert considerable influence on Western political thought. To explain the rising fundamentalization and Islamism, I think, it is necessary to take a step back in history.

Since the time of Islam's rapid expansion and reach for world hegemony—sparking off the rather unsuccessful counter-push, the crusades, as well as partially more successful episodes of repelling Muslim expansionist moves into Europe—the West by and large has remained wary of Islamic advances in the world. Military conquest meanwhile has given way to peaceful Islamic missionization of the dawa (or dakwah) kind; that is, using kindly persuasion to convert people with sweet words and good reasoning.[10] Christianity, though, continues to look with suspicion at peaceful Islamic missionary efforts in Africa, Asia, and America, but probably not with the intensity of the West's secular political interests. The vigilance acquired during World War I has certainly not lessened. Following the West's colonial intrusion into the classical Islamic world, its political potential had waned considerably; its doctrinally formulated worldly aspirations were of little consequence. Occasionally political phenomena in the Islamic world provoked some concerted response such as the so-called Suez crisis of 1956. The oil shocks in the 1970s, and the general tension, punctuated by outbreaks of open war between Palestinians and Israel—which remains one of the major sources for Muslims' dislike of the West and especially America—also captured a somewhat more lasting interest of the West. However, on the whole with the fragmentation of the Ottoman Empire at the end of World War I, the geopolitical potential of the Islamic world had been irreparably damaged. New insecure nation-states were created out of the detritus of the Ottoman Empire and, having been effectively emasculated they remained under the ideological tutelage of Western powers and at times under that of the Soviet Union. Bending the Turkish millet system[11] into new forms, Syria was created but Lebanon was split from it to give more weight to the Christian minority in the Levant. Three different, mutually hostile Muslim groups and some small minorities were forced together to create the new state of Iraq. Kuwait as much as Palestine and Transjordan were carved out rather arbitrarily and Palestine divided further to create a Jewish state in 1948. Kurdish ambitions for a national state were thwarted. France, Italy and Spain remained anchored in the Maghreb. The Western intervention in the "confrontasi" in Southeast Asia (1962–1966) saw to it that Indonesia, which had gained independence from the Netherlands after World War II, did not swallow up parts of the even more newly independent Malaysia. This pervading Western interventionism had one underlying motivation: that of utilizing the principle of fragmentation, and by cleverly utilizing sectarian and ethnic differences, to neutralize the growth of an orchestrated and noteworthy Islamic potency that might have endangered Western domination.

Add to the history of political interference an ideological dimension of more or less enforced secularization through unleashing various forces which cannot be controlled nor contained by Muslim authorities, and a picture of the present day reality emerges that gives a clue as to how Muslims might perceive their world. Thus in a political and ideological sense, the West is directly responsible for much of the shape the present-day Islamic world finds itself in. Consequently, the thrust of what is clearly recognizable as specifically Islamic politics now—collectively and with a sweeping generalization labeled Islamism—and which in its intent opposes the status quo, has arisen principally in response to the various forms in which the West exercises domination. Whether it is the existence of nation-states, its national boundaries and political mechanisms, the incomplete mission of modernization, fragmented secularization, unpopular political governance, in other words much of the sociopolitical and ideological reality, virtually all of the status quo, exudes the stench of Western interference in the nostrils of devout Muslims. If Islam wants to reassert itself politically and socially, it is practically forced to take a stance that is overtly or implicitly anti-Western. The West returns the favor by subsuming Islamism in its political taxonomy under the label extremism and tends to treat it as an aberrant phenomenon of revivalism, a suspect form of nativism, and a political pathology of which it hopes it will not last too long. (This certainly means ignoring moderate forms of Islamism. The Arab Spring and the democratic elections it has spawned in several countries do show that moderate Islamism is not necessarily the ferocious enemy of the West and of the democratic ideal as it was made out to be by Western opinion makers.)

In reality the broad sweep of re-Islamization and fundamentalization has brought to life a wide spectrum of political aspirations that somehow take their inspiration from Islam. Islamiyun (Islamists) are spread over a wide ideological arch and encompass a considerable range of ideas regarding means and ends.[12] Certainly, on one end there is the kind of fanaticism that wants to lead Muslims back into a ghetto of medievalism, but not all Islamic utopias are of the parochial Talebanic kind. Only extreme Salafism falls into the political rubric where even Sayyid Qutb's critical work is judged an illicit innovation and rejected as bida. (This is all the more remarkable as Islamism in general takes much inspiration from Qutb's and Mawdudi's work.)[13] The Islamist motto of din-wa-daulah, belief and state being coextensive, can draw on quite different conceptions from al-Qaeda's fanatical vision to Turkey's democratically based, current cautious re-Islamization program and similar efforts by the brief interregnum of Abdurahman Wahid's government in Indonesia a few years ago.

The most liberal versions just seek a cautious reorientation of society towards Islam's spiritual and moral values, while the more radical ones strive towards a total fusion of society and (conservative) theology. Current forms of fanatical adherence to Islam strongly reject the church-state separation. In their view the split is not sanctioned by the version of Islam they wish to implement. The takfiri (the excommunicated), the extreme jihadis, the committed salafis, all challenge the present forms of governance as Western inspired and would presumably also reject moderate forms of Islamism. They reject the legitimacy of the ruling elites and their regimes, be they dictatorial, aristocratic or quasi democratic, on the grounds that these are not in accord with Islamic principles of propriety, justice, and social order. Much of the present political leadership is summed up with the derogatory title of munafiqun (hypocrites). Taking the example of the Prophet, extreme Islamists envisage an ascetic leadership that is pure, God-fearing, and moral. Consequently, much of radical Islamism's power potential is directed against corrupt and despotic, semi-secularized regimes just as much as against undesirable Western influences.

Social justice is not unusually part of the revolutionary Islamic agenda. If one screens out Western propaganda and biased news reporting, some forms of Islamism have extensive welfare and education programs. On a social-moral front, the idea of social welfare—quite compatible with the idea of social welfare in a modern democratic state in comprising everything from medical care to education—is far from alien to Islam and is enshrined in the concept of zakat as an important religious duty and one of the five pillars of Islam. Charity and social welfare may conceptually be quite different but can practically be melded into one. Some forms of Islamism even agitate for free elections (where Islamists believe they can win democratically). In some ways Islamism has even assumed the mantle of liberation theology reminiscent of activist Catholicism in South America. Re-Islamization may also involve political aspects, which clearly are of a less laudable kind from a Western perspective. However, contrary to popular Western belief, there is nothing in Islam that constrains it so compellingly towards political autocracy, or despotism, and the unequal distribution of wealth and power that other options would not be possible. Despite the Prophet's iconic image of combining all powerful social functions in his hands, the absolute authority he exercised was willingly granted—one might say democratically ceded—by the faithful and not assumed by force. We shall look at the political paradox of the original Muslim community later.

Reforming Muslim society as programmatically demanded by Islamism, its radical as well as its moderate versions, either tacitly or overtly involves the strengthening of shariatic principles and their enforcement in law and social conventions. Paradoxically, an increase in democratic freedom may in some Muslim majority countries facilitate achieving this result, although one must realize that the intensity of the desired shariatization may vary a great deal. It is the principle of social reform on an entirely religious basis that makes Islamism stick out in a globalizing world piloted by a secularizing dynamic. There is no other society or non-Muslim country that has a religiously designed internal social reformation plan as conspicuous as Islamism has.

The most extreme fringe of Islamism dreams of the resurrection of the khilafa, the caliphate. Under globalized conditions it is not just envisaged to take the form of an office, which exercises spiritual leadership, but as a polity as well that unites most or all of the believers, reintroduces a strict code of conduct and brings back a golden era of Islam. As a powerful political entity it is expected to be a counterweight to the Western enterprise of globalization. In extreme visions, the territorial inclusiveness of this new Dar-al-Islam, the realm of Islam, may come to extend even to Western and other countries with large Muslim minorities. Abdullah Azzam, credited with being one of the founding fathers of al-Qaeda during the mujahidin campaign against the Soviets in Afghanistan, already seems to have envisaged the reconquest of a number of former Islamic lands:[14] Palestine, Bokhara, Lebanon, Chad, Eritrea, Somalia, Philippines, Burma, South Yemen, Tashkent, and even Andalucia.

ISLAMIC EXPANSIONISM

Seen in this light, recent population movements can be interpreted to play
into the hands of radical Islamist designs and to represent a revival of expansionary dynamics of Islam in premodern times. Hostile expansionism
through territorial conquest had been vitally important to the spread of Islam
in history. Until about three centuries ago, territorial conquest or in some
other way geographically extending the sphere of influence, went hand in
hand with campaigns of religious conversion, making spatial increase coterminous with religious growth. By this process Islam spread out of the Arab
peninsula through the Middle East to Western Africa, to central Asia and into
Europe. Despite some tolerance shown to some other religions, military conquest and political expansion gave the opportunity to exert pressure for the
sake of religious conversion. With it came the adoption of salient cultural
elements of the conqueror.[15] (This is not necessarily peculiar to Islam, but
represented a general truth prior to the onset of global secularization, which
separated the this-worldly political enterprise of expansion for strategic or
economic reasons from religious aspirations.) Meanwhile this process has
come to a halt—if one leaves aside the carving up of Cyprus into a Turkish
and a Greek part. Traversing into the slippery territory of Western paranoia,
it may be said that over the last two or three decades through mass migration,
as some Westerners have come to believe, a replay of Islamic expansionism
is happening. With more than a dash of tragic paranoia, some even call it a
surreptitious invasion. Recent decades have seen an influx of Muslims into
the West, in particular Western Europe, partly for reasons of security (fleeing
violence and persecution and seeking out the West as a safe haven) and
partly for economic reasons (attracted in particular by the booming econo-
mies of Western Europe). As the Muslim diaspora in the West has grown
now to sizable proportions, especially so in the more prosperous Western
countries of Europe, and, as some believe, has escalated alarmingly in numbers,[16] openly critical voices grow louder.[17] Political forces are being increasingly mobilized to stem this influx of cultural aliens, and to stifle the
growth of cultural Otherness amidst Europe. Muslim demands for cultural
and religious recognition and apparent resistance to assimilation, and even
integration, are taken as indications of an imminent hostile "take-over bid."
Fears are being vociferously articulated in some circles that this is a creeping
process of conquista to complete what could not be done centuries earlier. In
various ways fear has been expressed that the traditional identity of Europe is
under threat. This "angst" finds a curious and unexpected corroboration in
the utterances of some Muslim ideologues. When, for instance, Tariq Ramadan[18] pins the label of Dar-al-Dawa, the realm of proselytization, on the
West, it can be interpreted that it is not just meant as reassurance for Muslims

to feel at ease in the lands of the infidels, but to say the West can be prodded into adopting the right faith. Such remarks are suspected that they are not designed just to encourage Muslims to carve out a modest space for their religious survival under a policy of tolerance and multiculturalism, but to embolden them to assert a religio-cultural influence on the host society. This can not be done from a position of strength, but from a position of persistence, example, and persuasion. In calling the existence of Muslims in the West as being in Dar-al-Dawa,[19] Ramadan appears to be referring to the opportunity Muslims have through migration to exert a gentle if persuasive proselytizing effect on the encapsulating societies. He also refers to the new abode as being of shahada (profession of faith) and likens it to the Maccan period when Muslims as a minority were bearing witness. As most Westerners know in that situation a small minority grew into a world power.

At the moment the intelligentsia among Western Muslims, for the most part, seems more concerned with the maintenance of a separatist Muslim identity, shunning any pretensions of expansionism. In the host societies the insistence of a Muslim identity creates the suspicion that immigrant Muslims have no desire to even integrate, placing higher priority in the preservation of cultural and religious separatism. In a juridical respect, the melting pot theory and its practical demands cannot be upheld in the face of human rights, which entitle migrants and minorities to preserving their culture. (In the unrealiztic expectation that Muslims will become Westerners overnight, it is easily forgotten that wherever Europeans and Westerners went, adaptation to the "host society" hardly ever happened. In colonial times, dispensing their "civilizing" influence—replete with religious missionization—to the "natives," they were rather concerned with carving out enclaves in which European modes of living had dominant currency with minimal concessions to local conditions.[20] Little has changed in contemporary times.)

An increasing assertiveness of the Muslim leadership, insisting on their right to remain Muslim and rejecting mere tolerance as insulting condescension,[21] has fanned fears that cultural Europeanness is in peril. Not surprisingly with a mind-set poisoned with suspicion, the increasing appearance in the urban landscape of the mosques' Middle Eastern architecture, of minarets thrusting into the European sky, the niqab making an appearance in the street scenes, the demands for the right of having sharia courts, all seem to be harbingers of the approaching danger of Islamization.[22] Apart from pragmatic concerns about national security, there is the more intangible, if ubiquitous worry, about the national identity, the diminution of national and pan-European culture.[23] Most dramatically the noted Islamicist Bernard Lewis predicted that soon "Islam could be the dominant force in a Europe, which by being too politically correct had lost the battle for cultural and religious control." Churches have raised concerns that secularization has left a spiritual void, which Islam is all too ready to fill with its message. (On the other hand there are those stern voices that welcome the new firm morality pro-vided by Islam to replace the debauchery and loss of "moral compass" the West has suffered.) Here is not the space to analyze this phenomenon in detail. The relevant question in this context has to be this: does the right of immigrants to adhere to their cultural identity constitute a secret political agenda tantamount to an invasion of the host country? Does the human right for immigrants to retain the full integrity of their culture and religion facili-tate and even encourage its (mis)use as a strategy to alter the cultural compo-sition of the host society? And even if this is so, and the paranoid fears turn out to be true, can this endeavor legally be repulsed—for instance, through the enforcement of assimilationist regulations—without doing grievous dam-age to the whole intricate fabric of human rights and challenging the West's proud claim of having achieved a maximum of personal freedom unparal-leled in human history?

It can be of little surprise that this angst, finding a fertile ground in the West, turns to outright hostility—diffusely toward cultural Alterity and in a more focused way toward conspicuous Islamism.[24] Using a somewhat me-chanistic metaphor, it may be said that the demise of communism has freed up a potential of Western hostile attitudes, which could then be transferred to political Islam. Where previously Islam had been looked at with detached distrust and was even harnessed where possible as a useful force to contain Soviet expansionism,[25] now wherever politics appear to form a conspicuous extension of Islamic doctrine, as had previously been the case with the Tale-ban regime and continues with Iran, it provokes stiff opposition from the West. Recent significant political developments in Somalia, Pakistan, and Gaza show the familiar pattern. Such political phenomena, rightly or wrong-ly, do not only incite the Western antipathy towards religious fanaticism, but raise the spectre of al-Qaeda, the terrorist extension of radical Islam, trying to gain a foothold. In other cases, the suspicious unease exists about growing Shi'ite influence, which might foment destabilization and social unrest. Even when Islamic fervor on the global level is dampened by real political neces-sities, the appearance of Islamic doctrinal aspects in a country's political composition usually meets with opposition by the West-dominated world. The reasons are not altogether clear or logical. Human rights violations—often caused by the application of sharia—are usually cited. However, such claims lack in consistency and logic. Saudi Arabia and the Gulf States, sever-al subSaharan African countries and regions internally enforce an Islamic lifestyle that to a large extent is based on a conservative interpretation of classical sharia law and thus conflicts, practically as well as theoretically, with human rights and a Western perspective of justice. Many Muslim ma-jority countries as well as many non-Muslim countries of the Third World routinely violate human rights (as laid down in the United Nations charters) in one way or another by law and by virtue of organising social life in a way unsynchronized with the Western-controlled hegemony.

It is entirely conceivable that moderate Islamism may have some success across much of the Islamic world, and this may bring home the basically relativist cultural premises of globalization. It may even stall the mission of global "modernity" for a while and alter its direction in the long run. As Asia and Africa increasingly emancipate from Western dominance and the erst-while clear West-centeredness turns into eccentricity (at least in an economic sense), their social agenda begins to diverge from the trajectory mapped out by the West. Islam may yet come to play an important role in this process. At least more moderate forms of Islamism may be able to attract the tolerant latitude by the West to influence the course of globalization. The chances of success, however, are slim for the brand of extreme Islamism that takes its inspiration from Salafist ideas, which design a future that represents a return to social conditions extant at the Prophet's time. Returning to the Islamic version of a "flat-earth" worldview would appear to have little prospects of being more than an isolated, short-lived episode in the modern world. The Salafis who have a burning passion to reinvigorate the Prophet's mission by installing the divinely mandated society, as it existed more than a millennium ago, are far from being warmly embraced even by a majority of Muslims.

THE HEAVY HAND OF LEADERSHIP

The noted Islamic scholar Abdullahi Ahmed an-Na'im[26] writes,

> The tragedy of Islam today is that the Muslim leadership has locked itself into being intimidated by its extremist elements. These Muslim leaders, whose moral bankruptcy and weakness are represented by the opulent lifestyles of the Saudi Sheikhs [*sic*], live on the fringes of Islam as well as Western civiliza-tion. They lack the essence of either. In that sense, they are twice as corrupt and twice as Satanic as radical Muslims claim the West to be.

This is not an unusual view among Muslim intellectuals and reflects current realities—which now are partly being overturned by popular uprisings. How-ever, the conclusions, which Muslim intellectuals and aspiring leaders draw from it, can be quite different. So, what should proper Muslim leadership look like? And what are the supposed remedies they should introduce: relig-ious revolution and jihadism, khilafa utopianism, greater political adaptation to the Western model, and greater opening towards globalization?

To consider the topic of Muslim leadership, in relation to power and the specific Islamic character in which it is wielded and distributed, requires a brief description of historical political forms and precedents. Especially for an understanding of current types of Muslim leaders this is particularly relevant. Islam inclines Muslim society to a contradictory disposition in regard to political systematization and distribution of power. Doctrinally, Islam tends towards a relatively equal distribution of power in society, which shows fundamental affinities with political systems of a (premodern) democratic kind. On the other hand, the Prophet's personal historical example has left a subliminal taste for strong leadership, which seems to have influenced much of the recent political situation in the Islamic world by aiding the emergence of despots. This antinomious tendency, which goes well beyond a mere paradox and through which Islam harbors within itself a political contrast that is not easily reconciled, can only be sketched here by way of a brief analysis of the history of leadership and political systems.

Although Islamic doctrine inclines strongly to egalitarianism among the believers, it has never consequently been implemented. Spirit and partially also the letter of Islamic doctrine clearly spell out the equality of believers in several respects. Leaving aside for the moment gender differences, Islamic rules insist on legal equality: the sharia applies in equal severity and force to every Muslim regardless of rank or wealth. The idea of material equality is enshrined in the zakat, the religious tithe; one of the five pillars of Islam, this religious duty of giving alms in a certain proportion to one's wealth is intended to even out gross material differences. Significantly, it is not left to an individual sense of charity, but is doctrinally regulated. Islam also holds that there should be equality in status, as no one possesses higher prestige before God aside of that accorded to the pious, and in special cases to martyrs, as we shall see. Lastly, the ideal of equality is also enshrined in the preferred, legitimate political process. It is supposed to ensure equal influence (though confined to adult males) on decisionmaking in matters of governance through a shura system (convention or council) achieving ijma (consensus, agreement) in free deliberation. Good governance (hakimiya) is based on these processual principles as much as being in accord with doctrinal principles and virtues. Righteous leadership, based on such principles and arrived at through this process, entails taqlid, voluntary submission to sociopolitical and religious authority. The original Muslim community may have come close to this scriptural ideal under the Prophet's leadership, with the exception and proviso of the Prophet's exalted status and his powerful, charismatic persona having removed him from the ordinary process of selection. This was then exemplarily instituted by his immediate successors, providing the template for ordinary political processes. In this form of governance, exhibiting features of democracy, the ideals of Islamic social politics found their purest expression. Although formal voting and universal (gender) suffrage were absent, the ideal of ijma did balance to some extent the transcendentally underpinned power of the leading figure. This was no more than a potential, tantamount to a popular illusion about the individual Muslim's social weightedness and upholding the belief that the "Messenger's" authority was voluntarily ceded to him by his followers. Overall, this ideal political constellation, briefly realized in the original Muslim community bears a strong resemblance to the "democracy" in tribal societies. That is to say, the ideal political process and institutions share the characteristics with those traditionally extant in tribal societies of a more egalitarian bent (i.e., decision-making in council form, "elected" or chosen leadership, a certain degree of equality in influence varied to some extent through individual capabilities, etc.). The modern ideal of democracy is not quite achieved in these political systems as political councils with voting and decision-making powers are composed of delegates and representatives (such as respected elders, clan leaders, family heads, etc.) who are authorized to speak for others. (The well-known Afghan loya jirga is such a political constellation, and so are representative councils operating in Arab monarchies.)

Speaking to the ideal of (relative) equality in political debate among the believers, there was the recommendation that slaves who embraced Islam should be freed immediately. Doing so would remove gross status differences within the umma and allow all believers to contribute to ijma. In reality, however, the realization of the egalitarian dream remained just that: a dream. Apart from the gender division, Arab cultural tradition from the days of Islam's emergence was always strongly arraigned against the political amorphization of society. Islam presents in this regard a typical utopian agenda, which rarely gets to be implemented in completeness or for any length of time. In Islam's case the reality of Arab culture and society easily overruled doctrinal pretensions of egalitarianism. The Sunna intimates that already the second caliph, Umar, by his social background and personal psychological inclination was removed considerably from this ideal. Arab society, far from being homogenous, was rent with social status divisions that added to the complexities of tribal and religious divisions and differences arising from different economic foci. There were nomads, some specialized as camel herders, others as goat and sheep herders, merchants, agricultural farmers, and artisans. It would be surprising if these professional groups had enjoyed equality in status and esteem.[27] Slaves formed a class apart and had few rights. Probably women, too, in some groups, may have suffered social disadvantages. There were persons of noble birth (sharif), noble lineages and tribes (nasab), and client tribes and groups (da'if) who had to pay protection money (khuwa). Ahl-al-bayt, ruling houses, which formed the leadership elite every tribe had, competed among themselves for predominance and prestige, forming opportunistic alliances (hilf) and warring against each other. There were religious aristocracies, whose leaders (mansib) controlled sacred places (haram), acted as arbiters in disputes, and exploited their prestige for political influence.[28] To compress this social complexity into a community of equals was an experiment that was bound to fail.

At the beginning of Islamic history stands quite conspicuously the unity of leadership functions culminating in a hagiocracy. All power was concentrated singularly in the person of the Prophet, no important function was significantly delegated to others. Muhammad was a warrior-prophet, spiritual father figure, diplomat, and military strategist, all at the same time. Political leader, supreme judge, father confessor, prophetic speaker of God's will—he synchronized every leading social and political function with his supernatural message. It provided the rationale, explanation, and authority for his unique exercise of comprehensive power. For some years after his death, his impressive example was emulated by his immediate successors who demonstrated the ideal of the khilafa, which is still the guiding utopian vision for some fundamentalists. However, the four Rashidun caliphs, although their powers and leadership attributes were still closely modeled on the Prophet's life, deviated already in one basic aspect from the Prophet's example. Although in some features the Muslim community resembled some crude form of democracy, subtle changes of the political structure became apparent. The caliphs' authority was derived completely from a kind of plebiscite, public acclamation of sorts, but no longer from a recognition of the presence of divine grace. In other words, their position was no longer by God's choice; in their person divine sovereignty had in fact been usurped by man. While a modicum of charismatic qualities was still important to the assumption of a leadership role, caliphs no longer manifested the stamp of divine approval as clearly as the Prophet had done. The early part of Islam's history is an object lesson how supreme, divinely-granted personal charisma gradually turns into the much less flamboyant "office charisma," to use Max Weber's term, sustained in the end more by military force than gnostic respect.

Islam's history shows clearly the changing interplay between power concentrated in the hands of one man, who may or may not have held a divine mandate, and democratic impulses working towards the dispersal of power and surfacing in schismatic and anti-authoritarian efforts. The idea of a basic, divinely-derived unity of power was lost soon after the Prophet's demise and is retained now only in the messianic dreams of Shi'ism[29] and the utopian vision of a certain form of Islamism that wishes to find back to the original Golden Age. With the end of the exemplary and foundational career of the Prophet and the tradition-setting actions of his immediate successors, the Rashidun caliphs surrounded by al-salaf al-salih (the virtuous forebears), the Prophet's contemporaries, leadership of the rapidly expanding Muslim community became more and more diverse as its functions were split up into several specialized roles. Coherence was lost also as the Muslim community was pulled into several ideological directions and as factionalism increased. Imam Hussein had tried for a while, in vain as it turned out, not only to avoid a religious schism, splitting the growing Muslim community doctrinally and politically, but to retain spiritual and political-military leadership in his own hand. On a more abstract level, and cutting through the tangle of ideological and political diversity that consequently unfolded, leadership branched into specialized roles: that of political and military leadership wielding secular power (to some extent military leadership also became a separate domain although remaining largely under the control of secular authority) and of a clerical class, the jurist-scholars and theological experts. The caliphate assumed the trappings of secular power trying to exert a controlling influence on the independently working theological elite. Not unusually there was considerable tension between the two sides as both vied for supreme authority and both sides remained dependent to some extent on the approval of their legitimacy by the other. Despite the fact that the classical figurehead of the caliph nominally retained the attributes of top position in all matters, actual and active leadership divided into two specializations: theological or ideological guardianship was provided by the ulama, the muftis, mujtahids, and the fuqaha, and the secular political and military power was in the hands of others (sultans). Islamic clerics and scholar-jurists, openly competing with each other, are not ordered into an ecclesiastical hierarchy, have no councils to harmonize authoritative views, no machinery to check and recheck canonical law and creed.[30] These were a class of men who in their views were not coordinated, held widely different views, and obeyed no supreme authority. As a class of people they shared a diffuse professional awareness that they were the vessels of theology and law and were held together only by a joint interest not to do anything to jeopardize their privileged position in society by engaging themselves in radical innovation.

Every religious schism that convulsed Muslimhood brought about new forms of leadership legitimated in different ways. None of them came even close to the original ideal. The specialization of roles led to acute expressions of rivalry and friction: Islamic moralists demanding greater fidelity to doctrinal principles in state and personal matters of the ruling elites, and these in turn sought to exercise control over religious exegesis so as to gain or retain, as the case may be, legitimacy. This contradicted the original condition and the intrinsic ideal of Islam that demands the unification of spiritual and worldly leadership on the basic premise that worldly affairs should be tightly guided by religious doctrine and ethics.

The vision of the perfect society under one perfect, divinely appointed leadership, yet incorporating public approval, briefly realized in history, had shattered. It remained as a faint institutional afterglow in the millenarianism of the Shi'a emulating Ali's caliphate. Iran embodies in political reality the Shi'a ideal of the supreme Imamship of Ali and Hussein, combining in one person the qualities of theological and political leadership. The supreme Ayatollah, as the nation's spiritual leader and the highest ranking cleric in Shi'ism, is also the supreme, popularly unelected head of state and in his constitutional powers, superseding even the president, commands also considerable secular clout.[31] Ayatollah Ruhollah Khomeini in spectacular fashion combined clerical leadership and secular power skillfully manipulating, on a theological basis, a diffuse rejection of the Shah's regime into a successful political revolution. If Western reports are true, many Iranians believed, at least for some time, he was the expected final Imam. His successor, the Grand Ayatollah Ali Khamenei, as Supreme Leader exercises a supervising and controlling function over the government including the president and has the power with his advisory board to check all functions of governance, jurisprudence, and so on. for their doctrinal correctness. Yet, the present leadership is far from being regarded the incarnation of the returned Imam. Among the Sunni the utopian vision of an all-encompassing leadership also remains unfulfilled. As wishful thinking it inspires the most fanatical of Islamists who carry the maxim din wa daulah (belief and state) on their banner and dream of a khilafa. Their plan to reunite sacred and secular authority, by now probably surpasses the hope of resurrecting a classical institution of realiztic proportions, and has assumed redemptive and messianic expectations.

A few times in the past, ecstatic messianic phenomena emerged among Muslims when quasi charismatic persons claimed a leadership role in temporal as well as spiritual matters. The Mahdi "uprising" in Sudan had such features with military, anti-colonialist aspects added in. The most recent case was the takeover of the Masjid al-Haram, the Grand Mosque of Macca, in November 1979 by a group of armed Saudis whose leader Abdullah Hamid Mohammad al-Qahtani claimed to be the Mahdi. After a siege of two weeks, the mosque was cleared by police and military with many of the occupying militants killed and the Mahdi captured and later executed. In many cases of this kind thaumaturgical and soteriological expectations seem to have been abandoned or were destroyed by outside intervention almost as soon as they arose. In some cases where redemption beliefs did crystallize into a firm messianism—mainly in the Shi'a tradition—the followers are denied the dignity of being universally recognized as fellow Muslims: the Ahmadis, Druze, Alewis, and Alawis are often considered outside Islam proper because of their beliefs that their messianic expectation has been fulfilled and—similar to the Baha'i—that the Prophet's message has later been enhanced further. The Twelfer and Fiver Shi'ites continue to expect their messiahs at an unspecified time in the future.

The Taleban displayed, and still do, a close synergy between the spiritual and the political by combining it in the role of the amir-al-munimin (leader of the believers), although no pretense has been made that this resurrects the classical caliphate. In other cases, for instance and most successfully in the case of Wahhabism, religious renewal saw the wisdom in forming a symbiosis with secular power which, in turn, realized the advantage in aligning itself closely with religion for raison d'etat and for the legitimation of its rule. The history of the nation-state of Saudi Arabia is the narrative of this success of combining, yet never merging, secular political power and puritanical religious conservatism. Only in more recent years does this bifurcate power show signs of cracks as a split appears episodically between the royal house of Saud and some factions of the clerical elite who show sympathy for the radicalism of al-Qaeda or preach the virtues of a more Spartan lifestyle to behove the royal house. This has led to a situation in which the political leadership now is moved to exercise some tighter control over religion insofar as the state sets certain parameters of religiosity; yet at the same time is treading cautiously not to oppose the entire religious elite. In everyday life, the religious police have extraordinary powers and in some respects is above the state law and thus somewhat extraneous to the ruling clique. On the other hand, some high-ranking clerics appear to have been censored and even imprisoned for sanctioning a very radical brand of Islam and combining it with social critique.

Most expressions of leadership in the Islamic world today not only show the deep bifurcation of leadership, but display the fragmentation accrued over Islam's history. The creation of nation-states has produced new, additional forms of political leadership, some elected and most unelected. The ideological plane also shows a great variety of leadership roles, many of them contesting the same ideational and political ground, very few bridging deeply entrenched sectarian and ethnic divisions. Adding a novel dimension, in radical Islam a type of leadership emerges, and gains in prominence, which seems to emulate the features of the original Muslim community. It is a Shaykh-al-Islam that seeks to combine active political guidance with theological learning: performing a role that draws on expertise in theological matters, provides spiritual leadership, and combines it with radical political activism not to the exclusion of involvement in military and extremist activity. When Osama bin Laden remarked that the Prophet's law is emulated by the jihadists, what he may have had in mind is a reference to the belligerent aspects of the Prophet's leadership. Just as the Prophet was also a warrior, this type of leadership is not adverse to the use of the gun. Beyond regulating war by divine decrees, the Prophet was, as the Sunna makes plain, personally involved in fighting, devising battle strategies and leading his army. Despite his spiritual role he maintained a closeness to political and military action that placed him directly in harm's way. Combining theological learning not only with functions of political decision and planning but emphatically also action has become a defining ideal inspiring this type of leadership. Jihadism implicitly has adopted a doctrinal manifesto that recommends that spiritual leadership come out of the "ivory tower" and stay close to the physical fight. Bin Laden provided the role model having taken his cue from the example of others before him and from the Prophet himself.

Let us look at this development in a wider perspective on the clerical class. Through nationalization of sharia in many Muslim-majority countries, ulama, the traditional spiritual leaders and jurist-scholars, have lost their social position as guardians of the law.[32] As the administration of justice has passed into the hands of professional jurists (in the Western sense), the ulama have lost much of their erstwhile social status. Modern state law is only partly based on classical sharia concepts of jurisprudence and a traditional Islamic sense of justice. The political aspects of leadership are under the control of regimes, which are only to some, sometimes very limited, extent influenced by Islamic doctrine. (The decline of religious influence on formal law and political rule does not apply to Saudi Arabia and Iran. In both countries religion still exercises a controlling influence in all spheres of social life including jurisprudence. Turkey shows ambiguous features in that it is secularized by state constitution thus theoretically keeps religious doctrine from infusing politics and state law. On the other hand the current government is composed of a religious party.) Some muftis exercise the traditional role in still dispensing tafsir, ijtihad, and fatawa relating to legal as well as political matters, but states normally do not closely adhere to these views if not ignoring them altogether. On the other hand, the informal social influence of some religious experts has increased. They often use modern technological means of the electronic internet, in this manner reaching well beyond what would otherwise be the traditional confines of their influence. Thus their influence, paradoxically, has both increased as well as diminished. Their personal reach in the private sphere has considerably transcended traditional limitations, while their official influence has declined.

In the course of the re-Islamization of Muslim society, the religious elite begins to reclaim their traditional role as educators and guardians of the law. Following this broad trend, in the search for Islamic authenticity a reshaped leadership emerges, which is both representing a new form of hierocracy and a recourse to ancient precedent. The new leadership, though often less well versed in the intricacies of Islamic doctrine, and less adept to the many versions represented by the madhahib and the voluminous literature on fiqh, has greater political alertness and personal involvement. Touched by globalization, their awareness of wider political realities meets with their conservative interpretation of Islam. Skillfully combining religious tenet with political objectives, they manage to keep their followers enthralled, molding idealist minds and leading the willing devotees. Through their inspirational skills their words and thoughts resemble the revelations of esoteric secrets. Like initiands in tribal societies are made privy to the higher mysteries, the Muslim novices begin to see their existence in a new light, as if a veil has been taken from their eyes. Joining the ranks of the devotees is like a rebirth through conversion, emerging as an immaculate, morally cleansed new person in possession of a shining new identity and a new purpose in life that transcends poverty, social failure, and vacuous aimlessness. This new identity is not only forged by fiery words and slogans, but then has to be hardened by action.

Outstanding scholars such as Abul'Ala' Mawdudi, Sayyid Qutb, and Hassan al-Banna combined religious erudition with political programs. More recent times have produced scholar-politicians who have spread their not inconsiderable skills over theology as much as over active political leadership. What is more, they are, or in some cases were, keeping close to the fight to implement their ideals—some paying with their lives. Abdullah Azzam (a forerunner if not founding father of al-Qaeda), Ayman al Zawahiri (al-Qaeda's former no. 2 and now its leader), Osama bin Laden, the Taleban visionary Mullah Muhammad Omar, assassinated Palestinian leader Shaykh Ahmed Yassin, the Indonesian radical ustadz Abu Bakar Ba'asyir[33] (accused of being the architect of the Bali bombing), the Shi'a cleric Muqtada al Sadr in Iraq, the American born Yemeni Anwar al-Awlaki,[34] and countless radical imams. Several of them were fire hardened as mujahidin fighting the Soviet army in Afghanistan. Some of them, still bearing the scars acquired from their days as mujahidin, are teaching in the West, serving as mosque imams and preaching violent jihad. Madrasah teachers and scholars have managed to mesmerize and politically galvanize a sufficient number of Muslims to keep the world in fearful suspense. Combining a grasp of Islamic doctrine with strong political viewpoints about today's world and its perilous condition, they become a source of inspiration of sorts to individuals who search for a meaningful commitment to Islamic goals and causes in whose service they feel they can make a difference. Many of this type of leader have a checkered career of climbing the heights of adulation among followers willing to die for the cause insinuated to them, and descending to humiliation through show trials, imprisonment, and violent death. Dying by execution, assassination, car bomb, and drone seems to be a frequent fate but does not seem to deter them.[35] Obviously such a fate is considered a sacrifice worth bringing as martyrdom beckons as an ideological beacon of supreme value. It is an iconic phenomenon understood across cultural boundaries for its capacity to grant "immortality" and posthumously give meaning to human existence. The martyr's death is also of incalculable propagandist value.

While the steep rise of this kind of religious leadership astounds and occasions derision of the gullibility of so many ordinary people in blindly accepting clerical guidance to violence, it is easily forgotten that secularization in the West is not an unambiguous and all-encompassing phenomenon that has transformed all Westerners into religious skeptics, selfish pragmatists, and coldly rational thinkers. While Europe (including Russia), Australia, Canada, and New Zealand seem firmly embarked on a course of intensifying secularization, the United States is steering their own course between secularism and religious devotion—a devotion that admits the crossover of religious faith and secular power, even if expressed in a militaristic manner. In the conservative reaches of American society, one can find a cryptic bond between religiously fired up devotion and patriotic belligerence. It manifests itself, for instance, in the political affinity evangelical Christianity has had, throughout successive American administrations, with the formulation of aggressive policies.[36] Apocalyptic visions of Armageddon seem to be powerfully engraved in the American psyche.

The phenomenon of crowds being galvanized by a combination of religious exhortations and political rhetoric, as has become an almost daily occurrence somewhere in the Islamic world, may trigger astonishment and alarm in the West. Enigmatic and difficult to understand may be the fact that not only large numbers are attracted, but that they exhibit often unusual and sometimes rapturous behavior. Mass hypnosis and the mysterious workings of mass mentality[37] are known to generate remarkable reactions. As thousands spill from the doors of mosques shouting condemnation of America or their own regime, they exhibit the hypnotized, hysterical behavior of religious devotees. (One cannot help but be reminded of the fans of rock and pop music who in mass concerts become seemingly entranced by the occasion and exhibit symptoms of mass hysteria.) They demonstrate the facility of humans to come under the spell of intoxicating words and by their lingering effect be prepared to lay their lives on the line.

The ability of Muslim leaders to gather around them scores of devotees and to instill in them such commitment and even fanaticism is causing great concern. Exemplary demonstrations of this kind were given by Ayatollah Khomeini through his ability to stir thousands of young men—and their mothers—to become willing cannon fodder in the Iran-Iraq war. Fiery speeches of Muslim religious leaders have galvanized masses of people and continue to do so. A khutba (religious sermon) in a mosque or a lecture in a pesantren may seem far-fetched to become an electrifying motivator. It is easily overlooked that in the United States evangelical preachers propounding a very conservative message can allegedly attract congregations of twenty thousand admiring people every Sunday. If we are to believe journalistic reports, congregations, buildings, and budgets grow bigger and bigger every year. Not all of those listening eagerly and entranced to the homilies may in their daily lives be faithful to the values and ideas presented to them, yet still they are living demonstrations of the mesmerizing power of rhetoric. In the recent European past it was extremist political leadership, which in mass rallies unleashed the hypnotic powers of megalomaniac ideas. Fanatical, incendiary devotion manifested in these phenomena does throw a characteristic light on the human capacity for falling under the spell of words and ideas, especially when strung together by rousing rhetoric and grandiose concepts of divine will and destiny. Muslims and Westerners alike can be mesmerized by the pathfinder in the eternal quest of finding certainties in the insoluble connexion between faith and existential reason.

NEW DOCTRINAL PROPAGANDA

Islam is not just a religion in the sense of a hermetically closed system of beliefs, techniques of worship, transcendental ideas, and doctrinal assumptions of considerable clarity. It is a discursive field in which contesting powers, interests, and interpretations meet and compete. Exegesis of the dogma is necessary so as to translate doctrinal ambiguities into certainties that are able to inspire and guide action. Subjectivity and individual intentionality fill the spaces where sociopolitical agendas can grow and compete for legitimacy. Theological interpretations—a tafsir—can be extracted so as to deliver a useful framework of reference within which information and data can be understood, strategies can assume authenticity, and even utter violence can be justified as a doctrinal command. Information about the world and its here-and-now is slotted into the doctrinally defined pigeonholes giving it depth and existential meaning. As it fills the spaces of exegetical assumptions it provides up-to-date corroborating relevance for this framework.

An important part of the objective is the creation of an Islamic domain in which manifestations of Westernism and its "decadence" have been expunged, the "predatory intervention" of the West in Muslim affairs has been unmasked and thus further incursions thwarted. In this domain, purged of evil, the dominant position of ilm, essential knowledge, used to decipher God's creation and to live in accord with the divine design plan, has been reestablished. More ideological than theological, the millenarian nature of this vision arises out of and requires a type of leadership that can bestride two paths simultaneously by being spiritually uplifting and politically astute. Recreating the missionary zeal of the founding fathers, and marrying it with the revival of the vision of the perfect society and a perfectly ordered, just world, this intent fits a well-known pattern. The similarities with minor millenarian prophets who made claims to have knowledge of "Essential Man" and ideal society, divinely ordained, are obvious. Third World, the West, and Islamic world meet in unison in terms of the type of pseudo-charismatic leadership that claims to combine spirituality and sociopolitical program.[38]

The Islamic utopian reformation driven by visionary leadership, the purveyors of "true Islam," seeks to remoralize Muslim society by a revitalization of the Islamic doctrinal fiber. Contemporary Islamic society is believed to be in crisis, supposedly having been deformed by internal decay as well as powerful external forces. The benchmark in this assessment of what the ills of contemporary Islam and Muslim society are, is provided by a conservative understanding of what essential Islam is, which social, political, and moral values Quran and Sunna convey, and in what order of priority they need to be obeyed. The purpose is not a recalibration of Islamic doctrine to accord it with modernity and its requirements, but to change the givens of sociopolitical reality so as to bring them into harmony with the vision of "essential Islam."

The political and theological agenda in this visionary program combine in a new way. In incongruous juxtaposition, its exegetical viewpoints tend to be hyperconservative, its scriptural interpretation even reactionary, but its temporal intent is modern and forward looking. The formulation of a sociopolitical agenda, set on a fundament of conservative theology, is radically reformatory and propounds a hierophany of a social order that is both heavily traditionalist and futuristic. By this seeming contradiction I mean to say that it responds to the givens of modernity by being anti-globalizt, anti-modernist, and anti-Western on the basis of an appropriately conservative tafsir and that it envisages a revitalized, remoralized Muslim society that espouses traditional principles programmatically in a modern world. This kind of vision can emerge seemingly whimsically under any social circumstances, from among the Saudi economic elite to mosque imams in the West, where they may be labeled "hate-preachers," to Afghan village mullahs. Islam—especially Sunni Islam—having no established, formal authority structure and no encompassing hierarchy admits to a wide variety of theological views all of which may claim legitimacy and manage to attract a wide following, while holding at bay the censorious criticism of peers. No formal theological credentials are required. (It may, however, help to have academic credentials from one of the outstanding and prestigious places of learning in the Islamic world. To have studied at Qom or having trained at al-Azhar university or at a theological college in Saudi Arabia's heartland may be a career advantage.) Ideology thus comes to be regulated and endorsed from below and not above, being subject to fierce competition and contestation, and remains independent of the approval by an established elite.

This type of leadership and the ideology it spreads are greatly aided by modern technological means of mass communication. Khomeini's influence during the final years of Shah Reza Pahlavi's rule grew substantially through the dissemination of his sermons on audiotape. The Taleban regime, in its anti-modernist, anti-Western, and luddite frenzy, banned modern technological devices (television, tapes, computers, cell phones), though paradoxically allowing and using modern weaponry. The success of its ideological message came about through its close affinity with the conservative Pashtunwala, the culturally dictated way of thinking of the southern Afghan tribal world. However, the Taleban were unique in their extreme technoclastic "purism." The ultraconservative techno-Salafism for which the Taleban were renowned, has been rejected even by other hard-core Salafis as counterproductive on the basis of a different interpretation of Islamic doctrine and its relation to technological innovation. Of major importance is the distinction whether technology is regarded as aiding the cause of Islam or as frivolous playthings that divert from Islamic duties.[39] The regret that conservative Muslim clerics usually have is that modern electronic media (especially television) are not used more to spread their kind of message, instead of providing "cheap" entertainment.

The use of means of mass communication (cell phone, internet) has energized the political process, as the "Arab Spring" shows. However, technology being neutral, it can be used for any "moral" or "immoral" purpose: for instance, for organizing mass criminal action such as serial looting and burning as much as rallying people to demonstrate for democracy. Equally sobering, mass dissemination of information (images distributed by cell phone, internet, Twitter, Facebook, etc.) does not necessarily only contribute to the democratization of information as one might have expected; nor does it effectively enhance its truth value. While one effect of the electronic media in particular appears to be the relatively free flow of information and the increasing inability of elites or states to control information dissemination, radical messages enjoy the same liberties and often remain effectively unchallenged. The internet especially, more so than other communication means, has been expected to be a vital instrument in the liberated flow of information and the free and informed formation of opinion for the betterment of humanity, but this is not necessarily the case.

Radical Islam puts electronic communication and the associated difficulty of suppressing the flow of information to good use. Circumventing censorship, its messages though do not grossly falsify information (as was traditionally done in the authoritarian and autocratic regimes)—which under conditions of a much freer flow of information could be unmasked as mendacious and which would blunt the effect of the message. Instead it works by insinuating and spreading certain perspectives that have the ability to slant factual information but are not in open contradiction to facts that can easily be checked through the information highway, the electronic media, and the like. Communication technology is used to disseminate ideologically prejudiced information of a kind that is not in obvious discord with verifiable facts but tends implicitly or overtly to interpret them in a way that is not amenable to empirical checks but in which axiomatic Islamic doctrine provides a reference framework. Ephemeral counter-evidence, if and when it fleetingly surfaces and may create doubt, is discredited as propaganda, deliberate deception, and lies. One should remember that in the West, too, mistrust of official sources and the news media is widespread. To cultivate cynicism about the messages they disseminate, their truthfulness and motives, is considered to show good sense and intelligence. Governments and politicians are routinely suspected of dishonesty–a lesson painfully learned at first from Watergate, and as this new-found skepticism is applied to history and current events, more "revelations" and more surprises emerge. Particular parts of the print media and some television channels are especially well known that they strongly represent partisan political and economic interests. This kind of distrust of the surface meaning of information and the expectation that information is not given out in a fair and dispassionate way seems well entrenched among Muslims with regard to Western sources and those controlled by West-sponsored regimes, but does not extend to sources with Islamic credentials. Information from sources known to represent conservative Islamic interests tends to be credited with a high degree of veracity and to be taken at face value.

THE METHODOLOGY OF RADICALISM

The methodology envisaged to realize utopian dreams and other less ambitious aspirations of reinvigorating society with Islamic doctrine may diverge widely. Some goals are to be achieved with peaceful informal education (of the kind conducted by Tabligh Jamat),[40] or through Islam-friendly state schooling. However, if a spontaneous re-Islamization of Muslim society is to be achieved, it cannot be done through dawa, a peaceful but slow education process; it requires some time-adequate strategies to inculcate the necessary perspectives so as to achieve regime change and replace entrenched hegemonic patterns with authentically Islamic ones in the near future. In this atmosphere, doubts are raised not only about the legitimacy of the ruling political elite and the education system it has installed, but also about the state-supported ulama who cannot be trusted to inculcate the correct version of Islam.

To satisfy the impatience to bring about the desired change in mind-set quickly, initiatives other than kindly dawa may be required, such as casting education in the forms of indoctrination. This strategy draws on utilitarian ideas about the end justifying any didactic method, even pressing the concept of jihad into service, to refer to a battle with all available means for the minds and hearts to gather up converts for the cause. From fiery Friday khutbas (sermons) offered at the salat-al-jummah in mosques to mass rallies in sports stadiums, from evening classes to "summer camps" and weekend retreats, from ideologically committed pesantren and madrasahs (religious schools) to internet communication between continents, they can all serve as means to convey appropriate instruction. Winning adherents by some of these means may even stray into the area of overly vigorous conversion techniques and conjure up shades of brainwashing akin to strategies found in some present-day NRMs in the West.[41]

A fine example of an extremist educational institute was Pondok Nguruki (or Pesantren Islam al-Mukmin), an Islamic boarding school in Surakarta, Central Java, Indonesia. It was called an "ivy league" for Jemaa Islamiya recruits by the International Crisis Group, in reference to its reputation as a training institution for aspirants of Indonesian extremism. A number of people who had been educated there were implicated in terrorist attacks. Head of the school and co-founder was ustadz Abu Bakar Ba'asyir who, in 2004, was indicted as the mentor of the group of terrorists carrying out the first Bali bombing that killed nearly two hundred people. The school was said to store weapons and have jihadist slogans (such as, "it is honorable to die in the cause of Allah") decoratively painted on the walls. Around that time I was staying in the area, but I did not have the opportunity to visit the compound—the ongoing police investigation made it impossible, but I could pay a visit to another pesantren (boarding school) not far away. It had a more moderate reputation. Nonetheless, a large picture of Osama bin Laden, prominently displayed on the wall in the style of a religious icon, betrayed the school's ideological sympathies. It was difficult to ignore despite the director's laughing assurance that it meant nothing. According to reports it is such religious schools in Pakistan that continue to supply the Taleban with new recruits. They are well educated—in conservative Islamic terms, which is to say, their education has a heavy emphasis on knowledge that is not only Islamic in character, but also biased towards radical presumptions.

The didactic language used at such places endeavors to elevate global jihad to the status of universal panacea—a bifurcate jihad that is directed domestically to purge Muslim leadership and purify society as well as combating the West, the external source of corruption and immorality. Almost comically, a sizable part of the corroborative evidence, as I found, is gleaned from a caricature picture of what Western culture is all about. This image is drawn from the large pool of Western movies and television programs that depict rampant sexuality, violence, nudity, promiscuity, and vicious crime in sheer abundance; where homosexuality and brutality seem to be idolized greed, immorality, and crime appear to be rewarded with material affluence, and the like. Less world-wise minds accept this dubious offering as a true reflection of American and Western culture and unsurprisingly do not wish to have their society "polluted" with it. More scientifically minded demagoguery uses statistics about crime, alcohol abuse, poverty, and the like, rampant in the West behind its shining facade the death and destruction wrought on the world by Western-incited wars its global economic rapaciousness, and the injustice of supporting Israel against the legitimate claims of the Palestinians. Such arguments are usually exacerbated by the seemingly widespread belief that especially America is bent on fighting Islam to expunge it from humanity and that this was the true reason for invading Iraq and Afghanistan. Bringing up the Palestinian conflict also is always likely to arouse much passion welling up from the sense of Muslim solidarity, even in far away places as Indonesia, unaffected as this country and its people are by this unfortunate situation. Adding to the imaginary picture of the West's deviousness, the events of 9/11 are attributed to a vicious CIA plot to deliver to the American administration the desired pretext to attack the Islamic world. The opposing side, correspondingly, claims that Muslims in ascribing this kind of cynicism to the West in actual fact reveal something about their own mindset. They would resort to such a murderous deception against their fellow-Muslims if they thought this would help to realize their wider objectives. Indeed this argument does not seem to be wide off the mark. By a gigantic Machiavellianism, in the interest of achieving the greater objective, Islam's ethics do seem to permit deadly violence on a grand and indiscriminate scale. Incessant terrorist attacks, mainly by car and truck bomb, are so coarse in their execution that often both friend and foe suffer equally. (For instance, in the Bali bombing as many Balinese died as foreigners.) If a rationalization of this approach is needed the universally understood concept of sacrifice delivers the required excuse. This could be further sweetened with beliefs in a reward in the afterlife for those accidentally killed. When the Quran[42] says that helping a jihadi is like being one oneself, it extends the same rewards to accessories, which in a cynical reading perhaps could be extended even to the unintended victims of "collateral damage."[43]

Violence, unfortunately, is part of the palette of "normal" human interaction, deeply embedded in human nature as it is. Consequently it expresses itself both in informal personal interrelationships and in the highly formalized conduct of power politics, and in the official judicial enterprise of the state as much as in feuds and vendettas between social groups. Attempts to present violence as a manifestation of social pathology, as some scholars have tried to argue,[44] have not been convincing and have the ring of an unrealiztic, utopian vision of a society that can be cleansed of this blemish. It is more likely an innate expression of aggressive physicality, which can at best be hemmed in by social and ideological controls. Importantly, apart from its obvious pragmatic and tactical purpose, violence intrinsically also is a conveyor of symbolic meaning. In Islam's implicit theory of the perfect society, as much as in the strategies to achieve it, violence has its place in various shapes.

Radical Islam believes in political violence as a useful and morally defensible method. The methodology to which it will openly profess unashamedly relies on the success of calculated, strategic violence. In intensity this can range from the use of seemingly undirected, "mindless" petty violence of some Islamic organizations implementing a strategy of intimidation in the pursuit of purging society of evil, to the mass murder perpetrated by shadowy terrorist cells. The Front Pembela Islam (FPI) in Indonesia, for instance, occupies the lower rungs of violence. It has a well-earned reputation of using thuggery in the style of the Nazi SA (Sturm-Abteilung) to manifest and enforce its brand of Islamic morality. Beating up political opponents, committing arson against churches, vandalizing nightclubs and places where alcohol is consumed, and trashing courts of law when the organization is dissatisfied with verdicts are its standard repertory. The FPI seems to have an amazing ability to muster large numbers of thugs to descend locust-like on a place to lay waste to it, usually for the declared reason of enforcing Islamic morality, while apparently staying clear of the more deadly kind of terrorism. This activity is left to another organization, Laskar Jihad (The Jihad Soldiery), which considers itself the bulwark against Christianity. Its special brief seems to be to incite violence in places where Muslims and Christians are living side by side. On a more serious level, some Salafist and other radical organizations have also taken to tactics of harassment of non-Muslims, ranging from beatings and arson to murder. None of that, however, pernicious as it is, has reached the proportions of the activity of the Jemaa Islamiya, the Islamic Society "credited" with the two Bali bombings, as well as a range of other atrocities, too numerous to list here. Thus every niche in the scale of violence is occupied by a special organization. Like nature produces all conceivable biological specializations, the contested field of religion fills every niche with a particular form of ideology, varieties of aggressiveness, and types of missionary zeal.

The parochial nature of the execution of violence may surprise when seen in a global context. Beating up people, committing arson, bombing a hotel or embassy, and even killing some tourists and "expats" hardly changes the world. It may seem that radical Muslims lack the wider picture and do not have a realiztic appraisal of the magnitude of the West's hegemony; and that because of the lack of a proper universal gauge, they fight isolated and minor symptoms instead of addressing the real causes. In reality the leadership is realiztic—as well as educated—enough to understand that a contest of open violence with the West will not radically alter the balance of power, though it may have some effect in a very localized context where the powers are more evenly matched.[45] On a wider and global level the application of violence as an instrument of power is thought to be effective rather in a roundabout way by inflicting wounds each of which by itself is not deadly. Even as Islam's activism does not amount to guerrilla warfare, there are other fundamental reasons—more grounded in psychology than the physical world—that justify violence as a useful tool. Violence, rather than being merely a straightforward medium of forcefully expending energy, which impacts physically on an enemy, is the conveyor of messages. If violence is meted out sufficiently incisively and repeatedly, even if it cannot directly tip the balance of power, through the perseverance and viciousness it demonstrates has the ability to weaken and undermine the resolve of the opponent. On a smaller or local level this has been proven to be true in various contexts. (People tend to leave an area in which they are frequently subjected to acts of violence. The Madrid bombing has removed Spain from Iraq—or at least such a causation may be read into the events.) Another aspect of administering violence is that it is prized for its strong semiotic function. In standing up to a fierce adversary and carrying it out in the face of an overwhelming power, violence demonstrates strength of character and determination. Seen in this light, it satisfies the quest for self-confirmation and delivers affirmation of self-worth. Lastly, it serves to exact revenge for past injuries. Even if the violent action is far from inflicting a decisive blow, or is far from being an equivalent in severity to the original harm, it can restore at least a moral equilibrium. Exacting retribution for a past wrong reinstates the lost dignity suffered through an unjust act. (The idea of dueling between opponents in response to an insult and to restore honor can be found in many cultures.) Among radical circles in the Islamic world, the perceived reasons for generating a need for payback may extend as far back as the medieval crusades or may be historically as recent as the creation of the state of Israel; reasons may be as diffuse and general as a symbolic response to Western "unjust" domination or as particular as direct revenge for a particular military defeat or the assassination of an important leader.

The cultural roots of violence as a symbolic problem solver and as a restorer of honor and balance run deep in many traditional societies. Most premodern justice systems rely on this constellation. (The sharia in its most conservative form preserves the idea of unsublimated payback in the concept of qisas, i.e., prescribing a punishment that [ideally] is literally the equivalent of the crime and applies the judicial motto of "an eye for an eye" beyond a mere metaphor.) Indeed, it may be appropriate to see payback violence and the notion of restorative justice associated with it, as deeply grounded in a species-typical urge for revenge.[46] Although the word vendetta stems from the Mediterranean region, the concept of payback is truly universal. Often the roots of a chain of violent reciprocity involving generations are lost in the dim mists of the past and, in fact, the original reasons of the conflict become irrelevant as payback between social groups (clans, families) assumes the shape of a tradition. In keeping it alive notions of collective guilt, inherited guilt, and guilt by association often apply in equal measure obviating the need for finer distinctions or for tracing the chain to the original wrong. The vicious cycle of violence begetting violence in an absurdly ordered succession of events and unfolding in a controlled, almost ritualist fashion is not unfamiliar in many cultures.[47]

Traditional Middle Eastern society is no stranger to that open-ended method of "conflict resolution" in which violence is perpetrated for personal revenge or for the sake of collective retribution. The sense of justice in "underdeveloped" and rural areas still clings to violent methods: to settle disputes, restore honor, exact revenge, enforce shariatic rules, and so on—even though state law may seek to suppress it or tries to monopolize violence for its own purposes. In fact Islamic history from the beginning delivers paradigmatic events in which violence is supposed to solve religious conflicts or to satisfy the need for personal revenge. Assassination and murder accompany the history of the caliphs like a malodorous trail. Three of the Rashidun caliphs (Umar, Uthman, and Ali) died a violent death by murder, assassination, and in battle. Other caliphs and leaders suffered the same fate. The emergence of the Shi'a is steeped in an atmosphere of blood sacrifice; in particular Hussein's martyrdom in the battle of Kerbala at 680 AD is still commemorated in the Ashura celebrations and for Shi'ites has paradigmatic meaning of martyrdom.

The formation of the original Muslim community is marked by crucial and bloody battles (of Badr, Uhud, the "battle of the trench" at Madina and "of the camel" at Basra, and many more), engraved forever as decisive events in Islam's early history. They mark the bloody birth of a world religion as significant foundational cornerstones. Putting prisoners of war—or those who refused to embrace the new religion of the victorious Muslims—to the sword is also recorded history. Spreading the faith, or defending it, by sword and military might, was regarded a legitimate enterprise and as an effective means of proselytization, as legitimate as peaceful dawa.[48] Scholars see an ideological cleft between the first peaceful revelations, which were received at Macca, and a later more aggressive phase. Both phases are distinguishable in the Quran, even though they are obscured by a later process of ordering the records of suras and ayas in a manner that ignored the chronology of revelation. The mood of revelations changed dramatically at Madina; conciliatory suggestiveness gave way to a more strident, belligerent tone that lent support to a mounting assertive outlook on the world.

Violence, being woven from the start into incipient Islam, is also an integral aspect of the figure of the Prophet. He was not only a spiritual leader, a theological beacon rallying his community and subjecting them to a regime of strict rules of interaction, but his historical persona is also closely associated with violence. Breaches of the rules he propounded were violently punished within the community, for which he provided the rationale, just as externally the community's militarist defense and later expansionism link Islam and his efforts inextricably with the theme of violence. His role was instrumental in military matters as well as in others of an even more gruesome nature. Whole groups of people (usually called tribes though this seems doubtful) were put to the sword. The narrative of Islam's formative years (as conveyed by Quran and Sunna) with its deeply inscribed themes of violence can be expected to have shaped the mind-set of Muslimhood. Quite conceivably, it continues to exert influence over Muslims' perception of violence as a legitimate mechanism of defense and asserting religious supremacy. (This is, of course, not to say that all Muslims are violent or have a strong propensity toward it. Embellishing ecclesiastical history with violent and militaristic features, and celebrating them, is not confined to Islam, nor is this a compelling reason for people to act in a violent manner.) As can be expected, Muslims' perception of Christianity is tinged with the assumption that violence is also part and parcel of its dogma. For many Muslims the West's crusade, which in their view combines the aggressive promotion of Christianity with militarist features, has not ceased yet and still manifests itself in the numerous acts of assault on the Muslim world. Some Muslims are finding corroboration in recent history by pointing to (former) President George W. Bush's and (former) Prime Minister Tony Blair's professed strong religious belief. Their biographies, and interviews with them, make it plain that their Christian background played an important role in their lives. This can easily be linked, in one way or another, to these leaders' political decisions to enter into wars with Muslim countries—an interpretative step that many Muslims find easy to make. Both Islamic history and scriptures provide strong paradigmatic statements on violence, which can be employed in interpreting and understanding extra-Islamic circumstances and events.

Apart from violence for political reasons or personal revenge, on an interpersonal level the exercise of violence (in the sense of violation of the corporeal integrity of a person) is lawful and prominently prescribed in Islamic law. In Middle Eastern popular and conservative juridical conceptions the maxim of eye for an eye, the idea of retaliatory violent justice, is deeply engraved—in fact it tends to go across religious divisions. It has an ancient legitimacy, condoned and encouraged by several religious perspectives, codified in ancient texts and regulating fairly strictly the legal use of violence for punitive purposes. Monotheistically prescribed lawful violence has deep historical roots reaching back into the most ancient civilizations, which had codified systems of law. Islam follows this ancient tradition.

Violence in various forms is clearly prescribed by sharia as a legal means of punishment, and its official enforcement is underlined by traditionally being publicly demonstrated. Floggings, decapitation, hanging, stoning, and even hand amputation have in the past been executed in public and in some Muslim countries they still are. The principle of retributive violence can be mitigated through the payment of blood money, but at the same time the sharia also insinuates qisas, the concept that a crime be punished by a comparable and measured act of violence against the offender. This ancient law of appropriate retribution may be mellowed by the view, rather cryptically implied in the Islamic Sunna, that forgiveness has the greater merit,[49] but it is not as central to the Islamic sense of justice as in Christian philosophy is the paradigmatic importance of "turning the other cheek" and forgiving. Modern state law seeks to wrest the right of punishment—or forgiveness—from non-institutionalized discretion (private individuals acting in a vigilante style, rural communities and tribal councils, and other bodies not formally consti-tuted), and lodge it in dispassionate state functions and a justice system that obeys highly standardized, predetermined rules and has a clear taxonomy of crime and appropriate punishment. (The degree to which the state justice system is modeled on and faithful to the sharia can vary widely,[50] as can be the resistance of local communities, tribes, and so forth, to hand over the right of exercising justice.) This is of course not a specific Islamic problem and is not confined to Muslim states. Some regions are notorious for settling conflicts through interpersonal violence based on shariatic principles, which modern state law rejects or applies only in strongly modified form. If one is to believe informal sources (in the absence of statistics), this is so in the Islamic world predominantly with regard to certain gender-related misde-meanors. While unofficial viewpoints may favor the enforcement of rules that express gender inequality, official law may take a very different stance. Precisely for that reason, because it is believed that offences by women against traditional conduct are ignored by state law in its attempt to be even handed in gender matters, or because it is protective of a "new-fangled" notion of women's rights, some communities may be moved to "take the law into their own hands." (Radical Muslims tend to see the failure of the state legal system to act decisively in such matters as the cowardice of client regimes bowing to the juridical dictates of the West in order to curry favor and obsequiously secure financial assistance.) Another frequent source of tension between "customary" sharia law application and modern state law relates to the punishment of blasphemy. State law, when it is not exercising the death penalty in such matters, may be considered too lenient or remiss and provoke vigilante action with wider public support.[51]

The ancient tradition of violence as a direct expression of morality as well as a legitimate means of enforcement of moral standards has an unbroken continuity in the Islamic world from the past into the present. The imposition of death sentences is required for various crimes, not only murder but also apostasy, blasphemy, and adultery, and in pursuit of the restoration of family honor. On a lesser scale, amputation and other bodily interventions—in countries where this is still practiced in accord with conservative sharia inter-pretations—are now performed surgically under clinical conditions and can-ing and whipping as formal punishment are carried out under medical super-vision. Justice in an ultraconservative Islamic manner is spectacularly admin-istered in the public sphere as a salutary restoration of moral balance through a celebratory spectacle of violence. There are now few states or societies that adhere to the tactic of public execution. Saudi Arabia carries out judicial killing by beheading publicly. The erstwhile Taleban regime used to execute murderers by Kalashnikov rifle placed in the hands of a member of the aggrieved family. The executions were usually taking place, in the form of a public spectacle, in a sports stadium or other such public places. The bizarreness of displaying justice in action seems surpassed by Iran which not only punishes some "crimes" by public hanging, but then leaves the corpses suspended from cranes for the public to view for weeks afterwards. In Somalia, it would appear, in areas that are under control of Islamic radicals, stoning is still carried out in public.

From one point of view, Islam very clearly contains the idea of religiously mandated violence, be it in the form of the jihad (which will be considered in the next chapter) or following the punitive dictates of the sharia. Muslim history then delivers powerfully paradigmatic examples of how this is applied in legitimate conflict resolution, enforcement of justice, and consolidation of Islam. Counteractive doctrinal impulses designed to contain the emergence of violence and eliminate its need are comparatively weaker. From another viewpoint, responsibility for violence in the name of Islam is not placed with doctrine and law; instead particular sociopoltical circumstances are held responsible for inciting violence or provoking Islam to condone it. The famous international mufti Yusuf Al-Qaradawi—widely consulted by Muslims all over the world—has blamed the Muslim use of violence in the political arena and the absence of peaceful, dialogical, and constructive strategies promoted by Muslim leadership on the oppressive approach to ideological innovation and reformation used by existing regimes.[52] This interpretation, allotting responsibility rather widely, suggests that the political situation prevents leaders with peaceful ideas from emerging. This shifts the blame conspicuously away from Islam itself. Al-Qaradawi seems to studiously avoid the question of whether peaceful ideas can sufficiently overcome stimuli towards violence contained in Islamic doctrine itself. Yet, there seems merit in the assumption that the tensions and aggression contained in the current social conditions do little to negate impulses towards violence from wherever they may be emitted. Weber's sociological concept of elective affinity can provide a useful frame of interpretation of this phenomenon. There is a cultural substratum around the legitimacy of traditional forms of violence, which is corroborated in recent times by political strategies that apply militaristic, violent means to solve problems and to seek political solutions rather than dialogue. This ideological and sociological environment is not congenial to creating traction for peaceful reformatory ideas. Thus the emergence of effective leadership that devises and promotes effective peaceful strategies is made rather difficult, if not impossible. It is not only traditional and internal societal violence, a large example of the usefulness of violence in solving problems is also delivered by the modern state in suppressing dissent and not least by external political factors that seek a solution through the application of aggressive militaristic means. Palestine, Kashmir, Chechnya, the sad fate of Iraq and Afghanistan—to name only a few—deliver paradigmatic examples of "resolving" differences by violent means. This part of the world echoes to the sounds of internecine warfare and outside military intervention. Thus the Islamic world is engulfed in violence in which peaceful conflict resolution, both on a microsocial and macrosocial level, appears anomalous.

WHITHER UNDER BETTER LEADERSHIP?

Wracked by internal problems, the Islamic world in recent years has not contributed much to global leadership, despite its economic clout and its numerical strength of comprising approximately one and a half billion of the world population. Some sections of radical Muslim leadership, much in the limelight of world attention for its endeavor to justify violence with religious underpinnings, harbor a fervent globalophobia. They try to shape Islam into a bastion against the universalization of culture, which they perceive to be entirely on Western terms. If any specific doctrinal justification is needed at all, the classical dichotomy of Dar-al-Islam and Dar-al-Harb can serve a most useful purpose. The faithful can never be part of the world of the infidels, bowing to their cultural dominance and acquiescing in their governance. The most conservative version of Islam thus does have a dialogue with globalization, but one of rejection and the maintenance of parochialism to engrave a boundary against infidels, kafirun, apostates, hypocrites, mushrikun, and idolators—for their world must never dominate the realm of Islam.

Yet, current reality disavows the future prospects of this vision. Millions of Muslims have left the Islamic fortress, the traditional Dar-al-Islam, and ventured into Dar-al-Harb in search of peace and prosperity. Gathering in the West, some jurist-scholars speak of the diaspora now as living in Dar-al-Ahd, Dar-al-Sulh, Dar-al-Amn (the realm of truce, covenant, treaty, or peace),[53] and the like, to give immigrant Muslims peace of mind despite living under infidel governance. Some, however, now pine for the culture they have left behind, finding hope in the myth of return, longing to become muhajirun (those returning from infidel lands to the Islamic domain), and some bold ones even dream of changing the West into a more Islam-congenial environment. The most disillusioned and fanatical ones even seek to harm and destroy the West, the source of their frustration. Finding their dreams shattered, some Western Muslims then fall prey to the kind of leadership that has contributed much to the upheaval in the Islamic world in the first place.

They feel they are marginalized, their faith and culture disrespected, and that they are bereft of a political voice. A victim mentality begins to fester and becomes receptive to radicalized ideas.[54]

Muslims need guidance from within their own ranks in matters of peaceful global empowerment, democracy, and global secular humanism that transcends religious divisions—all of which requires a bold ijtihad. Exhortations to create a Euro-Islam[55] or to extrapolate the essence of Islam so as to make it congenial to Western conditions[56] have so far had only limited success. Guidance in this process, much of it seen by many Muslims as hostile to Islamic culture and faith, and steering through its difficulties has to come from within the Muslim intellectual elite. It cannot be provided from the outside.

One of the big challenges to Islam today is not another religion, but the fact that without a serious effort of reformation it is not fully compatible with the realities of a new world. The challenge is not the increasing expansion of rationalism over faith, and the effects of secularization shrinking the social influence of religion, nor new political opportunities, but it is the need for Islam to adjust to this in a meaningful way, to embrace these phenomena and adjust to them. Even as a privatized faith, and rid of political ambitions, it needs readjustment—especially for Western Muslims. Belief, morals, and leadership, every aspect of Islam demands a dialogue with modernity, the modernity that spreads around the world through globalization. Although the perception of its needs may grow, the clear articulation of a modernized Islam has not taken hold as yet. Even though challenges to globalization and West-guided modernity—already weakened by postmodernity—are posed almost everywhere, attempting to substitute specifically Western values and goals with others, and proposing a specifically Asian modernity or an African alternative, conservative Islamic faith and culture have not bravely rallied to the same task beyond simply resisting it.

The Muslim minority in the West, small as it may be in comparison to global Muslimhood, potentially has a vital role to play. It is best placed to enter into a dialogue with globalization, modernity, and secularization—because it is already vitally affected and has gathered valuable experience. About the intra-Islamic effort to modernize and reform Islam as a whole, a Muslim author has this to say:

> Muslims in the West are well placed to be the vanguard of this overdue intellectual effort, and despite [or because of] the various challenges they need to be proactive. By linking Islamic civilizational traditions with the humane values of Western modernity, diasporic Muslim intellectuals and activists can offer linkages between the world of Islam and the West. Their encounter can augur a new era of peace and prosperity and a departure from anguish and conflict. The ongoing polarization of various Muslim groups, banking on the primacy of their religious identity over everything else, including national/

ethnic/class identity, has been a painful experience. Yet, it is equally important to define modernity in its larger theoretical context before we may proceed to see the nature of the emerging Muslim discourse.[57]

Islam has not started yet to energetically bestride this road. High-rise buildings and technology sit uneasily next to shariatic conservatism based on premises of justice as ancient as the Old Testament. Bassam Tibi's[58] reasonable demand that Islam, if it wishes to be a legitimate part of the twenty-first century, has to drop its political aspirations, runs exactly counter to the most lively dynamics in the Islamic world. His warning that Islam has to become a religion in the Western sense has predictive merit, but only if one assumes the universality of secularization. This, in turn, may hinge on an Occidentalist slant, that is, the assumption that the development happening in the West presages the universal development pattern. That Tibi's exhortation will be heeded by Muslimhood at large in the short term seems rather remote, even though some researchers claim they detect the beginnings of Islam recasting itself as a religion that occupies the public space as one religion among others. [59] The privatization of religion is certainly recognized as an important step in the process of secularization,[60] but the Islamist fermentation for reform is clearly more active putting its propagandist tools to good use. As Tibi admitted in an interview in June 2011, his and his fellow moderates' ideas for a modernizing inner reform (islah) of Islam to advance a peaceful recalibration of Islamic doctrine so as to align it with global modernity and facilitate a harmonious coexistence with the West, find much less resonance in the arena of political ideas than radical political activism. Leaving aside inertia, equanimity and the quest for daily survival being a priority for the average Muslim, the forces of active secularist moderation, secular humanism, and rationalism have apparently not caught the imagination to the same extent as Islamism.

NOTES

1. There is also the Organization of Islamic Cooperation, the Muslim World League, and the League of Arab States, each containing several subbodies for coordinating education, economic cooperation, religious matters, jurisprudence, relief and charity, and so on. Member states vary in number and identity, but in toto they represent close to the majority of global Muslimhood. Each organization is saddled with numerous divisions and member countries rarely act in concert.

2. Fred Halliday, "The Politics of the Umma: States and Community in Islamic Movements." In *Shaping the Current Islamic Reformation*, B. A. Roberson (ed.). London, Portland, OR: Frank Cass, 2003; p. 29.

3. Halliday, "The Politics"; pp. 35–37.

4. On the whole, as Halliday ("The Politics . . ."; p. 39) argues, international relations cannot be adequately explained solely by cultural and ideational approaches that allot primacy to ideas, perceptions, and cultures. Thus also Huntington's approach must be flawed.

5. Patricia Crone, "The Tribe and the State." In *From Arabian Tribes to Islamic Empire.* Aldershot: Ashgate, 2008; esp. p. 454.

6. Huntington, *The Clash of Civilizations and the Remaking of World Order.* New York: Simon and Schuster, 1996.

7. Saudi leadership urged the United States to undertake military intervention against Iran.

8. See, e.g., James Piscatori, "Religion and realpolitik: Islamic Responses to the Gulf War." In *Political Islam: A Critical Reader,* F. Volpi (ed.). London, New York: Routledge, 2011. Although the war produced some surprising support for Saddam's Iraq, it split the Arab world into those nations that supported the allied attack and those that condemned it.

9. Afghan President Hamid Karzai, in October 2011, was reported to have declared that in case of an American attack against Pakistan, his country would side with the Muslim neighbor. In other words, any sense of gratitude to the Unites States would be set aside in the interest of Muslim solidarity. The reliability of this statement in realpolitical terms remains to be seen.

10. Based mainly on Quran 5/67: "Proclaim (the Message) which has been sent down to you from your Lord." And 16/125: "Invite to the way of your Lord with wisdom and fair preaching, and argue with them in a way that is better." For individuals to engage themselves in dawa(h) is considered a duty, fardh.

11. Following the classic dhimma system of recognizing religious minorities, the Ottoman millet system similarly granted local autonomy to ethnic and religious groups.

12. See, e.g., Asma Afsaruddin, "Demarcating Fault-lines within Islam: Muslim Modernists and Hardline Islamists Engage the Shari'a." In *Shari'a as Discourse,* J. Nielsen and L. Christoffersen (eds.). Farnham: Ashgate, 2010.

13. Asma Afsaruddin, "Demarcating fault-lines . . ." ; p. 30.

14. Fed Halliday, "The Politics of the Umma . . ." ; p. 35.

15. The expansion of Islam into Southeast Asia and the Indonesian archipelago has been by a different process. Though Islam was carried along by more or less peaceful missionization (it is assumed Sufi masters were the main vehicle of conversion from Buddhism and Hinduism), in its broader impact it was, however, still based on the classical rule (in the style of the Westphalian Peace of 1648) of "cuius regio eius religio" (in other words, governance dictates religious adherence). A more purist, less syncretic form of Islam may have been established not before the tenth century, and possibly much later. Some scholars have argued that it was not before contacts with Macca became closer and travel was becoming easier in the nineteenth century that a pure form of Islam took hold in Indonesia.

16. Estimates range from 20 to 25 million in Western Europe. As no official records of religious affiliation are being kept by secularized states, no exact statistics are available.

17. From Russia it is reported that it shows similar reactions to the influx of Muslims from its former provinces in the South and Southeast.

18. Ramadan, *Western Muslims and the Future of Islam.* New York: Oxford University Press, 2004.

19. Tariq Ramadan, *Western Muslims* ...; e.g., pp. 72–73. The whole world is Dar-al-Dawa, a place of "inviting people to God."

20. The circumstances of the Indian Raj provide one the finest examples of preservation of a British way of life amidst a vibrant "other" culture.

21. For instance, Tariq Ramadan (in his new book *The Quest for Meaning: Developing a Philosophy of Pluralism.* London: Allen Lane, 2010) proclaims that simple tolerance of Muslims, their religion and culture is not acceptable as it expresses the condescension of the dominant, while the relationship should be among equals. As critics say, this perspective expresses exactly this growing assertive climate generated by Muslims emboldened by "soft" multiculturalist policies.

22. This is so despite Muslims still forming a minority. See Arjun Appadurai's (*Fear of Small Numbers: An Essay on the Geography of Anger.* Durham, London: Duke University Press, 2006) analysis on the possible fate of ethnic and cultural minorities being threatened by paroxysms of violence in the name of cultural purism and ethnonationalism.

23. Bernard Lewis quoted from the *Jerusalem Post*, November 2, 2009. Earlier, he had already predicted that by century's end "at the very latest" Europe would be Islamic: see C. Caldwell, Islamic Europe, *Weekly Standard*, April 10, 2004, available at www.weeklystandard.com/Content/Public/Articles/000/000/004/685ozxcq.asp.
Francis Fukuyama, "A Year of Living Dangerously," *The Wall Street Journal,* November 2, 2005: 5. And "Identity, Immigration, and Liberal Democracy," *Journal of Democracy* 17/2 (2006): 5–20. His argument addresses the concerns that massive Muslim immigration in the West brings about a shift in cultural identity.

24. The rise in Islamophobia is a topical issue of unfortunate urgency. See, e.g., John Esposito and Ibrahim Kalin (eds.), *Islamophobia: the challenge of pluralism in the 21st century*. New York: Oxford University Press, 2011.

25. Even now it is doubtful whether Islamic fervor and patriotism, expressed in Afghanistan through opposition to what is conceived as a foreign occupation, can be neatly separated.

26. an-Na'im, "The Islamic Counter-Reformation." *New Perspectives Quarterly* 19/1 (2002): 29–35; p.30.

27. Especially traditional artisanry in premodern society enjoyed either higher or lower status than the social average. For instance, in the Hindukush area, where I did fieldwork, professional artisans such as blacksmiths, carpenters, potters, felt-makers, carvers, and even silver-smiths had a lower status.

28. Fred McGraw Donner, *The Early Islamic Conquests*. Princeton: Princeton University Press, 1981; pp. 30–37.

29. Most Iranians realize that Khomeini was not the hoped and prayed for returned Imam. Current Supreme Leader Ayatollah Ali Khamenei does not possess the charisma to raise the question.

30. This seems to have been a puzzle to Ernest Gellner in his book *Muslim Society*. Cambridge: Cambridge University Press, 1983; pp. 40–41. See also Sami Zubaida, *Beyond Islam*. London, New York: Tauris, 2011; pp. 38–48.

31. If newspaper reports and commentaries are to be believed, this was borne out when earlier in 2011 differences between President Ahmadinejad and Grand Ayatollah Ali Khamenei were finally settled in compliance with Khamenei's wishes rather than the president's.

32. Rudolph Peters, "From Jurists' Law to Statute Law or What Happens When the Shari'a is Codified." In *Shaping the Current Islamic Reformation*, B. A. Roberson (ed.). London, Portland, OR: Frank Cass, 2003; p. 93.

33. Erich Kolig, "Radical Islam, Islamic Fervour, and Political Sentiments in Central Java, Indonesia." *European Journal of East Asian Studies* 4/1 (2005): 55-86.

34. He is "credited" with having inspired three of the 9/11 attackers, as well as the Christmas Day bomber Umar Farouk Abdulmutallab, major Nidal Malik Hasan of the U.S. military installation Fort Hood, and Faisal Shahzad, the Time Square bomber. Allegedly he is one of only very few U.S. citizens on the CIA targeted kill list. (He was killed in October 2011.)

35. In Osama bin Laden's case the classification of his demise (on May 2, 2011) is difficult. The line is heavily blurred between "justice having been done" (as proclaimed by U.S. president Obama) and extrajudicial killing or assassination. Several conflicting aspects are muddling the waters: ethically justified action, the action allowed under the aegis of warfare (thus evoking shades of the war on terror, revoked by President Obama), revenge killing, and political assassination (both illegal under modern Western legal systems). The explanation of "attempted arrest gone badly wrong" seems hardly applicable.

36. It may also explain a possible connexion between the arms manufacturing industry and Christian fundamentalism. In 2009 for example, it was detected that armaments produced by a particular well-known United States firm had cryptic references to Biblical verses, referring to death and destruction, engraved on them.

37. See Elias Canetti, *Crowds and Power* (various editions and translations).

38. Ranging from Jim Jones' People's Temple, The Branch Davidians at Waco (Texas), Aum Shinri Kyo in Japan, HauHau, Ringatu, and Mihaia in New Zealand's history, and many more movements of the recent past.

39. Quran 17/64, 31/6, 53/61 specifically refer to wasting time through amusement like music and singing, which detracts from religious devotion.

40. Society for Spreading Faith, founded 1926 in India, an international and nondenominational movement directed towards re-Islamization.

41. New Religious Movements or so-called cults have been known to use pseudo-psychological and other robust techniques to win adherents. See William Sargent, *The Battle for the Mind*. London: Heinemann, 1957.

42. E.g., Quran 8/72, 74.

43. Alfred Guillaume, *The Traditions of Islam: An Introduction to the Study of the Hadith Literature*. Beirut: Khayats, 1966; p. 112.

44. More will be said about this topic later. It remains under-researched in anthropology, especially as to its symbolic meanings. Most modern studies concentrate on conflict resolution while older ones are either of the ethnobiological kind (firmly placing violence within ineradicable human nature) and mainly neo-Marxist studies (e.g., by Herbert Marcuse and Erich Fromm), which place it within the purview of social pathology. See, for instance, Hannah Arendt's classical study *On Violence*. London: Harcourt Brace Jovanovich, 1970.

45. My contention rests on my Indonesian research. Afghanistan is slightly different, as the West appears there as an invading force, which places the Western military alliance in the same category as the previous Soviet invasion. On the basis of this perception - rather than because of the attractiveness of extremist Islam - the Taleban can muster considerable popular support.

46. In fact animal primates have been observed retaining a grudge for some considerable time (if an immediate retribution is not possible) and acting on it eventually in a cathartic manner to punish the offender. The Christian message of "turning the other cheek" in this sense may be said to run counter to human nature and require the ultimate moral restraint.

47. Two traditional societies I am familiar with are the Australian Aboriginal and New Zealand's Maori society. Both have strongly ritualised forms of revenge—in Maori language called utu—and attach a high moral value to it. It is important that it be carried out as a duty (rather than merely to satisfy emotions) and be performed properly in an "orderly" fashion and in accordance with tribal protocol.

48. As recommended in the Quran 2/256, 5/67, 16/125.

49. Guillaume, *The Traditions of Islam*; p. 101.

50. See, e.g., Frank Vogel, *Islamic Law and Legal System: Studies of Saudi Arabia*. Leiden, Boston, Köln: Brill, 2000.

51. This has led to the assassination not only of philosophers and authors, but also of Muslim politicians who had been perceived to express religiously unacceptable ideas.

52. Jakob Skovgaard-Petersen, "The Global Mufti." In *Globalization and the Muslim World: Culture, Religion and Modernity*, B. Schaebler and L. Stenberg (eds.). Syracuse, NY: Syracuse University Press, 2004; p. 158.

53. Bernard Lewis, "Legal and Historical Reflections on the Position of Muslim Populations under Non-Muslim Rule." In *Muslims in Europe*, B. Lewis and D. Schnapper (eds.). London, New York: Pinter, 1994.
Gilles Kepel, *Allah in the West: Islamic movements in America and Europe*. Cambridge: Polity Press, 1997 (French ed. 1987).

54. See, e.g., Bashy Quraishy, "Immigration, Integration and Islam." *Aotearoa Ethnic Network Journal* 2/2 (2007): online. Mustafa Malik, "Islam in Europe: Quest for a Paradigm." *Middle East Policy* 8/2 (2001); and "Muslims Pluralize the West, Resist Assimilation." *Middle East Policy* 11/1 (2004): online.

55. See Bassam Tibi's numerous publications.

56. Tariq Ramadan, *Western Muslims. . . .*

57. Iftikhar H. Malik, *Islam and Modernity: Muslims in Europe and the United States*. London: Pluto Press, 2004; p. 6.

58. This is a major theme in Tibi's voluminous writing and recurs in several of his books.

59. Olivier Roy, *Secularism Confronts Islam*. New York: Columbia University Press, 2007 (original French ed. 2005).

60. Thomas Luckmann (*The Invisible Religion*. New York: Macmillan, 1967) identifies three main features of secularization effective in the religious sphere: unchurchedness, privatization of belief, and church-state separation.

Chapter Eight

Sacred Violence, Martyrs, and Secret Societies

SAD FACTS OF RELIGIOUS VIOLENCE

In his 2006 Regensburg address, Pope Benedict XVI in rather brusque and undiplomatic fashion raised the question of the concept and value of violence in Islam.[1] Conjuring up the distant past, he referred to the Byzantine Empire collapsing under the onslaught of the Ottoman Turks. Then going further, he placed violence near the core of Islam, insinuating that it was an integral element of this belief system. Needless to say, he meant to "re-litigate" the concept of jihad and its connection to terrorism in a sensible and considered way, but instead managed to cause considerable insult. Some centuries earlier the same comment may have been taken as a compliment. Perpetrating violence as a means of expansion of faith would have been taken as a sign of commendable vigor, proof of the vitality of belief, and if accompanied by success also as vindication of dogmatic correctness and testament to the veracity of the founding revelation.[2] No moral wrong would have been seen in spreading faith by the sword. Today such measures are frowned upon as an unacceptable method of proselytization. The value of coercion and armed conflict for purely religious purposes has fallen victim to a global hegemony that attributes legitimacy to the use of organized violence for quite different purposes. (The state has assumed the right to violence and exercises it for economic interests, self-protection, and more recently for the protection of human rights.) Religious conversion, as much as the preservation of faith, is supposed to happen by means of peaceful persuasion rather than the use of force. Duress of any kind in religious matters is utterly tabooed. Official Islam concurs and insists that dawa (proselytization) be carried out with

319

"sweet words" and inducements, but eschewing strong-arm tactics by any means. The doctrinal basis is provided by the Quran verse (2/256) "there is no compulsion in religion," and (16/125) "invite people to the way of your Lord (i.e., Islam) with wisdom and fair preaching." The worldwide Tablighi organization, for instance, concentrates on inner missionization to strengthen the faith among Muslims through mass rallies and public preaching in a peaceful way, while a wide range of other initiatives concentrates on external dawa. Saudi Arabia spends petrodollars lavishly around the world to spread its brand of Wahhabism, through financing educational programs, sponsoring imams and university chairs, and building mosques. While sometimes this leads to suspicions that this brand of enthusiastic Wahhabism does not necessarily have peaceful intentions, officially it disavows any connection to sinister, violent motives. Several Muslim countries pursue similar strategies of peaceful inner and external missionization, although not being able to draw on an equally rich funding base. Fanatical acts aimed at persuasion by force are left to violent fringe phenomena within Muslimhood, excepting, of course, that state law in some Muslim-majority countries circumscribes religious freedom openly or clandestinely. It may take a dim view on individual cases of apostasy or apply "lawful" pressure on religious minorities. Be it through the law or individual initiatives belligerent friction for religious reasons seems to be never far from the surface—despite official proclamations of peaceful intents.

It does not require a strong magnifying lens to perceive violence as tightly woven not only into Islam, but present in most religions. Religion totally devoid of even the smallest aspect of violence, I would maintain, is unthinkable. It may not manifest itself through openly aggressive, belligerent behavior, and instead could lurk on a more cryptic level of religious practice and belief. Violence is multifaceted, ubiquitous, and multidirectional in religion. It can be expressed in doctrinal, mythical, historical, and current sociopolitical forms; and it may be physical or symbolic. Here I will attempt to give a brief overview before looking in greater detail at the concept of jihad as the major doctrinal manifestation of violence in Islam.

As has been discussed already in the previous chapter, one does not have to dredge history very hard to find that atrocity, violent military conquest and forceful proselytization do not seem to be strangers to each other. The lust for power and religious conviction sometimes make dangerous bedfellows as is easily gleaned not only from Islamic history. Quite obviously, it is not always the necessities of physical survival and material existence, nor even the greed for wealth and resources, or the vision of a better and easier life, that drives people to wage war. Sometimes it is but the spurious belief in a religiously mandated imperative that causes people to clash violently. Matters of religious faith may drive people to confront, suppress, and exterminate others with stunning ruthlessness; and, alternatively, it may be the unshakeable firmness of their belief that drives them to stubbornly resist forcible conversion to the point of their own destruction.

Historically, religion-sponsored violence and faith-induced brutality is nothing new to humanity. Many religions at times seem to have employed violence for the purpose of defending or spreading their message.[3] Sometimes acts of violence are cynically rationalized as beneficial and "ennobled" by giving them a false ethical gloss. It may be a sacred duty to wipe out unbelief or to strike at heathens, and it may be considered an act of beneficence to coerce people to assume the "true faith." Unashamed sophistry may be employed to explain why force may ultimately be of benefit to the victim. Forcing unbelievers at the tip of a sword into the arms of the "correct" belief may be done for their own good, so as to preserve their souls for eternity, or because a violent punitive death could be construed that it expunges sin and cleanses the victim. Sacrilegious insult offered to the divine by the sheer existence of "infidels" or by their actions is another "good" reason for retributive violence. Another rationale may be that the spiritual purity of nation, ethnicity, or culture may be at stake. Many such "ethical" reasons exist, which can motivate and excuse the killing of not only whole groups and populations, but also individuals like apostates, heretics, witches, communities of religionists of other faiths, and the like, under all kinds of excuses exonerating the perpetrator and glorifying sadism at the same time.

Some of the motives for religious conflict hark back to the connection, discussed earlier, between knowledge and power; the idea that knowing something—believing in a religious sense being tantamount to knowing[4] —confers power on the believer. It is a valuable resource that needs to be protected and defended, perhaps tested in real life—or shared with others even if they are unwilling. In a fashion, this was expressed already by Sir Francis Bacon's remark[5] that possessing scientific knowledge equals power, which became a generalized aphorism that sums up this idea succinctly. Making this connection can result in various social phenomena: for instance, elevating religious secrecy to great importance. As knowledge confers power, one is loath to share it. Protecting it, and preserving the religious monopoly, may justify the use of violence. But the belief of possessing something of great value can also lead to the mercurial endeavor to spread a belief system as widely as possible, be it to enhance one's own power over like-minded individuals or to convince others, who may at first be unwilling to believe, of this value. In any case, the dispensation of knowledge, or alternatively withholding the blessing, relates to power—a power so precious that it warrants the use of violence. Tribal religiosity tends to be adverse to organized proselytization, a mercurial, missionary endeavor, which may at times be enthusiastically extended into the area of open and violent coercion. Instead it tends to rely on exclusivity and restrictions on admission. Yet, in one form or another all types of religiosity embrace the use of violent coercion for the sake of exercising control over the dissemination of its knowledge substance. Esoteric religious information is maintained by secrecy and protected by violence; forceful means are used in recruiting adepts and violence then accompanies religious revelation. Tribal initiation into esoteric, religious knowledge for the youth is neither voluntary nor based on informed consent. Induction ceremonies, in "grabbing" young boys and girls, are sometimes deliberately brutal. Ritualized initiation itself, the organized revelation of esoteric matter, is usually based on aspects of extreme violence. (Circumcision, for instance, lends itself to being interpreted as an act of assault.) In tribal societies, the reluctant initiand, unwilling to submit to the impending cruelty, lacking perhaps in the requisite courage—in the rare cases that this happens—becomes an outcast, subject to taunts and sanctions or may even be executed. Without going into ethnographic detail, it is important to realize that religion, its dogma as much as its practice through ritual and in the way it is applied in social life, usually is intimately interwoven with aspects of power and violence in one form or another.

The threshold of religious violence in Muslim society generally is lowered on account of the fact that religious belief is still attributed with major social significance and that correct social conduct has religious significance. Thus issues concerning the propriety of social conduct, its correctness in terms of, and compliance with, doctrinal commands with some inevitability tend to touch on religious sensitivities and are likely to trigger strong measures. In a more secularized society, which has abandoned the religious value of social behavior—or never had the intimate connectedness between doctrine and particular forms of social conduct—flashpoints that provoke violence would be situated differently and be less likely found in the minutiae of social behavior.

From a Marxist point of view religious motivation may only be an outer expression veiling underlying causes of a material order, but it certainly does not appear so to religious fanaticism that is ready to inflict violence solely in the imaginary defense or advancement of a subtle point of doctrine. Not much has changed in the modern world. In January 2010, churches were petrol-bombed in Malaysia—presumably by Muslim extremists—over no more than the use by Christians of the word Allah to refer to "their" God. Muslims were incensed that a local Christian journal had adopted the Arabic word (which simply means "God") to refer to the Christian God. To make matters worse the Christians had been supported in this "sacrilegious act" by the Malaysian high court, which issued a verdict that this was not illegal and did not constitute blasphemy. Obviously some Muslims found themselves in violent disagreement with this ruling and considered the word a "brand" that belongs only to Islam. The Islamic world in general takes a dim view on cases when there is suspicion that its spiritual territory is being infringed on by another religion and reacts violently when non-Islamic organizations or individuals attempt to convert Muslims or by their mere existence in the midst of Muslims offer an insult to the true faith. Similar incidents are not rare. The constant violent bickering on some Indonesian islands where Muslims and Christians live in close proximity to each other comes to mind and the persecution the Christian and Ahmadi minorities suffer in Pakistan and Middle Eastern societies. Reminiscent of the Malaysian fight over words, in July 2011 riots broke out in Bangladesh in protest against a recent amendment to the constitution which dropped the words "absolute faith and trust in Allah."

The globalized world is resonating with violence in many forms. Much of it is widely accepted with resignation or even with a sense of necessity. However, violence directly in the service of religion has become a phenomenon of salutary rarity within the West.[6] There has been a faint afterglow of religious violence though in very recent times in highly secularized Europe. The sectarian warfare in Northern Ireland and the infamous "ethnic cleansing" on the Balkans have conjured up shades of religious conflict. In both cases ethnic and political motivations were the real causes but had been augmented by religious differences. Religion contributed to the horrid melee by throwing the ethnic differences and the political crisis they provoked into sharper relief. To the surprise of many, religion turned out still to be a major ingredient in identity formation, even in the highly secularized conditions of Europe. However, it was not for religious reasons that conflict arose in the first place.

The Islamic world is incomparably more convulsed by sectarian altercations. In the Middle East the ten-year war between Saddam Hussein's Iraq and Iran—in addition to the traditional Arab—non-Arab divide and the long standing territorial dispute between the two countries—contained undertones of a sectarian clash between Sunni, and Shi'ites. The several wars and skirmishes India and Pakistan have fought since independence also have a religious background, and so has the unrest in Kashmir. Islam is involved in secessionist movements in the southern Philippines, mainland Southeast and Central Asia, and in China. Lebanon is rent into three main religious camps hostile to each other: Christians (of various denominations), Sunni, and Shi'ites; as well as some subgroups such as Druze, and Palestinian refugees without hope of ever being integrated. The religiously and ethnically complex pastiche of the Middle East also contains Syriaks, Kurds, Alevis, and Alawites, to name only some, who as minorities among engulfing majorities traditionally have always been in a difficult position. Not only in recent years have Christians (in Iraq, Pakistan, Indonesia, Malaysia, and Egypt) repeatedly become a target for Muslim fanatics. In Africa hotspots of religiously inspired tension are festering in Sudan, Somalia, and Nigeria. In many cases, as was recently the case in Europe, religious tension is exacerbated by underlying ethnic differences. However, in India, apart from the crisis in Kashmir and the chronic standoff with Pakistan, Hindu nationalists, Christians, and Muslims seem to be continuously at each others' throats despite being of one cultural and ethnic stock. Many more examples could be cited as evidence for the contention that religion is still responsible for many conflicts in the modern world and especially so in the Islamic world.

As has been outlined before, Islam's history is rich in violence almost from the moment of its inception. The narrative of the original, growing community of Muslims is punctuated by important battles, such as that of Badr, Uhud, and the "battle of the camel." Not only defense against hostile outsiders and battles for survival, also differences internal to Islam, rivaling religious exegeses, schismatic rifts provoking mutual recriminations of heresy, have repeatedly stirred this faith into bloody confrontations. The painful separation of Sunnism and Shi'a Islam, and continuous frictions between them ever since, the persecution of the Karejites and more recently the Baha'i in Iran and the Ahmadis in Pakistan and (to a minor extent in) Indonesia, sometimes bloody suppression of Sufism, Alawites, and Alevis represent the more prominent chapters of Islam's history. Sectarianism provides still important markers of Muslim identity of an intensity that collectively spills over into violence more easily than is the case in other religious identity formations. This fact that violence is often directed against other Muslims whose creed is scarcely distinguishable, adds to Islam's appearance as anachronistic in today's world. If it were quantifiable, the violence perpetrated within Islam internally for sectarian reasons would be many times that directed towards the West. The sectarian dimension of conflict though may not always stand by itself, but may augment socioeconomic and political reasons. The Sunni-Shi'a antagonism is mainly sectarian in character, but in some cases is linked with political and economic deprivation. (This is the case in Saudi Arabia and some Gulf states where Shi'ites feel disadvantaged by the ruling Sunni elite.) Sometimes sectarian differences may have a separatist dimension. The bombing of Shi'a mosques (in July 2010) in Zahedan, Iran, by Sunnis, for instance, is part of the political fight of Sunni Baluchis for independence. Kurdish independence from Turkey and the dream of a Kurdish national state comprising not only parts of Turkey, but also of Iraq, Syria, and Iran has pitted Kurds against fellow Muslims for many years. In a wider sense then this meandering and braided stream of bloody violence, seems deeply inscribed in the life world of Islam.

Seen globally, in the ever-shrinking category of religiously inspired violence, it is Islam's unfortunate position to stick out by the magnitude and frequency in which this religion is somehow connected with acts of violent conflict. It is equally striking that not unusually theological arguments are made to justify this connection. While religious reasoning in promoting and justifying violence has virtually disappeared from the arsenal of the West's political tactics, this proposition enjoys a dubious revitalization in radical forms of Islam. It may episodically be openly expressed, while subliminally sectarian differences are simmering below the surface of politics all the time. It is even more remarkable that religion is not only used as a rationale for its own use of violence but, somewhat absurdly, is also used as an explanation of the motives of the West. The impact of the West's episodic military incursions and robust interventions in the Islamic world are not necessarily seen as an accidental by-product of its exercise of global domination, or in terms of economic and strategic interests, but as a ploy of Christianity to diminish a religious rival and thus facilitate its own expansion. In this implausible and rather contradictory explanation, Western interventionism, its lust to interfere aggressively, is not only promoting secularism, but is deeply rooted in Christian expansionism.[7] When radical Islam speaks of a Western "crusade" (salibiyah), not unusually, this is understood in terms of this dual—and to the analytical mind contradictory—function.

A particularly compelling concept of violence perpetrated in the service of religion is that of crusade, the holy war waged against people of another faith. Spiritual necessity to the believer at times does appear to demand the employment of forceful means on a large scale. In a truly Machiavellian sense, the noble goal of preserving the faith may justify the vilest cruelties. Violence and fanaticism can powerfully grow when belief and political ambition or economic interest are fused in an explosive combination. Both the Islamic expansion—despite the doctrinal maxim of "there is no compulsion in religion"—and "Christian" aspects of colonialism provide good examples. The violent mass conversion of Meso- and South American Indians by Catholic Spain and its emissaries, the conquistadores, and Europe's medieval crusades against the "Mohammedan heathens" weave an especially bloody tapestry of history. Sectarian wars in Europe and religious purges acted out interchangeably between Catholics and Protestants, witch hunts, bloody personal religious feuds among clerics, prophets, and reformers, are all part of the nature of holy war.

The thrust of the Ottoman Empire into the Balkans and into central Europe to the doors of Vienna (first in 1524 and then again in 1683) could be seen as just another war, a strategy for "conflict resolution through its exacerbation," which to Europe then was not unfamiliar. But it held another dimension of even greater fear to Europeans: that of the religious and cultural Otherness pressing forward, advancing on the back of hostile hordes of loathsome "Moors" and "saracens," to subjugate the Occident to an alien, "aberrant" faith. It was that aspect that struck terror into the hearts of the European defenders. The ultimate prospect of succumbing in military defeat to a detested religion inspired a fear that was equal to the fear of death. (It is moot to speculate whether the victorious Turks would have been content with recognizing the vanquished people as dhimmi and leaving them their faith or would have forced them to convert on pain of death.) A person's horror of becoming a victim of massacre in these times seemed equal to the prospect of losing the traditional identity as Christian Occidental and becoming submersed into the vast ungodly cauldron of Turkicized Muslims. In both alternatives it meant to be destined for damnation. It would have seemed like Hobson's choice to die for one's Christian faith and redeem one's soul or convert and surely go to hell. Historical evidence suggests that this was a vital incentive in stiffening the stubborn resistance, more so than mere patriotism or "defending one's patch" against an invader would have done.

HIDDEN FEATURES OF RELIGIOUS VIOLENCE

Violence may be said to be integral to most—if not all—religions, either by the way they have been practiced or because it is doctrinally intimated. Despite protestations to the contrary, the monotheistic religions of the Middle East are no exception. One does not have to search among exotic religions such as Thugism (the worship of the Hindu goddess Kali) and the thirst for innocent victims this cult generated, or the Aztec worship of Quetzalcoatl and its demand for human hearts, or Aum Shinri Kyo's dry-run demonstration of the apocalypse in Tokyo's subway.[8] Violence often is multidirectional. Some Christianity-derived cults, when challenged, used violence not only to ward off an external enemy, but also towards their own membership.[9] The acceptance of violence as being somehow part of God's scheme is also a familiar feature. Self-destructive violence pervades the history of all three major monotheistic religions and is given by all of them a high moral value. Jewish zealots, early Christians and later reformers, Karejites and Shi'a martyrs bear historical testimony not only to their self-denying and willing demise but also to the iconic value placed on accepting violence as God's will. In Middle Eastern monotheism fundamental doctrinal issues, which provide subliminal corner stones of belief, are grounded in expressions of mythical violence. In many cases the value is not placed on inflicting violence—although this occurs too—but on submitting to it and accepting violent death as one's sacrifice to a higher purpose. From Abraham's readiness to commit the intended human sacrifice as an act of devotion, to the Christian crucifixion as the foundation act of a faith, Old and New Testament are riddled with celebrations of violence in the form of events of salvific or soteriological importance. Ritual reenactments and commemorations indirectly celebrate ancient forms of violence and keep the iconic notion alive. Divine vengeance of the Biblical flood, the horrific punishment inflicted on Egypt and the pharaoh, the unequal fight between David and Goliath leading to one of the combatant's demise, the persecution of early Christians under Emperor Nero, to the bloody history of Christian saints, religious themes celebrate violence in various forms. Historical and mythical cases of violence are commemorated in ritualized form through passion plays, the Shi'a festivity of Ashura, and reenacted through the sacrifice brought at eid-al-adha—all of which ultimately are celebrations of violence. The sublimation of violence through ritualization and symbolization does not diminish the cryptic message, eternally intertwining the sacred with violence, that acts of violence may be good in serving a divine purpose. Mythical events, acted out in ritual, elevate the theme of suffering, as a consequence of violence, to soteriological and iconic significance. (It is not too far-fetched to see ritual self-harm, rifat, practiced in some Sufi sects as an extension of this trope.) More will be said later about the embracement of violence in creating the sacred role of the martyr.

Sacred violence is not always inter-sectarian or inter-religious and may have connotations other than sacrificial. Violence may be directed as a form of straightforward punishment to those co-religionists considered nonconformists, heretics, apostates, and blasphemers and those who are considered to be breaking divine laws. Conservative versions of Islamic law condone and even demand violence as legal punishment, which they see as prescribed by God's ordinance. The penal code of the sharia fundamentally deems all crimes to be of a nature that defies religion—offenses against divine command—and therefore punishable with utter severity, but reserves the harshest punishment for insults directly offered to God, that is, heresy (altering or falsifying the word of God), apostasy (rejecting God's message), and blasphemy (insulting the sacredness). The severity of these offenses justifies the gravest response. But not only the death penalty, demanded by strict sharia rules for such crimes, is a form of violence; much of the Islamic penal armory such as amputations, application of reciprocal retribution qisas (based on the Biblical maxim "an eye for an eye"), and flogging are violations of the bodily integrity of a person and represent legitimized, exemplary demonstrations of violence.

THE ORGANIZATIONAL FACE OF VIOLENCE

Having reviewed past and present with a not-too-fine-grained global perspective (fleetingly pointing to historical narratives and ritualized representations of violence), it seems fair to say that much of the religiously inspired violence in the present-day world seems to emanate primarily from Islam. The previous antagonistic tension between the two superpowers, the United States and Soviet Russia, representing a global ideological dichotomy, by and large had diverted attention from what seemed to be crises of smaller magnitude. With the disappearance of this tension, the full glare of the

West's attention falls on upheavals in the Islamic world (including now also the diasporic situation of Muslims living in and closely interacting with the West). The arising unflattering attention is giving the issue an almost evolutionary gloss. A distorted essentialization of Islam not only caricatures this religion's image, but also gives Islam the appearance of being mired in an era of religious violence, which Western society has left behind. Secularization and modernization that have affected Christianity so profoundly, making it peaceful as well as emasculating it socially, seem to have bypassed Islam, or rather have not reached it yet. The idea of waging a crusade on religious, Christian grounds—to physically defend the faith or annihilate a religious dissenter—seems utterly ridiculous if not futile and is certainly illegal. While at least the mainstream of Christianity has lost its gusto for violent confrontation for doctrinal reasons, Islam does not appear to have undergone the same kind of transformation. Christianity has moved on to embracing an ideology in which aggressive acts even remotely reminiscent of violence—like burning copies of the Quran—have become relegated to the social and lunatic fringes. Characteristically, most of today's proselytization work is not only peaceful, but combined with welfare and healthcare work, exemplary deeds of active caring. (In the eyes of fanatical Muslims this makes Christian missionarydom even more insidious. Charity and active compassion is seen to be bribery to bring people under the West's domination in yet another cunning way.)

The brand name of Islamic violence is supplied by al-Qaeda. Most probably it is wrong to think of al-Qaeda as an organization in the traditional meaning of the term. Although it emerged from the international army of mujahidin fighting in Afghanistan and in the process adopting the most brutal, merciless methodology conceivable, over the years it metamorphosed into a new form. It may be more apt to think of it as an ideological locus [10] that through a worldwide connectivity subcontracts the execution of terrorist acts to only loosely affiliated groups and cells which have little awareness of each others' existence. "The camp" refers to an ideological position, a standpoint in relation to the world and its political and ideological conditions. Whatever al-Qaeda as organization may be—cohesive, structured organization or loose-knit circle of ideologically like-minded individuals operating in autonomous cells with only some core ideas held in common and financially fed from one central source—it represents now the foremost physical manifestation of religious violence and consummate aggressive fanaticism. The name al-Qaeda has become virtually synonymous with a posture of murderous religious fanaticism, and so has the name of its (former) main ideologue, Osama bin Laden, presumed founder and self-styled theological expert until his death in 2011. The so-called "bin Laden factor" has done much damage to the reputation of Islam as a whole and has significantly lessened its acceptance in the West as just another religion of the same respectability as Christianity or Buddhism.

In a broader sense, harnessing theology for fanatical ends is not just the preserve of al-Qaeda. Thus it is not justified to blame it for all violence perpetrated in the name of Islam. The Islamic ordinariate of brutality is much wider and terrorist methods are not the monopoly of al-Qaeda proper. Countless other Islamic organizations and movements fit into this mold. There are extremist movements fighting for political causes such as independence (the North Caucasus Islamists, or organizations in the southern Philippines, for example), or to establish locally an extreme fundamentalist regime (the Pakistani and Afghani Taleban, northern Nigerian [the Buku Haram movement] and Somali groups [the al-Shabaab and Islamic Court movements], Saudi Arabian and Yemeni extremists, the Indonesian Jemaa Islamiyah), which look up to al-Qaeda as their teacher but probably have only intermittent and opportunistic contacts with it. These groups may draw at times on al-Qaeda's assistance, receive finance, intelligence, and inspiration, and perhaps maintain some loose connections with it but operate independently of any central command structure. Some groups may have global or international ambitions, and others may pursue a local or regional agenda. What they have in common is the use of violence under the pretense of having a mandate from Islam and conducting a holy war in its name.

In terms of actions and philosophies, this extremist category is very wide. Depending on definition, it is not just comprising such organizations, which now are subject to anti-terrorist legislation in many countries. Khomeini's revolutionary theology implemented in 1990 to create the God-state of present-day Iran also displayed similarly violent features, but meanwhile has become legitimized by being foundational to the modern theocratic state of Iran. Outside organized extremism, among Muslims there is a wide spectrum of conservative attitudes, which have considerable sympathy for aggressive action be it against the West or other Muslims, and thus provide an almost inexhaustible potential resource for extremism. (Thus effectively fighting extremism cannot be based on killing and interning as many extremists as possible, but on altering the balance of ideology.)

It is the seemingly all-pervading linkage between Islam and various forms of violence, historic and current, defensive and aggressive, which blights the reputation of this religion as a whole. Because of the absence of a more subtle and informed awareness of Islam's nuances and historical changes, it fails to be considered as harmless and benevolent a religion as Christianity, whose basic kindliness is only matched by its social irrelevance. This perception is of vital importance in a situation of globalized interlocking of vital geopolitical and economic interests and even more drastically in situations in which Muslims are no longer geographically separated from the West, but as sizable diasporic minorities have become part of it. Suspicion and distrust in matters of national security, rejection of Muslims as fellow-citizens, and Islamophobic emotions are the result.

THE DOCTRINE OF HOLY WAR

There is another important aspect to religious violence—violence that is not used for aggressive purposes but used purely for defense. This gives violence morally a more readily defensible position. The violation of secrecy—a core value in most tribal religions which needs to be vigorously defended—usually is punished very harshly and without mercy. Even defending precious belief against insult and denigration can have its ethical defense. The use of force to protect the integrity of a faith, even from a modern perspective, carries some considerable moral legitimacy. This is certainly a prominent feature in present-day Islam and the standard rationale used by jihadis. Most leading Muslim theologians will concur on the point that if Islam is threatened in any way the use of force is justified. Defending the faith by any means in principle is a doctrinal requirement of high priority, deeply anchored in the scriptures. Disagreement, however, lies in what constitutes a threat that makes defensive action mandatory and what degree or means of force are permissible. (In the highly secularized circumstances in which Christianity seeks to survive, this rationale is not officially recognized by mainstream churches.) The scriptures, and in particular the Quran, do not clearly separate the two motives—aggressive and defensive intentions—perhaps in recognition of the principle that attack is the best defense. (Certainly, this was a truism at the time Islam emerged and attempted to consolidate itself.) The concept of jihad potentially encompasses both and is quite ambiguous about the two motives. Mainstream interpretation today though gives in-principle primacy to the defensive kind. Doing so, however, is a matter of exegesis. Arranging attitudes toward the uses of violence on a spectrum, it becomes clear that peaceful interpretations (especially some Sufi versions) on one extreme disregard altogether the belligerent aspects contained in the scriptures, while radical Islam, on the opposite end, dwells heavily on them and seeks them out to justify violent action.

Today's extremist Salafis (relying on the example of the very first generations of Muslims), in pursuing an aggressive jihadist agenda, find ample justification for their actions in the sacred scriptures.[11] The military exploits under the Prophet's command were mainly for defensive reasons to ward off attack or buy some time to allow the fledgling Muslim community to consolidate. In some cases, however, military action went considerably beyond securing survival and pursued expansionist or other tactical aims.[12] Both

Quran and Sunna provide justification and precedent for strong-arm tactics to secure the faith and preserve the community of believers, and in doing so go well beyond defense in the very narrow sense of warding off aggression of an external enemy. Beyond physical defense, when the lives of the believers are threatened, the imperative of providing protection for the faith supplies a rich matrix from which all kinds of justification may be deduced. Although theoretically one may make a distinction between preserving the substance of religion and protecting those practicing it, radical Islam blurs the two sides and often proceeds from the assumption that because Muslims are physically and spiritually in peril—for a variety of reasons—Islam per se requires to be protected, if necessary, by a violent jihad. Usually, when radical Muslims refer to the purity of Islam (which is in danger somehow) they have in mind a particular version of it and implicitly define "true" faith, purity of dogma, and correct worship in a narrow, highly idiosyncratic manner. The danger may be believed to emanate from external, impersonal forces of change, cultural influences imposed by outsiders, or possibly may stem from illicit conditions within Muslimhood itself. It does not require a physical threat. What may be labeled heresy, for instance, can be perceived to pose such a threat to Islam itself, or an un-Islamic regime, as much as, in a concrete sense, corrupting the Muslim youth with Western popular culture and the false allure of materialism or even a liberal interpretation of Islamic doctrine.

Today's legitimacy of a global jihad, from a radical Muslim point of view, firmly rests on the perception that Islam is under attack—an attack emanating mainly from the West as well as corrupt regimes in the West's pay. Bad governance by pseudo-Muslim administrations is considered as anti-Islamic and as much of an attack on true Islam as the subversive cultural impulses arising from the West, the humiliating defeats it inflicts time after time on the Islamic world and the corrosive secularization it promotes. One requires as strong a rebuttal as the other. Extreme views condemn as similarly pernicious and dangerous attempts within Muslimhood to enter into a dialogue with modernity, rationalism and globalizm to reform and modernise Islamic tenet. Labeling such initiatives blasphemy and heresy (kufr and bida) ultraconservatives respond with violent rejection. When they find the state unresponsive to this "crime," vigilante action appears entirely justified. To stifle individual initiatives of "subverting" the true faith, even assassination is considered a legitimate strategy. Such subversion from within may be judged to be even worse than the decadence insinuated by Western popular culture or the uncouth proximity of members of another sect. The range of possibilities by which something may be construed as a spiritual attack on Islam is sheer unlimited. And in a physical sense, when looked at from this perspective, there are many examples where Muslims, as groups, nations, and collectively, have been humiliated, routed and subjugated in every conceivable way by the powers of the West. All this provides rich nourishment to the belief that Islam is under attack and in dire need of vigorous defense.

It is essential for a consideration of conservative Islam to take a critical look at the defense mechanism couched in the doctrine of jihad. As a term jihad has become a byword of terrorism in today's world. The concept of jihad, paradigmatic for Islamic violence, has been made familiar in the West at first by bin Laden's declaration of a "Jihad against Crusaders and Jews" in 1998. The term has entered now the Western standard vocabulary as a word of loathing. In translation the semantic combination of holy and war seems oddly incongruous in a secularized West. In response it has produced the eponymous expression "unholy war" referring to its odious reputation of an indiscriminately murderous, unjust campaign. [13]

Jihad is often called the sixth pillar of Islam in recognition of its doctrinal importance. Jihadis have elevated it above the other five pillars (shahada—profession of faith; salat—prayer; alms—zakat; fasting—sawm; and pilgrimage—haj) giving it focal importance as a sacred duty, a fardh. The sacred scriptures contain many ambiguities, not least in relation to jihad, which allows various and quite contradictory interpretations. By a small twist of exegesis, the concept ostensibly gives support to aggressive ideas that Islam or Muslims are somehow under threat and in need of being defended at all cost. The call to an all out "cosmic war" can be deduced from the Quran just as easily as a quietist, resigned attitude that shuns aggression. [14]

The call to fight in order to defend the faith is doctrinally underpinned by Islam's inherent conviction of its spiritual and moral superiority. In other words, its belligerent side can only be fully understood by recognizing some specific doctrinal issues to do with its sense of having a mission in the world and occupying a superior position among humanity. While this in itself is not a call to arms, one can imagine that it generates a readiness to defend this central value and prove its truth by engaging in action—in other words, it implies an imperative of assertive self-preservation. Central in insinuating an inclination towards activism driven by a sense of superiority is the declaration of the Quranic verse 3/110, which says, "You are the best community created for mankind, enjoining what is right and forbidding what is wrong." A sense of superiority is further reinforced in verse 3/104: "Let there arise out of you a group of people inviting to all that is good [Islam], enjoining Al-Ma'ruf [i.e., Islamic monotheism and all that Islam orders one to do] and forbidding Al-Munkar [polytheism and disbelief and all that Islam has forbidden]. And it is they who are successful."

Among others, Bassam Tibi, himself a Muslim, draws specific attention to the "superiority complex" instilled by conservative Islamic teaching. He himself in his early years has had the "benefit" of this teaching, he explains. [15] The message of collective superiority of Muslims and Islam is most impressively summed up in the Qur'anic verse (3/110) where Muslims are reminded that they are the cream of humanity and are of exemplary significance to the world.[16] It is easy on this basis to understand why many Muslims see a discrepancy between this proclamation and the actual reality in the modern world. This then can readily be construed not only as a deficiency that has to be regretted but also as entailing a divinely demanded duty to rectify the situation. Self-righteous condescension towards "infidels" needs to be nourished by empirical facts.

In this vein, Quran verse 9/123 admonishes Muslims: "O believers, fight the unbelievers who are near to you, and let them find in you a harshness; and know that God is with the God-fearing." Such doctrines do not encourage a sense of humility to emerge; they make it incumbent for the believer to assume a dominant position. There is no suggestion in these and other verses of yielding gracefully or being content with a condition of equality with others. Turning an advantage into an offer of peace is rejected in verse 47/35: "so be not weak and ask for peace while you are having the upper hand. Allah is with you." Ayat 3/21 chooses similar tones: "Verily! Those who disbelief in the Ayat of Allah and kill the Prophets without right, and kill those men who order just dealings, . . . then announce to them a painful torment." And 32/18 says, "Is he who is a believer like him who is an evil-liver? They are not alike."

Such exhortations clearly promote a message of supremacy and a quest for domination, if necessary by force. It is obvious that such doctrinal points and what ambiguities they may generate can be relatively easily molded into an aggressive posture. One only needs to detach these verses from the historical context and ignores a reasoned asbab-an-nusul. A possible ambiguity if such exhortations really do apply to the present world can also be "clarified" by the appropriate mind-set.

Muslim minds, offended by the current global situation, find encouragement and incitement in such decontextualized statements contained in the Islamic scriptures—in fact they do not see ambiguity, but clarity. In particular some passages can be interpreted to contain the demand to take up arms in the defense of the faith. When the Quran (9/38) proclaims, "O you who believe! What is the matter with you, that when you are asked to march forth in the cause of Allah [i.e., Jihad] you cling heavily to the earth? Are you pleased with the life of this world rather than the Hereafter? But little is the enjoyment of the life of this world as compared to the Hereafter," it is a clarion call to fight in the "just" cause, and not to spare one's own life. Self-preservation has to be set aside. As Quran verse 4/95 specifically reminds the believer, "Do not sit at home [unless disabled], God prefers the one who fights with his wealth and with his life—his is the paradise." The hadith commands, "He who does not care about the state of the Muslim umma, is not part of the Muslims." Therefore to the attackers on Muslims " announce . . . a painful torment" (Quran 3/21); and the Muslims are further reminded of their duty: "Fight against them so that Allah will punish them by your hands and disgrace them and give you victory over them and heal the breasts of a believing people" (9/14). And as verse 3/104 promises to those people who do good and prevent evil, it is "they who are successful." Victory is theirs.

If one searches, one can find in the Quran even harsher imperatives, such as "kill the mushrikun [unbelievers, idolaters] wherever you find them, and capture and besiege them, and lie in wait for them in each and every ambush" (Quran 9/5); "Fight against the mushrikun . . . collectively, as they fight against you collectively" (9/36); "Fight the unbelievers until there is no longer any fitnah [sedition, disbelief, polytheism] and religion is all for God" (2/ 193; 8/39); and "Cast [the disbelievers] into hell[fire]" (8/37). All this, when isolated from the historical context in which Muslims were called to the defense of Islam in times of dire need, as existed at the Prophet's time, may seem to convey an eternally valid message of aggression and implacable hostility. By a stretch of the imagination, such a situation of Islam's need might be perceived to exist as the West militarily, economically, and ideologically appears to oppress Muslims. In this perceived crisis, the call for restraint, which clearly is also contained in the Quran, is easily ignored: for instance, when it says "Fight in the way of Allah those who fight you, but transgress not the limits. Truly, Allah does not like the transgressors" (2/ 190).[17]

As argued before, Islam is emphatically this-worldly in its intent, yet it also has an inherent tendency, as most religions do, to transcendentalize the meaning of human existence. By proposing a kind of other-worldliness that gives meaning to human life, it relativizes and diminishes the importance of individual existence in comparison with God's grandiose design plan. Religious devotion of some intensity tends to magnify the transcendence of the meaning of human existence and concomitantly to downplay the here-and-now as just a transitory phase to be replaced with something of far greater durability and significance. "Untempered by secularism, the brevity and ephemerality of this life is ranged in unequal contest against the prospect of divine judgment, and subsequent eternal paradisical reward or hellish damnation."[18] Everlasting bliss can be earned by performing one's duty. This creates a mentality that makes it easy for the fervent believer to depart from this world for the sake of attaining eternal bliss. At the same time it gives ethical license to coerce others, whose life's meaning is equally supposed to be located in the afterlife, to do the same so as to hasten them towards God's final judgment. The practical result means blurring the distinction between martyrdom and homicide. The anthropocentric world view of the West, which has long left behind such medievalist religious fervor and rejected the view that this life is just a test with an ulterior purpose, fails to empathize with this position not only in its own name, but condemns its inherent incompatibility with an ethically and ideologically globalizing world. The values globalizm, grounded in this-worldliness and empiricism, tries to espouse are in stark contradiction to the fanatical Muslim philosophical position.

Jihad is usually translated as holy war—or by Christianizing the concept, crusade. It actually means struggle of an unspecific kind and refers to a morally justified act. The word war, harb, is associated rather with unjust fighting as it characterizes the pointlessly violent activities of the "unbelievers." Hence their abode is that of Dar-al-Harb. Although jihad is also translated as "fighting" (or "fighting in the cause of Allah") and "striving with your life," it does not necessarily refer to armed or violent struggle. It is a hallmark of radicalism that this aspect has been put into the foreground of present-day teaching.

Tradition and scriptures distinguish between lesser and greater struggle, the latter by definition being the more demanding and the more meritorious. This kind of struggle—a fight with one's inner enemies as it were—refers to personal growth and the endeavor to become a better Muslim through self-discipline, and a faithful and painstakingly correct adherence to Islamic articles of faith and to prescribed behavior. In this sense it refers to the duty of every Muslim without gender distinction to strive towards personal perfection. The foremost duty, one may infer, is to rise to moral excellence and virtue in practical life. What the Prophet had apparently considered to be the more exacting and morally higher form of a Muslim's duty has retreated into the background in the course of Islam's recent radicalization. Extremist interpretations of jihad, inspired by the view that Islam is in peril or that Muslims are suffering oppression, have led to the lesser aspect of the concept gaining pre-eminence. Thus the role of mujahidin (the people carrying out jihad) is predominantly understood now in terms of waging armed struggle, and, in garnering world attention, it has led to the neologism of jihadist, a word synonymous with terrorist. This Islam-specific morality not only demands moral rectitude, self-discipline, and self-sacrifice from the jihadi, but even excuses homicide, whether in the course of war or terrorism, as a legitimate commitment to jihad.

Even among apologists of violence, the more temperate view on this theological point holds that jihad is not necessarily intended to be of the Machiavellian kind that holds that the end justifies the means and thus every kind of violence is permitted. The Quran (2/190–93, 9/36) takes care to spell out rules of engagement. For instance, non-combatants—women, children, and the elderly—held to be innocent of armed aggression are to be spared; the opponent's means of sustenance are not to be destroyed, and if the enemy surrenders, to make peace. Mindful of such edicts, some Muslim scholarly authorities reject the legitimacy of unconditional, indiscriminate jihadism. However, the extremist view perceives justification in the belief that there are no innocents among its enemies; all share in the collective culpability of being hostile to the true faith. Even Muslims who do not follow the call to engage in jihad or do not share in the particular radicalised version of Islam may be seen to have joined the ranks of the enemy and become legitimate targets.

Dehumanizing the enemy is the usual device of war propaganda, and particularly vicious forms demonize the enemy by ascribing to them the attributes of evil, which is supposed to inspire even greater efforts to vanquish them. Conceiving a conflict in Manichaean terms of good fighting against evil is an old propaganda trick (still employed in the wars of the twentieth century) that stiffens one's resolve. The Iranian rhetoric of America being the Great Satan—ridiculously hackneyed as this may sound in the secularized West—is not just a figure of speech but falls into this rubric of war propaganda couched in extreme religious jargon.

THE ANTHROPOLOGY OF SACRED VIOLENCE

Depending on the meaning attributed by believers to the concept of jihad, a more peaceful or alternatively a more radical, belligerent form of Islam emerges. Neither will seriously contradict the core elements of belief. Moderate Islam understands jihad as an inner fortitude that rejects being translated into physical violence. From another point of view belief without action is meaningless. As the ahadith admonish, seeing injustice perpetrated on fellow Muslims and not intervening is tantamount to reneging on one's own Muslimness. Neutrality is as impossible an option as siding with the enemy. What we can observe in this context of Islam doctrinally activating violence is more than just using it as a functional tool to achieve a tactical end. It represents the ritualization of violence; in other words, the elevation of violence to the status of a sacred instrument. The violence into which the energies of the religious adepts are to be channelled is given a special liturgical meaning. Struggling in the cause of God lends itself readily to the instrumentalization of violence as a companion of sacrality. Such an interpretation of jihad, although this is by no means self-evident or cogent, fits seamlessly into a broader understanding of Islam and shapes it decisively.

The important point to make is that for radical Islam the violence that is associated with its understanding of the essential meaning of jihad, holy war, is enriched with a distinctly sacred, liturgical meaning. It possesses a redemptive quality as well as containing aspects of sacrifice. Rene Girard[19] has examined the close connection between violence and the sacred and the manifestation of this in the religious triumvirate of violence, sacrality, and sacrifice. Not all violence perpetrated by Muslims, though, is sacrificial in intent and carries some symbolic connotations. It may be purely pragmatic, unsublimated, and opportunistic, and by heaping chaos upon chaos, may simply be a social release valve to respond to an unjust, bewildering, or oppressive situation. In this sense of expressing inner rage, it may manifest undirected social pathology, no more than pent-up aggression suddenly unleashed. But crusades or holy wars are essentially of a different kind: in obeying a sacred duty, meting out suffering and death means offering a sacrifice. In a gruesome manner this universal trope of human sacrifice can be seen manifest in the slaughter of captives by cutting their throats. Some such acts perpetrated by Muslim extremists have been videotaped and broadcast on the internet (mainly in the aftermath of the Iraq war and the ensuing brutal anomie). Through their resemblance to the ritual halal slaughter of animals, such acts can be recognized as being more than just sadistic executions, but as ritualized murder containing distinct undertones of sacrifice.

For the jihadist suffering literally is a self-sacrifice offered for a higher glory. Suffering death is the "ultimate" sacrifice, and like all sacrifice brought in the name of a sacred cause, some reward is expected. Sacrifice plays on the universal theme of reciprocity; it is a transaction in which both sides, sacrificer and supernatural agency, enter into a relationship of obligation and mutuality. This expectation may be divine intervention in assisting the sacred cause or more concretely a reward may be expected to fall personally to the sacrificer. Martyrdom clearly is the most meritorious form of self-sacrifice, promising the highest rewards; it is of a kind that ennobles even the suicide bomber, the human bomb, and lifts them above the contemptible act of suicide. In this religious lexicon killing oneself and others is a sacrificial act that is beatified by the highest ethical reason and bathed in a mellow moral glow under an approving divine canopy.

The martyr is promised immediate salvation and eternal reward in paradise. Martyrs do not die, their earthly demise merges seamlessly with an afterlife of bliss and affluence. Believers are urged not to weep for them, for "they have not died." For the more simple-minded and materially orientated ones among the martyrs, the favors of hordes of huri, flawless virgins with "swelling bosoms," beckon—although for female martyrs no equivalent, opposite-gendered reward is promised. Their torn and tortured bodies—unwashed as it is prescribed for martyrs—miraculously resurrected and unblemished immediately enter paradise where in youthful form the martyrs at once partake of wonderful provisions. For the more educated, these rather earthly delights are metaphors for unimaginable spiritual wonders awaiting the select few. In this intoxicating perspective, moral shadings vanish. Even naked, unspeakable brutality becomes excusable, canonized by the purity of its intent and diminished by the magnitude of reward. More will be said later of the mysterious mind-set of the suicide bomber.

Purity of intent and motive to perform a sacred duty, and violence may combine in bizarre, unspeakable combinations. Violence thus performed is instrumental in achieving a desirable, perhaps divinely commanded, goal whereby the cruelty of methods may befit the magnitude of the purpose, yet make it completely ethical through its ritualistic execution. In serial Aztec human sacrifice as much as in the horrors of the Holocaust, these elements are inseparably intertwined. The destruction of countless lives becomes rationalizable as indeed necessary, a duty to be performed, for the survival of society, or the nation as well as for the greater glory of serving a higher authority (be they gods or destiny). Nourishing the gods with the hearts and blood of victims was considered necessary to retain divine help and thus keep the Aztec nation strong—as well as eliminating scores of enemies. Eliminating the enemies of the Nazi state, who in Nazism's murderous eugenics were obstacles to the attainment of the perfect, cleansed nation, eliminated a corrosive and dangerous threat to its health and strength. Deranged visions of the sacred importance of global jihad, in my view, show some uncanny similarity by being based on conceptions of sacrifice, ethically pure violence, and sacrality of objective.

Sadistic violence of this kind raises anxious questions. Whether it is sublimated to a higher purpose or appears to be simply unrefined, atavistic destructiveness, it raises a nagging question: is it innately present in the human condition—and, therefore, will inevitably show up in some form or other—or is it coming from a "capital of violence" that is built up by uncongenial social conditions? It could be generated by particular social agencies, institutions, and constellations[20] or, always slumbering in the deeper reaches of human nature, could be called forth by conflict situations. Is violence inevitably inherent in every society or can a society without violence be designed? There are many questions, none having been answered with finality. Some critics of Islam tend towards the view that violence may be brought to fomentation by doctrinal flash points contained in this religion, such as the ones I have highlighted before. Islam seems to serve somehow as a catalyst. The ex-Christian West entertains the expectation that religion be restraining, an institution that dissipates or suppresses violent energies and helps in subduing what may be seen as a naturally occurring "volcanic" quality of human nature. This makes Islam suspect, as it appears to cause the opposite effect. However, one should not overlook that the moral imperatives of peace, tolerance, understanding, and humility have risen to doctrinal prominence in the (mainstream) Christian churches not so long ago and that opposite impulses do still exist. Some "fire and brimstone" preachers exemplify the persistence of liturgical belligerence at least in word, if not in action. The assumption that religion intrinsically is pacifying and has a socializing mission—in which destructive violence is kept at bay—is wrong. Most religions openly or cryptically "preach" violence—which is to say, contain belief elements that ritualize, iconisize, or allude to violence, or doctrinally conjure up images of violence and its results. These belief elements can be instrumentalized to activate and justify violent behavior in any form. The fallacious expectation that religion is a medium that encourages a harmonious sociability can be found in both Emile Durkheim's and Karl Marx's thinking about religion. In this respect they meet in unison, even though one thought religion was objectively necessary and beneficial for society and the other that its tranquilizing, "opium-like" effect was pernicious. Both may have been wrong in presuming that religion's intrinsic purpose is the pacification of human nature.

POWER THAT GROWS FROM THE BARREL OF DOCTRINE

The questions, whether Islam is prone to generating violence and whether its edicts are inciting aggression loom large. The concept of jihad is often identified as the source of violence. Clearly, radicals see it as an open invitation, religiously sanctioned and of supreme ethical value, to be violent. Because of scriptural ambiguity gaining clarity depends on interpretation and often this is achieved by removing the reference from its wider, historical context. Extremists ignore the so-called Greater jihad, a concept derived from the ahadith in which the Prophet is described having said, after a successful military campaign, that the greater and more difficult task is still ahead: the believers' personal struggle to moralize their existence. At the same time it may be argued that the infusion of Islamic morality into human existence creates a duty to take up arms to defend this morality when it is threatened by jahiliya (immorality, decadence, ignorance) and heresy. Crisis may create a confluence of both forms of jihad: to be moral may require taking up arms. The duty to struggle in the name of Islam is supplemented and underpinned by a scriptural claim to supremacy. A heightened sense of its own superiority intricately woven into the fabric of Islamic doctrine adds both pungency and urgency to the imperative of jihad in the present global circumstances.

In this sense, undeniably, the sacred texts contain doctrinal impulses towards the employment of violent means. They could be overcome or set aside, but some interpretations choose not to do that. Such impulses are contained especially in three concepts: the moral duty of jihad, the exaltedness of the virtue of martyrdom, and the certain expectation of paradise through acts of violence. It would require a determined counter-exegesis to weaken and deactivate the divine imperatives, which jump out at the believer who experiences alienation and wishes to embrace Islam wholeheartedly as a panacea.

One suspects that for many, but in particular for radical Islamists, Quranic phraseology is not empty rhetoric, grandiloquence without meaning. It represents a hard-edged imperative: submission under God's will, not in the form of resignation (a kismat), but as a clarion call to live up to one's duty for action. In this it is important to realize that the Salafist leanings of today's radicals usually do not seem to concern themselves with the rich philosophical and contemplative literature that Islam has accumulated over centuries. It is primarily the Quran and the Sunna (the collection of ahadith) that form the basis of the Salafis' collective belief and from which they seem mainly to draw inspiration. In addition, the writings of Qutb, al-Banna, and Mawdudi may be consulted, to strengthen their belief that the West has to be resisted, but some extreme Salafism even rejects these sources as illicit innovations. The more nuanced and liberal nature of the works from the classical and the Spanish period eludes this search for the fundamentals of the faith.

The doctrinal exhortation to assume an activist stance is further corroborated by the sacred scriptures giving specific instructions about how to deal with infidels in the defense of religion and Muslim co-religionists. Constant vigilance is advised, both defensively and offensively, for instance, in Quran verse 3/200: "Guard your territory by stationing army units permanently at the places from where the enemy can attack you, and fear Allah, so that you may be successful." Such verses may be of dubious tactical value in today's world, but they seem to issue eternally valid commands never to let one's guard down in relation to "infidels." Instructions are seemingly always given from a position of strength, never considering compromise, seeking mutual rapport based on tolerant understanding. Instead a tone of belligerence is paramount, so impressively articulated in verse 9/123: "O believers, fight the unbelievers who are near to you, and let them find in you a harshness; and know that God is with the god-fearing."

Even more openly aggressive imperatives are not hard to find, such as "Kill the mushrikun [unbelievers, idolaters] wherever you find them, and capture and besiege them, and lie in wait for them in each and every ambush" (Qur'an 5/9); and "fight against the mushrikun . . . collectively as they fight against you collectively" (Qur'an 9/36), which, when isolated from their historical context, may seem to convey a message of implacable hostility and command belligerence towards people of other faiths. It is not difficult to understand how fanatical aggressiveness can grow from a certain understanding of Quranic passages. Thus justification of forceful defensive action for the fanatic turns into a duty of unmitigated, proactive aggression. On this basis a sense of victorious supremacy turns from a hoped-for prospect, a longing for a divine promise yet to be met, to an unshakeable, preordained certainty.

Passages surrounding articles of faith like these taken from the Quran—but elaborated and exemplified in the exegetical Islamic literature—provide doctrinal foundations that lend themselves to being exploited by ideologues to shape a jihadi's frame of mind. Flexibility of interpretation hardens into the shapes of eternal truths. Especially if the historical contextualization of divine revelation is denied, as fundamentalism is inclined to do, it lacks the awareness that the scriptures may relate to the original precariousness of the Muslim community. Instead it creates the belief that eternal truths have been formulated, which apply in unchanged form to contemporary situations and convey an urgency to validate them. Rejecting contextualization means accepting the unconditionally exemplary value of historical events and giving them the status of sacred precedence to be emulated faithfully. Indeed, this is the perspective one finds time and time again in the utterances of extremists.

The scriptures also supply rules of engagement, a fact which can be misconstrued as underpinning the necessity to engage in warfare. Such rules may seem to preach fairness, such as to spare noncombatants, women and children, the elderly, not to destroy the enemy's means of livelihood, and the like. But these rules of fairness lend themselves to be interpreted in various ways. They can easily be understood to further corroborate the divinely intended need towards violent conduct. By recommending aggression to be carried out in an orderly and prescribed manner, it moralizes this violence, and legitimizes it with the divine seal. For the jihadist it strengthens a sense of "doing the right thing." And in another sense, these rules can entirely and legitimately be suspended, for instance, if the adversary is considered to fight without rules or constraints, or commands overwhelming power. An additional rationale—providing a telling background to bin Laden's fatawa—is to ascribe to the West, and especially America, a collective culpability without exceptions. People have the government they elect or deserve, and thus there are no innocents that should not be harmed. Through this convenient rationale not only is democracy condemned, but also terrorism justified in striking indiscriminately. Targets like airplanes, marketplaces, and underground trains become legitimate venues for attacks.

The point to be made here is that Islam is what people make of it. To blame Islam per se as a religion for the violence is alluring but overly simplistic. There is no simple causal connection between Islamic doctrine and violent acts of extremism and terrorism. Doctrine, appropriately interpreted, provides a comfortable justification for any action. Add to this a perception of duty to address injustice or suffering, a sense of powerlessness in using ordinary channels of protest, a sense of being a victim of hegemonic oppression, deprivation, and aggression. Certainly, the perception is widespread of the hegemonic oppression of the Islamic world by the West and that the Christian-secularized West is waging a religious war against Islam. This provides both incentive and broad license for harsh measures and retribution.

The Quran (5/33) seems to condone this where it says, "The recompense of those who wage war against Allah and His messenger and do mischief in the land is only that they shall be killed or crucified or their hands and feet be cut off from opposite sides, or be exiled from the land." This, for some, is justification for the fiercest response imaginable, leaving little excuse for leniency, concession or compromise, while from another angle of interpretation this may have no gravity, failing to relate to present conditions.

Doctrine may provide a justification and perhaps even a methodology, but not a cause. As with any ideology, the time has to be rife for doctrine to become influential. In the confluence of Max Weber's[21] elective affinity (of the congruency of ideas and material circumstances creating an interestedness[22]) and Antonio Gramsci's[23] idea of how dominance of an ideology (i.e., hegemony) is achieved (namely by consensus and persuasion—not enforcement—through which a client culture or group or society accepts the domination by another),[24] lies the explanation for the rise of Islamic militancy. The belief in osmotic empowerment does not hinge on the octruization of ideology. Ideas of the need of Islam to defend itself with all means possible against infidel incursion and the injustices of the modern world can only take hold if there is some basis in empirical reality, if there are conditions that lend themselves to this interpretation and make these ideas seem reasonable and full of explanatory cogency. In such circumstances it does not need blunt coercion to rally people; instead seductive reasoning, the intellectual allure of seemingly sound explanations and promised solution provide the pull of the ideological force field. Thus even the sweet dawa recommended in the Islamic methodology suffices.

Islamic extremism occupies a broad front against the West's political and cultural dominance. Bin Laden's fatwa addressing the West as crusaders uses the reference to a historical situation to point to a contemporary danger posed by the West. As the crusades once threatened to re-Christianize the "Holy Land" and the Levant, the West's current engagement in the Islamic world needs to be repulsed now to prevent the destruction of Islam. Pushing America and its allies out of the Islamic realm is even more important in a very specific sense. Infidel troops are already dangerously close to Hijas, the holy inner precinct of the Islamic world that includes Macca and Madina. The presence of nonbelievers is not tolerated there. Establishing infidel dominance over Islam's core area from where it spread would pollute its purity and make muhajirun (refugees from infidel rule) of all devout Muslims. No other world religion is less inviting to its inner sanctum, although some secretive cults also like to surround themselves with extreme exclusiveness. For conservative Muslims the intrusion of infidels into the heartland from where Islam sallied forth to conquer wide swathes of geography, is unthinkable.

The scriptural example and the law schools suggest that Muslims should not live under infidel rule. They should rather follow the Prophet's example of hijra (his emigration from Macca to Madina), which occurred in the year 622 AD and signifies the year zero in the Islamic calendar. The issue of good Muslims having to live under non-Muslim governance has remained a thorny issue.[25] It is not difficult to understand that on this basis a readiness for assimilation under minority conditions cannot easily grow despite the doctrine of darura (necessity),[26] clever interpretations of maslaha (the common good), and the scriptural concession that there should be no hardship in religion. While this is plainly obvious when Muslims form a diaspora in the West, some extend this notion, and its ethical problems, to the globalized future: what to do when the whole world is under Western domination?

From the defensive thinking of conservative Islam also grows the ambitious vision of a reestablishment of a global khilafa, a caliphate that encompasses large parts of the world, thus spreading a political umbrella over all Muslims. It bans the specter of devout Muslims having to live under non-Islamic rule. In this realm Islamic governance should replace infidel governance. Reclaiming Palestine, Chechnya, and Dagestan, separating the Muslim southern islands from Catholic Philippines, freeing southern Muslim Thais from Buddhist rule, liberating Xinjiang's Uighurs from Han-dominated communist China would make sure that no Muslims would have to live under infidel rule.

From a partisan viewpoint it seems painfully obvious that many Muslims are victimized and persecuted by the West. As I could observe firsthand by attending a mujahidin conference in Indonesia,[27] it is only a small step, aided by a convoluted logic, to the assumption that the West's aggressive stance in the world at large is directed against Islam as a religion and a way of life.[28] Some Muslims sincerely believe the time is upon them to defend both.

Objective facts suggest that it is a tiny minority, perhaps as little as a few thousand, among the 1.3 or 1.4 (according to some estimates 1.6) billion Muslims, who have fully and fanatically embraced the violent extremist creed to make them into active terrorists. There is a much larger resource of sympathizers who embrace this point of view and who form a shadowy reserve army from which active extremists might be drawn. Perhaps there are also some thousands who driven by a misguided sense of patriotism and perhaps by poverty can be bought to do the Taleban's bidding in the mountains of Afghanistan and Pakistan. Not all extremists and militants are fighting the West in some form. There are more Muslims who direct their aggression towards other Muslims. But it remains a statistical fact that the vast majority of Muslims must be peaceful or at least are not actively involved in violent action. However, this seems to do little to rectify the West's widely held view of Islam as a violent religion that seduces people to commit terrible crimes. Perhaps it is true that many Muslims have in recent years been polticized and radicalized in their perception of the world, stirring mightily anti-Western, and especially anti-American, sentiments; that they have become entranced by radical doctrines and form now a reservoir of potential recruits for extremism. Yet, it is still unjustified to allot blame solely to Islam as a system of belief that incites violence.[29] The relation between Islamic faith and violence may be traceable to the scriptural doctrines but is not compelling enough to blame Islam per se. Like other religions, the Islamic faith may contain stimuli towards violence, which, however, are not potent enough inevitably to lead to violence on a grand scale. As in other religious doctrines and traditions, there are doctrinal ambiguities that can be exploited by radical ideologues to form a dogmatic imperative for extremism, but by the same token the inherent plasticity of religious doctrine does also allow it to be shaped into a foil for moderation. As the "counter-reformer" Abdullahi an-Na'im,[30] offering an alternative view, states, "the notion of aggressive jihad has become morally untenable as a means of conducting international relations."

TERRORISM AND ITS SYMBOLIC LANGUAGE

Terrorism has sometimes been called the power of the powerless. This certainly contains a valid assessment. In a contest one of the opponents, unable to match power and to injure and weaken the enemy in open combat, seeks strategic advantage or recompense by devious tactics. If successful they may sap the enemy's strength and even if they are failing, they may still undermine his resolve. One of terrorism's prominent functions is to serve a psychological purpose: through its ubiquitousness and unpredictability terrorist violence can be unsettling and even cause fear far beyond its physical impact. In their physical effectiveness individual attacks may amount to no more than pinpricks, yet that can be demoralizing—just as ants or mosquitoes can drive you from the lovely picnic spot you have discovered. Comparing this nuisance with terrorism may amount to terminological hyperbole, but in a methodological respect it goes to the heart of the matter. The psychological effect in sum total exceeds the damage: the terror that grips a nation is bigger than the bomb's impact. And at the risk of sounding heartless, it may be said that worldwide many more people die in road accidents or from a smoker's lung than by the terrorists' bombs. Yet the fear generated by terrorism is greater and so is its social impact. (Actual loss of life through attacks on airplanes, for instance, though relatively small, has led to a complete revolution in airport security systems at enormous expense, while tobacco smoking has not been banned as a dangerous drug.)

The psychological impact is exactly the reason why terrorism is condemned by international conventions and laws. It does not come as a surprise that terrorists, well aware of the usefulness of this method, disregard the ban. Some Islamic authorities explicitly condone this tactic and even encourage it because of its psychological effectiveness. One of the foremost Sunni spiritual authorities, the mufti Yusuf al Qaradawi, has not only welcomed the conquest of Europe and America through peaceful dawa, but specifically and in several versions theologically welcomed suicide operations as heroic martyrdom and declared the spreading of terror an acceptable method to unsettle and discourage the enemy. Terrorism in this view is a legitimate war tactic to even the chances. Given the sheer impossibility of swaying the hegemonic juggernaut of the West by conventional means, Muslim terrorism with somewhat greater plausibility has been called the language of despair.

In addition to its rational function of spreading fear, terrorist action contains a symbolic aspect and acts as a device of communication. In a seemingly unequal contest between opponents of quite different strength the weaker side may try to match the more powerful on a level of symbolic action. Blowing up airplanes, trains, and offices does not militarily weaken the West (or shake an unloved pseudo-Muslim satrap regime to the core) and as such has little effect on the hegemonic imbalance, but it has a theatrical effect that exceeds the sum total of people killed and maimed, or the material damage inflicted. Car bombs and suicide vests by themselves do not unseat an unwanted government, but they do send a powerful symbolic message of the resolve and punch of its opponents. Destroying tall buildings with flying incendiary devices full of people is priceless in terms of creating a brutal iconography. Its semiotic multivocality is of powerful expressiveness on several levels: from the theatrical performance value of spectacularly crumbling skyscrapers and the sacrificial immolation of thousands, to the encrypted message about the destruction of the seat of financial power from which economic world domination is exercised. (The attack on the military seat of power, the Pentagon, did not quite succeed; nor, as far as one can surmise, did the attack intended to strike at the center of political power, the White House.) No less spectacular is the demonstration of the ability to geographically match the enemy's reach and penetration, thrusting a dagger into his very heart. Yet, most effective was the creation of graphic images of destruction. They have been used to great propagandist effect in the cyberspace communications following the 9/11 attacks. Even if jihad cannot muster the same military might as the West, it has shown itself capable of creating a lasting symbol of its effectiveness.

The Islamic world itself came perilously close to suffering a demonstration of such symbolic magnitude. This happened when the Masjid al Haram, the Grand Mosque of Macca containing the innermost sanctum, the Ka'aba, was temporarily seized by terrorists in 1979. A belief in the return of the

Mahdi had led a group of fanatical devotees to act on an apocalyptic vision and to seize the mosque in a surprise attack. What better way to symbolize the dawn of a new era than by occupying the supreme icon of Islam and dedicating it to the Mahdi? Police and military units, over several days, laid siege to the armed Muslim terrorists holed up inside. In the ensuing battle the sacred precinct was heavily damaged. It caused many casualties and severely desacralized the holiest of holy shrines. Ultimately, the terrorists were vanquished; some were killed during the fighting and others taken prisoner (the presumed Mahdi among them) and later executed by beheading. The attack may not have been successful, but it managed to leave an indelible impression, even though few Muslims like to be reminded of it.

As two antagonists grapple with each other, the language of power becomes a shared factor in the competitive relationship. This language does not just draw on physical violence, but uses tactics of symbolic value such as seizing or destroying an iconic item. The symbolic meaning of such an act is understood across cultural differences. Yet, a combative discourse and measuring power by symbolic means can only really take place when the two opponents use the same "language"; that is to say, use commonly understood symbols as a means of communication. Constructing a common "language" to enter into a discourse together may depend on the weaker group accepting paradigms and symbols of the dominant group.[31] When cultures are too different, the actions they inspire may remain chronically misunderstood— devoid of the symbolic significance intended—by the opposing side, or even worse, may be ignored. A good example taken from Europe's colonial history is the summary landgrab by which the Australian continent was expropriated from the indigenous people.[32] Starting with a total incomprehension on the part of the colonizing power of the Aborigines' modus operandi of distributing, owning, and using land, their language of resistance was totally brushed aside as inconsequential, irrelevant, indeed was not understood as a legitimate means of either patriotism or defense of their ownership right. Partly because of its ritualistic nature and partly because of its, in a practical military sense, pitiful ineffectiveness, resistive action taken by the Aborigines was not even understood as guerrilla warfare let alone as a legitimate attempt to protect their "natural" rights of ownership.[33] Aborigines in turn failed to comprehend the meaning of being dispossessed in a colonialist enterprise. Bereft of opportunities—even of the few reluctantly tendered by the dominant society—to help and express themselves in terms comprehensible to the dominant group, Aborigines slowly and painfully had to learn to speak the symbolic language of the conqueror so as to be able to convey their objection to their being dispossessed. It took over a hundred years. The tragic lesson to be learned is that it behoves the weaker opponent to find means and ways to communicate with the more powerful and to do so by assimilating some of the symbolic vocabulary of the language of hegemony.[34]

This language used in the current struggle between the West and Islam (or rather, some extremist Muslims) for ideological supremacy draws on grandiose symbols and rituals of power, imageries of war, ostentatious displays of destruction, visions of doomsday and Armageddon in the form of arrays of bombs and missiles, magnificent explosions, and fields of ruins. All this is delivered through theatrical performances of war, designed to impress and demoralize the opponent, and smash their resolve into early submission. (At times this tactic was given verbal dignity with the epithet "shock and awe.") Muslims responded with a similar display of airplanes crashing in a fireball and of burning and crumbling buildings. The attack on New York's twin towers revealed something of the self-aggrandizing character of Islamic extremism trying to match the West's array of symbols. It was an event—at the risk of sounding frivolous, a happening—that was meant to rival in magnitude aggressive manifestations staged by the West. Perhaps by hyperbolizing Kant's concept of moral reciprocity and symmetry it may be said there is a competition of terror between America and radical Islam. The attack's dimension succeeded in indelibly inscribing it in history as a Muslim ritual of power. In terms of display of destructive potency it certainly exceeded the impact of individual airoplane crashes (even of the Lockerby kind), carbombs, and exploding suicide vests; it was even larger a prize than the iconoclastic destruction of the Bamiyan Buddhas, which clearly was intended as a signal of victory over unbelief.[35] Not surprisingly, America, raising the stakes, responded to the destruction of its modernist icon and the failed attack on its heart of military might, the Pentagon, with an even bigger display of power: by bringing down a whole country (Afghanistan) and in quick succession repeating the lesson in even greater magnitude by destroying another (Iraq). The orgiastic display of firepower, charred ruins, tens of thousands of casualties, and thoroughly destroyed despotic governance produced a symbol difficult to match in its magnificence.

Some Muslims, approving the destruction of the twin towers, offered another path to intellectualize these events and lift them above the motivation of sheer brutality and senseless display of force. They pointed out that this was payback for the violence and injustice inflicted on the Islamic world by the West and in particular the United States.[36] Payback should always be proportional to the injustice perpetrated. While physical proportionality can hardly be achieved in the struggle between Muslims and the West, some symbolic balance can be aimed for. Befitting the fundamentally different ethos of the contesting cultures, while Islam is suffering spiritually at the hands of the West, the damage inflicted on the West is to its pride and haughtiness. Not only has the myth of its invulnerability been disproved, at least symbolically its hold on financial world domination has also been dented. The universal significance of proportional payback has been discussed before. Measured in these terms, the reciprocal attack was extremely modest, even restrained; and in order to address the injustice properly and to restore balance, in this view, more attacks of a similar magnitude should follow. Rationalizing this atrocity, intellectualizing its ferocity, and thus to provide some moral justification, seems to be of some concern to thinking Muslims. One argument questioning the morality of this action has been that if Muslims are concerned with justice, where is the justice in killing thousands of innocents, people who have done no harm to Muslims? The Islamic response counters by portraying the towers as places of evil; places where the sin of riba (banking with interests) was cultivated. The towers represented the financial wheeling and dealing of the West, where IMF and World Bank operated, carrying out their sinful business of world strangulation by which the Muslims were shackled in poverty. Such highly immoral financial machinations being carried out in this place would have kept pious Muslims at bay, hence no pious Muslims could have suffered in this inferno. (In this dimly thought-out scenario the oil wealth accumulated by the Arab elites assumes the same moral sinfulness but is considered of lesser global harm.) Both global financial institutions are held culpable in enslaving the Islamic world financially and making it subservient to the rapacious capitalism of the West. Thus there are no innocent victims in this tragedy.

According to Islamic rules of fairness in conducting jihad, noncombatants should be spared, as should women and children, the elderly, the frail and the sick. No such rules apply in bomb warfare. In this sense blowing up tall buildings, the Dresden fire bombing, and dropping the "fat boy" on Hiroshima belong in the same category. One might reject the close kinship between them and yet there is some similarity that unites them. In bomb warfare as much as in suicide bombing, targets may be chosen arbitrarily and opportunistically, but they are important for their psychological and symbolic effect. The attacks are meant to send a powerful message, their enormous destructiveness being a symbolic, exemplary measure of the sender's power. All three bomb attacks were planned and carried out for the same reason: a ritual act of power to reveal the potential destructive might in an impressive, irresistible demonstration.

The symbolic act happens to be indiscriminately lethal, but that hardly matters. (Even drones are not exactly high precision instruments, just as the expression "surgical strike" metaphorically suggestive of precisely targeted medical intervention, is misleading.) From the sweeping perspective of the modern jihadi moralizing his deed, murderous acts may appear to be targeted. Shi'a processions, or Sunni mosques, chosen as targets have a good chance of inflicting damage to the sectarian adversary. In the struggle between Islam and the West there are no innocents on the side of the West— hence there is no moral dilemma. To some extent, paradoxically, democracy is to blame. Democratic systems, giving rights to vote and thus determining governance, spread responsibility and guilt over the whole society. Radical

Muslims rationalize the absence of precise targeting by assuming that in democracies people are collectively responsible for the government—they possess the governance they deserve. Thus no one is innocent. Their guilt is either of the collective kind or by association and both spread culpability to all Westerners. (A Norwegian imam's ruling that extremists should not target the respective Western country that gives them shelter, sounds rather quaint and apparently is unheeded if one looks at Muslim attacks in the West.) However, seen in this light, the ethical ground which might justify the frequent car bombs exploding in the Islamic world, in highly frequented places like busy streets and marketplaces, and which usually kill large numbers of Muslims without sectarian or ethnic distinction, still remains a mystery. So-called "collateral damage" may justify methods of modern warfare, but to my knowledge it is not an Islamic concept.

THE MYSTERIOUS MIND-SET OF MARTYRS AND SUICIDE BOMBERS

Several scriptural references refer to a physical and moral elevation of those who give their lives for the cause of Islam. A great reward awaits them. "They are not dead" the Quran promises; "do not weep for them."[37] Self-sacrifice "in the way of Allah" is considered a high virtue. The martyrdom of the shahid, dying in pursuit of "the just cause," awaits much prestige and above all transcendental reward, according to the Quran (22/58–59; 2/154; 3/157–58, 169–71). The mustashhidin (martyrs) are assured instantly to become the beneficiaries of divine largesse. (With some recalibration this issue may well apply not only to the martyrs among Muslim extremists, but also to the demonstrators and fighters in the Arab Spring uprisings whose bravado suggests a comparison with the death-defying ethos of suicide bombers. These people share the willingness to die a martyr's death regardless of the political motivations.) Looking beyond the doctrinal gloss, on closer inspection, martyrdom harbors a moral dilemma.

As present-day terrorist methods often do not spare the attacker's life—and are not designed to do so—the theological problem arises: is this condemnable suicide and should be forbidden, or is it virtuous self-sacrifice to be recommended? Can the human bomb be a killer, a committer of suicide, a saint, a martyr, a sinner and a legitimate warrior all at the same time—and emerge spiritually unscathed to reap eternal rewards?

In this respect Islam manifestly posits a contradiction inherent in its tenet: it condemns suicide (intihar) as a sinful act—as it says in a hadith, "Your body has rights over you," and in the Quran (2/195), "Do not bring about your own destruction." Yet, a person's death in the course of a jihad, fighting for Allah, is praised as a highly valued form of martyrdom (shahada). The willing death of the mustashhidin (the self-sacrificers), engaged in a suicidal mission, then—amounting to voluntary self-destruction—is an obvious moral conundrum. Does the suicide vest represent a tool of self-destruction or a weapon to harm an enemy in pursuance of a just cause?

The desired resolution rests on a "mysterious" transformation. Though in both its design and execution tantamount to suicide, and, therefore, to be condemned, the act performed for the higher purpose of defending Islam embodies the virtue of ultimate self-sacrifice (istishhad), the highest ethical act of the jihad. The defining difference is the intent and its ethical gravity. Thus it offers to resolve the nagging problem: if martyrdom plainly is achievable only by planned suicide, which in itself undoubtedly is a sinful act rejected in the scriptures, how to value a voluntary certain death in the pursuit of "the just cause." The terrorist's suicide mission containing a grave moral contradiction, bears the stigma of self-harm—as integral to the heroic act is the certainty of death, not just an exponential increase of risk through the nature of the operation—but at the same time wears the halo of supreme morality in the form of self-sacrifice (istishhad). How can that act elevate him or her to the status of mustashhidin for whom paradise awaits? For some this tactic of modern warfare has opened up an acute ethical problem that has occasioned some learned debate—publicly accessible in the various websites of Islamic authorities. Overwhelmingly those who deal with this issue agree: if the religious warrior is certain of his own demise, it is the nature of the cause for which he or she surrenders their life that determines the ethical value. For other scholarly minds the fine dividing line between the death-wish and the urge to defend the faith as the guiding principle—a subtle distinction between the behavior's Thanatos and religious ecstasy—is blurred for the sake of the practical need for a relentless, no-holds-barred jihad. The extraordinariness of the fight and the magnitude of danger to true faith requires special dispensations. It seems in the face of this awareness the question of theological correctness pales somewhat into insignificance. Whatever scholarly opinion may be, an amazing number of people, in taking the ultimate step, seem to have found a clear answer. Some Muslim scholars, however, remain unconvinced of the deed's ethical merit.

Apart from the imaginative forms of violence this phenomenon of self-sacrifice generates, of particular interest is the formation of this mind-set and its causes. The religiously motivated act that leads to the voluntary, fully envisaged and intended destruction of the perpetrator in its personal motives remains mysterious, especially to the secularized Western mind. How does the (extremely) devout progress from refusing suicide as sinful to embracing it for the sake of a higher priority? How does an educated suburban dweller, a student, a housewife slide into the role of suicide bomber?

How to understand the willingness of men and women to become the human bomb? In the name of Islam, fanatics have driven explosives-laden trucks and cars, hiding explosives in vests and belts, in turbans, under burqas, in shoes and underpants, even in body cavities, thus making certain of their own horrible if instant demise. (This may seem slightly preferable to self-cremation, as some contemporaneous protesters have chosen—among them the young Tunisian man whose sacrifice sparked off the so-called Arab Spring. In historical times this was the preserve of Christian reformers and their suicidal insistence on being burned at the stake for refusing to recant. Of one such hapless martyr, Johann Hus, it was said that he suffered for the duration of the Lord's Prayer.)

This stubborn insistence on setting aside the basic instinct of self-preservation is not only a manly thing. Although men clearly are the main candidates, women also choose this path of personal redemption. In Russia they are notoriously known as the "black widows," so called for the color of their dress.[38] The Moscow underground bombing of March 2010, apparently, was carried out by two black widows with suicide vests. But they represent a new development. The Quran cites women as noncombatants who are to be spared. And while Khomeini in the Iran-Iraq war escalated the suicide mission of young men to epic proportions (they were given cardboard keys to paradise, to hang around their necks when they marched through minefields), women were excluded. Their self-sacrifice was considered un-Islamic. Since about the year 2000 Hamas, the Palestinian and Chechen jihad, and al-Qaeda—apparently in contravention of the basic sacred scriptures—recruit women for this purpose.[39]

A rational explanation of this phenomenon—which defies natural instinct of self-preservation as well as fundamental Islamic doctrine—is difficult and elusive. In modern times it is particularly hard to understand. As the absolute certainty of eternal life in a splendid beyond-world and wonderful heavenly rewards, titillating with their delights, has diminished in an increasingly secularized world, where does this courage, this sangfroid to stare death in the face come from? It may have been easier in the past when the firmness of religious belief and the attractiveness of paradise were hardening the resolve. But when this kind of religious fanaticism has obviously lost some of its soteriological currency in the world, the flowering of this phenomenon in Islam seems hard to grasp. Under the relentless onslaught of hegemonic rationalism, this extreme sense of commitment in the West is confined to religious pathology and insanity. Yet there seems to be an endless supply of people who are inspired by the conviction that this action is religiously and ethically supremely justified and that it is of extreme merit to spill their own and others' blood.

In today's hegemonic discourse acts of martyrdom may, for some causes, inspire fleeting admiration because of their apparent idealism, but tend quickly to become consigned to the category of insanity. Hedonism and preoccupation with physical well-being are of supreme value. On the collective political and military planning level, loss-and-gain calculations do not count on self-sacrificial martyrdom in the achievement of a goal. (The world was astounded about the idealism of the first wave of workers, immediately after the Chernobyl disaster, trying to contain the fallout. They seem to have been well aware that they would be doomed.) State violence is pursued usually only after a risk assessment in relation to factors of survivability, and avoids to ask for self-sacrificial acts of heroism. (Such acts, by and large, have become the stuff of Hollywood films, but not of real life.) The hegemonically desired benefit of risky operations is based, in Max Weber's terms, on Zweckrationalitaet (instrumental rationality, which is the pursuit of rational gains in the empirical world to be achieved with rational means), and not Wertrationalitaet (value rationality in which a higher transcendental value is pursued regardless of material, empirically verifiable gains in real life). Pursuit of virtue through self-harm in a religious context is considered the last convulsion of a vanishing world.

What seems so incomprehensible, perhaps even repulsive, to the modern rationalist discourse, is that the believing mind puts a different value on the concept of suffering and self-sacrifice for the attainment of a transcendental goal. Empathetic understanding for such motives has drastically diminished in modernity. The suffering of the martyr is an offering made to a higher power inviting reciprocity in the form of blessing or more tangible rewards. It would go too far exploring the whole complexity of self-harm in a universal cultural context. It touches on issues of universal human psychology—or to put not too fine a point on it, masochism and sadomasochism. It also summons up universal tropes of suffering and its redemptive value and of extreme asceticism and its connection with the wish for spiritual and cognitive enlightenment. A short sketch has to suffice to demonstrate the universality of this cultural phenomenon—which has suffered a drastic decline in the West.

The hope for higher insights—or rewards of some kind—through suffering is universally expressed in various ways. It is quintessentially practiced in the Shamanic and Fakir traditions. The Shamanic vision quest in addition to hallucinogenic drugs may be aided by suffering some deliberately inflicted agonizing pain. In the Hindu, Buddhist, and Sufi traditions, the range of calculated discomfort endured by Fakirs for the sake of enlightenment is considerable: from inflicting wounds on one's body, skewering one's flesh, lying on a bed of nails, to pulling a car with one's penis—the range of possibilities is only limited by one's imagination. Beyond that, most traditional cultures show features where some form of extreme bodily discomfort or even torture, deliberately and ritually inflicted, delivers revelatory experiences, or special wisdom, or a promise of divine reward. Mythology of various cultures celebrates this theme (for instance, Odin's suffering hanging from the world tree Yggdrasil for the sake of gaining wisdom). A well-known paradigmatic example is the sun-dance ritual of the Mandan Indians in which the devotees are skewered through the skin on their backs and suspended from above. (This technique has been revived by a small group of Western devotees.) Pain inflicted in this and countless other rituals of calculated suffering may be expected to create altered states of consciousness and ecstasy that have soteriological as well as enlightening purposes. In the Catholic tradition there are many customs that celebrate the redemptive trope of suffering and self-denial: from relatively harmless features of asceticism (fasting, vows of silence, celibacy, arduous pilgrimages, wearing hair shirts and sack cloth, fetters, etc.) to practices of self-torture, so-called corporal mortification (for instance, through flagellation).[40] Pilgrimages covering long distances on one's knees are practiced in Catholicism and Buddhism.[41] Acts of extreme and violent self-denial, regardless of whether they are done as an intellectualized painful penance to atone of concupiscence or simply to satisfy neurotic urges, can range from wearing the crown of thorns, using a metal cilice, the realiztic reenactment of Christ's passion carrying a heavy cross, and even actual crucifixion (which sometimes goes beyond symbolized staging; it may be performed even with real nails). In some rare instances, instead of gaining prestige in the respective religious community, this has led to the death of the victim. In a few cases it raised the suspicion that death was not accidental, but had been intended by the victim: in other words, religious ecstasy was planned to culminate in suicide. Needless to say, the official church frowns on such displays of extreme devotion. Wider secularized society shows even less respect for such ecstatic behavior.

Islam also has features of ritual castigation (apart from Sufi rituals which practice self-harm). Shi'ism celebrates Ashura on the tenth day of Muharam with mass demonstrations of self-flagellation in various forms. Even the fasting, sawm, at Ramadan is amenable to the interpretation that it is an act of self-chastisement, making a sacrifice of one's bodily comfort, for spiritual gain. Devout religious conduct in many cultures is full of symbolic and real acts of self-denial and asceticism to the point of self-harm. Religiously induced ecstasy is a fascinating psychological phenomenon, which can be channelled by culture into various activities and expressions. Considered in this light, the human bomb cannot be taken as a new phenomenon of moral depravity.

On the theme of religiously blessed suffering, one may wonder about the torture of waterboarding and other methods of inflicting suffering on Muslim prisoners (suspected of terrorism) in order to extract information. Do they perceive this treatment in religious terms as being of redemptive quality? Do they see their fate as that of a martyr? It would be conceivable, even though I have not found any corroborating information.[42]

The shahid enjoys high esteem and a prestige that is hard to fathom in a more secularized society such as the West. And, of course, there is the promise and expectation of paradise, graphically imagined by many to be full of earthly—and even sexual—delights, which must be an allurement for the aspirants to martyrdom. The videotapes and letters left behind by suicide bombers (successful ones and thwarted ones) speak a clear language of religiously induced ecstasy and the expectation of a metaphysical reward. In the farewell videotapes of intending martyrs, there are few hints of sadness and depressive foreboding—only joyful anticipation and acceptance of a religious duty. Training tapes and propaganda videos issued by the ideologues of terror, as a rule, emphatically play on religious doctrines and beliefs that support martyrdom and expectations of reward in order to create the necessary fervor and consummate obedience to divine command.

The renowned scholar Bernard Lewis[43] put forward the opinion that at the root of suicide bombing is sexual frustration. For the time being at least, this must remain a very speculative, if not facile, hypothesis. Expectations of a carnally wonderful afterlife, he proposed, would provide the major incentive for young Muslim men to lay down their lives. Because there is no casual sex in the Arab-Muslim world, young men are left with either marriage or visits to a brothel. Both options may be financially unaffordable leaving only the alluring and compensatory mirage of sexual fulfilment in a martyr's paradise. A large number of virgins with "swelling breasts" and "wide, lovely eyes,"[44] as promised in the scriptures, may indeed feature in the sexual fantasies of contenders to martyrdom, but whether this is the main motif in choosing this career is far from certain. Lewis' overly Freudian explanation, placing libido near the wellspring of religious violence, may be tempting by its simplicity, but ultimately falls down for exactly that reason. Human beings are not so uncomplicated that one deep psychological cause can mechanistically account for such motivations as suicide-murder. With equal justification one may point to the absence of alcohol as an ameliorating social lubricant that if more freely available may take the edge off people's irascibility.

Osama bin Laden recorded a feeling of calm and serenity when during the mujahidin's campaign against the Soviets in Afghanistan, a grenade landed next to him. In the event it did not explode and bin Laden lived to pursue his fighting career. As the explosive lay next to him, he registered a sense of tranquillity and an elevated being of otherness going beyond a mere sense of detachment or extra-body experience. In Arabic this describes the sensation of sakina,[45] not only feeling disconnected from the physical world, but in a state of utter calmness and serenity. The concept of sakina referring in this way to a feeling of detached exhilaration is clearly related to the notion of religious enrapture. Some people, experiencing the numinous vividly, are capable of feeling they are in the presence of divinity. In Quran (48/4 and 48/ 26) it says, "He it is Who sent down al-sakinah into the hearts of the believers" and it endowed "the Messenger" and the believers with a quality which elevated them above the pride and haughtiness of disbelievers. Al-sakinah as an intoxicating and fortifying, yet calming, quality is accessible only to believers. It can be imagined that suicide bombers in their mental preparation strive towards this desirable sensation that steels them for the task, makes them indifferent to the result, and assures them of possessing divine grace. Having not experienced this, what seems to be, a trancelike condition, or religious rapture or any form of extraordinary exultation, I cannot say whether at least terminologically it may be called intoxication with the sacred.

Historically, today's suicide bombing is not a recent Islamic invention. As far as the use of explosives in this enterprise is concerned, the dubious honor belongs to Sri Lankan Tamil Elam fanatics. Theirs may in fact have been a reinvention as in wider history the idea of deliberate, violent self-sacrifice in the pursuit of a sacred goal seems to reach back to a Muslim sect of several centuries ago. Members of the Hashhashin sect were sent on assassination missions from which it was impossible to return. In the twelfth and thirteenth century this Nizari sub-sect of Shi'ism in northern Persia pursued strategies of daring assassination that made it virtually impossible for the perpetrator to survive. In recent times this tactic was used in the Middle East by Fedayin militias in Palestine and with devastating effect by the Shi'ite Hezbollah in Lebanon. They developed the first truck bombs that led to the hasty retreat of the American and French marines in 1983. Perhaps the best-known suicide warriors of recent history—who went far beyond the ordinary bravery of soldiers in the line of duty and patriotism—were Japan's Kamikaze pilots in World War II. Islamic suicide bombers may be said to be the Kamikaze of the postmodern era. Kamikaze died for nationalism and patriotic glory, not religion, but seen in a different way, there is an ingredient they share with Muslim suicide bombers: Kamikaze were idealists of the highest order, acting in defense of what they were taught to be of supreme value. Giving their lives and making a principled stand elevated them as individuals beyond what they could achieve, or ever hope to be, as ordinary soldiers. As martyrs their personal glory would remain unsurpassed.

Jihadis, similarly, see themselves as legitimate warriors in a legitimate war, not as terrorists. In their understanding their acts are liturgical, sanctifying even murder-suicide, and of symbolic value, beyond merely inflicting damage to the enemy. Even from a point of view of pragmatics, this tactic may have a place: with a display of extreme violence that includes self-destruction a demonstration is given of the unrelenting, unshakable commitment of the warriors, which may shock and intimidate. Whether this works is debatable. The Western hegemonic perspective tends to see present-day suicide bombers as contemptible criminals of low moral status. (The comparison with individuals committing mass murder and then shooting themselves, as seems to happen with disturbing frequency, is not only tempting but leads to a perspective that sees this kind of action as a form of psychological aberration.) Their bravado lacks the admirable gloss of heroism in the eyes of non-Muslims. This perception logically arises from a socially determined partisan standpoint. Ideology—to which ethics and values belong as integral parts—tends to arise from—or at least is intimately connected with—a socioeconomic position. One does not have to cling "religiously" to a Marxist position, to assume that the Western socioeconomic "infrastructure" supports an ideological proclivity in which the glorification of individual enterprise for material gain produces little sympathy for human self-destruction for a spurious "spiritual" cause. Individualism, materialism, capitalism, and secularization together produce an ideological "climate" in which religiously motivated suicide bombing would struggle to ascend to a supreme value of idealistic heroism. Obviously, the globalized world, despite efforts to entrench a certain hegemonic worldview, has not yet managed to eradicate rival values and ideals. In fact, their persistence could be seen as becoming iconic in anti-globalizing and anti-hegemonic endeavors. In the sense that jihad becomes a major ideological ingredient in the resistance to globalization, it can be expected that this dynamic develops features of a "counterculture" in which some aspects purposefully imitate the rejected hegemon, and others deliberately contrast with it.

AMERICA'S FIRST SUICIDE BOMBER

Confirmation of sorts of the value of suicide bombing as a powerful symbolic act came to radical Muslims from an unexpected quarter. The world news media, early in 2010, reported a spectacular homicide-suicide attack on a taxation office in Austin (Texas, USA) in which a man crashed his light airplane into the office building killing some people and himself. Allegedly, he believed the IRS (Internal Revenue Service), the federal agency of taxation, had gratuitously ruined him. Shortly afterwards, New Zealand's electronic Dawa eNewsletter[46] commented on this event with a newsflash.

It portrayed the event as a legitimate act of majoritarian discontent in America. The article cited a "Rasmussen Poll [that] indicates that the vast majority of Americans are convinced that "their" government is totally unresponsive to them, their concerns, and their needs." It went on to say that "only 21 percent of the American population agree that the U.S. government has the consent of the governed, and that 21 percent is comprised of the political class itself and liberals [*sic*]. Rasmussen concludes that the gap between the American population and the politicians who rule them "may be as big today as the gap between the colonies and England during the eighteenth century." This is not only a rather idiosyncratic reading of internal American politics, but interestingly, it contradicts the notion, mentioned earlier, that in a democracy all are collectively responsible for the form of governance they have.

Citing the incident with tacit but readily apparent approval, the article voiced the view that only extreme violence will get the attention of the Western world. The important ingredient is the theatrical effect, the artfulness of execution, the shock waves—while the number of people killed is supplementary to this purpose.

"Indications are that Joseph Stack [the suicide pilot] was sane," the article says. "Like Palestinians faced with Israeli jet fighters, helicopter gunships, tanks, missiles and poison gas, Stack realized that he was powerless. A suicide attack was the only weapon left to him." The article argued that the suicide note explaining his motivation segregated him from the deranged people who randomly commit mass murder. It intimated that in this case violence has become an act of sanity, even rationality.

"The [U.S.] government and its propaganda ministry [*sic*] do not want to call Stack a terrorist," the article maintained.

> Terrorist is a term the government reserves for Muslims who do not like what Israel does to Palestinians and the U.S. government does to Muslim countries. . . . But Stack experienced the same frustrations and emotions as Muslims who can't take it any longer and strap on a suicide vest. "Violence," Stack wrote, "not only is the answer, it is the only answer." Stack concluded that nothing short of violence will get the attention of a government that has turned its back on the American people.

Clearly, this interpretation is not totally devoid of some logic, yet it puts a gloss on the incident, which is unlikely to be shared by the predominant Western view—for several reasons. Not least among them is the reluctance, discussed before, of attributing commendable value to acts of murderous self-destruction, although it may agree that there may be some theatrical effect in its execution. There might be more agreement in the assumption that grandiose acts of violence garner attention.

Clearly, this incident was modeled on the events of 9/11. It also makes transparent another aspect of extremism. It draws attention to the fact that violence is a language, a form of communication when other forms of communication fail. Conflict resolution, therefore, first and foremost has to find a common language, agreed-on common symbols. When Theo van Gogh was shot in the streets of Amsterdam by a Muslim extremist, who had taken exception to a film the Dutch filmmaker had made with Ayaan Hirsi Ali (the Dutch-Somali apostate), in his dying moments he famously asked his assailant, "Can't we talk about this?" He did not realize killing him was the language of the enraged and aroused fanatic. Murder is not necessarily always a negotiable phenomenon of greed, instinctive rage, opportunism—but may be a cerebral communicative device that employs a universally understandable symbol; it is speaking for the powerless or those mute with rage who are incapable of other forms of articulation. Lacking in legitimate power and lost for words, there seems to be only one language left that can be understood by the powerful adversary.

TERRORISTS, GANGS, AND SECRET SOCIETIES

In this section I wish to consider two particular social aspects, which seem to be eminently characteristic for the militant organizations and functions of Islamic extremism. In various combinations these aspects can be detected in various other social phenomena.

The average age of suicide bombers is said to be around twenty-five, and for the majority it is less than thirty. Even though I cannot vouch for the absolute accuracy of these statistics (and I doubt that anyone else can), the youthfulness of the human bomb, ensuring their death as martyrs in various lethal ways, must be an object of reflection.

There are several more or less clandestine Islamist organizations that use suicide bombing and other extremist tactics. Some are notorious throughout the world. Others have a more localised relevance and may not be so well known to the outside world. The overwhelming majority of them operate deep in the shadows of secrecy, barely known by a few snippets of inside information about their clandestine nature and goals. Their individual members leave the shadows of anonymity only to execute acts of terror and destruction, and when they are caught as a result, or their torn and mangled remains are identified.

Al-Qaeda is probably somewhat atypical in that it probably is no coherent organization, but rather a loose network of autonomous cells that receive orders and finances from a more or less centralized "brain." It approves and contracts out "projects" making it difficult to trace the initiative back to the blessing it received from the al-Qaeda hierarchy and the funds it may have attracted from its paymasters. (This seems to have been the situation of bin Laden's modus operandi as observed shortly before his demise at the hands of the American military death squad.) Thus under the label al-Qaeda there is a whole host of only loosely affiliated groups of varying size—from large paramilitary organizations in places like Yemen and Somalia to secret cells of three or four individuals in Western cities—and with different degrees of militancy. Al-Qaeda is probably best known for using suicide bombers. The

Middle Eastern conflict zones of Iraq, Palestine-Israel, Afghanistan, and Pakistan are well acquainted with this tactic. India is also familiar with this phenomenon. Farther East, Jemmaa Islamiyah[47] has become infamously known for the so-called Bali bombings as well as other atrocities in Southeast Asia some of which involved suicide missions. It has a program of re-Islamization (mainly of Malay society) and establishing a Southeast Asian khilafa.

The Taleban fighters[48] in Afghanistan and Pakistan are a very different type of organization. This is a relatively openly military organization with wide grassroot support from mainly within the tribal society of the Pashtun (in both Afghanistan and Pakistan). Ideologically, it represents not only a very conservative, Wahabbism-influenced version of Islam, but also incorporates many cultural idiosyncrasies of tribal pashtunwala. Death-defying prowess and extreme courage have always been admired character traits, which are put to good use now in the internecine warfare. (In its form today it revives the previous Pashtun—Tajik division. Having been pushed into the underground through the military successes of their Western and Tajik opponents, more recently they are reemerging with increasing vigor and extending their field of operation and strategic interests deep into Pakistan.) In Afghanistan—conjuring up shades of the mujahidin resistance to the Soviet invasion—Taleban political philosophy is strengthened by claims to a patriotic duty to defend the country against the occupation force of Western infidels.

There are many more or less well-organized groups with varying degrees of inner cohesion and fanatical dedication. Internally motivated by a joint sense of purpose, their objectives may differ in focus and ultimate intent. Broadly, they have in common the character of secret or semi-secret societies inspired by fanatical religious belief, and a commitment to violence as a legitimate tactical means. Other features that are present to varying degrees of intensity and spectacularity are a sociocritical or rebellious agenda, and the use of violent theatrics to broadcast their intentions.

The shadowy army of Muslim militants, and in particular the terrorist cell, embody two significant social phenomena—or perhaps better referred to as sociological tropes: the youth gang, which apart from youthful age brings a destructive and rebellious potential into the frame, and the secret society, which has discipline, order, and structure and is gathered around a central mission or agenda that motivates its existence. This is not to say that gangs are totally unstructured. But the destructive force of its rebellious spirit discharges in a more or less aimless, untargeted manner. In modern society this phenomenon can be found in the formation of youth street gangs and the (semi-) delinquent subculture it engenders.[49]

In a wider perspective it becomes readily obvious that in hybrid form and in various combinations these phenomena are widespread. By placing less emphasis on the specific religious background of Muslim extremism and lifting its seemingly rebellious, violent agenda and clandestine mode of operation into the focus, one finds that history and the contemporary world abound with kindred phenomena. In a phenomenological sense, these phenomena are not precisely identical by sharing all of the ideological and sociological features, which would make them immediately subsumable under one category, but rather are joined by a family resemblance. Organizations like the Ku Klux Klan, the IRA (Irish Republican Army), and ETA (the Basque separatist organization) come readily to mind as paradigmatic for violent, shadowy organizations with a rebellious political agenda. Similarly, in Europe and the United States, urban guerrilla groups of the 1960s, 1970s, and early 1980s pursued revolutionary sociopolitical goals, in their philosophy and sociocritical agenda operating under cover of secrecy on the extreme left of the political and ideological spectrum. In South America this tradition continues. These shadowy organizations demonstrate the thin line between what may be considered a cause of social justice and the tactics that clearly stem from a terrorist textbook.

Another shadowy organization showing some of the common features with strong religious undertones was Aum Shinri Kyo (Supreme Truth) in Japan. Although clearly a millenarian religious sect under charismatic leadership, it bluntly manifested its terrorist agenda through its doomsday-inspired attack in Tokyo's subways in 1995.[50] Subsequent investigations revealed an enormous secret organization with a large following, secret laboratories, and production facilities no one outside the cult seems to have known about. The way this organization functioned provides a useful link to appreciate similarities in other respects between secretive cults and radical Islamism: they share certain recruitment techniques. The attraction to the semi-secret nature of radical and extremist organizations is not solely based on its mystique or the lure of adventure, and it does not arise only from a rational embracement of its mission in protest against the political and social status quo. As has often been observed with NRMs (or so-called cults), successful recruitment to a large extent is based on the tactical use of certain psychological techniques to persuade prospective adepts. The indoctrination process can be facilitated by various artificially provided circumstances. Among them, the physical separation from society and community is important in order to control the learning input effectively and provide an environment that not only shuts out contravening influences but also produces the appropriate stimuli. (Youth initiation practiced in tribal society employs similar principles.) Fundamental to the learning experience of this kind is gathering the novices in camps where they can be isolated from the influences of the wider community and new patterns of understanding can be implanted in them while at the same time keeping disturbing influences at bay—at least for some time, perhaps long enough for the new ideas to be bedded down.[51] Physical detachment and distance from the outside world is an effective means of influencing minds. The stereotypical cults seeking to indoctrinate receptive young minds in isolated camps, force them to cut off ties with family and friends. This practice is used also in the education scenario of radical Islam. Closed learning institutions, such as madrassas (religious boarding schools) or paramilitary training camps, which provide the ideal physical and intellectual confinement, provide the ideal environment to implant the appropriate worldview and value system. Evening sessions in mosques and weekend training courses are only imperfect imitations, but can achieve similar results in generating total commitment to a worldview that is more or less askew to the "mainstream."

Scanning history, social phenomena of rebellious youth groups with violent agendas can be found at various points in the past and pursuing various social and political agendas. In the aftermath of World War I, out of the chaos of defeat, formations of extremist political organizations can be found in Germany and Austria—some of them illegal and pseudo-secret. As long ago as in the Middle Class revolution of 1848 in several German cities, we find similar motives of violent rebellion against an established order nurtured by semi-secret cells. (The young and idealistic Karl Marx was prominently involved in the failed uprising and had to flee to England where freedom of thought enjoyed greater respect.) These groups exemplify an important point: the desire to become instrumental in the elimination of politically or ethically unwanted conditions does not necessarily always attract primarily the economically most deprived and undereducated groups—in Marx's terminology, the Lumpenproletariat. Deprivation features may play a role in recruiting "foot soldiers." Material deprivation is present, for instance, in the life story of the surviving Bombay attacker who came from humble Pakistani circumstances and was attracted by monetary reward as much as by the promised adventure that allowed him to break out of his miserable, humdrum existence. It is also a factor in the recruitment of Taleban fighters among the poor peasantry who are lured by regular pay and other pecuniary inducements. Material poverty certainly helps in recruiting drives, but that should not deceive that the leadership, as well as many of the followers, are relatively well educated and usually do not come from a socioeconomically deprived background. Looking at the life stories of terrorists, and those aspiring to it, who have come to the notice of the West, makes it clear that they had a good, and in some cases above-average, education. Obviously, it is not necessarily the search for financial and economic gain that drives people into the arms of radical organizations. Not infrequently it is a mixture of fanatical ethics, rage about injustice, and youthful impetuosity that moves people to rebel against society and the dominant world order, and to fall in with the pursuit of utopian visions of a better, more just, more ethical world.[52]

This phenomenon of violent rebellion against the sociopolitical status quo by secret groups of relatively well-educated young people has a long history, although it may lack the radical and organized socio-critical agenda. The existence of rebellious and violent youth gangs, often students (organized in so-called semi-secret student societies, called Burschenschaften in German language areas) in several European countries, spreading at times terror among the sedate burghers, can be traced back into postmedieval times. Although these groups of educated youths did not act on a clear ideological plan of radical social reform, they did manifest rebellion against the prevailing social order. Social phenomena of extreme violence, often directed against their own community, perpetrated by youth gangs can even be found in premedieval times in Europe. Ancient precursors may be seen in the so-called berserkers in Scandinavian society[53] around the ninth and tenth century and, according to Tacitus's description of Teutonic tribal society, such an element was present already in Roman times. These were cadres of young men spreading fear among opponents in battle through their crazed and frenzied behavior. Half-naked and gnashing their teeth in rage, often foaming at the mouth (possibly from drug taking)[54] they believed themselves to be invulnerable as well as invincible. They were feared as much by their own community as by the enemy in battle.[55] Other similar phenomena crop up episodically in Europe's later history. Culture historians[56] see this tradition perpetuated, for instance, in the Bavarian Black Riders, a secretive group riding on black horses with a skull on top of their helmets, in the Thirty Years War.[57] The destructive potential of such groups could be directed inwardly against their own society as much as outwardly.

Clandestine, violent organizations can crop up in the most unexpected places. Underground resistance movements in cases of war are a well-known phenomenon, as is the general trope of the "Fifth Column." In rare cases the state makes use of this "rebellious" potential for defensive purposes. It is little known that in 1940 a special branch of the British Home Guard—or Dad's Army, as it was also known (it did not only recruit old men into its ranks, but also those with vital functions who could not be spared to serve at the front)—was created to fight a guerrilla war. Under Churchill's direct command, this clandestine organization was known, if at all, as the Scallywags. Its members, respectable and professional citizens for the most part, were trained in sabotage, assassination, and spying with a view to resisting an impending German occupation in every possible way. Highly secret and befittingly financed by MI5, it comprised about six thousand members whose identities were generally not known to the wider society, nor very much to each other. They were organized in small cells with as few members as possible knowing of each other so that betrayal would not endanger the whole organization. It was in effect a terrorist suicide squad, as it was expected that hardly anyone would survive their personal mission, once the organization began doing its job.

What these rabble-rousing groups, secret societies, and clandestine organizations have in common is the ritualization of violence, opposition to an existing social condition or social order, and harnessing a degree of idealism and moralistic fervor for destructive purposes. In some cases one has to dig deep to discern features of idealism under the thick surface of gratuitous violence. The destructive zeal and the lust for power through terror may often come to overshadow any other more laudable features.

A common feature of such social elements is that it involves a certain age bracket (as well as predominantly the male gender). Perhaps for obvious reasons, mainly young men are attracted to such groups and organization. This is another sociological aspect of interest in this context. If one casts the net even wider, one may include here football hooliganism and skinhead groups both of which display prominently features of (often "mindless" and untargeted) violence. The underlying philosophy of skinheadism in fact is vaguely connected with a rebellious, if at times only vaguely formulated political program. The opposition to the sociopolitical status quo may be in terms of anti-immigration, white supremacy, racism, anti-multiculturalism, extreme nationalism, and the like. Often, acts of violence seem to be untargeted and random and hardly in support of any articulated political cause. Young men are attracted for various reasons ranging from socioeconomic deprivation (although this is usually more of a subjective state of mind) to the desire to pursue what they may see as ultimate social justice with a Machiavellian moral elasticity. In any case, a personal sense of disenfranchisement from society at large—often for imaginary, or fictitious reasons—lies at the root.

In modern Western society the potential of youthful enthusiasm can grow into violent fanaticism when goaded along by unscrupulous leadership. However, the formation of (semi-) secret societies associated with extreme violence forming an important part of their agenda, points to a sociological syndrome that is more widespread and has deeper roots in human nature than would appear on first sight. (Whether one wants to attach a Freudian significance to it, as Bernard Lewis has tried to do, is another matter.) Alienation of male youth ventilating itself in aggression is probably a universal phenomenon, although maintaining this means moving onto anthropologically tricky ground. It invokes the old nature-versus-nurture debate and conjures up visions of a "classical" anthropological debate two decades ago. The notion of a harsh and bitter human nature stood against the description of the harmonious, lovely Samoan society, which had made the American anthropologist Margaret Mead famous.[58] In her narrative Samoans of her time were living in an easy-going, carefree society without violence and social stresses—

which came to be bitterly disputed by others who claimed she had been deceived. It is not improbable, however, that in culturally, socially, and economically very homogenous societies the alienation, which seems to act as a catalyst for violent rebellion in the young generation, is minimized to the point of appearing to be absent. On the other hand, some societies and historical contexts may have offered an instituted possibility to harness the destructive potential and ritualize the violence of male youth groups by channelling it into socially more useful enterprises. This may have been defensive endeavors from which the whole society or group may have benefited, or aggressive, offensive adventures—such as youth initiation groups of the Massai being traditionally occupied with killing lions and stealing cattle from outsiders. The wandering years of trade apprentices, the journeyman's perambulations, obligatory in European societies in previous decades, may be a more peaceful version of the same initiative. In some Australian Aboriginal societies young men in the course of youth initiation were expected, for the duration of several years, to live in groups alone, segregated from family and community, and to fend for themselves. In chance encounters with others, they were expected to keep their distance, observe avoidance rules, and in communicating with others use changed (falsetto) voices to disguise their identities. In other words, the meaning of such institutionalized customs of temporary expulsion may be found to lie in deflecting potentially destructive energies, dissipating them, or directing them towards external conflicts. As gang studies have shown such groups are not amorphous, but have a firm internal structure, a set value system, common symbols, and hierarchies of respect. Access to success, status, and in-group respect is of a kind different from the analogous concepts in mainstream society and more often than not is based on aggressive bravado. Exactly this ethos can be expected to be present in modern extremist groups.

In an unspecific, amorphous sense there is a youthful reservoir of aggression and excitability that can be tapped for generating a more organized and focused form of violence, which may be harnessed for various purposes and commissioned to pursue any goal. Mobilization of the aggressive potential young men offer can happen through evocation of idealism (in support of causes believed to be worthwhile) and by glorifying destructive acts. (As far as one can tell, the twin tower attack with its strong visual imagery has become emblematic in the world of terrorism.) Islam's often violent history can supply the sacred precedents. Together with the plasticity of Islamic doctrine that allows interpretations that elevate aggressive tendencies to highest ethical and sanctified prominence, goals can be articulated by the appropriate ideologues, to try and change the world by any means.

NOTES

1. See Erich Kolig, *New Zealand's Muslims and Multiculturalism*. Leiden: Brill, 2010; p. 174–177.

2. This is not to overlook that many religions have always shunned not only forcible conversion, but any kind of organized missionization. Hinduism, Judaism, and many tribal religions, on the contrary, cultivate(d) a sense of exclusivity, which makes admission not easy.

3. See Mark Juergensmeyer. *Terror in the Mind of God: The Global Rise of Religious Violence*. Berkeley: University of California Press, 2003.

4. The contradiction involved in knowing and believing in this context is only semantic. Their distinction, however, is integral to modern epistemology, while in traditional versions it is irrelevant. In a traditional, theocentered epistemology, the cognitive act of believing in something (of an intangible, nonempirical kind) is identical with knowing something (in an empirical, verifyable sense). The modern religious believer is also disinclined to make a profound distinction, thus giving belief the status of firm knowledge.

5. (1561–1626). To be precise, he was referring to scientific knowledge, which gives power over nature. Much of Michel Foucault's argument, in particular, draws on this notion of a power-knowledge connection, though in a much wider, sociological sense.

6. Catholic-Protestant wars fought over purely religious differences have ceased centuries ago and pogroms against Jews on purely religious grounds have become unthinkable. Unfortunately, visceral xenophobism can adopt quite different rationales. (See Arjun Appadurai, *Fear of Small Numbers*. Durham and London: Duke University Press, 2006.) The Northern Irish conflict and the Balkan wars of the 1990s largely had political reasons, with religion providing the outer varnish as it were.

7. As I found in my own research, both sides of this argument may be held simultaneously by a person. As so often, cognitive dissonance may not result in discarding one side or stimulate urgent attempts to somehow harmonize both and to resolve a logical contradiction.

8. In the attack in 1995, twelve persons died and allegedly five thousand were injured by the release of Sarin gas.

9. An outstanding example is the People's Temple, which in 1978 in Guyana, after having killed a U.S. congressman (suspected of spying), committed collective suicide (though as it turned out afterwards not always entirely voluntarily) of 918 members. Similarly, the destruction of the Branch Davidian community in Waco, Texas, caused about one hundred persons' death, in 1993. There are many more examples of Christian, inspired cults committing not only assault in the name of upholding a self-styled law, but also lethal violence internally against the membership. There is a huge literature on NRMs (New Religious Movements). See for example, Christopher Evans, *Cults of Unreason*. London: Harrap, 1974; Rodney Stark (ed.), *Religious Movements*. New York: Paragon, 1985; Bryan Wilson and Jamie Cresswell (eds.), *New Religious Movements*. London, New York: Routledge, 1999.

10. Rohan Gunaratna, *Inside al Qaeda*. New York: Columbia University Press, 2002. Zachary Abuza, *Militant Islam in Southeast Asia*. Boulder, London: Riemer, 2003.

11. Asma Afsaruddin ("Demarcating Fault-lines within Islam: Muslim Modernists and Hardline Islamists Engage the Shari'a." In *Shari'a as Discourse*, J. Nielsen and L. Christoffersen (eds.). Farnham: Ashgate, 2010; p.35) mentions that radical Islamists emphasize violent jihad and despise as impotent those who prefer a more peaceful interpretation.

12. There was also an ingredient of revenge, for instance when two Jewish tribes were put to the sword for perceived wrongs they did to the Muslim community.

13. John Esposito's, *Unholy War: Terror in the Name of Islam* (Oxford, Oxford University Press, 2002) presents a comprehensive view on the subject.

14. The terms "cosmic war" stems from Reza Aslan, *How to Win a Cosmic War*. New York: Random, 2009. Aslan argues that jihadism is not based on the Quran, but rather the writing of Hassan al-Banna, Sayyid Qutb, and Ahmed ibn Taymiyyah (p. xviii). However, on pp. 3–4 he reproduces the letter the 9/11 bombers received from their "handler." In it they are instructed to

remember the Quran and its commandments. Some Salafis who emphatically wish to return to the doctrinal basics of the Quran and embrace the notion of a violent jihad, do reject Qutb's work.

15. See, for instance, Bassam Tibi, *Political Islam, World Politics and Europe*. London, New York: Routledge, 2008; p. 37–38, where he draws specific attention to this.

16. John Esposito, *Islam the Straight Path*. New York: Oxford University Press, 1991; p. 30 has a more elegant translation.

17. Aslan, *How to Win . . .* (p. xix) renders this ayat as "Fight in the way of God those who fight you, but do not begin hostilities. God does not like the aggressor."

18. Erich Kolig, *New Zealand's Muslims . . .* ; p. 247. This section repeats the threads of thought on jihad laid out in this book.

19. Girard, *Violence and the Sacred*. Baltimore and London: John Hopkins University Press (orig. 1972), 1977.

20. As, for instance, Erich Fromm causally connected extreme human destructiveness with certain societal forms (*The Anatomy of Human Destructiveness*. London: Cape, 1974).

21. The concept of "Wahlverwandtschaft" is used by Weber in a rather vague sense, but most conspicuously in his explanation of the rise of the capitalist ethos. For a summary see, e.g., Herbert Howe, Max Weber's "Elective Affinities: Sociology within the Bounds of Pure Reason." *Americam Journal of Sociology* 84/2 (1978): 366–385.

22. L. Mannheim (ed. by Paul Kecskemeti), *Essays on the Sociology of Knowledge*. London: Routledge & Kegan, 1952; p. 183 on the concept of "interestedness."

23. Gramsci, *Selections from the Prison Notebooks*. New York: International Publishers, 1971.

24. Rarely is it conversion by force, though hegemony may also be "armored with coercion" (P. Anderson, "The Antimonies of Antonio Gramsci," *New Left Review* 100 (1976-1977): 5–78; p.13). But ultimately consent and collaboration by the subordinate class are indispensable in the exercise of hegemony (Joseph Femia, "Hegemony and Consciousness in the Thought of Antonio Gramsci." *Political Studies* 23 (1975): 29–48).

25. See Bernard Lewis, "Legal and Historical Reflections on the Position of Muslim Populations under Non-Muslim Rule." In *Muslims in Europe*, B. Lewis and D. Schnapper (eds.). London, New York: Pinter, 1994. See Tariq Ramadan's (*Western Muslims and the Future of Islam*. New York: Oxford University Press, 2004; p. 65–73. justifications for allowing Muslims to live in the West, and the recourse to traditional concepts such as Dar-al-Ahd, Amn etc.

26. The concept of necessity in times of need allows for a reasonable reduction in the total adherence to Islamic prescriptions.

27. Organised by Majelis Mujahidin Indonesia, a radical Islamic organization founded by Abu Bakar Ba'asyir (accused to be the instigator of the first Bali bombing). This party was teetering on the brink of political legality. See Erich Kolig, "Radical Islam, Islamic Fervour, and Political Sentiments in Central Java, Indonesia." *European Journal of East Asian Studies* 4/1 (2005): 55–86.

28. The whole tenor, for example, of Iftikhar Malik's book (*Islam and Modernit . . .*) is of this kind: it claims that from the beginning the West has been hostile towards Islam.

29. Opinions are strongly divided on this question. It is hardly surprising that one view holds Islam and its doctrines responsible for the violence perpetrated in its name. See Abdelwahab El-Affendi, "The Terror of Belief and the Belief in Terror: On Violently Serving God and Nation." In *Dying for Faith*, Madani Al-Rasheed and Marat Shterin (eds.). London, New York: Tauris 2009.

30. an-Na'im, The Islamic Counter-Reformation. *New Perspectives Quarterly* 19/1 (2002): 29–43; p. 33

31. David Kertzer, *Ritual, Politics, and Power*. New Haven, London: Yale University Press, 1988. Anthropological essays analyzing the acceptance by a subaltern group of paradigms and symbolic language of the dominant group are, for instance, Roger Keesing, "Creating the Past: Custom and Identity in the Contemporary Pacific." *The Contemporary Pacific* 1/1 (1989):19–42; and Allan Hanson, "The Making of the Maori: Culture Invention and Its Logic." *American Anthropologist* 91/4 (1989): 890–902 to name only two.

32. Very briefly put, this was the "terra nullius" declaration by the British Crown in 1788, which pronounced the continent a colony. In subsequent years and by further declarations the Crown extended its assumption of sovereignty from the original eastern parts of the continent incrementally further West. By this act the Aborigines were regarded as only occupiers of the land without property rights and without claim to sovereignty. The symbolism of this act—with far reaching consequences—was totally incomprehensible to the indigenous people.

33. See Erich Kolig, *Dreamtime Politics: Religion, World View and Utopian Thought in Australian Aboriginal Society*. Berlin: Reimer, 1989.

34. Ghandi's passive resistance was a symbolic language of power that was understood by the British hegemon. Perhaps its paradigm of peaceful objection struck a responsive chord in the Christian background of the colonial power.

35. Unbelief here not only in the sense of Buddhism or the forbidden representation of the human form, but also victory over the Shi'ite Hazara who in their "seditious unbelief" had tolerated the figures to remain for so long.

36. Equally popular was the hypothesis that the destruction was staged and self-inflicted by the United States so as to have an excuse to attack the Islamic world or to divert attention from the actions of Israel.

37. Quran 22/58–59; 2/154; 3/156–58, 169–71.

38. These are women fighters, often the widows of jihadis, from the North Caucasus area of Dagestan and Chechnya fighting for an Islamic state independent from Russia—or in some cases possibly as an act of personalized vengeance.

39. See Margaret Gonzalez-Perez, "The False Islamization of Female Suicide Bombers." *Gender Issues* 28 (2011): 50–65. The argument that women with psychological problems, immature young girls, and economically unsupported women become primary targets of recruitment would need more empirical corroboration.

40. Church authorities (such as the Vatican) do at times speak out against extreme practices.

41. A particularly arduous form of pilgrimage in Tibetan Buddhism is to move along a sacred path by continuous prostrations.

42. I deliberately abstain here to discuss the legality of this controversial action, legalized by the George W. Bush administration in the course of the "War on Terror" policy. It has been condemned as a human rights violation and at the same time defended—in Machiavellian terms; for instance, by a Harvard law scholar, Alan Dershowitz (*Why Terrorism Works*. Melbourne: Scribe, 2003).

43. Interview in the Jerusalem Post, February 25, 2011, www.jpost.com/Opinion/Columnist/Article.aspx?id=209770.

44. Hadith and Quran 44/54, 52/20.

45. This seems to be related to the Hebrew Shekhina which refers to God's presence in the world. It also relates to the name Sakaina, one of the daughters of imam Hussein. See for example Robert Lacey, *Inside the Kingdom*. London: Random Arrow Books, 2009; p. 118.

46. Of March 1, 2010. This normally is a moderate medium of distributing Islamic news.

47. Zachary Abuza, *Militant Islam in Southeast Asia*. . . .

48. Ahmed Rashid, *Taliban: The Story of Afghan Warlords*. London: Tauris, 2000. In the meantime more relevant literature has accumulated.

49. See William Foote Whyte, *The Street Corner Society*. Chicago, University of Chicago Press, 1943; Fredric Thrasher, *The Gang*. Chicago: University of Chicago Press, 1927; Robert Merton, "Social Structure and Anomie." *American Sociological Review* 3 (1938): 672–682.

50. Sect members released lethal sarin gas in underground trains in March 1995 on the order of the charismatic leader and prophet Shoko Asahara, causing seven deaths, seriously sickening 144, and reportedly injuring a further 5000. See, e.g., Ian Reader, *Religious Violence in Contemporary Japan*. Richmond: Curzon, 1999.

51. This holds true regardless of whether one agrees to call the attendant learning process learning in the ordinary semantic meaning, indoctrination, or brain washing.

52. The mix of youthful rebellion, search for belonging, and idealism striving towards a just society is clearly noticeable in Ed Husain's story of becoming an "Islamist." (Ed Husain, *The Islamist*. London: Penguin, 2007.)

53. Berserksgangr in Norse.

54. Other explanations are that this was a pathological syndrome associated with epilepsy.

55. This social phenomenon is mentioned in the Egils and Ynglynga Sagas as well as other sources. They were possibly associated with Odin (or Woden) worship and showed interesting ritual features such as the wearing of bear or wolfskins (which merges into the werewolf myth), and engaged in symbolic violence such as drinking blood and eating raw meat.

56. Such as Hans Peter Duerr. *Ueber die Grenze zwischen Wildnis und Zivilization*. Fankfurt a.M.: Suhrkamp, 1985; p. 103.

57. One might see a faint echo in the Nazi SS troops and their emblematic black uniform and skull and crossbone symbol.

58. Margaret Mead, *Coming of Age in Samoa*. New York: William Morrow, 1928. Later, her thesis of freewheeling sexuality preventing adolescence crises was attacked by Derek Freeman (*Margaret Mead and Samoa: The Making and Unmaking of an Anthropological Myth*. Cambridge: Harvard University Press, 1983.) Their difference of ethnographic interpretation became a celebrated controversy between Mead and Freeman and their admirers.

Epilogue

Robin Wright prefaces her book *Sacred Rage*[1] with a bon mot by John Stuart Mill: "One man with belief is equal to a thousand with only interests." This clever remark has an assured validity where the effectiveness and drive to action of a fervent believer is concerned. It is a worthy companion to the adage "belief can shift mountains," but applied to the fanaticism of the Muslim extremists of whom Wright's book speaks, it refers to the grim reality that a few fanatics can hold the world to ransom. The people "with belief" referred to in the book are a sad example of what impact fanatical belief can have. Most reasonable people would prefer any number of people "with interests" to those few fervent believers. Having a strong belief may be comforting to the believer, but may be of small merit beyond that. Yet, it is the strength of belief, the commitment and the action based on it that makes Islam a fascinating topic. The fanatics it produces hold the world enthralled. What motivated this system of beliefs to emerge and how does its present-day authenticity—such as it is—fit into the modern world? And how can a basic, common humanness account for the existence of such beliefs?

No sooner had I written this paragraph, the Oslo mass murder occurred (in July 2011). The Norwegian, a confused Christian right-wing extremist Islamophobe, who wanted to save Western Europe from the "Muslim take-over," so as to get his message of grave concern across, killed between seventy and eighty people. The reality is that he is not alone in that some Europeans feel they have been overrun by the Muslim diaspora. This xenophobia had now borne terrible fruit. Interestingly, this terrorist also referred to John Stuart Mill's adage on his Twitter account. Slightly modifying it he wrote, "One person with a belief is equal to the force of 100,000 who have only interests." How attractive one sentence can be to the extremist mind, finding reassurance and incentive in it. Osama bin Laden to my knowledge never referred to it, and it is doubtful that he read John Stuart Mill, but it seems to be made for him and the likes of him.

Did the Prophet Muhammad through his labors intend to foster an excessive dedication, which seamlessly merges with a kind of fanaticism that flies in the face of all natural decency and compassion? Did he intend to spawn a fanaticism through which thousands are killed fourteen centuries later? From an anthropological viewpoint, Islam's original motivations, the semiotic functions of its cultural patterning lying in the cradle of this faith, are shrouded in the mysterious darkness of distant history which can be lifted, ever so slightly, into the light only by conjecture. For the believer there is more certainty; a certainty, however, which is only individually experienced, but rarely shared widely, let alone universally accepted.

The emergence of Islam fits the charismatic revitalization patterns which seek to establish a perfect society on an "up-to-date" building plan. Such plans are usually syncretistic combining old with new, the familiar with the radically new. The normal dynamics of social and cultural replication to maintain internal continuity and unbroken identity over time give anthropology a difficult subject to comprehend. Even more impenetrable are episodic bursts of radical cultural innovation by charismatic leaders whose revolutionary efforts cannot be explained by environmental and social necessities or other "rationally" graspable circumstances. It is chronically difficult to explain the sudden quixotic appearance of reformatory or revolutionary ideas, striking out boldly to identify new ideals, implement new moral standards, install new social patterns, and drastically reorganize collective existence. And why are some ideas, like Islam's, enormously successful and others are not?

Explanations that rely on the conjectural understanding of social, political, or economic circumstances of the time when Islam emerged are on terra infirma because the intricacies of social and ideological discourses of that time and society remain largely hidden. Was there an urgent expectation for further divine revelation, was the society pregnant with hope for divine intervention and radical change? Only by extrapolating from a general anthropology of chiliasm, and the rough grid it can produce, can some broadly generalized insights be gained. For the believer, of course, origin and purpose are clear and require no investigation. In fact explanatory attempts, which go beyond an unquestioning and uncritical acceptance of the divine nature of revelation, may encounter resentful rejection.

The uncertain ground on which speculation about the motivational origins of Islam and the meaning of its symbolist creation is moving, is even more uncertain when one attributes a highly generative, causal role to the founding figure. In other words, personalizing intent and reducing motivations to the inspirational idiosyncrasy of a charismatic figure increases the difficulties of explanation exponentially. Intentions, hopes, and dreams of the charismatic founder can only be subject of intense speculation. There is a profound difference between the materialist perspective that attributes little independent relevance to the prophet and a Weberian point of analysis that values the spontaneous creativity of the charismatic and ascribes to him or her a profoundly causative role. The believer's view that the charismatic is simply the conveyor of a divine message—a view which exaggerates as much as underplays the creativity of this role—is on a different level altogether.

Today, Islam is of world-spanning significance. It has weathered the changes, brought on throughout the centuries, better than Christianity, especially in retaining some of the social importance for which it seems to have been generated originally. It has more strongly remained faithful to its original intent of bringing an earthly salvation by introducing to humanity cultural configurations and social patterns considered perfect, because they seemed pregnant with divine intent and God's design plan for an ideal human existence. This sense of perfection today is the source of some difficulty. The globally prevalent ideas of what constitutes desirable forms of social interrelationships and international conviviality have changed drastically. Comparative standards used by the modern kind of assessment in the course of globalization are quite different. International thinking has introduced new moral standards, legal benchmarks, and concepts of justice and personal freedom, laid down above all in the various human rights agendas sponsored by the United Nations, but also in more or less binding conventions of international relations. (One of the fundamental clashes here may be between the right to religious freedom and the personal rights of individuals. The liberty of religion to be collectively exercised and the liberty of individuals to opt out or vary its rules can stand in stark opposition as I have indicated here and there in this book with regard to particular religious features.) In many aspects these new "products" of human creativity diverge in paradigmatic gravity from the divinely received and instituted patterns of Islam, even though one may understand and sympathize with the original intent by which they were inspired. Above all, there has been a global change in the meaning of human existence as secularized anthropocentric comfort and materialist pragmatism are making enormous inroads into theocentric devotion, obedience to divine will, religious asceticism, and the expectation of other-worldly compensations.

If one leaves aside supernatural pretensions, there is no unanimity why and with what purpose certain cultural features characteristic for Islam emerged. What is clearer is the fact that whatever meaning and relevance these features once possessed do not necessarily fit the modern world. This is so for various reasons: be it because of the particular hegemonic trajectory the world is embarked on and which is guided to a large extent by a different culture; or be it because globalization brings a profound change in the

world's self-awareness, a self-consciousness against which the strictures and
values of conservative Islam uncomfortably chafe. Correspondingly, reformatory attempts to place Islam within the twenty-first century, by Muslim
scholars themselves, are very diverse in intent and degree of boldness—and
so far have failed to get the traction that would marginalize the overly conservative and the fanatics to a dwindling, insignificant minority.

In many places where Muslims form a diasporic minority, rightly or
wrongly, they are met with distrust, suspected of harboring hostile plans and
of being encouraged in this by aggressive doctrinal exhortations. The West
looks with growing alarm at the numerical growth of its Muslim minority.
Perceptions of Muslims' reluctance to adjust to the dominant host culture[2] or
that they pose a security risk, though hardly having a basis in actual factual
observation, grow stronger.[3] For the greatest part it is the panhuman trait of
distrust and hostility to the cultural Other, which modern, globalized ethics
and laws have only insufficiently overcome. Especially European identity
and self-definition, both in their collective as well as national forms, have
hardened in contours of a dichotomous distinction between "we" and Muslimness. Encrusted by centuries of Islamophobia such ingrained self-awareness does not change easily. Other considerations also play a role in the
"Occident's" rejection of Muslims and with them a mistrust of Islam. It
seems hard to overcome the perceptions of Islam's misogyny, its restrictions
on the freedom of personal choice, and of its alleged anti-democratic political
inclination. There is a belief that its doctrines are inherently radical and prone
to extremism. All of this seems to conflict with dominant discourses in the
West and in the globalized world at large. While this certainly augments the
anti-Islamic rhetoric, the strongest motif for rejection is what is seen as
Islam's embracement of violence doctrinally mandated by the iconic concept
of jihad. Adherents to Huntington's tenet of a clash of civilizations find their
beliefs of the dangerous nature of Islam vindicated by the expressions of
violence emanating from the Islamic world. On a thin basis of facts, demonizing Islam can grow rampantly. [4] Political parties in European countries
have crystallized around Islamophobia and some politicians have nailed their
colors to this mast. To add to the ideological confusion, sections of the
Western left wing find themselves defending Islamic terrorism as a form of
rejection of Western capitalism.

Feeble attempts by some leading politicians to draw a line between mainstream Islam and radicals who are prepared to fly airplanes into tall buildings
have failed in the past to convince Muslims the West is not opposed to Islam.
President Barack Obama in 2009, shortly after his inauguration, reiterated
this assurance in Turkey and Cairo. Even if a majority of Muslims would like
to believe such assurances, few of the West's actions seem to support them.
From a skeptical point of view, the West, through its destabilizing effect and
its incessant interventions in the Islamic world, has provoked the violence,

which is now endemic in Muslim society.[5] The wars unleashed in Iraq and Afghanistan have certainly been of benefit to the recruitment drive for idealistic Muslims to join the ranks of extremists.[6] The latest clear example (in June 2010) was the U.S. citizen of Pakistani origin who, comfortable, educated, and middle class in his background, ineptly tried to detonate a car bomb in New York's Times Square. When caught he stated that it was his demonstration against U.S. militarist policies in the Middle East and Asia. From a mild-mannered, modern-minded Muslim who had just received American citizenship he had turned into a terrorist to show his disgust with America's foreign policy in the Islamic world.

Even when hostilities perpetrated in the name of Islam eventually cease, as one hopes they will, it will take time to overcome the accumulated mistrust towards this religion. A balanced rational view of Islam is unlikely to return for some time. Perhaps this book is able to make a helpful step in this direction.

NOTES

1. *The Wrath of Militant Islam*. New York, London, etc.: Touchstone, 1985 (ed. 2001).

2. See, e.g., Mustafa Malik, "Muslims Pluralize the West, Resist Assimilation." *Middle East Policy* 11/1 (2004): 70–84. Jocelyne Cesari, *When Islam and Democracy Meet*. New York: Palgrave Macmillan, 2004. Yvonne Haddad and Jane Smith (eds.), *Muslim Minorities in the West: Visible and Invisible*. Walnut Creek CA: Altamira, 2002.

3. The events of 9/11 and other terrorist attacks deliver the main rationale for the West's dislike of Islam. See Jocelyne Cesari (ed.), *Muslims in the West after 9/11: Religion, Politics and Law*. London, New York: Routledge, 2009.

4. There are many examples. Ophelia Benson and Jeremy Stangroom, *Does God Hate Women?* London, New York: Continuum, 2009; pp. 160–166. Melanie Phillips, *Londonistan*. London: Gibson Square Books, 2006. Bat Ye'or, *The Dhimmi* (Rutherford, NJ: Fairleigh Dickinson, 1985; *Islam and Dhimmitude: Where Civilizations Collide*. Cranbury, NJ: Assoc. Univ. Presses, 2002; *Eurabia: The Euro-Arab Axis*. Canbury NJ: Assc. Univ.Presses, 2005. Many authors feel justified to engage in exaggerated polemics to press home the point of Islam's dangers.

5. See, for instance, Iftikhar Malik, *Islam and Modernity*. London, Sterling, VA: Pluto, 2004; p.5.

6. Eliza Manningham-Buller, director of MI5 between 2002 and 2005, was reported to have told the British enquiry in July 2010 that the unjustified war in Iraq gave Osama bin Laden the reason to wage jihad and drove many to join al-Qaeda. It increased the risk of terrorism in the UK and allowed al-Qaeda to move into Iraq where it had not been before.

Index

About the Author

Erich Kolig is an Honorary Fellow in Religion, University of Otago, New Zealand; a former senior lecturer (reader) in social anthropology at that university and visiting professor of cultural anthropology, University of Vienna. Among his recent books, he has authored *New Zealand's Muslims and Multiculturalism* (Brill, 2010) and edited (with V. Angeles and S. Wong) *Identity in Crossroad Civilisations: Ethnicity, Nationalism and Globalism in Asia* (University of Amsterdam Press, 2009). Apart from his numerous publications on mainly indigenous politics and religion, he has written extensively on Islam (in general, in New Zealand and in Indonesia), multiculturalism, and Islamic Law in Western liberal democracy. For over forty years, he has conducted field research in Afghanistan, Australia, Austria, Indonesia, New Zealand, and Vanuatu. He has also traveled widely in the Islamic world.

CPSIA information can be obtained at www.ICGtesting.com
Printed in the USA
BVOW070613270312

286117BV00002B/1/P

9 780739 174241